The Best
AMERICAN SHORT STORIES 1997

GUEST EDITORS OF
THE BEST AMERICAN SHORT STORIES

The Best AMERICAN SHORT STORIES 1997

Selected from
U.S. and Canadian Magazines
by E. ANNIE PROULX
with KATRINA KENISON

*With an Introduction
by E. Annie Proulx*

HOUGHTON MIFFLIN COMPANY
BOSTON • NEW YORK 1997

ISSN 0067-6233
ISBN 0-395-79866-3
ISBN 0-395-79865-5 (PBK.)

Printed in the United States of America

QUM 10 9 8 7 6 5 4 3 2 1

Contents

Perceived Social Values

Rites of Passage

Foreword

EACH YEAR since 1915, *The Best American Short Stories* has brought together in book form a selection of the best short fiction to have appeared in print in the previous year. In the course of the century, the process has changed little. The first two editors of the series, Edward J. O'Brien and Martha Foley, made the selections themselves. After Martha Foley's death in 1977, her successor, Shannon Ravenel, initiated the custom of inviting a guest editor to choose the final stories.

When I became the fourth series editor, in 1990, the job seemed, if a bit overwhelming, at least clearly defined. There were then some 250 nationally circulated magazines and journals in the United States and Canada that regularly published short fiction. I would read the stories in those magazines and pass on 120 or so to the guest editor, who would then choose twenty for the book.

How quickly, it seems, this enterprise has changed. The boundaries of what constitutes publication have undergone a major shift, the reading load has swelled as a result, and, in many cases, the magazines themselves have been transformed, expanded, or superseded by electronic technology.

This year I began to read fiction on the Internet. During the same period, I also began reading the entire century's worth of back volumes of *The Best American Short Stories*. That I find myself simultaneously engaged in these two disparate pursuits is a coincidence, but a significant one. As the end of the century approaches, it is only fitting that we look back and gather together into one volume (to be published on the eve of the millennium) the most enduring stories published in this series since 1915. At the same time, faced with an explosion of on-line publishing, it seems fitting that we pay attention to the body of literary fiction that is being published electronically. If ever I needed proof of Marshall McLuhan's maxim that the medium is the message, I have found it in the juxtaposition of these two reading experiences.

The early volumes in this series, which I have assembled with the help of various used-book sellers, librarians, and the Houghton Mifflin archives, testify to the value accorded to the printed word at a time when books were treasured possessions. Blow off the dust and behold a handsomely bound blue volume, its cover stamped in gold, its ribbon bookmark still intact, often as not a printed bookplate carefully pasted inside the front cover, affirming ownership. All together, these books compose a remarkable picture of our century, a picture that emerges through the stories of the times. I read them with a deepening respect for our literature, for the journals and periodicals that have survived this century by virtue of their ongoing commitment to high literary standards, and for my three predecessors. To an extraordinary extent, the stories they chose — twenty, fifty, even eighty years ago — still speak to us today.

My reading on the World Wide Web is invariably done late at night. As I click from one Web site to another, I feel rather like a dowser, my restless mouse the divining rod. There are now scores of electronic magazines publishing literary fiction, and just as many editors who see on-line publication as the way of the future. The economics are irresistible: there are no printing or distribution costs, hence no need to add subscribers before increasing the print run. While small literary journals struggle to pay their bills and find enough readers to justify their existence, E-zines are instantaneously accessible, at virtually no cost, to thousands. The publishing process is nearly instantaneous too. Work is submitted on line, accepted, contracted for, "typeset," and published on line, all in a matter of hours or days.

There are no stories from E-zines in this year's collection, but that is not to say that there never will be. My on-line reading has not yet yielded gold — only the realization that while the number of stories being offered for public consumption is growing exponentially, the best literary fiction is still finding its way into print. This is good news for those of us who prefer the aesthetics of an elegantly produced literary journal to Web-based computer graphics and who prefer to make their discoveries by turning the page rather than clicking on a hyperlink.

Meanwhile, editors of traditional journals are grappling with the question of not only what to publish, but where to publish it. Virtually every major periodical in the country has established some sort of presence on the Internet. But smaller publications are going on line as well. *The Mississippi Review,* for example, publishes some fiction in its on-line edition that does not appear in the magazine. Journals such as *Glimmer Train, Ploughshares,* and *DoubleTake* try to raise awareness of their publications by offering excerpts and background information on line. Facing dwindling institutional support, the disappearance of grant money, and increasing paper costs, others consider giving up their print editions altogether. And the majority of E-zines — *Blue Moon Review, Enterzone, Oyster Boy,* and *Crisp,* to name a few — have no print counterparts whatsoever.

The Georgia Review, by contrast, has, in its fiftieth year of publication, taken a stand against the new technology — indeed, it is still typeset in hot metal and printed by letterpress. Stanley Lindberg, its editor, has written: "It's hard to see how the future of literary quarterlies depends on the ability to transmit facts more rapidly. . . . The greater cultural need, in our opinion, is for more journals that can offer intellectually authoritative selections of information already sorted and synthesized, placed in meaningful perspective, made relevant to new understanding, and written in ways that are aware of (and sometimes even revel in) the evocative power and beauty of language."

As Mr. Lindberg eloquently reminds us, publishing is about more than transmitting — it is also, and perhaps most importantly, about interpreting and selecting. Few would argue that the daily onslaught of information makes anyone any happier or any smarter. On the contrary, as the flow has increased in speed and volume, many of us have experienced a general sense of unease, a feeling that there is so much coming at us that we can never hope to stay on top of it. After all, the transmission of information has speeded up, but human beings don't read any faster than they ever did. We must still select for ourselves, and we must look to the selections of others. More is not better, it is just more, which means that the task of selection, for editors and readers alike, grows ever more challenging.

E. Annie Proulx read this year's stories with an exacting critical eye and an informed respect for the particular challenges and possibilities of the form. Not only did she select the stories for this volume, she also arranged them in a way that allows the reader to consider her choices in a broader literary context. We are grateful for her efforts.

The stories chosen for this anthology were originally published in magazines issued between January 1996 and January 1997. The qualifications for selection are (1) original publication in nationally distributed American or Canadian periodicals; (2) publication in English by writers who are American or Canadian, or who have made the United States or Canada their home; (3) original publication as short stories (excerpts of novels are not knowingly considered). A list of magazines consulted for this volume appears at the back of the book. For readers interested in on-line fiction, I recommend eSCENE, an annual anthology of Internet fiction edited by Jeff Carlson, who offered invaluable assistance as I made my own foray into the universe of electronic publications (http://www.etext.org/Zines/eScene/).

K.K.

Introduction

THE SHORT STORY is a difficult literary form, demanding more attention to control and balance than the novel. It is the choice of most beginning writers, attracted to its brevity, its apparent friendliness (a deception) to slender themes, or even its perceived function as a testing ground before attempting the five-hundred-page novel. Then, too, the casual endings that first appeared in *The New Yorker* many decades ago — stories that, to paraphrase Randall Jarrell,* do not so much end as stop — seem to offer easy exit routes, though these soft endings, if not competently handled, can reduce a story to an anecdote. To see it done well, read Jeffrey Eugenides's "Air Mail." This loose ending, now commonly used, can convey both the fluidity of time and the particular of circumstance, letting us appreciate the story as a small dot on the continuum of human experience. It is a subtle form that challenges the reader to hold the page against what he or she knows of life.

This under-the-breath ending seems also to be contributing to the redefinition of the American short story as an excerpt from something — a life, a memoir, a novel. A surprising number of so-called short stories are literally excerpts from larger works; in some publications, notably *The New Yorker,* a chapter or section of a forthcoming novel, not identified as such, is sometimes presented as a short story. One of the criteria for this annual collection is that the works must have been conceived by their authors as short stories — pull-out selections from larger works are not eligible. Two

---

* Randall Jarrell, *Kipling, Auden & Co.,* in reviewing Wright Morris's 1954 novel, *The Huge Season,* wrote, "But though the book pretends to end, it only stops."

pieces in this collection, Jonathan Franzen's "Chez Lambert" and Karen Bender's "Eternal Love," were written as short stories, but since publication the authors have begun developing them as novels. This progression from story to novel is not uncommon, partly, I suspect, because of the more malleable shape of the new short story. The situation is reminiscent of Salman Rushdie's *Haroun and the Sea of Stories,* where the Water Genie speaks of the Ocean of the Streams of Story: "And because the stories were held here in fluid form, they retained the ability to change, to become new versions of themselves, to join up with other stories and so become yet other stories."

Still, in the short story there lingers a faint sense of example, a trimmed, useful tautness implying a function for the reader beyond entertainment. Its focus on an event is, in part, why few stories weather as well as novels — the problems they present, the messages encoded in their sentences, lose application and utility as the *Zeitgeist* shifts and social attention turns to other matters. The reader comes to the short story subliminally expecting enlightenment; that is, we accept the idea that there is some nugget of embedded truth in a short story, and this acceptance partially sponges off the label of fiction in a way that does not occur with the novel in its detailed examination of character.

The stories in this collection might be sorted into categories, though most are complex enough to fit in several or defy all pigeonholes. I suggest them chiefly as a reminder of the rich possibilities of the story form, the endless variations on the events of life, time, and place, the vast and ancient miscellany of human experience from which writers draw.

Manners and Right Behavior stories are often written *via negativa* and present situations of betrayal, lies, cheating, sharp practice, false charges, imposture, infidelity, gross neglect of hygiene, and so forth to make their points. Robert Stone's powerful "Under the Pitons," which draws strength from subtleties and nuance as much as the elemental contest, fits here, and perhaps also Ha Jin's unusual and wry story of vengeance, "Saboteur." Here too we might put Jonathan Franzen's sardonic "Chez Lambert" with its festering Yuban cans of the wrong stuff, and Carolyn Cooke's daedal "Bob Darling" riding the fastest, the last and lonely train with plates of chicken breast on his knee.

Identifying the Stranger satisfies our innate curiosity to know what blood, clan, country, street, mental, emotional, or psychological predilection claims the Unknown One in our midst. Read Michelle Cliff's fresh and exquisitely spare "Transactions" with its lonely traveler and his sudden bizarre act. These stories may be drawn with cruel relish, as Richard Bausch's sharp-toothed "Nobody in Hollywood," Cynthia Ozick's savagely funny "Save My Child!" and Karen E. Bender's cringe-inducing "Eternal Love." Leonard Michaels's "A Girl with a Monkey" has interesting parallels with "Bob Darling," but the weight of the story falls in the other corner.

Perhaps the most common bin through which North American short story writers rummage for subject matter is one we might call *Perceived Social Values.* From here come the stories of families dysfunctional or ideal, stories about the way we face or turn from incurable illnesses or madness or loss through broken heart or death, abortion, divorce, racial discrimination, the striking down or slow dissolution of childhood innocence, expressions and denials of parental love and neglect and abuse, interpretations of right and wrong. A very popular story in recent decades presents the infidelity of a parent through the hindsight observations of a sensitive child-now-grown-up narrator. But few such stories are as finely graven as the one in this collection, Donald Hall's "From Willow Temple." Junot Díaz's "Fiesta, 1980," essentially the same story, seems radically different not only because of Díaz's distinctive style, but because it is in brilliant cultural, ethnic, and class contrast. T. Coraghessan Boyle's "Killing Babies" is a blowtorch playing over contemporary abortion controversies, while the dark and comic "Send Me to the Electric Chair" by Clyde Edgerton catches a sorting of life into right and wrong in a particular regional context, and tags the very high price of bad behavior. "Missing Women" by June Spence roasts all of us. Pam Durban's rich, deeply layered "Soon" examines the dissolution of a family over three generations, spiteful acts, and love transposed.

Many short stories deal with *Rites of Passage* and are perhaps as ancient as human experience. Here are stories of initiation, sexual awakening, seminal journeys, entrance into adulthood and other stages of life, stories of hunts, tests of self against others or natural forces, stories of marriage, divorce, of religious ceremony and realization, identification and recognition of self, and the great curtain raisers and last acts, birth and death. Michael Byers's tense and glowing "Shipmates Down Under" takes the reader to the brink of several crucial life-stage situations, leaves some achingly unresolved. "Powder," a highly compressed virtuoso work from Tobias Wolff, mixes elements of rites of passage stories and trickster tales and ends on a note of sudden and wonderful high exuberance. The falcon of fiction loops the loop over a character in Tim Gautreaux's sly "Little Frogs in a Ditch," a character who throws our pity in our grateful teeth.

The long story is not very often successful; few writers can handle these sustained works that are neither short stories nor novellas. Alyson Hagy's "Search Bay" is a rare example that works, where the power of the story builds through measured unfolding. It is one of two stories in this collection — the other is Lydia Davis's beautiful "St. Martin" — that effectively uses geographical place to deepen meaning and move the events. It has, moreover, the architecture of a complete story rather than the scantling feel of an excerpted novel section.

The process of choosing stories for this collection was simple enough: one reads, sorts, reads again, considers, sorts, scribbles, tears out hair, reads again. Roughly 130 tearsheets arrived in three batches. Katrina Kenison suggested I follow the recent tradition of reading blind — that is, of reading the stories with the authors' names effaced, designed as an exercise in democratic equality. It did not work for me. It seemed absurd that any reader charged with this task of selection would choose stories because of an author's name or reputation, or would neglect a story because he or she had not read the writer's work earlier. (I suspect the more practical reason is to avoid the awkward situation where one might be faced with rejecting a story by a writer friend.) So these stories were read as anyone might read them, with knowledge of the names of the ones who wrote them, but no particular weight on that information.

Of the large pile of stories that were put aside, two or three were strong but marred by anachronisms and careless errors of fact. Of the others, many were competent but not outstanding, some were weak anecdotes, not stories at all. Not a few were written in chatty, slangy conversational style, a kind of facile, TV-dialogue-like jabber characterized by short, hard little sentences with the rhythm of a woodpecker in a dead tree. First-person narrator and present tense grew tiresome. Too many were formulaic: sensitive girls or sensitive ex-cons set against someone ill, or old, or handicapped, or peculiar; mawkish urban and suburban love affairs; college students at intro-to-life summer jobs; the sensitive watcher-child observing mother's or father's adultery; insensitive kids making fun of sensitive kids of different ethnicity. And the same images and characters and actions appeared over and again — university-professor fathers (usually professors of history, literature, or the classics, never science or math), dead mothers (almost never were they university professors), heart attack victims, boys building airplanes, youths sitting in wrecked vehicles in which friends or relatives have died, aged couples featured in photographs taken decades earlier, many, many barking dogs, clove cigarettes, and banal, folksy, one-liner advice given by old dad.

The final selection depended on the strength and vigor of the story, good writing, the story's architectural balance, and a certain intangible feel for the depth of human experience, not uncommonly expressed through a kind of dry humor. There were several finely written stories on familiar themes that were reluctantly put aside in favor of more vigorous and interesting work. I kept the reader in mind as this collection came together and believe that here are provocative and satisfying stories, some of the best of last year's published short American fiction.

E. ANNIE PROULX

Manners and Right Behavior

HA JIN

Saboteur

FROM THE ANTIOCH REVIEW

MR. CHIU and his bride were having lunch in the square before Muji Train Station. On the table between them were two bottles of soda spewing out brown foam, and two paper boxes of rice and sautéed cucumber and pork. "Let's eat," he said to her, and broke the connected ends of the chopsticks. He picked up a slice of streaky pork and put it into his mouth. As he was chewing, a few crinkles appeared on his thin jaw.

To his right, at another table, two railroad policemen were drinking tea and laughing; it seemed that the stout, middle-aged man was telling a joke to his young comrade, who was tall and of athletic build. Now and again they would steal a glance at Mr. Chiu's table.

The air smelled of rotten melon. A few flies kept buzzing above the couple's lunch. Hundreds of people were rushing around to get on the platform or to catch buses to downtown. Food and fruit vendors were crying for customers in lazy voices. About a dozen young women, representing the local hotels, held up placards that displayed the daily prices and words as large as a palm, like *Free Meals, Air Conditioning,* and *On the River.* In the center of the square stood a concrete statue of Chairman Mao, at whose feet peasants were napping with their backs on the warm granite and with their faces toward the sunny sky. A flock of pigeons perched on the chairman's raised hand and forearm.

The rice and cucumber tasted good and Mr. Chiu was eating unhurriedly. His sallow face showed exhaustion. He was glad that the honeymoon was finally over and that he and his bride were heading for Harbin. During the two weeks' vacation, he had been

worried about his liver because three months ago he had suffered
from acute hepatitis; he was afraid he might have a relapse. But
there had been no severe symptom, despite his liver being still big
and tender. On the whole he was pleased with his health, which
could even endure the strain of a honeymoon; indeed, he was on
the course of recovery. He looked at his bride, who took off her
wire glasses, kneading the root of her nose with her fingertips.
Beads of sweat coated her pale cheeks.

"Are you all right, sweetheart?" he asked.

"I have a headache. I didn't sleep well last night."

"Take an aspirin, will you?"

"It's not that serious. Tomorrow is Sunday and I can sleep longer.
Don't worry."

As they were talking, the stout policeman at the next table stood
up and threw a bowl of tea in their direction. Both Mr. Chiu's and
his bride's sandals were wet instantly.

"Hooligan!" she said in a low voice.

Mr. Chiu got to his feet and said out loud, "Comrade policeman,
why did you do this?" He stretched out his right foot to show the wet
sandal.

"Do what?" the stout man asked huskily, glaring at Mr. Chiu while
the young fellow was whistling.

"See, you dumped water on our feet."

"You're lying. You wet your shoes yourself."

"Comrade policeman, your duty is to keep order, but you pur-
posely tortured us common citizens. Why violate the law you are
supposed to enforce?" As Mr. Chiu was speaking, dozens of people
began gathering around.

With a wave of his hand, the man said to the young fellow, "Let's
get hold of him!"

They grabbed Mr. Chiu and clamped handcuffs around his
wrists. He cried, "You can't do this to me. This is utterly unreason-
able."

"Shut up!" The man pulled out his pistol. "You can use your
tongue at our headquarters."

The young fellow added, "You're a saboteur, you know? You're
disrupting public order."

The bride was too terrified to say anything coherent. She was a
recent college graduate, had majored in fine arts, and had never

seen the police make an arrest. All she could say now was "Oh please, please!"

The policemen were pulling Mr. Chiu, but he refused to go with them, holding the corner of the table and shouting, "We have a train to catch. We already bought the tickets."

The stout man punched him in the chest. "Shut up. Let your ticket expire." With the pistol butt he chopped Mr. Chiu's hands, which at once released the table. Together the two men dragged him away to the police station.

Realizing he had to go with them, Mr. Chiu turned his head and shouted to his bride, "Don't wait for me here. Take the train. If I'm not back by tomorrow morning, send someone over to get me out."

She nodded, covering her sobbing mouth with her palm.

After removing his shoelaces, they locked Mr. Chiu into a cell in the back of the Railroad Police Station. The single window in the room was blocked by six steel bars; it faced a spacious yard in which stood a few pines. Beyond the trees two swings hung from an iron frame, swaying gently in the breeze. Somewhere in the building a cleaver was chopping rhythmically. There must be a kitchen upstairs, Mr. Chiu thought.

He was too exhausted to worry about what they would do to him, so he lay down on the narrow bed with his eyes shut. He wasn't afraid. The Cultural Revolution was over already, and recently the Party had been propagating the idea that all citizens were equal before the law. The police ought to be a law-abiding model for common people. As long as he remained cool-headed and reasoned with them, they might not harm him.

Late in the afternoon he was taken to the Interrogation Bureau on the second floor. On his way there, in the stairwell, he ran into the middle-aged policeman who had manhandled him. The man grinned, rolling his bulgy eyes and pointing his fingers at him like firing a pistol. Egg of a tortoise!, Mr. Chiu cursed mentally.

The moment he sat down in the office, he burped, his palm shielding his mouth. In front of him, across a long desk, sat the chief of the bureau and a donkey-faced man. On the glass desktop was a folder containing information on his case. He felt it bizarre that in just a matter of hours they had accumulated a small pile of writing about him. On second thought, he began to wonder whether they had kept a file on him all the time. How could this have happened? He lived and worked in Harbin, more than three hundred miles away, and this was his first time in Muji City.

The chief of the bureau was a thin, bald man who looked serene and intelligent. His slim hands handled the written pages in the folder like those of a lecturing scholar. To Mr. Chiu's left sat a young scribe, with a clipboard on his knee and a black fountain pen in his hand.

"Your name?" the chief asked, apparently reading out the question from a form.

"Chiu Maguang."

"Age?"

"Thirty-four."

"Profession?"

"Lecturer."

"Work unit?"

"Harbin University."

"Political status?"

"Communist Party member."

The chief put down the paper and began to speak. "Your crime is sabotage, although it hasn't induced serious consequences yet. Because you are a Party member, you should be punished more. You have failed to be a model for the masses and you —"

"Excuse me, sir," Mr. Chiu cut him off.

"What?"

"I didn't do anything. Your men are the saboteurs of our social order. They threw hot tea on my feet and my wife's feet. Logically speaking, you should criticize them, if not punish them."

"That statement is groundless. You have no witness. How could I believe you?" the chief said matter-of-factly.

"This is my evidence." He raised his right hand. "Your man hit my fingers with a pistol."

"That can't prove how your feet got wet. Besides, you could hurt your fingers by yourself."

"But I told the truth!" Anger flared up in Mr. Chiu. "Your police station owes me an apology. My train ticket has expired, my new leather sandals are ruined, and I am late for a conference in the provincial capital. You must compensate me for the damage and losses. Don't mistake me for a common citizen who would tremble when you sneeze. I'm a scholar, a philosopher, and an expert in dialectical materialism. If necessary, we will argue about this in the *Northeastern Daily*, or we will go to the highest People's Court in Beijing. Tell me, what's your name?" He got carried away by his harangue, which was by no means trivial and had worked to his advantage on numerous occasions.

"Stop bluffing us," the donkey-faced man broke in. "We have seen a lot of your kind. We can easily prove you are guilty. Here are some of the statements given by the eyewitnesses." He pushed a few sheets of paper toward Mr. Chiu.

Mr. Chiu was dazed to see the different handwritings, which all stated that he had shouted in the square to attract attention and refused to obey the police. One of the witnesses had identified herself as a purchasing agent from a shipyard in Shanghai. Something stirred in Mr. Chiu's stomach, a pain rising to his ribs. He gave out a faint moan.

"Now, you have to admit you are guilty," the chief said. "Although it's a serious crime, we won't punish you severely, provided you write out a self-criticism and promise that you won't disrupt public order again. In other words, whether you will be released will depend on your attitude toward this crime."

"You're daydreaming," Mr. Chiu cried. "I won't write a word, because I'm innocent. I demand that you provide me with a letter of apology so I can explain to my university why I'm late."

Both the interrogators smiled with contempt. "Well, we've never done that," said the chief, taking a puff of his cigarette.

"Then make this a precedent."

"It's unnecessary. We are pretty certain that you will comply with our wishes." The chief blew a column of smoke at Mr. Chiu's face.

At the tilt of the chief's head, two guards stepped forward and grabbed the criminal by the arms. Mr. Chiu meanwhile went on saying, "I shall report you to the provincial administration. You'll have to pay for this! You are worse than the Japanese military police."

They dragged him out of the room.

After dinner, which consisted of a bowl of millet porridge, a corn bun, and a piece of pickled turnip, Mr. Chiu began to have a fever, shaking with a chill and sweating profusely. He knew that the fire of anger had got into his liver and that he was probably having a relapse. No medicine was available, because his briefcase had been left with his bride. At home it would have been time for him to sit in front of their color TV, drinking jasmine tea and watching the evening news. It was so lonesome in here. The orange bulb above the single bed was the only source of light, which enabled the guards to keep him under surveillance at night. A moment ago he had asked them for a newspaper or a magazine to read, but they had turned him down.

Through the small opening on the door, noises came in. It seemed that the police on duty were playing poker or chess in a nearby office; shouts and laughter could be heard now and then. Meanwhile, an accordion kept coughing from a remote corner of the building. Looking at the ballpoint and the letter paper left for him by the guards when they took him back from the Interrogation Bureau, Mr. Chiu remembered the old saying, "When a scholar runs into soldiers, the more he argues, the muddier his point becomes." How ridiculous this whole thing was. He ruffled his thick hair with his fingers.

He felt miserable, massaging his stomach continually. To tell the truth, he was more upset than frightened, because he would have to catch up with his work once he was back home — a paper that was to meet the publishing deadline next week, and two dozen books he ought to read for the courses he was going to teach in the fall.

A human shadow flitted across the opening. Mr. Chiu rushed to the door and shouted through the hole, "Comrade guard, comrade guard!"

"What do you want?" a voice rasped.

"I want you to inform your leaders that I'm very sick. I have heart disease and hepatitis. I may die here if you keep me like this without medication."

"No leader is on duty on the weekend. You have to wait till Monday."

"What? You mean I'll stay in here tomorrow?"

"Yes."

"Your station will be held responsible if anything happens to me."

"We know that. Take it easy, you won't die."

It seemed illogical that Mr. Chiu slept quite well that night, though the light above his head had been on all the time and the straw mattress was hard and infested with fleas. He was afraid of ticks, mosquitoes, cockroaches — any kind of insect but fleas and bedbugs. Once in the countryside, where his school's faculty and staff had helped the peasants harvest crops for a week, his colleagues had joked about his flesh, which they said must have tasted nonhuman to fleas. Except for him, they were all afflicted with hundreds of bites.

More amazing now, he felt he didn't miss his bride a lot. He even enjoyed sleeping alone, perhaps because the honeymoon had tired him out and he needed more rest.

The back yard was quiet on Sunday morning. Pale sunlight streamed through the pine branches. A few sparrows were jumping on the ground, catching caterpillars and ladybugs. Holding the steel bars, Mr. Chiu inhaled the morning air, which smelled meaty. There must be a restaurant or a delicatessen nearby. He reminded himself that he should take this detention with ease. A sentence that Chairman Mao had written to a hospitalized friend rose in his mind: "Since you are already in here, you may as well stay and make the best of it."

His desire for peace of mind originated from his fear that his hepatitis might get worse. He tried to remain unperturbed. However, he was sure that his liver was swelling up, since the fever still persisted. For a whole day he lay in bed, thinking about his paper on the nature of contradictions. Time and again he was overwhelmed by anger, cursing aloud, "A bunch of thugs!" He swore that once he was out, he would write an article about this experience. He had better find out some of the policemen's names.

It turned out to be a restful day for the most part; he was certain that his university would send somebody to his rescue. All he should do now was remain calm and wait patiently. Sooner or later the police would have to release him, although they had no idea that he might refuse to leave unless they wrote him an apology. Damn those hoodlums, they had ordered more than they could eat!

When he woke up on Monday morning, it was already light. Somewhere a man was moaning; the sound came from the back yard. After a long yawn, and kicking off the tattered blanket, Mr. Chiu climbed out of bed and went to the window. In the middle of the yard, a young man was fastened to a pine, his wrists handcuffed from behind around the trunk. He was wriggling and swearing loudly, but there was no sign of anyone else in the yard. He looked familiar to Mr. Chiu.

Mr. Chiu squinted his eyes to see who it was. To his astonishment, he recognized the man, who was Fenjin, a recent graduate from the Law Department at Harbin University. Two years ago Mr. Chiu had taught a course in Marxist materialism in which Fenjin had been enrolled. Now, how on earth had this young devil landed here?

Then it dawned on him that Fenjin must have been sent over by his bride. What a stupid woman! What a bookworm, who knew only how to read foreign novels. He had expected that she would talk to the school's security section, which would for sure send a cadre here. Fenjin held no official position; he merely worked in a private law firm that had just two lawyers; in fact, they had little business except for some detective work for men and women who suspected their spouses of having extramarital affairs. Mr. Chiu was overcome with a wave of nausea.

Should he call out to let his student know he was nearby? He decided not to, because he didn't know what had happened. Fenjin must have quarreled with the police to incur such a punishment. Yet this would not have occurred if Fenjin hadn't come to his rescue. So no matter what, Mr. Chiu had to do something. But what could he do?

It was going to be a scorcher. He could see purple steam shimmering and rising from the ground among the pines. Poor devil, he thought, as he raised a bowl of corn glue to his mouth, sipped, and took a bite of a piece of salted celery.

When a guard came to collect the bowl and the chopsticks, Mr. Chiu asked him what had happened to the man in the back yard. "He called our boss 'bandit,'" the guard said. "He claimed he was a lawyer or something. An arrogant son of a rabbit."

Now it was obvious that Mr. Chiu had to do something to help his rescuer. Before he could figure out a way, a scream broke out in the back yard. He rushed to the window and saw a tall policeman standing before Fenjin, an iron bucket on the ground. It was the same young fellow who had arrested Mr. Chiu in the square two days before. The man pinched Fenjin's nose, then raised his hand, which stayed in the air for a few seconds, then slapped the lawyer across the face. As Fenjin was groaning, the man lifted up the bucket and poured water on his head.

"This will keep you from getting sunstroke, boy. I'll give you some more every hour," the man said loudly.

Fenjin kept his eyes shut, yet his wry face showed that he was struggling to hold back from cursing the policeman or that he was probably sobbing in silence. He sneezed, then raised his face and shouted, "Let me go take a piss."

"Oh yeah?" the man bawled. "Pee in your pants."

Still Mr. Chiu didn't make any noise, holding the steel bars with both hands, his fingers white. The policeman turned and glanced at the cell's window; his pistol, partly holstered, glittered in the sun. With a snort he spat his cigarette butt to the ground and stamped it into the dust.

Then the cell door opened and the guards motioned Mr. Chiu to come out. Again they took him upstairs to the Interrogation Bureau.

The same men were in the office, though this time the scribe was sitting there empty-handed. At the sight of Mr. Chiu the chief said, "Ah, here you are. Please be seated."

After Mr. Chiu sat down, the chief waved a white silk fan and said to him, "You may have seen your lawyer. He's a young man without manners, so our director had him taught a crash lesson in the back yard."

"It's illegal to do that. Aren't you afraid to appear in a newspaper?"

"No, we are not, not even on TV. What else can you do? We are not afraid of any story you make up. We call it fiction. What we do care is that you cooperate with us; that's to say, you must admit your crime."

"What if I refuse to cooperate?"

"Then your lawyer will continue his education in the sunshine."

A swoon swayed Mr. Chiu, and he held the arms of the chair to steady himself. A numb pain stung him in the upper stomach and nauseated him, and his head was throbbing. He was sure that the hepatitis was finally attacking him. Anger was flaming up in his chest. His throat was tight and clogged.

The chief resumed, "As a matter of fact, you don't have to write out your self-criticism. We had your crime described clearly here. What we need is just your signature."

Holding back his rage, Mr. Chiu said, "Let me look at that."

With a smirk the donkey-faced man handed him a sheet, which carried these words: "I hereby admit that on July 13 I disrupted public order at Muji Train Station, and that I refused to listen to reason when the railroad police issued their warning. Thus I myself am responsible for my arrest. After two days' detention, I have realized the reactionary nature of my crime. From now on, I shall continue to educate myself with all my effort and shall never commit this kind of crime again."

A voice started screaming in Mr. Chiu's head, "Lie, lie!" But he shook his head and forced the voice away. He asked the chief, "If I sign this, will you release both my lawyer and me?"

"Of course, we'll do that." The chief was drumming his fingers on the blue folder — their file on him.

Mr. Chiu signed his name and put his thumbprint under his signature.

"Now you are free to go," the chief said with a smile, and handed him a piece of paper to wipe his thumb with.

Mr. Chiu was so sick that he didn't stand up from the chair at the first try. Then he doubled his effort and rose to his feet. He staggered out of the building to meet his lawyer in the back yard. In his chest he felt as though there were a bomb. If he were able to, he would have razed the entire police station and eliminated all their families. Though he knew he could do nothing like that, he made up his mind to do something.

"Sorry about this torture, Fenjin," Mr. Chiu said when they met.

"It doesn't matter. They are savages." The lawyer brushed a patch of dirt off his jacket with his trembling fingers. Water was still dribbling from the bottoms of his trouser legs.

"Let's go now," the teacher said.

The moment they came out of the police station, Mr. Chiu caught sight of a tea stand. He grabbed Fenjin's arm and walked over to the old woman at the table. "Two bowls of black tea," he said, and handed her a one-yuan note.

After the first bowl, they each had another one. Then they set out for the train station. But before they walked fifty yards, Mr. Chiu insisted on eating a bowl of tree-ear soup at a food stand. Fenjin agreed. He told his teacher, "Don't treat me like a guest."

"No, I want to eat something myself."

As if dying of hunger, Mr. Chiu dragged his lawyer from restaurant to restaurant near the police station, but at each place he ordered no more than two bowls of food. Fenjin wondered why his teacher wouldn't stay at one place and eat his fill.

Mr. Chiu bought noodles, wonton, eight-grain porridge, and chicken soup, respectively, at four restaurants. While eating, he kept saying through his teeth, "If only I could kill all the bastards!" At the last place he merely took a few sips of the soup without tasting the chicken cubes and mushrooms.

Fenjin was baffled by his teacher, who looked ferocious and muttered to himself mysteriously, and whose jaundiced face was covered with dark puckers. For the first time Fenjin thought of Mr. Chiu as an ugly man.

Within a month, over eight hundred people contracted acute hepatitis in Muji. Six died of the disease, including two children. Nobody knew how the epidemic had started.

ROBERT STONE

Under the Pitons

FROM ESQUIRE

ALL THE PREVIOUS DAY, they had been tacking up from the Grenadines, bound for Martinique to return the boat and take leave of Freycinet. Blessington was trying to forget the anxieties of the deal, the stink of menace, the sick ache behind the eyes. It was dreadful to have to smoke with the St. Vincentian dealers, stone killers who liked to operate from behind a thin film of fear. But the Frenchman was tough.

Off Dark Head there was a near thing with a barge under tow. Blessington, stoned at the wheel, his glass of straight Demerara beside the binnacle, had calmly watched a dimly lighted tug struggle past on a parallel course at a distance of a mile or so. The moon was newly risen, out of sight behind the island's mountains, silvering the line of the lower slopes. A haze of starlight left the sea in darkness, black as the pit, now and then flashing phosphorescence. They were at least ten miles offshore.

With his mainsail beginning to luff, he had steered the big ketch a little farther off the wind, gliding toward the trail of living light in the tug's wake. Only in the last second did the dime drop; he took a quick look over his shoulder. And of course there came the barge against the moon-traced mountains, a big black homicidal juggernaut, unmarked and utterly unlighted, bearing down on them. Blessington swore and spun the wheel like Ezekiel, as hard to port as it went, thinking that if his keel was over the cable nothing would save them, that 360 degrees of helm or horizon would be less than enough to escape by.

Then everything not secured came crashing down on everything

else, the tables and chairs on the afterdeck went over, plates and
bottles smashed, whatever was breakable immediately broke. The
boat, the *Sans Regret*, fell off the wind like a comedian and flapped
into a flying jibe. A couple of yards to starboard the big barge raced
past like a silent freight train, betrayed only by the slap of its hull
against the waves. It might have been no more than the wind, for all
you could hear of it. When it was safely gone, the day's fear welled
up again and gagged him.

The Frenchman ran out on deck cursing and looked to the
cockpit, where Blessington had the helm. His hair was cut close to
his skull. He showed his teeth in the mast light. He was brushing his
shorts; something had spilled in his lap.

"Qu'est-ce que c'est là?" he demanded of Blessington. Blessington
pointed into the darkness where the barge had disappeared. The
Frenchman knew only enough of the ocean to fear the people on it.
"Quel cul!" he said savagely. "Who is it?" He was afraid of the Coast
Guard and of pirates.

"We just missed being sunk by a barge. No lights. Submerged
cable. It's okay now."

"Fuck," said the Frenchman, Freycinet. "Why are you stopping?"

"Stopping?" It took a moment to realize that Freycinet was under
the impression that because the boat had lost its forward motion
they were stopping, as though he had applied a brake. Freycinet
had been around boats long enough to know better. He must be
out of his mind, Blessington thought.

"I'm not stopping, Honoré. We're all right."

"I bust my fucking ass below," said Freycinet. "Marie fall out
of bed."

Tough shit, thought Blessington. Be thankful you're not treading
water in the splinters of your stupidly named boat. "Sorry man," he
said.

Sans Regret, with its fatal echoes of Piaf. The Americans might be
culturally deprived, Blessington thought, but surely every cutter in
the Yankee Coast Guard would have the sense to board that one.
And the cabin stank of the resiny ganja they had stashed, along with
the blow, under the cabin sole. No amount of roach spray or air
freshener could cut it. The space would probably smell of dope
forever.

Freycinet went below without further complaint, missing in his ignorance the opportunity to abuse Blessington at length. It had been Blessington's fault they had not seen the barge sooner, stoned and drunk as he was. He should have looked for it as soon as the tug went by. To stay awake through the night he had taken crystal and his peripheral vision was flashing him little mongoose darts, shooting stars composed of random light. Off the north shore of St. Vincent, the winds were murder.

Just before sunrise, he saw the Pitons rising from the sea off the starboard bow, the southwest coast of St. Lucia. Against the pink sky, the two peaks looked like a single mountain. It was hard to take them for anything but a good omen. As the sudden dawn caught fire, they turned green with hope. So many hearts, he thought, must have lifted at the sight of them.

To Blessington, they looked like the beginning of home free. Or at least free. Martinique was the next island up, where they could return the boat and Blessington could take his portion and be off to America on his student visa. He had a letter of acceptance from a hotel-management school in Florida but his dream was to open a restaurant in the Keys.

He took another deep draft of the rum to cut the continuing anxieties. The first sunlight raised a sweat on him, so he took his shirt off and put on his baseball hat. Florida Marlins.

Freycinet came out on deck while he was having a drink.

"You're a drunk Irishman," Freycinet told him.

"That I'm not," said Blessington. It seemed to him no matter how much he drank he would never be drunk again. The three Vincentians had sobered him for life. He had been sitting on the porch of the guesthouse on Canouan when they walked up. They had approached like panthers — no metaphor, no politics intended. Their every move was a dark roll of musculature, balanced and wary. They were very big men with square scarred faces. Blessington had been reclining, tilted backward in a cane chair with his feet on the porch rail, when they came up to him.

"Frenchy?" one had asked very softly.

Blessington had learned the way of hard men back in Ireland and thought he could deal with them. He had been careful to maintain his relaxed position.

"I know the man you mean, sir," he had said. "But I'm not him, see. You'll have to wait."

At Blessington's innocuous words they had tensed in every fiber, although you had to be looking right at them to appreciate the physics of it. They drew themselves up around their hidden weaponry behind a silent, drug-glazed wall of suspicion that looked impermeable to reason. They were zombies, without mercy, and he, Blessington, was wasting their time. He resolved to count to thirty but at the count of ten he took his feet down off the rail.

Freycinet turned and shaded his eyes and looked toward the St. Lucia coast. The Pitons delighted him.

"Ah, là. C'est les Pitons, n'est-ce pas?"

"Oui," said Blessington. *"Les Pitons."* They had gone south in darkness and Freycinet had never seen them before.

The wind shifted to its regular quarter and he had a hard time tacking level with the island. The two women came out on deck. Freycinet's Marie was blond and very young. She came from Normandy and she had been a waitress in the bistro outside Fort-de-France, where Freycinet and Blessington cooked. Sometimes she seemed so sunny and innocent that it was hard to connect her with a hood like Freycinet. At other times she seemed very knowing indeed. It was hard to tell, she was so often stoned.

Gillian was an American from Texas. She had a hard, thin face with a prominent nose and a big jaw. Her father, Blessington imagined, was one of those Texans, a tough, loud man who cursed the Mexicans. She was extremely tall and rather thin, with very long legs. Her slenderness and height and interesting face had taken her into modeling, to Paris and Milan. In contrast, she had muscular thighs and a big derriere, which, if it distressed the couturiers, made her more desirable. She was Blessington's designated girlfriend on the trip but they rarely made love because, influenced by the others, he had taken an early dislike to her. He supposed she knew it.

"Oh, wow," she said in her Texas voice, "look at those pretty mountains."

It was exactly the kind of American comment that made the others all despise and imitate her — even Marie, who had no English at all. Gillian had come on deck stark naked, and each of them, the Occitan Freycinet, Norman Marie, and Irish Blessington, felt scornful and slightly offended. Anyone else might have been forgiven. They had decided she was a type and she could do no right.

Back on Canouan, Gillian had conceived a lust for one of the dealers. At first, when everyone smoked in the safe house, they had paid no attention to the women. The deal was repeated to everyone's satisfaction. As the dealers gave forth their odor of menace Marie had skillfully disappeared herself in plain view. But Gillian, to Blessington's humiliation and alarm, had put out a ray and one of the men had called her on it.

Madness. In a situation so volatile, so bloody *fraught*. But she was full of lusts, was Texan Gillian, and physically courageous, too. He noticed she whined less than the others, in spite of her irritating accent. It had ended with her following the big St. Vincentian to her guesthouse room, walking ten paces behind with her eyes down, making herself a prisoner, a lamb for the slaughter.

For a while Blessington had thought she would have to do all three of them but it had been only the one, Nigel. Nigel had returned her to Blessington in a grim little ceremony, holding her with the chain of her shark's-tooth necklace twisted tight around her neck.

"Wan' have she back, mon?"

Leaving Blessington with the problem of how to react. The big bastard was fucking welcome to her but of course it would have been tactless to say so. Should he protest and get everyone killed? Or should he be complacent and be thought a pussy and possibly achieve the same result? It was hard to find a middle ground but Blessington found one, a tacit, ironic posture, fashioned of silences and body language. The Irish had been a subject race, too, after all.

"I gon' to make you a present, mon. Give you little pink piggy back. Goodness of my ha'art."

So saying, Nigel had put his huge busted-knuckle hand against her pale hard face and she had looked down submissively, trembling a little, knowing not to smile. Afterward, she was very cool about it. Nigel had given her a little Rasta bracelet, beads in the red, yellow, and green colors of Ras Tafari.

"Think I'm a pink piggy, Liam?"

He had not been remotely amused and he had told her so.

So she had walked on ahead laughing and put her palms together and looked up to the sky and said, "Oh, my Lord!" And then glanced at him and wiped the smile off her face. Plainly she'd enjoyed it, all of it. She wore the bracelet constantly.

Now she leaned on her elbows against the chart table with her bare bum thrust out, turning the bracelet with the long, bony fingers of her right hand. Though often on deck, she seemed never to burn or tan. A pale child of night was Gillian.

"What island you say that was?" she asked.

"It's St. Lucia," Blessington told her. "The mountains are called the Pitons."

"The Pee-tuns? Does that mean something cool in French?" She turned to Blessington, then to Freycinet. "Does it, Honoré?"

Freycinet made an unpleasant, ratty face. He was ugly as cat shit, Blessington thought, something Gillian doubtless appreciated. He had huge soulful brown eyes and a pointed nose like a puppet's. His military haircut showed the flattened shape of his skull.

"It means stakes," Blessington said.

"Steaks? Like . . ."

"Sticks," said Blessington. "Rods. Palings."

"Oh," she said, "stakes. Like Joan of Arc got burned at, right?"

Freycinet's mouth fell open. Marie laughed loudly. Gillian looked slyly at Blessington.

"Honoré," she said. "*Tu es un dindon.* You're a *dindon*, man. I'm shitting you. I understand French fine."

It had become amusing to watch her tease and confound Freycinet. Dangerous work and she did it cleverly, leaving the Frenchman to marvel at the depths of her stupidity until paranoia infected his own self-confidence. During the trip back, Blessington thought he might be starting to see the point of her.

"I mean, I worked the Paris openings for five years straight. I told you that."

Drunk and stoned as the rest of them, Gillian eventually withdrew from the ascending spring sun. Marie went down after her. Freycinet's pointed nose was out of joint.

"You hear what she say?" he asked Blessington. "That she speak French all the time? What the fuck? Because she said before, '*Non,* I don't speak it.' Now she's speaking it."

"Ah, she's drunk, Honoré. She's just a bimbo."

"I 'ope so, eh?" said Freycinet. He looked at the afterdeck to be sure she was out of earshot. "Because . . . because what if she setting us up? All zese time, eh? If she's *agent.* Or she's informer? A grass?"

Blessington pondered it deeply. Like the rest of them he had thought her no more than a fatuous, if perverse, American. Now, the way she laughed at them, he was not at all sure.

"I thought she came with you. Did she put money up?"

Freycinet puffed out his hollow cheeks and shrugged.

"She came to me from Lavigerie," he said. The man who called himself Lavigerie was a French Israeli of North African origin, a hustler in Fort-de-France. "She put in money, *oui*. The same as everyone."

They had all pooled their money for the boat and to pay the Vincentians. Blessington had invested $20,000, partly his savings from the bistro, partly borrowed from his sister and her husband in Providence. He expected to make it back many times over and pay them off with interest.

"Twenty thousand?"

"Yes. Twenty."

"Well, even the Americans wouldn't spend twenty thousand dollars to catch us," he told Honoré. "We're too small. And it isn't how they work."

"Now I think I don't trust her, eh?" said Freycinet. He squinted into the sun. The Pitons, no closer, seemed to displease him now. "She's a bitch, *non?*"

"I think she's all right," Blessington said. "I really do."

And for the most part he did. In any case he had decided to, because an eruption of hard-core, coke-and-speed-headed paranoia could destroy them all. It had done so to many others. Missing boats sometimes turned up on the mangrove shore of some remote island, the hulls blistered with bullet holes, cabins attended by unimaginable swarms of flies. Inside, *tableaux morts* not to be forgotten by the unlucky discoverer. Strong-stomached photographers recorded the *tableaux* for the DEA's files, where they were stamped NOT TO BE DESTROYED, HISTORIC INTEREST. The bureau took a certain satisfaction. Blessington knew all this from his sister and her husband in Providence.

Now they were almost back to Martinique and Blessington wanted intensely not to die at sea. In the worst of times, he grew frightened to the point of utter despair. It had been, he realized at such times, a terrible mistake. He gave up on the money. He would settle for just living, for living even in prison in France or America. Or at least for not dying on that horrible bright blue ocean, aboard the *Sans Regret*.

"Yeah," he told Freycinet. "Hell, I wouldn't worry about her. Just a bimbo."

All morning they tacked for the Pitons. Around noon a great crown of puffy cloud settled around Gros Piton and they were close enough to distinguish the two peaks one from the other. Freycinet refused to go below. His presence was so unpleasant that Blessington felt like weeping, knocking him unconscious, throwing him overboard, or jumping over himself. But the Frenchman remained in the cockpit though he never offered to spell Blessington at the wheel. The man drove Blessington to drink. He poured more Demerara and dipped his finger in the bag of crystal. A pulse fluttered under his collarbone, fear, speed.

Eventually, Freycinet went below. After half an hour, Gillian came topside, clothed this time, in cutoffs and a halter. The sea had picked up and she nearly lost her balance on the ladder.

"Steady," said Blessington.

"Want a roofie, Liam?"

He laughed. "A roofie? What's that? Some kind of . . ."

Gillian finished the thought he had been too much of a prude to articulate.

"Some kind of blowjob? Some kind of sex technique? No, dear, it's a medication."

"I'm on watch."

She laughed at him. "You're shitfaced is what you are."

"You know," Blessington said, "you ought not to tease Honoré. You'll make him paranoid."

"He's an asshole. As we say back home."

"That may be. But he's a very mercurial fella. I used to work with him."

"Mercurial? If you know he's so mercurial how come you brought him?"

"I didn't bring him," Blessington said. "He brought me. For my vaunted seamanship. And I came for the money. How about you?"

"I came on account of having my brains in my ass," she said, shaking her backside. "My talent, too. Did you know I was a barrel racer? I play polo, too. English or western, man, you name it."

"English or western?" Blessington asked.

"Forget it," she said. She frowned at him, smiled, frowned again. "You seem, well, scared."

"Ah," said Blessington, "scared? Yes, I am. Somewhat."

"I don't give a shit," she said.

"You don't?"

"You heard me," she said. "I don't care what happens. Why should I? Me with my talent in my ass. Where do I come in?"

"You shouldn't talk that way," Blessington said.

"Fuck you. You afraid I'll make trouble? I assure you I could make trouble like you wouldn't believe."

"I don't doubt it," Blessington said. He kept his eyes on the Pitons. His terror, he thought, probably encouraged her.

"Just between you and me, Liam, I have no fear of dying. I would just as soon be out here on this boat now as in my little comfy bed with my stuffed animals. I would just as soon be dead."

He took another sip of rum to wet his pipes for speech. "Why did you put the money in, then? Weren't you looking for a score?"

"I don't care about money," she said. "I thought it would be a kick. I thought it would be radical. But it's just another exercise in how everything sucks."

"Well," said Blessington, "you're right there."

She looked off at the twin mountains.

"They don't seem a bit closer than they did this morning."

"No. It's an upwind passage. Have to tack forever."

"You know what Nigel told me back on Canouan?"

"No," Blessington said.

"He told me not to worry about understanding things. He said understanding was weak and lame. He said you got to *overstand* things." She hauled herself and did the voice of a big St. Vincentian man saddling up a white bitch for the night, laying down wisdom. "You got to *overstand* it. *Overstand* it, right? Funny, huh."

"Maybe there's something in it," said Blessington.

"Rasta lore," she said. "Could be, man."

"Anyway, never despise what the natives tell you, that's what my aunt used to say. Even in America."

"And what was your aunt? A dope dealer?"

"She was a nun," Blessington said. "A missionary."

For a while Gillian sunned herself on the foredeck, halter off. But the sun became too strong and she crawled back to the cockpit.

"You ever think about how it is in this part of the world?" she asked him. "The Caribbean and around it? It's all suckin' stuff they got. Suckin' stuff, all goodies and no nourishment."

"What do you mean?"

"It's all turn-ons and illusion," she said. "Don't you think? Like coffee." She numbered items on the long fingers of her left hand. "Tobacco. Emeralds. Sugar. Cocaine. Ganja. It's all stuff you don't need. Isn't even good for you. Perks and pick-me-ups and pogy bait. Always has been."

"You're right," Blessington said. "Things people kill for."

"Overpriced. Put together by slaves and peons. Piggy stuff. For pink piggies."

"I hadn't thought of it," he said. He looked over at her. She had raised a fist to her pretty mouth. "You're clever, Gillian."

"You don't even like me," she said.

"Yes I do."

"Don't you dare bullshit me. I said you don't."

"Well," Blessington said, "to tell you the truth, at first I didn't. But now I do."

"Oh, yeah? Why?"

Blessington considered before speaking. The contrary wind was picking up and there were reefs at the south end of the island. Some kind of monster tide was running against them, too.

"Because you're intelligent. I hadn't realized that. You had me fooled, see? Now I think you're amusing."

"Amusing?" She seemed more surprised than angry.

"You really are so bloody clever," he said, finishing the glass of rum. "When we're together I like it. You're not a cop, are you? Anything like that?"

"You only wish," she said. "How about you?"

"Me? I'm Irish, for Christ's sake."

"Is that like not being real?"

"Well," he said, "a little. In many cases."

"You are scared," she said. "You're scared of everything. Scared of me."

"Holy Christ," said Blessington, "you're as bad as Honoré. Look, Gillian, I'm a chef, not a pirate. I never claimed otherwise. Of course I'm scared."

She made him no answer.

"But not of you," he said. "No. Not anymore. I like you here. You're company."

"Am I?" she asked. "Do you? Would you marry me?"

"Hey," said Blessington. "Tomorrow."

Freycinet came up on deck, looked at the Pitons, then up at Blessington and Gillian in the cockpit.

"*Merde*," he said. "Far away still. What's going on?"

"We're getting there," Blessington said. "We're closer now than we look."

"Aren't the mountains pretty, Honoré?" Gillian asked. "Don't you wish we could climb one?"

Freycinet ignored her. "How long?" he asked Blessington.

"To Martinique? Tomorrow sometime, I guess."

"How long before we're off les Pitons?"

"Oh," Blessington said, "just a few hours. Well before dark so we'll have a view. Better steer clear, though."

"Marie is sick."

"Poor puppy," Gillian said. "Probably all that bug spray. Broth's the thing. Don't you think, Liam?"

"Ya, it's kicking up," Blessington said. "There's a current running and a pretty stiff offshore breeze."

"*Merde*," said Freycinet again. He went forward along the rail and lay down beside the anchor windlass, peering into the chains.

"He's a cook, too," Gillian said, speaking softly. "How come you're not more like him?"

"An accident of birth," Blessington said.

"If we were married," she said, "you wouldn't have to skip on your visa."

"Ah," said Blessington, "don't think it hasn't occurred to me. Nice to be a legal resident."

"Legal my ass," she said.

Freycinet suddenly turned and watched them. He showed them the squint, the bared canines.

"What you're talking about, you two? About me, eh?"

"Damn, Honoré!" Gillian said. "He was just proposing." When he had turned around again she spoke between her teeth. "Shithead is into the blow. He keeps prying up the sole. Cures Marie's mal de mer. Keeps him on his toes."

"God save us," said Blessington. Leaning his elbow on the helm, he took Gillian's right hand and put it to her forehead, her left shoulder, and then her right one, walking her through the sign of the cross. "Pray for us like a good girl."

Gillian made the sign again by herself. "Shit," she said, "now I feel a lot better. No, really," she said when he laughed, "I do. I'm gonna do it all the time now. Instead of chanting *Om* or *Nam myoho renge kyo.*"

They sat and watched the peaks grow closer, though the contrary current increased.

"When this is over," Blessington said, "maybe we ought to stay friends."

"If we're still alive," she said, "we might hang out together. We could go to your restaurant in the Keys."

"That's what we'll do," he said. "I'll make you a sous-chef."

"I'll wait tables."

"No, no. Not you."

"But we won't be alive," she said.

"But if we are."

"If we are," she said, "we'll stay together." She looked at him sway beside the wheel. "You better not be shitting me."

"I wouldn't. I think it was meant to be."

"Meant to be? You're putting me on."

"Don't make me weigh my words, Gillian. I want to say what occurs to me."

"Right," she said, touching him. "When we're together you can say any damn thing."

The green mountains, in the full richness of afternoon, rose above them. Blessington had a look at the chart to check the location of the offshore reefs. He began steering to another quarter, away from the tip of the island.

Gillian sat on a locker with her arms around his neck, leaning against his back. She smelled of sweat and patchouli.

"I've never been with anyone as beautiful as you, Gillian."

He saw she had gone to sleep. He disengaged her arms and helped her lie flat on the locker in the shifting shade of the mainsail. Life is a dream, he thought. Something she knew and I didn't.

I love her, Blessington thought. She encourages me. The shadow of the peaks spread over the water.

Freycinet came out on deck and called up to him.

"Liam! We're to stop here. Off les Pitons."

"We can't," Blessington said, though it was tempting. He was so tired.

"We have to stop. We can anchor, yes? Marie is sick. We need to rest. We want to see them."

"We'd have to clear customs," Blessington said. "We'll have bloody cops and boat boys and God knows what else."

He realized at once what an overnight anchorage would entail. All of them up on speed or the cargo, cradling shotguns, peering into the moonlight while they waited for *macheteros* to come on feathered oars and steal their shit and kill them.

"If we anchor," Freycinet said, "if we anchor somewhere, we won't have to clear."

"Yes, yes," Blessington said. "We will, sure. The fucking boat boys will find us. If we don't hire them or buy something they'll turn us in." He picked up the cruising guide and waved it in the air. "It says right here you have to clear customs in Soufrière."

"We'll wait until they have close," said Freycinet.

"Shit," said Blessington desperately, "we'll be fined. We'll be boarded."

Freycinet was smiling at him, a broad demented smile of infinitely self-assured contempt. Cocaine. He felt Gillian put her arm around his leg from behind.

"*Écoutez,* Liam. *Écoutez bien.* We going to stop, man. We going to stop where I say."

He turned laughing into the wind, gripping a stay.

"What did I tell you," Gillian said softly. "You won't have to marry me after all. 'Cause we're dead, baby."

"I don't accept that," Blessington said. "Take the wheel," he told her.

Referring to the charts and the cruising guide, he could find no anchorage that looked as though it would be out of the wind and that was not close inshore. The only possibility was a shallow reef, near the south tip, sometimes favored by snorkeling trips, nearly three miles off the Pitons. It was in the lee of the huge peaks, its coral heads as shallow as a single fathom. The chart showed mooring floats; presumably it was forbidden to anchor there for the sake of the coral.

"I beg you to reconsider, Honoré," Blessington said to Freycinet. He cleared his throat. "You're making a mistake."

Freycinet turned back to him with the same smile.

"Eh, Liam. You can leave, man. You know, there's an Irish pub in Soufrière. It's money from your friends in the IRA. You can go there, eh?"

Blessington had no connection whatsoever with the IRA, although he had allowed Freycinet and his friends to believe that, and they had chosen to.

"You can go get drunk there," Freycinet told him and then turned again to look at the island.

He was standing near the bow with his bare toes caressing free-board, gripping a stay. Blessington and Gillian exchanged looks. In the next instant she threw the wheel, the mainsail boom went crashing across the cabin roofs, the boat lurched to port and heeled hard. For a moment Freycinet was suspended over blank blue water. Blessington clambered up over the cockpit and stood swaying there for a moment, hesitating. Then he reached out for Freycinet. The Frenchman swung around the stay like a monkey and knocked him flat. The two of them went sprawling. Freycinet got to his feet in a karate stance, cursing.

"You shit," he said, when his English returned. "Cunt! What?"

"I thought you were going over, Honoré. I thought I'd have to pull you back aboard."

"That's right, Honoré," Gillian said from the cockpit. "You were like a goner. He saved your ass, man."

Freycinet pursed his lips and nodded. "Bien," he said. He climbed down into the cockpit in a brisk, businesslike fashion and slapped Gillian across the face, backhand and forehand, turning her head around each time.

He gave Blessington the wheel, then he took Gillian under the arm and pulled her up out of the cockpit. "Get below! I don't want to fucking see you." He followed her below and Blessington heard him speak briefly to Marie. The young woman began to moan. The Pitons looked close enough to strike with a rock and a rich jungle smell came out on the wind. Freycinet, back on deck, looked as though he was sniffing out menace. A divi-divi bird landed on the boom for a moment and then fluttered away.

"I think I have a place," Blessington said, "if you still insist. A reef."

"A reef, eh?"

"A reef about four thousand meters offshore."

"We could have a swim, non?"

"We could, yes."

"But I don't know if I want to swim with you, Liam. I think you try to push me overboard."

"I think I saved your life," Blessington said.

They motored on to the reef, with Freycinet standing in the bow to check for bottom as Blessington watched the depth recorder. At ten meters of bottom, they were an arm's length from the single float in view. Blessington cut the engine and came about and then went forward to cleat a line to the float. The float was painted red, yellow, and green. Rasta colors like Gillian's bracelet.

It was late afternoon and suddenly dead calm. The protection the Pitons offered from the wind was ideal and the bad current that ran over the reef to the south seemed to divide around these coral heads. A perfect dive site, Blessington thought, and he could not understand why even in June there were not more floats or more boats anchored there. It seemed a steady enough place even for an overnight anchorage, although the cruising guide advised against it because of the dangerous reefs on every side.

The big ketch lay motionless on unruffled water; the float line drifted slack. There was sandy beach and a palm-lined shore across the water. It was a lonely part of the coast, across a jungle mountain track from the island's most remote resort. Through binoculars Blessington could make out a couple of boats hauled up on the strand but no one seemed ready to come out and hustle them. With luck it was too far from shore.

It might be also, he thought, that for metaphysical reasons they presented a forbidding aspect. But an aspect that deterred small predators might in time attract big ones.

Marie came up, pale and hollow-eyed, in her bikini. She gave Blessington a chastising look and lay down on the cushions on the afterdeck. Gillian came up behind her and took a seat on the gear locker behind Blessington.

"The fucker's got no class," she said softly. "See him hit me?"

"Of course. I was next to you."

"Gonna let him get away with that?"

"Well," Blessington said, "for the moment it behooves us to let him feel in charge."

"Behooves us?" she asked. "You say it *behooves* us?"

"That's right."

"Hey, what were you gonna do back there, Liam?" she asked. "Deep-six him?"

"I honestly don't know. He might have fallen."

"I was wondering," she said. "He was wondering, too."

Blessington shrugged.

"He's got the overstanding," Gillian said. "We got the under." She looked out at the water and said, "Boat boys."

He looked where she was looking and saw the boat approaching, a speck against the shiny sand. It took a long time for it to cover the distance between the beach and the *Sans Regret.*

There were two boat boys, and they were not boys but men in their thirties, lean and unsmiling. One wore a wool tam-o'-shanter in bright tie-dyed colors. The second looked like an East Indian. His black headband gave him a lascar look.

"You got to pay for dat anchorage, mon," the man in the tam called to them. "Not open to de public widout charge."

"We coming aboard," said the lascar. "We take your papers and passports in for you. You got to clear."

"How much for the use of the float?" Blessington asked.

Suddenly Freycinet appeared in the companionway. He was carrying a big French MAS 36 sniper rifle, pointing it at the men in the boat, showing his pink-edged teeth.

"You get the fuck out of here," he shouted at them. A smell of ganja and vomit seemed to follow him up from the cabin. "Understand?"

The two men did not seem unduly surprised at Freycinet's behavior. Blessington wondered if they could smell the dope as distinctly as he could.

"Fuckin' Frenchman," the man in the tam said. "Think he some shit."

"Why don' you put the piece down, Frenchy?" the East Indian asked. "This ain't no Frenchy island. You got to clear."

"You drift on that reef, Frenchy," the man in the tam said, "you be begging us to take you off."

Freycinet was beside himself with rage. He hated *les nègres* more than any Frenchman Blessington had met in Martinique, which was saying a great deal. He had contained himself during the negotiations on Canouan but now he seemed out of control. Blessington began to wonder if he would shoot the pair of them.

"You fucking monkeys!" he shouted. "You stay away from me, eh? Chimpanzees! I kill you quick . . . *mon,*" he added with a sneer.

The men steered their boat carefully over the reef and sat with their outboard idling. They could not stay too long, Blessington

thought. Their gas tank was small and it was a long way out against
a current.

"Well," he asked Gillian, "who's got the overstanding now?"

"Not Honoré," she said.

A haze of heat and doped lassitude settled over their mooring.
Movement was labored, even speech seemed difficult. Blessington
and Gillian nodded off on the gear locker. Marie seemed to have
lured Freycinet belowdecks. Prior to dozing, Blessington heard her
imitate the Frenchman's angry voice and the two of them laughing
down in the cabin. The next thing he saw clearly was Marie, in her
bikini, standing on the cabin roof, screaming. A shotgun blasted
and echoed over the still water. Suddenly the slack breeze had a
brisk cordite smell and it carried smoke.

Freycinet shouted, holding the hot shotgun.

The boat with the two islanders in it seemed to have managed to
come up on them. Now it raced off, headed first out to sea to round
the tip of the reef and then curving shoreward to take the inshore
current at an angle.

"Everyone all right?" asked Blessington.

"Fucking monkeys!" Freycinet swore.

"Well," Blessington said, watching the boat disappear, "they're
gone for now. Maybe," he suggested to Freycinet, "we can have our
swim and go too."

Freycinet looked at him blankly as though he had no idea what
Blessington was talking about. He nodded vaguely.

After half an hour Marie rose and stood on the bulwark and
prepared to dive, arms foremost. When she went, her dive was a
good one, straight-backed and nearly splash-free. She performed a
single stroke underwater and sped like a bright shaft between the
coral heads below and the crystal surface. Then she appeared pret-
tily in the light of day, blinking like a child, shaking her shining
hair.

From his place in the bow, Freycinet watched Marie's dive, her
underwater career, her pert surfacing. His expression was not affectionate but taut and tight-lipped. The muscles in his neck stood
out, his moves were twitchy like a street junkie's. He looked exhausted and angry. The smell of cordite hovered around him.

"He's a shithead and a loser," Gillian said softly to Blessington.
She looked not at Freycinet but toward the green mountains. "I

thought he was cool. He was so fucking mean, I, like, respected that. Now we're all gonna die. Well," she said, "goes to show, right?"

"Don't worry," Blessington told her. "I won't leave you."

"Whoa," said Gillian. "All right!" But her enthusiasm was not genuine. She was mocking him.

Blessington forgave her.

Freycinet pointed a finger at Gillian. "Swim!"

"What if I don't wanna?" she asked, already standing up. When he began to swear at her in a hoarse voice she took her clothes off in front of them. Everything but the Rasta bracelet.

"I think I will if no one minds," she said. "Where you want me to swim to, Honoré?"

"Swim to fucking *Amérique*," he said. He laughed as though his mood had improved. "You want her, Liam?"

"People are always asking me that," Blessington said. "What do I have to do?"

"You swim to fucking *Amérique* with her."

Blessington saw Gillian take a couple of pills from her cutoff pocket and swallow them dry.

"I can't swim that far," Blessington said.

"Go as far as you can," said Freycinet.

"How about you?" Gillian said to the Frenchman. "You're the one wanted to stop. So ain't you gonna swim?"

"I don't trust her," Freycinet said to Blessington. "What do you think?"

"She's a beauty," Blessington said. "Don't provoke her."

Gillian measured her beauty against the blue water and dived over the side. A belly full of pills, Blessington thought. But her strokes when she surfaced were strong and defined. She did everything well, he thought. She was good around the boat. She had a pleasant voice for country music. He could imagine her riding, a cowgirl.

"Bimbo, eh?" Freycinet asked. "That's it, eh?"

"Yes," Blessington said. "Texas and all that."

"*Oui,*" said Freycinet. "Texas." He yawned. "*Bien*. Have your swim with her. If you want."

Blessington went down into the stinking cabin and put his bathing suit on. Propriety to the last. The mixture of ganja, sick, roach spray, and pine scent was asphyxiating. If he survived, he thought, he would never smoke hash again. Never drink rum, never do speed or cocaine, never sail or go where there were palm trees and too many stars overhead. A few fog-shrouded winter constellations would do.

"Tonight I'll cook, eh?" Freycinet said when Blessington came back up. "You can assist me."

"Good plan," said Blessington.

Standing on the bulwark, he looked around the boat. There were no other vessels in sight. Marie was swimming backstroke, describing a safe circle about twenty-five yards out from the boat. Gillian appeared to be headed hard for the open sea. She had reached the edge of the current, where the wind raised small horsetails from the rushing water.

If Freycinet was planning to leave them in the water, Blessington wondered, would he leave Marie with them? It would all be a bad idea because Freycinet was not a skilled sailor. And there was a possibility of their being picked up right here or even of their making it to shore, although that seemed most unlikely. On the other hand he had discovered that Freycinet's ideas were often impulses, mainly bad ones. It was his recklessness that had made him appear so capably in charge, and that was as true in the kitchen as it was on the Raging Main. He had been a reckless cook.

Besides, there were a thousand dark possibilities on that awful ocean. That he had arranged to be met at sea off Martinique, that there had been some betrayal in the works throughout. Possibly involving Lavigerie or someone else in Fort-de-France.

"Yes," said Blessington. "There's time to unfreeze the grouper."

He looked at the miles of ocean between the boat and the beach at the foot of the mountains. Far off to the right he could see white water, the current running swiftly over the top of a reef that extended southwesterly, at a forty-five-degree angle to the beach. Beyond the reef was a sandspit where the island tapered to its narrow southern end. On their left, the base of the mountains extended to the edge of the sea, forming a rock wall against which the waves broke. According to the charts, the wall plunged to a depth of ten fathoms, and the ocean concealed a network of submarine caves and grottoes in the volcanic rock of which the Pitons were composed. Across the towering ridge, completely out of sight, was the celebrated resort.

"I'll take it out of the freezer," Blessington said.

A swimmer would have to contrive to make land somewhere between the rock wall to the north and the reef and sandspit on the right. There would be easy swimming at first, through the windless afternoon, and a swimmer would not feel any current for the first mile or so. The last part of the swim would be partly against a brisk current, and possibly against the tide. The final mile would seem much farther. For the moment, wind was not in evidence. The current might be counted on to lessen as one drew closer to shore. If only one could swim across it in time.

"It's all right," said Freycinet. "I'll do it. Have your swim."

Beyond that, there was the possibility of big sharks so far out. They might be attracted by the effort of desperation. Blessington, exhausted and dehydrated, was in no mood for swimming miles. Freycinet would not leave them there, off the Pitons, he told himself. It was practically in sight of land. He would be risking too much, witnesses, their survival. If he meant to deep-six them he would try to strike at sea.

Stoned and frightened as he was, he could not make sense of it, regain his perspective. He took a swig from a plastic bottle of warm Evian water, dropped his towel, and jumped overboard.

The water felt good, slightly cool. He could relax against it and slow the beating of his heart. It seemed to cleanse him of the cabin stink. He was at home in the water, he thought. Marie was frolicking like a mermaid, now close to the boat. Gillian had turned back and was swimming toward him. Her stroke still looked strong and accomplished; he set out to intercept her course.

They met over a field of elkhorn coral. Some of the formations were so close to the surface that their feet, treading water, brushed the velvety skin of algae over the sharp prongs.

"How are you?" Blessington asked her.

She had a lupine smile. She was laughing, looking at the boat. Her eyes appeared unfocused, the black pupils huge under the blue glare of afternoon and its shimmering, crystal reflection. She breathed in hungry swallows. Her face was raw and swollen where Freycinet had hit her.

"Look at that asshole," she said, gasping.

Freycinet was standing on deck talking to Marie, who was in the water ten feet away. He held a mask and snorkel in one hand and a pair of swim fins in the other. One by one he threw the toys into the water for Marie to retrieve. He looked coy and playful.

Something about the scene troubled Blessington, although he could not, in his state, quite reason what it was. He watched Freycinet take a few steps back and paw the deck like an angry bull. In the next moment, Blessington realized what the problem was.

"Oh, Jesus Christ," he said.

Freycinet leaped into space. He still wore the greasy shorts he had worn on the whole trip. In midair he locked his arms around his bent knees. He was holding a plastic spatula in his right hand. He hit the surface like a cannonball, raising a little waterspout, close enough to Marie to make her yelp.

"You know what?" Gillian asked. She had spotted it. She was amazing.

"Yes, I do. The ladder's still up. We forgot to lower it."

"Shit," she said, and giggled.

Blessington turned over to float on his back and tried to calm himself. Overhead the sky was utterly cloudless. Moving his eyes only a little, he could see the great green tower of Gros Piton, shining like Jacob's ladder itself, thrusting toward the empty blue. Incredibly far above, a plane drew out its jet trail, a barely visible needle stitching the tiniest flaw in the vast perfect seamless curtain of day. Miles and miles above, beyond imagining.

"How we gonna get aboard?" Gillian asked. He did not care for the way she was acting in the water now, struggling to stay afloat, moving her arms too much, wasting her breath.

"We'll have to go up the float line. Or maybe," he said, "we can stand on each other's shoulders."

"I'm not," she said, gasping, "gonna like that too well."

"Take it easy, Gillian. Lie on your back."

What bothered him most was her laughing, giggling a little with each breath.

"Okay, let's do it," she said, spitting salt water. "Let's do it before he does."

"Slow and steady," Blessington said.

They slowly swam together, breaststroking toward the boat. A late afternoon breeze had come up as the temperature began to fall.

Freycinet and Marie had allowed themselves to drift farther and farther from the boat. Blessington urged Gillian along beside him until the big white hull was between them and the other swimmers.

Climbing was impossible. It was partly the nature of the French-made boat: an unusually high transom and the rounded glassy hull made it particularly difficult to board except from a dock or a dinghy. That was the contemporary, security-conscious style. And the rental company had removed a few of the deck fittings that might have provided hand- and footholds. Still, he tried to find a grip so that Gillian could get on his shoulders. Once he even managed to get between her legs and push her a foot or so up the hull, sitting on his neck. But there was nothing to grab on to and she was stoned. She swore and laughed and toppled off him.

He was swimming forward along the hull, looking for the float, when it occurred to him suddenly that the boat must be moving. Sure enough, holding his place, he could feel the hull sliding to windward under his hand. In a few strokes he was under the bow, feeling the ketch's weight thrusting forward, riding him down. Then he saw the Rastafarian float. The float was unoccupied, unencumbered by any line. Honoré and Marie had not drifted from the boat — the boat itself was slowly blowing away, accompanied now by the screech of fiberglass against coral. The boys from the Pitons, having dealt with druggies before, had undone the mooring line while they were sleeping or nodding off or scarfing other sorts of lines.

Blessington hurried around the hull, with one hand to the boat's skin, trying to find the drifting float line. It might, he thought, be possible to struggle up along that. But there was no drifting float line. The boat boys must have uncleated it and balled the cleat in nylon line and silently tossed it aboard. They had been so feckless, the sea so glassy, and the wind so low that the big boat had simply settled on the float, with its keel fast among the submerged elk-horn, and they had imagined themselves secured. The *Sans Regret*, to which he clung, was gone. Its teak interiors were in another world now, as far away as the tiny jet miles above them on its way to Brazil.

"It's no good," Blessington said to her.

"It's not?" She giggled.

"Please," he said, "please don't do that."

She gasped. "What?"

"Never mind," he said. "Come with me."

They had just started to swim away when a sudden breeze carried the *Sans Regret* from between the two couples, leaving Blessington and Gillian and Honoré and Marie to face one another in the water across a distance of twenty yards or so. Honoré and Marie stared at their shipmates in confusion. It was an embarrassing moment. Gillian laughed.

"What have you done?" Honoré asked Blessington. Blessington tried not to look at him.

"Come on," he said to Gillian. "Follow me."

Cursing in French, Freycinet started kicking furiously for the boat. Marie, looking very serious, struck out behind him. Gillian stopped to look after them.

Blessington glanced at his diver's watch. It was five-fifteen.

"Never mind them," he said. "Don't look at them. Stay with me."

He turned over on his back and commenced an artless backstroke, arms out straight, rowing with his palms, paddling with his feet. It was the most economic stroke he knew, the one he felt most comfortable with. He tried to make the strokes controlled and rhythmic rather than random and splashy to avoid conveying any impression of panic or desperation. To free his mind, he tried counting the strokes. As soon as they were over deep water, he felt the current. He tried to take it at a forty-five-degree angle, determining his bearing and progress by the great mountain overhead.

"Are you all right?" he asked Gillian. He raised his head to have a look at her. She was swimming in what looked like a good strong crawl. She coughed from time to time.

"I'm cold," she said. "That's the trouble."

"Try resting on your back," he said, "and paddling with your open hands. Like you were rowing."

She turned over and closed her eyes and smiled.

"I could go to sleep."

"You'll sleep ashore," he said. "Keep paddling."

They heard Freycinet cursing. Marie began to scream over and over again. It sounded fairly far away.

Checking on the mountain, Blessington felt a rush of despair. The lower slopes of the jungle were turning dark green. The line dividing sun-bright vegetation from deep-shaded green was withdrawing toward the peak. And it looked no closer. He felt as though they were losing distance, being carried out faster than they could paddle. Marie's relentless screeches went on and on. Perhaps they

were actually growing closer, Blessington thought, perhaps an evening tide was carrying them out.

"Poor kid," Gillian said. "Poor little baby."

"Don't listen," he said.

Gillian kept coughing, sputtering. He stopped asking her if she
was all right.

"I'm sorry," she said. "I'm really cold now. I thought the water was
warm at first."

"We're almost there," he said.

Gillian stopped swimming and looked up at Gros Piton. Turning
over again to swim, she got a mouthful of water.

"Like . . . hell," she said.

"Keep going, Gillian."

It seemed to him as he rowed the sodden vessel of his body and
mind that the sky was darkening. The sun's mark withdrew higher
on the slopes. Marie kept screaming. They heard splashes far off
where the boat was now. Marie and Honoré were clinging to it.

"Liam," Gillian said, "you can't save me."

"You'll save yourself," he said. "You'll just go on."

"I can't."

"Don't be a bloody stupid bitch."

"I don't think so," she said. "I really don't."

He stopped rowing himself then, although he was loath to. Every
interruption of their forward motion put them more at the mercy
of the current. According to the cruise book it was only a five-knot
current but it felt much stronger. Probably reinforced by a tide.

Gillian was struggling, coughing in fits. She held her head up,
greedy for air, her mouth open like a baby bird's in hope of nourishment. Blessington swam nearer her. The sense of their time
ticking away, of distance lost to the current, enraged him.

"You've got to turn over on your back," he said gently. "Just ease
onto your back and rest there. Then arch your back. Let your head
lie backward so your forehead's in the water."

Trying to do as he told her, she began to thrash in a tangle of her
own arms and legs. She swallowed water, gasped. Then she laughed
again.

"Don't," he whispered.

"Liam? Can I rest on you?"

He stopped swimming toward her.

"You mustn't. You mustn't touch me. We mustn't touch each other. We might . . ."

"Please," she said.

"No. Get on your back. Turn over slowly."

Something broke the water near them. He thought it was the fin of a blacktip shark. A troublesome shark but not among the most dangerous. Of course, it could have been anything. Gillian still had the Rasta bracelet around her wrist.

"This is the thing, Liam. I think I got a cramp. I'm so dizzy."

"On your back, love. You must. It's the only way."

"No," she said. "I'm too cold. I'm too dizzy."

"Come on," he said. He started swimming again. Away from her.

"I'm so dizzy. I could go right out."

In mounting panic, he reversed direction and swam back toward her.

"Oh, shit," she said. "Liam?"

"I'm here."

"I'm fading out, Liam. I'll let it take me."

"Get on your back," he screamed at her. "You can easily swim. If you have to swim all night."

"Oh, shit," she said. Then she began to laugh again. She raised the hand that had the Rasta bracelet and splashed a sign of the cross.

"*Nam*," she said. "*Nam myoho renge kyo.* Son of a bitch." Laughing. What she tried to say next was washed out of her mouth by a wave.

"I can just go out," she said. "I'm so dizzy."

Then she began to struggle and laugh and cry.

"Praise God, from whom all blessings flow," she sang, laughing. "Praise Him, all creatures here below."

"Gillian," he said. "For God's sake." Maybe I can take her in, he thought. But that was madness and he kept his distance.

She was laughing and shouting at the top of her voice.

"Praise Him above, you heavenly host! Praise Father, Son, and Holy Ghost."

Laughing, thrashing, she went under, her face straining, wide-eyed. Blessington tried to look away but it was too late. He was afraid to go after her.

He lost his own balance then. His physical discipline collapsed and he began to wallow and thrash as she had.

"Help!" he yelled piteously. He was answered by a splash and Marie's screaming. Perhaps now he only imagined them.

Eventually he got himself under control. When the entire mountain had subsided into dark green, he felt the pull of the current release him. The breakers were beginning to carry him closer to the sand, toward the last spit of sandy beach remaining on the island. The entire northern horizon was subsumed in the mountain overhead, Gros Piton.

He had one final mad moment. Fifty yards offshore, a riptide was running; it seized him and carried him behind the tip of the island. He had just enough strength and coherence of mind to swim across it. The sun was setting as he waded out, among sea grape and manchineel. When he turned he could see against the setting sun the bare poles of the *Sans Regret*, settled on the larger reef to the south of the island. It seemed to him also that he could make out a struggling human figure, dark against the light hull. But the dark came down quickly. He thought he detected a flash of green. Sometimes he thought he could still hear Marie screaming.

All night, as he rattled through the thick brush looking for a road to follow from concealment, Gillian's last hymn echoed in his mind's ear. He could see her dying face against the black fields of sugarcane through which he trudged.

Once he heard what he was certain was the trumpeting of an elephant. It made him believe, in his growing delirium, that he was in Africa — Africa, where he had never been. He hummed the hymn. Then he remembered he had read somewhere that the resort maintained an elephant in the bush. But he did not want to meet it, so he decided to stay where he was and wait for morning. All night he talked to Gillian, joked and sang hymns with her. He saved her again and again and they were together.

In the morning, when the sun rose fresh and full of promise, he set out for the Irish bar in Soufrière. He thought that they might overstand him there.

CAROLYN COOKE

Bob Darling

FROM THE PARIS REVIEW

BOB DARLING spent the day and the evening on the fastest train in Europe. The train lugged slowly through yellow towns, then it began to pull together its force and go. The landscape slid past. In one stroke the train braced and broke through the air into a river of dinning sound. It climaxed at 380 kilometers per hour. Darling heard this news from a German across the aisle, but he sensed the speed in a deeper bone. His body was attuned to the subtle flux of high speed, to the jazz pulse, the fizz.

He closed his eyes, registered the scrape of the antimacassar against his brittle hairs, and dozed. Dying tired him, so did the drugs he took to keep from urinating on the seat. But he never let himself go that far, to close his eyes, unless the buzz of speed was in him, the drone of engines, the *zhzhzh* of jets.

On the seat beside him lounged a young woman named Carla. So far she had not given him too many terrible disappointments. Otherwise, she was a baby, vague on facts and ahistorical; she talked too much, she pouted when she didn't get her way, she disliked opera, and she drank. But overall Darling felt they had been compatible. Paris, coming up, would be the last leg of their trip. Darling planned the Tuileries, the Orangerie, an afternoon at the Louvre, couscous in the Latin Quarter, two nights at the Hôtel Angleterre.

That would be the end of it, then, no further obligation. Back home they would pass each other on the usual streets, exchange shrill pleasantries, pat each other's dogs. Sometime, perhaps, in the future, he could take her out to dinner at their old place on Bleecker Street and afterward press himself upon her as a lover.

(With liquor enough, she had a sentimental heart.) But one day she would move, get a job, find a lover, change her life. She would look at her calendar and think she had not seen him on the street. But she would be afraid, so she would procrastinate about calling him until she was sure that he was dead. Then she would realize it must have happened a year, two years ago. And this way she would not mourn his passing.

(What would that be like? What if he didn't know, if the end of it was not-knowing, if not-knowing was the surprise? What if there was nothing afterward, and he didn't know? Where would the information go he had put into his head over the years — the names of kings, the taste of food, the memory of his mother and his father, that *Louvre* is early French for "leper," lava is mainly water, loose facts, what Thoreau said: "Our moulting season, like that of fowls, must be a crisis in our lives," the names of women, the names of small hotels? Would the contents of his busy head be wasted, lost?)

He opened his eyes. A crowd of old men on bicycles crashed by outside the window and were gone. Carla in the seat beside him leaned into the *Blue Guide;* the lemony point of her nose and the book vibrated perceptibly to the motion of the train. Her eyes were puffy, from sleep maybe. She still had on her dress from the evening before — it was an absurd dress for day — and some cosmetic residue sparkled on her throat. Her sharp perfume hung on the air. She could sit for hours that way, a packet of French cigarettes and a bottle of Perrier balanced on the seat beside her, her bare feet crossed in her lap. She read any trash for hours and ignored the view. Travel, Darling thought irritably, was a vacation for her.

"The *Train à Grande Vitesse,*" she said now, out of nowhere.

"The TGV, yes, that's the train we're on now," he said.

"You called it the *Très Grande Vitesse,*" said Carla, looking up at him, frowning. "Actually it's *train,* not *très.*"

"That's what they call it informally, I guess," he said, looking across Carla's lap at the blur of France. "Very Great Speed."

"Informally they call it the TGV. And I know what *très* means, thank you."

She was a little bulldog, round face, skinny as a refugee, knees like knuckles in stripey tights. Long arms, down to her knees. Twenty, twenty-two. He was not an old man, Darling, but compared to her.

But in her eyes. From that first afternoon he thought he could get her into bed if he remembered to call her Carla, not Paula.

He had found her in a funny way, unconscious on another train. There were two of them almost exactly alike. It was a hot summer day; they looked as if they had been to the beach. Sun sparkled on the backs of their necks and the strings of their bathing suits dangled down, one red checked, the other pale blue. The strings held up the brassieres of their suits, the only word for it he knew.

They hung from the handstraps, limp as fringe. First one girl went down. The shoes of interested citizens chattered like sets of teeth around the head. Then the second girl dropped straight as a rope. The shoes, aroused by one girl unconscious, lost interest. Two girls down stank of conspiracy. No one besides Bob Darling wanted to be taken in.

He hiked his trousers so they would not be damaged by his knees and squatted to greet the girls when they woke. In the dangerous and unpredictable city, maybe this gesture had saved their lives. He ought to be able to get one of them into bed.

The first one opened her eyes, and he saw a flattening out of the tube of her pupils, her vision narrowing to familiar and unimaginative suspicions. "What did I, pass out?" she said.

"You seemed to fall," Darling said.

The girl blinked at him. "My wallet still here?" She slapped her body with her hands, then quieted them in a leather pouch around her belly. "Miracle."

"You want air," he said.

She shook her head. "I've got to go to work downtown." It was a shame, Darling thought, because the first girl really was the up-and-comer.

"What do you do? I mean that respectfully," Darling assured her, because he thought she might be a dancer, and Paula had been the most marvelously uninhibited dancer. His response to her dancing had always been sexual, but in the most respectful sense.

"Legal proofreading," said the girl.

The second girl opened her eyes and he looked away from the first girl into her face. She was a bulldog, but not bad looking.

The first girl changed trains to downtown. Darling marveled at how they bussed each other's cheeks, then one went off to read legal documents in an office, sand still sparkling on the back of her neck. That pale blue string.

He walked the second girl — Carla — up from the underground. He held her arm. He liked to think he knew the why and
the how of the city. Did she know the Such-and-Such Café? The
apple cake was the thing to eat. Did she like apple cake? He guided
her into the café's perimeter by the arm.

But Carla didn't want apple cake. She said she was bored without
drinks. She sat across a round table, behind a tumbler of yellow
wine.

He was old enough that she would not be shocked by the news
of his death, or the idea of his illness. "Things break down," she
would think with a shrug. But Darling was still young enough —
and the news was fresh enough — that it came as a shock, a surprise. Barely two hours before he found her, his GP, Carnevali, had
sighed deeply and told Darling to
                       Concentrate
                   on the probability
                     of mortality.
Darling had buttoned down his shirt, top to bottom. He covered up
his lung, his large intestine, his small intestine, his appendicitis scar.
He put on his sweater and his leather jacket. He was about to hail a
taxi on Park when suddenly he wanted to live, live. His eyes flailed
like arms, grasping at the colors of the city. He had crossed over to
Lexington, and grabbed the subway downtown.

His apple cake lay in crumbs before him on a plate. "Let me show
you something," he said, throwing out a spark of spit. He removed
a black leather book and a fountain pen from inside his jacket
pocket. A lozenge flew out too and rolled wildly into the gutter.
He leaned over the book, showing it to her, partially blocking her
view with his body, intent. "This is Dwight Sterling," he said, and
pointed to a list of numbers. "First-rate accountant." He looked at
Carla. "You don't do your own taxes, do you? This is his office, this
is home — his wife's name is Paula, you'll like her, she is very
uninhibited. This is their number in Springs. Dwight can get a
message to me anytime. Now here is Jane, she is the astrologer who
walks my dog — you can call her. This is Herb Witter, he's a philosopher. He left academia to sell industrial properties in Elizabeth,
New Jersey. These are people who can get a message to me anytime," he said.

He closed the book and slid it across the table. "You take it. I know all these numbers." Her hand flickered on the table. "Please," he said. "Even if you don't *want* to leave a message I will know you *can* leave a message."

"See your pen?" she said. He handed it over. She opened his little address book to a blank page near the *W*s and rolled the pen across it experimentally. Then she drew an outline of the couple at the next table, and the table, and a vase with a few flowers in it.

Darling jiggled his leg. "You're an artist," he said.

"Naah." She ran blue lines through her drawings. He watched her bear down on the nib. He smiled, sipped his coffee. "That's a hundred-and-fifty-dollar pen," he said.

Her face emptied. She slipped the cap on the pen and slid it across the table.

"No, no, you use it," he said.

Her finger touched the marbled end.

Darling scraped his chair on the concrete, hobbled it over in a series of shrieks and told her his name. "You can call me Bob, or you can call me Darling. I mean that respectfully. Most people call me Darling. Not just women. Men."

"Darling," she said. "Like the girl in Peter Pan."

"What? Peter Pan?" Darling said excitedly.

"The girl's name — the one who goes to Never-Never Land with Peter Pan."

"Not Mary Martin?"

"No — I meant — the Disney," she said.

Darling sniffed. "Life is too short to talk about Walter Disney," he said.

"Fine," she said. She looked at the pen.

It was their first *frisson*. Darling savored it with coffee. Together they watched the couple she had drawn eat a big meal at the next table, two halves of chicken — but possibly not the same chicken. They sat across from each other, looking at their dinners. The man ate delicately, pulling the underdone meat away from the bone with the point of his knife and actually penetrating his mouth with the blade. He fixed his yellow eyes impersonally on the food. The woman ate quickly, as if other duties called to her. His thin white shirt strained to girdle him, and through the fabric the white loops of his undershirt were legible. The woman wore a transparent blouse that magnified her white arms and the vastness of her brassiere. Once she stopped chewing, looked up at him and said something. The man didn't look at her, but barked out a laugh. "I'm not feeling flush tonight," he said.

They ate the skin off their chicken, buttered their bread and rolled it up so more fit into their mouths in one bite. When all the food was gone they wiped their lips with their napkins and waited with all their attention until the waiter came and cleared their plates away.

When the waiter came back with pie and coffee on a tray their hands flew up to make room for the dishes, fingers like birds' wings. They took turns using the cream and sugar. The woman stirred her coffee. "Everything I've dreamed of for forty years, it's coming true," she said loudly.

Darling squeezed Carla's hand. "Are you hungry?" he asked.

"Oh, no. I never eat at night," she said.

He climbed six flights of stairs to her one room of Chinese paper lanterns and museum posters and her futon on the floor, battened down with sheets and a quilt and ropes of lingerie and clothes. They sat on the futon, which was all of her furniture. There was an old coal fireplace with a flue out one side, but the blue rug ran into it. She served him a glass of yellow wine. Everything she had, she offered.

She played Stravinsky's *Firebird* on her boom box and rolled pink lipstick over her lips. When she stood and rolled her thin sweater up her arms and called him to her bed, he realized he was already there. The slug of strong sensations — desire, hope, *virility* — brought tears of sorrow to his eyes, which Carla mistook for gratitude.

He hoped to keep his bag of sensations light. Only the most intense sensations interested him. He had looked forward to this train because it was the fastest train. He had been very clear with Carla about this from the start. He wanted to ride the fastest train in Europe. That was one. Two was, he wanted to eat the wonderful six-course dinner they served on the train. If they went together, this was something he definitely wanted to do. He asked her all about it before they left the city, while they were still in the planning stages.

"Fine Bob, whatever," Carla said when he asked.

Some afternoons they sat under a sun umbrella at the Such-and-Such Café. Her accent, when she ordered *caffè macchiato*, was perfect. Darling spread out the map like a tablecloth under their cups and crumbs and napkins and brought out sheets of onionskin scribbled over in pencil with the itinerary, flight numbers, train routes, and the names and telephone numbers and addresses of hotels. He noticed that Carla used these things carefully. She brushed his cake crumbs from the countries on the map.

She had never heard of Versailles, Père-Lachaise. She had never heard of Jim Morrison. Her ignorance was vast, ecumenical. He drew on the paper cloth with a mechanical pencil — he had given over his fountain pen and hadn't seen it since. He sketched dreamily, from memory.

"What's that?" she asked.

"It's a baguette, a kind of long French bread."

"Oh, Bob, I know *baguette*. I thought you were drawing a canoe."

But then he thought she spoke Italian, from her seamless demand for *macchiato*. She shrugged and said she didn't know a word of it — just liked the bitterness. He wondered whether she had broken his pen, bearing down on the nib, or sold it. He would have liked to show her how the ink went in so that if the pen had stopped working she would not worry that she was to blame. His heart ached, imagining her humiliation and shy gratitude.

"You have to speak up — it won't be any good unless we do things you want to do," he told her. "We have to plan everything together. You have to tell me where you want to go, what you want to see."

Carla had never been there before. "I don't know," she said. Her white dress was ancient unto transparency. Her shoulders looked like two milk bottles.

He had read that the dinners on the train were sometimes oversubscribed. You could eat a *croque monsieur* in the bar car, but that wasn't the thing to do. The thing to do was to get the dinner on the train.

"Fine, whatever," Carla said. "I don't care what I eat."

He leaned across the table, angry, closed his fingers around Carla's wrist, and squeezed.

She pulled his hand off in a smooth, strong gesture that surprised him and pulled her arm into her lap. "I eat anything. Scraps," she said.

He sat up late at night on the floor, walled in by forty years' worth of the *New York Times* and creased hotel brochures. He called her at two o'clock in the morning. "Do you want to go to the Sabine Hills or the Villa d'Este at Tivoli? Tell me what you want to do."

There was a pause on the line, a certain flattening out in the expectant air. "Who is this, please?" she said.

And yet, in Europe, it turned out Carla had a terrible instinct for knowing exactly what she wanted to do. In Venice she saw the Lido from a speedboat and wanted to go there. "What is it?" she said, and he told her.

"Oh, Bob, I want to go and spend a day," she said.

But she had agreed already, he reminded her, buttoning his shirt, to walk with him through the Collezione Peggy Guggenheim, and to take a vaporetto to the cathedral at Torcello. Anyway, the last time he had been to the Lido, the water was full of white fuzzballs and nobody would swim.

"But I want to go to the Lido," she objected. "Just rent a beach chair if it isn't too expensive. I just want to be there, Bob." She jumped up and down on the bed, then jumped off and ran to the window and pulled back the heavy curtain.

"I doubt you can even get your lunch out there," he said. "I thought we could sit at a table at the Piazza San Marco."

"Oh, Bob, I don't want to eat!" Carla said. "I could just go out on the boat taxi and meet you later."

They stood barefoot on the rug, facing each other across the unmade bed.

"If that's what you would like to do," he said.

"It is, it is," she said.

And it was done.

He spent the day on foot, a blind day of moving through the crowds at the Piazza San Marco, leaning on the arm of the vaporetto, sliding through the viscous water to the mudflats, on foot again across the Bridge of Sighs. Always water swelled under him, undulating, filthy blackness. He smelled his own sweat through the leather jacket and tasted in his mouth the temperature of his boiling insides. After lunch in a trattoria in Dorsoduro he went out in the air and coughed two drops of blood on a Kleenex. He folded the Kleenex into the pocket of his leather jacket and went on to the piazza, where he threw the Kleenex away.

Hours later he opened the door to his room with his key. The ether of wine was like a fog, an Oriental smokiness. Carla was sitting straddled across the bidet with just the top of the bikini on that she had bought in a newsstand at the beginning of their trip, before they left the United States, even. Even then he had been shocked by that crudeness, that lack of care. He remembered paying a hotel bill while she went off into the newsstand, sliding a card from his wallet, signing his name. That unpleasantness, a woman beside him with a bag in one hand and a bottle of mouthwash in the other, having some trouble about her bill, putting the bottle of mouthwash down on the cashier's polished desk, and raking a hand through her bag, her hair ugly around the neck of her coat, muttering *"Merde, merde . . ."*

Carla's skin was burnt red around the bathing suit top and she had long scratch marks up and down her back. She turned slowly away from the sound of running water to look at him in the door. Twisting her chin over her shoulder pulled cords in her throat which opened her mouth. She seemed to be manipulated by strings.

Some bleary look in her eyes got in the way of his concern for her.

He folded his leather jacket over his arm. He stood in the doorway with the door in one hand. "I may just meet you downstairs," he said.

Carla rolled her eyes and turned away. He went out, closing the door behind him. He bought a postcard at the front desk and sat down at a narrow writing desk.

"Dear Paula," he wrote. "It is now six o'clock Sunday evening. The clock atop the Italian steps has struck those hours with an ancient quality. An array of birds with a multiplicity of sounds is announcing their departure this evening. The light is muted and pink, the city overall is waiting." He read it over — it all seemed beside the point somehow. She had been so direct with him in her postcard from Helsinki, the small block letters: "You are an elf, darling. But I am not really interested in elves."

He folded the card over and over itself and slipped it into his pocket just as Carla appeared in the doorway. She had on her small black thrift-store dress; she had pushed her yellow hair back behind tiny pearls in her ears. But under her eyes looked yellow-blue. They had Pellegrino water together, then dinner at a place on one of the canals, pasta first, then calamari in ink and, at Darling's suggestion, three bottles of wine. "How many bottles do we need?" Darling asked Carla. "I mean that respectfully. I want to get drunk too." They drank fast out of tiny green glasses. Bob Darling shouted, "I'm drunk! Pow! Life is a glorious mist!"

He ordered cake and a gondola, and then the ancient wooden walls began to close in around him. His vision closed down on her dress, which seemed to have no front or back. Someone had laid a round plate of cake on her chest (between her breasts, nipples like eyes), which one of the waiters passed to the gondolier on the boat after he passed Carla, who was laughing, out.

She held his arm on the ride back to the hotel. Looking out over the black water, he pictured the way he would open the world to her, the blown-glass choker he would fit around her neck, the lire liquid in his hand, pouring into her. His fingers spread around the knuckle of her knee.

"You want to know what my landlady said about you, Bob?"

"If you like," he said.

"It was the time you told that terrible joke, remember? She said, 'I don't trust one single thing about that man.'" She squeezed his arm.

On the way out of the gondola she slipped and her leg sank into the black liquid up to her knee. Walking up the narrow stairs to their room, he heard the sucking sound of her shoe. Then she was asleep, painful looking, red. He tried not to look at her, at the red marks on her back. Instead he lay back on his pillow, unable as ever to sleep in silence, and turned pages in the blank book he had bought for her to record her trip. "He was his own whole world," she had written. "He wore neat black suits, bikini underwear. Every day he sent his pajamas down to be washed — why? — and they came back ironed. He saved anything that had words on it — theater tickets, programs, newspapers, napkins — but he never read anything. He carried a skin change purse that I wanted. He could walk for hours without stopping, but only in the city. He gave out his telephone numbers to everyone."

Her hand flopped out and lay on his arm. He looked at her

things from the day, tossed out like ropes at sea — her bikini bottom, the black dress, the plate and fork and the remains of the cake
they had eaten on the boat, the Oriental smell of her perfume, the
ether of wine. He read more, snatches here and there — her block
letters were full of effort but difficult to read. "Asked if he could cut
me just a little bit on the thigh with his nail scissors." (His eye shot
up, electric, red, but fell again to the page.) "In an umber room /
he kissed my mouth / nibbled my mouth like an ant / carried me
away / like crumbs." He let Carla's hand lie on his arm until it felt
heavy, then he moved it away.

The argument was about the difference between naked and nude.
They had it in France, in the countryside, over dinner in a small
hotel. His cutlet had a crust on it, and it swam in a sauce. He drank
wine from a leaden pitcher.

"My friend Paula one time gave a dinner party," he said, mention-
ing Paula carefully, by name. "All her husband's clients, all their
Oriental rugs unrolled, and she just came into the room and un-
zipped this jumpsuit she was wearing and it just fell around her feet
like a puddle. I'll never forget it. She was naked, she was statuesque,
celebrating, inviting, brave. To say she was nude is an insult."

"What did people do?" Carla asked.

"Of course no one did anything. We were far too respectful. A
woman like Paula naked in a room like that is almost untouchable."

"But what was it for?" Carla asked.

"You mean, did she want to be an object of art or an object of sex?
Isn't that what you mean — you think these things are different?"

Carla said, "Poor Paula."

"Why?" He could hear the mockery in his voice. Spit formed
in the corner of his mouth. Was it finer to be painted by Picasso
than to stand naked at a window? Which picture would be finer,
better?

But the word he used was wrong, she argued. You would never say
a child was nude — it would be an offense to the child, it would be
obscene. Nudity corrupted nakedness with eyes, she said, climbing
up onto her high horse, conservative as a child.

Would she prefer the lighter and more moral state? he asked her,
mocking. Which was the more "natural" state? If nudity was more
artful than nakedness, wasn't it also less natural? So it followed,

since she was always interested in being more natural, that she would rather get naked than get nude.

"I am not interested in being more natural," she said.

He sent his dinner back twice. It was an impossible place. He went upstairs to the loo; through a hole in the floor he saw the top of her head, saw her spear a corner of his cutlet with her fork. Flies, flies. Standing over the urinal, he understood he was dying of foie gras and sauternes. Their room down the hall — she had flung the casement open and let in all the flies. But what could it matter? He buttoned up his pants and hell, hell, did not wash his hands.

After dinner she wanted to go for a walk — through the fields of sunflowers.

"All right," he said. He wanted to hurt her so she would remember him. But it was hard to walk without seeing his feet, through the wide yellow heads bobbling in his. His hand attached to her damp shoulder with a sound of suction.

"Your eyes are so Freud," she said.

"What did you say?"

"Freud. In German it means cold."

He took hold of the other shoulder.

"Do you think you tricked me? Do you think you're crafty?" she burst out. She pushed him off, away. He fell back, pulling the heavy-headed flowers down with him. He pulled at her arm with his hand, pulling her to him, calling her to bring him up. He felt the wide universe between him and the world. She yanked wildly at his arm and there was the door of the pension, the closed white stone.

The train reeled north at great speed. Carla opened her eyes, stretched her arms and yawned. She looked out of the window. "What time is it?" she asked.

"Five o'clock," he said. "We have dinner in half an hour."

She sat up now, serious, and rolled orange lipstick over her lips, examining her mouth in a pocket mirror inscribed, she had told him, to her mother by a lover: "A little bit every day." She closed the mirror and dropped it into one of her shapeless bags. "Oh, I can't eat at five-thirty, can you Bob? Let's go and have a drink in the bar."

It was unbelievable. He could have pulled out her eyes.

"I asked you a month ago about eating dinner on this train," he said.

"Don't you see what this is? All they are going to do is throw a tray at you," she said.

The train overtook its whistle. All sound now was behind his ears. He had an image of himself in black space, pinned on the back of a rocket. He put his arms down like two great weights on the arm-rests, to steady himself.

"Please, eat this dinner with me," he said.

"Look," said Carla. "Why can't we just go into the bar car and have a drink and a sandwich or something later, when we get hungry? I can't stand being crammed in this car like a sardine. Wouldn't it be more interesting to go and have a drink and look out the windows and talk to people?"

"I don't want to," Darling said. "What I want to do is what we arranged a month ago. I want to eat the dinner they serve on this train. I want to sit right here and eat the dinner they serve on the train!"

"Oh, I don't," she said.

"You wanted to a month ago when you said you would," he said.

"Oh, Bob, for God's sake, a month ago." She raked her hair with a hand and looked over the tops of the seats at the people sitting in seats all around them, at the oblivious heads.

"Eat dinner with me tonight. Please, Carla, just do it," he said.

"Why do you want me to do something I don't want to do? Why would you want that?" she said. Her eyes went everywhere but to him.

He looked at Carla until she ran out of places to look, until she couldn't go anywhere, until she looked at him. He sat in her path, in the aisle seat. Carla had the window. Her eyes floated over him.

"I don't see the point of asking me to sit here and eat my dinner on a tray when I am not hungry and I don't want to do it."

"Could you do something for me just because I ask you to, or do you think dinner is too much to ask? Because it wasn't too much to ask a month ago when I asked you. According to you it wasn't," he said. He looked at his fingers vibrating in his lap, melded into a warped hideous undifferentiated hand, a paw.

Her eyes glazed over. She looked past him.

He hugged his knees to his seat's edge and let her climb over him into the aisle. She stood up and stretched herself out limb by limb like an animal. He looked up, and she rolled her green eyes over him.

"I need francs," she said.

He reached into his shirt and pulled out the skin purse she had coveted. "Take it," he said.

She caressed the skin between her fingers, tears in her eyes. "Look, Bob, I'm sorry I've been this big disappointment to you on your trip," she said. "I did my best, okay?"

He looked into her face for any sign, but there was none.

"Okay, Bob?" Carla said again.

"Take the river Styx to hell!" he said.

She walked backward toward the bar car, against the speed and pull of the train. Her fingers moved over the skin purse; it was the scrotum of a lamb. A steward brought two trays — chicken breasts in white sauce, yellow beans, apple tarts.

He sat quietly, penned into his seat by his tray. He looked across the seat Carla had left and at the tray on the folding table in front of it, and beyond that, out of the window at the blur of France. He considered moving into her seat, but then considered the empty seat to be part of his view: not-Carla. He tasted his unpromising dinner and discovered that he was hungry, but still discerning.

He ate his dinner slowly, looking carefully across the empty seat at the blur, and at Carla's chicken, at her yellow bones. All right: it was the fastest train in Europe. The food was above average. Everything was moving. The landscape outside looked as if it were underwater, wet, bleeding green-yellow-blue. He gripped a tray in each hand and in one motion switched his empty tray with hers. He ate the second dinner more quickly than the first, kept the fork gripped in his hand and moving back and forth between the tray and his mouth until he had to confess he was glad she had left. He scooped up Carla's apple tart, then wiped the ooze from his lips with a napkin, virtuous. He looked at the outside from the inside of the train. There was no comparison between this train and other trains he had ridden. He was like a fish being carried upriver in a current faster than a fish could swim. In the cradle of this unanswerable motion, Bob Darling rested and slept. The river poured into his eyes.

JONATHAN FRANZEN

Chez Lambert

FROM THE PARIS REVIEW

ST. JUDE: that prosperous midwestern gerontocracy, that patron saint of the really desperate. The big houses and big cars here filled up only on holidays. Rain pasted yellow leaves to cars parked in blue handicapped slots. Teflon knees and Teflon hips were flexed on fairways; roomy walking shoes went squoosh, squoosh on the ramps and people movers at the airport.

Nobody laughed at seniors in St. Jude. Whole economies, whole cohorts, depended on them. The installers and maintainers of home-security systems, the wielders of feather dusters and complicated vacuums, the actuaries and fund managers, the brokers and tellers, the sellers of sphagnum moss and nonfat cottage cheese and nonalcoholic beer and aluminum stools for sitting in the bathtub with, the suppliers of chicken cordon bleu or veal Parmesan and salad and dessert and a fluorescently lit function room at $13.95 a head for Saturday night bridge clubs, the sitters who knitted while their charges dozed under afghans, the muscular LPNs who changed diapers in the night, the social workers who recommended the hiring of the LPNs, the statisticians who collated data on prostate cancers and memory and aging, the orthopedists and cardiologists and oncologists and their nurses, receptionists and bloodworkers, the pharmacists and opticians, the performers of routine maintenance on American-made sedans with inconceivably low odometer readings, the blue-uniformed carriers of colonial-handicrafts catalogues and pension checks, the bookers of tours and cruises and flights to Florida, the projectionists of PG-rated movies at theaters with Twilight Specials, the drafters of wills and the executors of irrevocable trusts, the radio patrolmen who responded to home-security false alarms and wrote tickets for violating minimum-speed postings on expressways, the elected state officials who resisted property-tax reassessment, the elected national representatives who kept the entitlements flowing, the clergy who moved down corridors saying prayers at bedsides, the embalmers and cremators, the organists and florists, the drivers of ambulances and hearses, the engravers of marble markers and the operators of gas-powered Weed Whackers who swept across the cemeteries in their pollen masks and protective goggles and who once in a long while suffered third-degree burns over half their bodies when the motors strapped to their backs caught fire.

The madness of an invading system of high pressure. You could feel it: something terrible was going to happen. The sun low in the sky, a mockery, a lust gone cold. Gust after gust of entropy. Trees restless, temperatures falling, the whole northern religion of things coming to an end. No children in the yards here. Shadows and light on yellowing zoysia. The old swamp white oak rained acorns on a house with no mortgage. Storm windows shuddered in the empty bedrooms. Distantly the drone and hiccup of the clothes dryer, the moan of a leaf blower, the smell of apples, the smell of the gasoline with which Alfred Lambert had cleaned the brush from his morning painting of the porch furniture. At three o'clock the fear set in. He'd awakened in the great blue chair in which he'd been sleeping since lunch. He'd had his nap and there would be no local news until five o'clock. Two empty hours were a sinus in which infections raged. He struggled to his feet and stood by the Ping-Pong table, listening in vain for Enid.

Ringing throughout the house was an alarm bell that no one but Alfred and Enid could hear directly. It was the alarm bell of anxiety. We should imagine it as one of those big cast-iron dishes with an electric clapper that sends schoolchildren into the street in fire drills, and we should imagine it ringing for so many hours that the Lamberts no longer heard the message of "bell ringing" but, as with any sound that continues for so long that you have the leisure to learn its component sounds (as with any word you stare at until it resolves itself into a string of dead letters), instead heard a clapper going ping-ping-ping-ping-ping against a metallic resonator, not a pure tone but a granular sequence of percussions with a keening overlay of overtones; ringing for so many days that it simply blended into the background except at certain early morning hours when one or the other of them awoke in a sweat and realized that a bell had been ringing in their head for as long as they could remember; ringing for so many months that the sound had given way to a kind of metasound whose rise and fall was not the beating of compression waves but the much, much slower waxing and waning of their *consciousness* of the sound. Which consciousness was particularly acute when the weather itself was in an anxious mood. Then Enid and Alfred — she on her knees in the dining room opening drawers, he surveying the disastrous Ping-Pong table — each felt near to exploding with anxiety.

The anxiety of coupons, in a drawer containing boxes of candles in designer colors, also utensils of pewter and silver in flannel bags. Overlaying these accessories for the dinner parties that Enid no longer gave was a stratum of furtiveness and chaos, because these dining room drawers often presented themselves as havens for whatever Enid had in hand when Alfred was raging and she had to cover up her operations, get them out of sight at whatever cost. There were coupons bundled in a rubber band, and she was realizing that their expiration dates (often jauntily circled in red ink by the manufacturer, a reminder to act quickly while the discount opportunity lasted) lay months and even years in the past: that these hundred-odd coupons, whose total face value exceeded $60 (potentially $120 at the supermarket on Watson Road that doubled coupons), and which she had clipped months *before* their expiration, had all gone bad. Tilex, 60 cents off. Excedrin PM, $1 off. The dates were not even *close*. The dates were *historical*. The alarm bell had been ringing for *years*.

She pushed the coupons back in among the candles and shut the drawer. She was looking for a letter that had come by registered mail some weeks ago. She had stashed it somewhere quickly because Alfred had heard the mailman ring the bell and shouted, "Enid! Enid!" but had not heard her shout, "Al, I'm getting it!" and he had continued to shout, "Enid!" coming closer and closer, and she had disposed of the envelope, presumably somewhere within fifteen feet of the front door, because the sender was The Axon Group, 24 East Industrial Serpentine, Schwenkville, PA, and some weeks or perhaps months earlier she had received a certified letter from Axon that for reasons known better to her than (thankfully) to Alfred she had been too anxious to open immediately, and so it had disappeared, which was no doubt why Axon had sent a second, registered letter subsequently, and this entire circumstance was something she preferred to keep from Alfred, because he got so darned anxious and was impossible to deal with, especially regarding the situation with Axon (which, thankfully, he knew almost nothing about), and so she had stashed the second letter as well before Alfred had emerged from the basement bellowing like a piece of earth-moving equipment, "There's somebody at the door!" and she'd fairly screamed, "The mailman! The mailman!" and he'd shaken his head at the complexity of it all.

She felt sure that her own head would clear if only she didn't have to wonder, every five minutes, what Alfred was up to. It seemed to her that he had become somewhat depressed, and that he ought, therefore, to try to take an interest in life. She encouraged him to take up his metallurgy again, but he looked at her as if she'd lost her mind. (She didn't understand what was so wrong with a friendly suggestion like that; she didn't understand why he had to be so *negative*.) She asked whether there wasn't some work he could do in the yard. He said his legs hurt. She reminded him that the husbands of her friends all had hobbies (David Schumpert his stained glass, Kirby Root his intricate chalets for nesting purple finches, Chuck Meisner his plaster casts of great monuments of the ancient world), but Alfred acted as if she were trying to distract him from some great labor of his, and what was that labor? Repainting the wicker furniture? He'd been repainting the love seat since Labor Day. She seemed to recall that the last time he'd painted the furniture it had taken him only a few hours to do the love seat. But he went to his workshop morning after morning, and after three weeks she ventured in to see how he was doing, and the only thing he'd painted was the legs. After three weeks! And he'd clearly missed a spot on one of the legs! He seemed to wish that she would go away. He said that the brush had gotten dried out, that that was what was taking so long. He said that scraping wicker was like trying to peel a blueberry. He said there were crickets. She felt a shortness of breath then, but perhaps it was only the smell of gasoline and the dampness of the workshop that smelled like urine (but could not possibly be urine). She fled upstairs to look for the letters from Axon.

Six days a week, several pounds of mail came through the slot in

the front door, and since nothing incidental was allowed to pile up
on the main floor — since the fiction of living in this house was that
no one lived here — Enid faced a substantial tactical challenge.
She did not think of herself as a guerrilla, but a guerrilla was what
she was. By day she ferried materiel from depot to depot, often just
a step ahead of the governing force. By night, beneath a charming
but too dim sconce at a too small table in the breakfast nook, she
staged various actions: paid bills, balanced checkbooks, attempted
to decipher Medicare copayment records and make sense of a
threatening Third Notice from a medical lab, which demanded
immediate payment of $0.22 while simultaneously showing an ac-
count balance of $0.00 carried forward and thus indicating that
she owed nothing and in any case offering no address and naming
no entity to which remittance might be made. It would happen that
the First and Second Notices were underground somewhere, and
because of the constraints under which Enid waged her campaign,
she had only the dimmest sense of where those other Notices might
be on any given evening. She might suspect perhaps the family
room closet, but the governing force, in the person of Alfred,
would be watching a network newsmagazine at a volume thunder-
ous enough to keep him awake, and he had every light in the family
room burning, and there was a non-negligible possibility that if she
opened the closet door a cascade of catalogues and *House Beautiful*s
and miscellaneous Merrill Lynch statements would come toppling
and sliding out, incurring Alfred's wrath. There was also the possibility that the Notices would not be there, since the governing
force staged random raids on her depots, threatening to "pitch"
the whole lot of it if she didn't take care of it, but she was too
busy dodging these raids ever quite to take care of it, and in the
succession of forced migrations and deportations any lingering
semblance of order was lost, and so the random Nordstrom's shopping bag that was camped behind a dust ruffle with one of its plastic
handles semi-detached would contain the whole shuffled pathos of
a refugee existence — non-consecutive issues of *Good Housekeeping*,
black-and-white snapshots of Enid in the 1940s, brown recipes on
high-acid paper that called for wilted lettuce, the current month's
telephone and gas bills, the detailed First Notice from the medical
lab instructing copayers to ignore subsequent billings for less than
50 cents, a complimentary cruise-ship photo of Enid and Alfred

wearing leis and sipping beverages from hollow coconuts, and the only extant copies of two of their children's birth certificates, for example.

Although Enid's ostensible foe was Alfred, what made her a guerrilla was the house that occupied them both. They had always aimed high in decorating it, and its furnishings were of the kind that no more brooked domestic clutter than a hotel lobby would. As without in prosperous St. Jude, so within chez Lambert. There was furniture by Ethan Allen. Spode and Waterford in the breakfront. The obligatory ficus, the inevitable Norfolk pine. Copies of *Architectural Digest* fanned on a glass-topped coffee table. Touristic plunder — enamelware from China, a Viennese music box that Enid out of a sense of duty and mercy every so often wound up and raised the lid of. The tune was "Strangers in the Night."

It's to their credit, I think, that both Lamberts were hopelessly ill-equipped to manage such a house, that something in each of them rebelled at the sterility. Alfred's cries of rage on discovering evidence of incursions — a Nordstrom's bag surprised in broad daylight on the basement stairs, nearly precipitating a tumble — were the cries of a government that could no longer govern. It was finance that betrayed him first. He developed a knack for making his printing calculator spit columns of meaningless eight-digit figures, and after he devoted the better part of an afternoon to figuring the cleaning woman's Social Security payments five different times and came up with four different numbers and finally just accepted the one number ($635.78) that he'd managed to come up with twice (the correct figure was $70.00), Enid staged a nighttime raid on his filing cabinet and relieved it of all tax files, which might have improved household efficiency had the files not found their way into a Nordstrom's bag with some misleadingly ancient *Good Housekeeping*s concealing the more germane documents underneath, which casualty of war led to the cleaning woman's filling out the forms herself, with Enid merely writing the checks and Alfred shaking his head at the complexity of it all.

It's the fate of most Ping-Pong tables in home basements eventually to serve the ends of other, more desperate games. When Alfred retired he appropriated the eastern end of the table for his banking and correspondence. At the western end was the portable color TV on which he'd intended to watch the local news while sitting in his great blue chair but which was now fully engulfed by *Good Housekeeping*s and the seasonal candy tins and baroque but cheaply made candle holders that Enid never quite found time to transport to the Nearly New consignment shop. The Ping-Pong table was the one field on which the civil war raged openly. At the eastern end Alfred's calculator was ambushed by floral-print potholders and souvenir coasters from the Epcot Center and a device for pitting cherries that Enid had owned for thirty years and never used; while he, in turn, at the western end, for absolutely no reason that Enid could ever fathom, ripped to pieces a wreath made of pine cones and spray-painted filberts and Brazil nuts.

To the east of the Ping-Pong table lay the workshop that housed his metallurgical lab, the industry underpinning the seamless prosperity of the house above. This workshop was now home to a colony of mute, dust-colored crickets that clustered and roiled in various corners. There was something fetal about these crickets, something provisional. When you surprised them, they scattered like a handful of dropped marbles, some of them misfiring at crazy angles, others toppling over with the weight of their own copious protoplasm, which had the color and texture of pus. They popped all too easily, and cleanup took more than one Kleenex. The Lamberts had many afflictions that they believed to be outsized, extraordinary, unheard of — unmentionable — and the crickets were one of them.

The gray dust of evil spells and the enchanted cobwebs of a place that time had forgotten cloaked the thick insulating bricks of the electric arc furnace, the Hellmann's Real Mayonnaise jars filled with exotic rhodium, with sinister cadmium, with stalwart bismuth, the handprinted labels browned and blasted by the leakage of vapors from nearby glass-stoppered bottles of sulfuric acid and aqua regia, and the quad-ruled notebooks with cracked leather spines in which the latest entry in Alfred's hand dated from that time, nearly twenty years ago, before the spell was cast, before the betrayal. Something as daily and friendly as a pencil still occupied the random spot on the workbench where Alfred had laid it in a different decade; the passage of so many years imbued the pencil with a kind of enmity. Worse than a palace in ruins is a palace abandoned and decaying and untouched: if it were ruined it could be forgotten. A ceramic crucible of something metallurgical still sat inside the furnace. Asbestos mitts hung from a nail beneath two certificates of U.S. patents, the frames warped and sprung by dampness. On the hood of a binocular microscope with an oil-immersion lens lay big chips of peeled paint from the ceiling. The only dust-free objects in the room were a wicker love seat on a dropcloth, a can of Rustoleum and some brushes, and a couple of Yuban coffee cans, which despite increasingly irrefutable olfactory evidence Enid chose not to believe were filling up with her husband's urine, because what earthly reason could he have, in a house with two and a half bathrooms, for peeing in a Yuban can?

Until he retired, Alfred had slept in an armchair that was black. Between his naps he read *Time* magazine or watched *60 Minutes* or golf. On weeknights he paged through the contents of his briefcase with a trembling hand. The chair was made of leather that you could smell the cow in.

His new chair, the great blue one to the west of the Ping-Pong table, was built for sleeping and sleeping only. It was overstuffed, vaguely gubernatorial. It smelled like the inside of a Lexus. Like something modern and medical and impermeable that you could wipe the smell of death off easily, with a damp cloth, before the next person sat down to die in it.

The chair was the only major purchase Alfred ever made without Enid's approval. I see him at sixty-seven, a retired mechanical engineer walking the aisles of one of those midwestern furniture stores that only people who consider bargains immoral go to. I see him passing up lesser chairs — chairs with frivolous levers, chairs that don't seem important enough. For his entire working life he has taken naps in chairs subordinate to Enid's color schemes, and now he has received nearly five thousand dollars in retirement gifts. He has come to the store to spend the better part of this on a chair that celebrates, through its stature and costliness, the only activity in which he is truly himself. After a lifetime of providing for others, he needs even more than deep comfort and unlimited sleep: he needs public recognition of this need. Unfortunately, he fails to consider that monuments built for eternity are seldom comfortable for short-term accommodation. The chair he selects is outsized in the way of professional basketball shoes. I see his fingers trembling as they trace the multiple redundancy of the stitching. It's a lifetime chair — a mechanical engineer's chair, a chair designed to function under extraordinary stress, a chair with plenty of margin for error. On the minus side, it's so much larger than any person who'd sit in it — is at once so yielding and so magnificent — that it forces its occupant into the postures of a sleeping child. In the coming years he won't settle into this chair so much as get lost in it.

When Alfred went to China to see Chinese mechanical engineers, Enid went along and the two of them visited a rug factory to buy a rug for their family room. They were still unaccustomed to spending money on themselves, and so they chose one of the least expensive rugs. It had a design from the *Book of Changes* in blue wool on a field of beige. The blue of the chair Alfred brought into the house a few years later vaguely matched the blue of the rug's design, and Enid, who was strict about matching, suffered the chair's arrival.

Soon, though, Alfred's hands began to spill decaffeinated coffee on the rug's beige expanses, and wild grandchildren from the Rocky Mountains left berries and crayons underfoot, and Enid began to feel that the rug was a mistake. It seemed to her that in trying to save money in life she had made many mistakes like this. She reached the point of thinking it would have been better to buy no rug than to buy this rug. Finally, as Alfred went to sleep in his chair, she grew bolder. Her own mother had left her a tiny inheritance years ago, and she had made certain investments. Interest had been added to principal, certain stocks had performed rather well, and now she had an income of her own. She reconceived the family room in greens and yellows. She ordered fabrics. A paperhanger came, and Alfred, who was napping temporarily in the dining room, leaped to his feet like a man with a bad dream.

"You're redecorating *again?*"

"It's my own money," Enid said. "This is how I'm spending it."

"And what about the money *I* spent? What about the work *I* did?"

This argument had been effective in the past — it was, you might say, the constitutional basis of the tyranny's legitimacy — but it didn't work now. "That rug is nearly ten years old, and we'll never get the coffee stains out," Enid answered.

Alfred gestured at his blue chair, which under the paperhanger's plastic dropcloths looked like something you might deliver to a power station on a flatbed truck. He was trembling with incredulity, unable to believe that Enid could have forgotten this crushing refutation of her arguments, this overwhelming impediment to her plans; it was as if all the unfreedom and impossibility in which he'd spent his seven decades of life were embodied in this four-year-old but (because of its high quality) essentially brand-new chair. He was grinning, his face aglow with the awful perfection of his logic.

"And what about the chair, then?" he said. *"What about the chair?"*

Enid looked at the chair. Her expression was merely pained, no more. "I never liked that chair."

This was probably the most terrible thing she could have said to Alfred. The chair was the only sign he'd ever given of having a personal vision of the future. Enid's words filled him with such sorrow — he felt such pity for the chair, such solidarity with it, such astonished grief at its betrayal — that he pulled off the dropcloth and sank into its leather arms and fell asleep.

(This is one way of recognizing a place of enchantment: a suspiciously high incidence of narcolepsy.)

When it became clear that both the rug and Alfred's chair had to go, the rug was easily shed. Enid advertised in the free local paper and netted a nervous bird of a woman who was still making mistakes and whose fifties came out of her purse in a disorderly roll that she unpeeled and flattened with shaking fingers.

But the chair? The chair was a monument and a symbol and could not be parted from Alfred. It could only be relocated, and so it went into the basement and Alfred followed. And so in the house of the Lamberts, as in St. Jude, as in the country as a whole, life came to be lived underground.

Enid could hear him upstairs now, opening and closing drawers. In the streaklessly clean windows of the dining room was chaos. The berserk wind, the negating shadows. Now, of course, she had control of the upper floors. Now, when it was far too late.

Alfred stood in the master bedroom wondering why the drawers of his dresser were open, who had opened them, whether he had opened them himself. He could not help blaming Enid for his confusion. For witnessing it into existence. For existing, herself, as a person who could have opened these drawers.

"Al? What are you doing?"

He turned to the doorway where she'd appeared. He began a sentence: "I am —" but when he was taken by surprise, every sentence was an adventure in the woods; as soon as he could no longer see the light of the clearing from which he'd entered, it would come to him sickeningly that the crumbs he'd dropped for bearings had been eaten by birds, silent deft darting things that he couldn't quite see in the darkness but which were so numerous and swarming in their hunger that it seemed as if *they* were the darkness, as if the darkness weren't uniform, weren't an absence of light but a teeming and corpuscular thing, and indeed when as a studious teenager he'd encountered the word *crepuscular* in *McKay's Treasury of English Verse,* the corpuscles of biology had bled into his understanding of the word, so that for his entire adult life he'd seen in twilight a corpuscularity, as of the graininess of the high-speed film necessary for photography under conditions of low ambient light, as of a kind of sinister decay; and hence the panic of a man betrayed deep in the woods whose darkness was the darkness of starlings blotting out the sunset or black ants storming a dead opossum, a darkness that didn't just exist but actively *consumed* the bearings he had sensibly established for himself, lest he be lost; but in the instant of realizing he was lost, time became marvelously slow and he discovered hitherto unguessed eternities in the space between one word and the next, or rather he became trapped in that space between words and could only stand and watch as time sped on without him, the mindless part of him crashing on out of sight blindly through the woods while he, trapped, the grownup Al, watched in considerable but oddly impersonal suspense to see if the panic-stricken little boy Freddie might, despite no longer knowing where he was or at what point he'd entered the woods of this sentence, still be fortunate enough to blunder into a clearing where Enid was waiting for him, unaware of any woods — "packing my suitcase," he heard himself say. This sounded right. Verb, possessive, noun. Here was a suitcase in front of him, an important confirmation. He'd betrayed nothing.

But Enid had spoken again. The audiologist had said he was mildly impaired. He frowned at her, not following.

"It's *Thursday,*" she said, louder. "We're not going till *Saturday.*"

"Saturday!" he echoed.

She berated him then, and for a while the crepuscular birds retreated, but outside the wind had blown the sun out, and it was getting very cold.

Identifying the Stranger

MICHELLE CLIFF

Transactions

FROM TRIQUARTERLY

I

A BLOND, BLUE-EYED CHILD, about three years old, no one will
know her exact age, ever, is sitting in the clay of a country road, as if
she and the clay are one, as if she is the first human, but she is not.

She is dressed in a boy's shirt, sewn from osnaburg check, which
serves her as a dress. Her face is scabbed. The West Indian sun,
even at her young age, has made rivulets underneath her eyes
where waters run.

She is always hungry.

She works the clay into a vessel that will hold nothing.

Lizards fly between the tree ferns that stand at the roadside.

A man is driving an American Ford, which is black and eating up
the sun. He wears a Panama hat with a red band around it. He
carries a different brightly colored band for each day of the week.
He is pale and the band interrupts his paleness. His head is balding
and he takes care to conceal his naked crown. In his business,
appearance is important.

He is practicing his Chinese as he negotiates the mountain road,
almost washed away by the rains of the night before. His abacus
rattles on the seat beside him. With each swerve and bump, and
there are many, the beads of the abacus quiver and slide.

He is alone.

"You should see some of these shopkeepers, my dear," he tells his
wife. "They make this thing sing."

His car is American and he has an American occupation. He is a traveling salesman. He travels into the interior of the island, his car packed with American goods.

Many of the shopkeepers are Chinese, but like him, like everyone it seems, are in love with American things. He brings American things into the interior, into the clearing cut from ruinate. Novelties and necessities. Witch hazel. Superman. Band-Aids. Zane Grey. Chili con carne. Cap guns. Coke syrup. Fruit cocktail. Camels.

Marmalade and Marmite, Bovril and Senior Service, the weekly *Mirror* make room on the shopkeepers' shelves.

The salesman has always wanted a child. His wife says she never has. "Too many pickney in the world already," she says, then kisses her teeth. His wife is brown-skinned. He is not. He is pale, with pale eyes.

The little girl sitting in the road could be his, but the environment of his wife's vagina is acid. And then there is her brownness. Well.

And then he sees her. Sitting filthy and scabbed in the dirt road as he comes around a corner counting to a hundred in Chinese. She is crying.

Has he startled her?

He stops the car.

He and his wife have been married for twenty years. They no longer sleep next to each other. They sleep American style, as his wife calls it. She has noticed that married couples in the movies sleep apart. In "Hollywood" beds. She prevails on Mr. Dickens (a handyman she is considering bringing into the house in broad daylight) to construct "Hollywood" beds from mahogany.

The salesman gets out of the car and walks over to the little girl.

He asks after her people.

She points into the bush.

He lifts her up. He uses his linen hanky to wipe off her face. He blots her eye corners, under her nose. He touches her under her chin.

"Lord, what a solemn lickle ting."

He hears her tummy grumble.

At the edge of the road there is a narrow path down a steep hillside.

The fronds of a coconut tree cast shadows across the scabs on her face. He notices they are rusty. They will need attention.

He thinks he has a plan.

At the end of the narrow path is a clearing, with some mauger dogs, packed red-dirt yard, and a wattle house set on cement blocks.

The doorway, there is no door, yawns into the darkness.

He walks around the back, still holding the child, the dogs sniffing at him, licking at the little girl's bare feet.

A woman, blond and blue-eyed, is squatting under a tree. He is afraid to approach any closer, afraid she is engaged in some intimate activity, but soon enough she gets up, wipes her hand on her dress and walks toward him.

Yes, this is her little girl, the woman says in a strangely accented voice. And the salesman realizes he's stumbled on the descendants of a shipload of Germans, sent here as convicts or cheap labor, he can't recall which. There are to this day pockets of them in the deep bush.

He balances the little girl in one arm, she weighs next to nothing, removes his hat, inclines his balding head toward the blonder woman. She lowers her blue eyes. One eye has a cloud, the start of a cataract from too much sun.

He knows what he wants.

The woman has other children, sure, too many, she says. He offers twenty American dollars, just like that, counting out the single notes, and promises the little girl will have the best of everything, always, and that he loves children and has always wanted one of his own but he and his wife have never been so blessed.

The woman says something he does not understand. She points to a small structure at the side of the house. Under a peaked roof is a statue of the Virgin Mary, a dish of water at her feet. On her head is a coronet of lignum vitae. She is rude but painted brightly, like the Virgins at the roadside in Bavaria, carved along routes of trade and plague. Her shawl is colored indigo.

"*Liebfrau,*" the woman repeats.

He nods.

The Virgin's shawl is flecked with yellow, against indigo, like the Milky Way against the black of space.

The salesman is not Catholic, but never mind. He promises the little girl will attend the Convent of the Immaculate Conception at Constant Spring, the very best girls' school on the island. He goes on about their uniforms. Very handsome indeed. Royal blue neckties and white dresses. Panama hats with royal blue hatbands. He points to the band around his own hat by way of explanation.

The royal blue will make his daughter's eyes bright.

This woman could not be more of a wonder to him. She is a stranger in this landscape, this century, she of an indentured status, a petty theft.

He wonders at her loneliness. No company but the Virgin Mother.

The woman extends her hand for the money, puts it in the side pocket of her dress. She strokes the head of her daughter, still in the salesman's arms.

"She can talk?"

"*Ja, no mus'?*"

A squall comes from inside the darkness of the house, and the woman turns, her dress becoming damp.

"Well, goodbye then," the salesman says.

She turns back. She opens her dress and presses a nipple, dripping, into the mouth of her little girl. "Bye, bye," she says. And she is gone.

He does not know what to think.

The little girl makes no fuss, not even a whimper, as he carries her away, and he is suddenly afraid he has purchased damaged goods. What if she's foolish? It will be difficult enough to persuade his brown-skinned wife to bring a white-skinned child into the house. If she is fool-fool, God help him.

Back at the car he tucks her into the front seat, takes his penknife and opens a small tin of fruit cocktail.

He points to the picture on the label, the glamorous maraschino cherry. "Wait till you taste this, darlin'. It come all the way from America." Does she have the least sense of what America is?

He wipes away the milk at the corners of her mouth.

He takes a spoon from the glove compartment.

"You can feed yourself?"

She says nothing, so he begins to spoon the fruit cocktail into her. Immediately she brightens and opens her mouth wide, tilting her head back like a little bird.

In no time she's finished the tin.

"Mustn't eat too fast, sweetheart. Don't want to get carsick."

"*Nein, nein,*" she says with a voice that's almost a growl.

She closes her eyes against the sun flooding the car.

"Never mind," he says, "we'll be off soon." He wraps the spoon and empty fruit-cocktail tin into a sheet of the *Gleaner,* putting the package on the floor of the back seat.

Next time he will pour some condensed milk into the tinned fruit, making it even sweeter.

There's a big American woman who runs a restaurant outside Milk River. She caters to the tourists who come to take the famously radioactive waters. And to look at the crocodiles. She also lets rooms. She will let him a room for the night. In turn he will give her the American news she craves. She says she once worked in the movies. He doesn't know if he believes her.

He puts the car in gear and drives away from the clearing.

His heart is full. Is this how women feel? he wonders as he glances at the little girl, now fast asleep.

What has he done? She is his treasure, his newfound thing, and he never even asked her name. What will you call this child? the priest will ask. Now she is yours. He must have her baptized. Catholic or Anglican, he will decide.

He will have to bathe her. He will ask the American woman to help him. He will take a bathroom at the mineral spring and dip her into the famous waters, into the "healing stream," like the old song says.

He will baptize her himself. The activity of the spring, of world renown, will mend her skin. The scabs on her face are crusted over and there are more on her arms and legs. She might well have scurvy, even in the midst of a citrus grove.

But the waters are famous.

As he drives, he alternates between making plans and imagining his homecoming and his wife's greeting. You must have taken leave of your senses, busha. She calls him busha when she's angry and wants him to stand back. No, busha. Is who tell you we have room fi pickney? He will say he had no choice. Was he to leave this little girl in the middle of a country road, covered with dirt and sores and hungry? Tell me, busha, tell me jus' one ting: is how many pickney you see this way on your travels, eh? Is why you don't bring one home sooner? Tell me that.

Everybody wants a child that favors them, that's all.

She will kiss her teeth.

If she will let him have his adoption, he will say, she can have the other side of the house for her and Mr. Dickens. It will be simple. Once he plays that card there will be no going back. They will split the house down the middle. That will be that.

Like is drawn to like. Fine to fine. Coarse to coarse.

There are great advantages to being a traveling salesman in this place. He learns the island by heart. Highland and floodplain, sinkhole and plateau. Anywhere a shopkeeper might toss up, fix some shelves inside a zinc-roofed shed, open shop.

He respects the relentlessness of shopkeepers. They will nest anywhere. You can be in the deepest bush and come upon a tin sign advertising Nescafé, and find a group of people gathered as if the shed were a town hall, which it well might be.

Everything is commerce, he cannot live without it.

On the road sometimes he is taken by what is around him. He is distracted by gorges, ravines possessed of an uncanny green. Anything could dwell there. If he looks closer he will enter the island's memory, the petroglyphs of a disappeared people. The birdmen left by the Arawak.

Once he took a picnic lunch of cassava cake and fried fish and ginger beer into the burial cave at White Marl, and left a piece of cassava at the feet of one of the skeletons.

He gazes at the remains of things. Stone fences, fallen, moss-covered, which might mark a boundary in Somerset. Ruined windmills. A circular ditch where a coffle marked time on a treadmill. As steady as an orbit.

A salesman is free, he tells himself. He makes his own hours, comes and goes as he pleases. People look forward to his arrival, and not just for the goods he carries. He is part troubadour. If he's been to the movies in town he will recount the plot for a crowd, despite the beauty of the stars, the screen washed in color.

These people temper his loneliness.

But now, now.

Now he thinks he'll never be lonely again.

II

The Bath is located on the west bank of Milk River, just south of where the Rio Bronte, much tamer than its name, branches off.

The waters of the Bath rise through the karst, the heart of stone. The ultimate source of the Bath is an underground saline spring, which might suggest a relationship with the sea. The relationship with the sea is suggested everywhere; the limestone that composes more of the land than any other substance is nothing but the skeletons of marine creatures.

"From the sea we come, to the sea we shall return." His nurse-maid used to chant this as he lay in his pram on King's Parade.

The water of the Bath is a steady temperature of ninety-one degrees Fahrenheit (thirty-three degrees Centigrade). The energy of the water is radiant, fifty-five times more active than Baden-Baden, fifty times more active than Vichy.

Such is the activity that bathers are advised not to remain immersed for more than fifteen minutes a day.

In the main building the bather may read testimonials to the healing faculties of the waters. These date to 1794, when the first bathrooms were opened.

> Lord Salisbury was cured of lowness of spirit
> Hamlet, his slave, escaped depraved apprehensions
> May 1797, Anno Domini

> Mrs. Horne was cured of the hysteria and loss of spleen
> December 1802, Anno Domini

> The Governor's Lady regained her appetites
> October 1817, Anno Domini

> Septimus Hart, Esq., banished his dread
> July 1835, Anno Domini

> The Hon. Catherine Dillon was cured of a mystery
> February 1900, Anno Domini

The waters bore magical properties. Indeed some thought the power of the Lord was in them.

The salesman's car glides into the gravel parking lot of the Little Hut, the American woman's restaurant. She named it after a movie she made with Ava Gardner and Stewart Granger. "A movie she made" sounds grandiose; she picked up after Miss Gardner, stood in for her during long shots.

She hears the car way back in the kitchen of the restaurant, where she's supervising Hamlet VII in the preparation of dinner. Tonight, pepper-pot soup to start, followed by curried turtle, rice and peas, a Bombay mango cut in half and filled with vanilla ice cream.

The American woman, her head crowned with a thick black braid, comes out of the doorway onto the verandah, which runs around the Little Hut, and walks toward the salesman's car.

"Well, well, what have we got here?" She points to the passenger seat in front. "What are you, a kidnapper or something?"

She's wearing a khaki shirt with red and black epaulets, the tails knotted at her midsection, and khaki shorts. The kitchen steam has made her clothes limp, and sweat stains bloom on her back and under her arms. Her feet are bare. She wears a silver bangle around one ankle.

"Gone native" is one of her favorite ways of describing herself, whether it means bare feet, a remnant of chain, or swimming in Milk River alongside the crocodiles.

Still she depends on the salesman to bring her news of home.

"I've got your magazines, your *Jets*," the salesman says, ignoring her somewhat bumptious remark.

It was late afternoon by now. A quick negotiation about a room for the night and then he would take his little sleepyhead, who has not stirred, to be bathed. He has great faith in the waters from all he has heard.

He asks the American woman about a room.

"There's only one available right now," she tells him. "I've been overrun."

The room is located behind the restaurant, next to the room where Hamlet VII sleeps.

The salesman — she remembers his name is Harold (he was called Prince Hal at school, he told her), hers is Rosalind — is not crazy about sleeping in what he considers servants' quarters, and tells her so.

"My daughter," he begins.

Rosalind interrupts him. "Look, this is all I have right now. You may as well take it."

He's silent.

"It's clean and spacious," she tells him, "lots of room for you, and for her." She nods in the direction of the little girl. She can't help but be curious, aware from his earlier visits that he said he had no children, that his wife had turned her back on him, or so he said, that he equated being a traveler for an import firm with being a pirate on the Spanish Main, right down to the ribbon on his hat and his galleon of a car.

"Footloose and fancy-free" was how he described himself to her, but Rosalind didn't buy it.

He seemed like a remnant to her. So many of them did. There was something behind the thickness of green, in the crevices of bone; she wore a sign of it on her ankle.

"Very well, then. I'll take it."

"You won't be sorry."

"I need to take her to the Bath presently. Will you come?"

"Me? Why?"

"I need a woman to help me with her."

"I thought you said she was your daughter."

"I did."

"What's wrong with her?"

"Her skin is broken."

"Well, they have attendants at the Bath to help you."

"Okay, then."

Rosalind had in mind a stack of *Jets*, a pitcher of iced tea, and a break into the real world, Chicago, New York, Los Angeles, before the deluge of bathers, thirsty for something beside radioactive waters, descended on her.

"It will be fine. Just don't let her stay in too long."

"I won't."

"How much do I owe you for the magazines?"

"Not to worry."

"Well, then, the room is gratis."

That was fair. He felt a bit better.

At the Bath, a white-costumed woman showed him and the little girl into a bathroom of their own. She unveiled the child and made no comment at the sores running over her tummy and back. As she dipped the child into the waters an unholy noise bounded across the room, beating against the tile, skating the surface of the waters, testing the room's closeness. *"Nein! Nein!"* the little girl screamed over and over again. The salesman had to cover his ears.

The waters did not bubble or churn; there was nothing to be afraid of. The salesman finally found his tongue. "What is the matter, sweetheart? You never feel water touch your skin before this?"

But the child said nothing in response, only took some gasps of breath, and suddenly he felt like a thief, not the savior he preferred.

"Nein! Nein!" she started up again, and the woman in white put her hand over his treasure's mouth, clamping it tight, and held her down in the temperate waters rising up from the karst.

She held her down the requisite fifteen minutes and then lifted her out, shaking her slightly, drying her, and only two bright tears were left, one on each cheek, and he knew if he got close enough he would be reflected in them.

The woman swaddled the child in a white towel, saying, "No need to return this." She glanced back, in wonder he was sure, then turned the knob and was gone.

If the waters were as magical as promised, maybe he would not have to return. He lifted the little girl up in his arms and felt a sharp sensation as she sank her baby teeth into his cheek, drawing blood.

The salesman had tied the stack of *Jets* tightly, and Rosalind had to work the knife under the string, taking care not to damage the cover of the magazine on top. The string gave way and the stack slid apart. The faces of Jackie Wilson, Sugar Ray Robinson, and Dorothy Dandridge glanced up at her. A banner across one cover read, "Emmett Till, The Story Inside." She arranged herself on a wicker chaise on the verandah and began her return to the world she'd left behind.

She took the photographs — there were photographs — released by his mother — he was an only child — his mother was a widow — he stuttered — badly — these were some details — she took the photographs into her — into herself — and she would never let them go.

She would burn the magazine out back with the kitchen trash — drop it in a steel drum and watch the images curl and melt against turtle shell — she'd give the other magazines to Hamlet as she always did — he had a scrapbook of movie stars and prizefighters and jazz musicians. The mother had insisted on the pictures, so said *Jet*.

This is my son. Swollen by the beating — by the waters of the river Pearl — misshapen — unrecognizable — monstrous.

Hamlet heard her soft cries out in the kitchen, over the steam of turtle meat.

"Missis is all right?"

She made no answer to his question, only waved him off with one hand, the other covering the black-and-white likeness of the corpse. She did not want Hamlet to see where she came from.

America's waterways.

She left the verandah and went out back.

Blood trickled from the salesman's cheek.

"Is vampire you vampire, sweetheart?"

"What are you telling me?"

They were sitting on the verandah after dinner, the tourists having strolled to Milk River guided by Hamlet to watch the crocodiles in the moonlight.

"Are they man-eaters? Are they dangerous?" one tourist woman inquired.

"They are more afraid of you than you could possibly be of them," Hamlet told her.

The little sharp-toothed treasure was swaddled in the towel from the Bath and curled up on a chaise next to Rosalind. Tomorrow the salesman would have to buy her decent clothes.

If he decided to keep her.

But he must keep her.

"I gave a woman twenty American dollars for her."

"What is she?"

What indeed, this blond and blue-eyed thing, filled with vanilla ice cream, bathing in the moonlight that swept the verandah.

Not a hot moon tonight. Not at all.

He rubbed his cheek where the blood had dried.

"Her people came from overseas, long time ago."

They sat in the quiet, except for the back noise of the tropics. As if unaware of any strangeness around them.

Silence.

His wife would never stand for it.

He might keep his treasure here. He would pay her room and board, collect her on his travels. A lot of men had outside children. He would keep in touch with his.

Why was he such a damn coward?

Rosalind would never agree to such a scheme, that he knew.

But no harm in asking.

It would have to wait. He'd sleep on it.

But when he woke, all he woke to was a sharp pain in his cheek. He touched the place where the pain seemed keenest, and felt a round hardness that did not soften to his touch but sent sharp sensations clear into his eyes.

When he raised his eyelids the room was a blur. He waited for his vision to clear but nothing came. The red hatband was out of sight.

He felt the place in the bed where his treasure had slept. There was a damp circle on the sheet. She was gone.

RICHARD BAUSCH

Nobody in Hollywood

FROM THE NEW YORKER

I WAS PUMMELED as a teenager.

For some reason, I had the sort of face that asked to be punched. Something about the curve of my mouth, I guess. It made me look like I was being cute with people, smirking at them.

I am what is called a late-life child. My brother, Doke, is twenty years older and played semi-pro football. But by the time I came along Doke was through as a ballplayer, and my father had given up on seeing a son play pro. I was a month premature, and very, very tiny as a child. Dad named me Ignatius, after an uncle of his that I never knew. Of course I didn't take to sports, though I could run pretty fast (that comes with having a face people want to hit). I liked to read; I was the family bookworm. I'm four feet nine inches tall.

Doke married young, divorced young, and had a son, Doke Jr., that the wife took with her to Montana. But Doke missed the boy and went out there to be near him, and when I graduated from high school he invited me for a visit. That's how I ended up in Montana in 1971. I'd gone to spend the summer with Doke, in a hunter's cabin up in the mountains. It was a little cottage, with a big stone hearth and knotty-pine paneling and color photos of the surrounding country. On a shelf above the hearth were some basketball trophies belonging to the guy who owned the place, a former college all-star now working as an ophthalmologist down in Dutton.

Doke taught me how to fly-fish. A fly rod had a lot of importance to Doke, as if being good with the thing was a key to the meaning of life or something. He had an image of himself, standing in sunlight, all beauty, fly rod in hand. He was mystical about the enterprise, although he didn't really have much ability.

While I was staying with Doke, I met Hildie, my eventual ex-wife. She was a nurse in the hospital where Doke took me the night I met his new girlfriend, Samantha. I met Samantha about two hours before I met Hildie.

Samantha had come home to Montana from San Francisco, where she'd been with her crazy mother. Before I met her — for many days before — Doke had talked about her, about how beautiful and sexy she was. According to Doke, I just wasn't going to believe my eyes. He'd met her in a bar he used to frequent after working construction all day in Dutton. She was only twenty-five. He told me all about her, day after day. We were drinking pretty heavy in the evenings, and he'd tell me about what she had gone through in her life.

"She's so beautiful to have to go through that stuff," he said. "Suicide and insanity and abuse. A lot of abuse. She's part Indian. She's had hard times. Her father was a full-blooded Cherokee. She's a genius. He killed himself. Then her mother went crazy, and they put her in this institution for the insane over in San Francisco. Her mother doesn't know her own name anymore. Or Samantha's. Pathetic, really. Think about it. And she looks like a goddess. I can't even find the words for it. Beautiful. Nobody in the world. Not even Hollywood."

At the time, I was worried about getting drafted into the army and was under a lot of stress. I didn't want to hear about Doke's beautiful girlfriend. "Man," he said. "I wish I had her picture — a snapshot of her — so I could show you. But the Indian blood means she has this thing about having her picture taken. Like it steals part of her soul. They all believe that."

He was talking about her the night she arrived, the traveling she'd done when she was a dancer for the Rolling Stones ("She knows Mick Jagger, man"), and the heavy things she'd seen — abused children and illicit drugs and alcohol — and also the positions she liked during sex, and the various ways they had of doing it together.

"She's an Indian," he said. "They have all kinds of weird ideas."

"Could we go out on the porch or something?" I said.

He hadn't heard me. "She wears a headband. It expresses her

people. She was six when her mother went crazy the first time. A white woman, the mother, right? This poor girl from Connecticut had no idea what she was getting into, marrying this guy, coming out here to live, almost like a pioneer. Only, the guy turned out to be a wild man. They lived on the reservation, and nobody else wanted anything to do with them because of how he was. A true primitive, but a noble one, too. You should hear Samantha talk about him. He used to take her everywhere, and he had this crazy thing about rock concerts. Like they were from the old days of the tribe, see. He'd go and dance and get really drunk. Samantha went with him until she was in her teens. She actually has a daughter from when they traveled with the Rolling Stones. The daughter's staying with her mother's sister back east. It's a hell of a story."

"She's only twenty-five?"

He nodded. "Had the daughter when she was seventeen."

"The Rolling Stones," I said. "Something."

"Don't give me that look," he said.

I smiled as big as I could. "No," I said. "Really. I wasn't. I'd just like to go outside. It's stuffy in here, isn't it?"

"Could be Mick Jagger's kid," my brother said, significantly. "Samantha knew him."

"Well," I said. "Hey. She'll be here soon. We better clean up a little."

He poured himself another drink. "What have we done in our lives?" he said, staring at the table and looking sad. "I've worked a few jobs. Bought a car here and there. Got married and got divorced. And you — you graduated from high school. Went to the prom, right? I mean, we haven't really experienced anything. Imagine having your father kill himself."

"How'd he do it?" I asked.

"I told you," he said. "He shot himself. Jesus, are you listening to me?"

A little while later, Samantha pulled in, and we went out to greet her. She'd been driving for two days, she told us. It was almost dark, but from what I could see she looked like death itself. We all went inside, and Doke poured more whiskey. He kept watching me, waiting for a sign, I suppose. I couldn't give him one. He'd built up so many of my expectations that I'd begun to think beyond what was really possible for a big, not too nice-looking former high school football star with a potbelly and a double chin. Samantha wasn't pretty. Not by a very, very, very long stretch. And it wasn't just the fact that she'd been sitting behind the wheel of a ratty carbon-monoxide-spewing car for two days. She could've just walked out of a beauty parlor after an all-afternoon session and it wouldn't have made any difference. She did have nice dark skin, but her eyes were set deep in her skull, and they were crossed a little. They were also extremely small — the smallest eyes I ever saw, like a rodent's eyes, black and with a scary glitter in them. They fixed on you as if you were something to eat and swallow. She was tall, and had long legs, and hips wider than Doke's. Her hair was shiny, crow black, and stiff. She'd let it grow wild, so it appeared that it hadn't seen a brush in her lifetime. She was not physically beautiful by any standard you care to name.

So there she was, and Doke stood by, staring, all moony-eyed and weepy with the booze and love, and I guess I couldn't keep the surprise out of my face. I had thought I was going to meet this beautiful woman; instead, I'd met Samantha.

"I have to go freshen up," she said after we'd been through the introductions. She went into the bathroom and closed the door. We heard what sounded like water being poured out of a big vat into other water.

Doke turned to me. "Well?" he said. "Right?"

"Jesus Christ," I said. I thought he meant the sound.

"Isn't she beautiful?"

I said, "Right." But I couldn't be as convincing as I wanted to be.

"You ever see anything —" he said. He was standing by the table, tottering a little, holding on to the back of the chair. "You know?"

I said, "Yeah."

He pulled the chair out and sat down and ran his hands through his hair. "Just," he said. "Really."

I nodded.

"Right?" he said.

I said, "Uh-huh."

He picked up the bottle and drank. Then shook his head. "Something."

"Wow," I said.

After another drink and a few seconds of staring off, he said, "What's the matter with you?" He still wasn't looking at me.

I said, "Nothing. Why?"

He poured more whiskey, then sat there and seemed to study it. "You got something to say?"

"Can't think of anything," I said.

He looked at me, and I sat down, too. "Well?" he said. "I don't like that look."

"She's been on the road," I said. "She's tired."

"Not her. You. I don't like *your* look."

I ran my hands over my face. I thought he might think I was smirking at him. "Oh," I said. "I'm okay."

"That isn't what I mean," he said.

I reached for the whiskey. "I think I'll have some more of that," I told him. "That's all right with you?"

He didn't answer. He was thinking.

Samantha came out of the bathroom. I didn't know what she'd done to freshen up. Nothing had changed at all. She sat down and leaned back in the chair and clasped her hands behind her head. "So this is your brother."

"That's him," Doke said.

"You're so little compared to Doke. It's strange." She went over and got herself a glass and brought it back to the table, where Doke poured her some whiskey.

"I told Ignatius about your dad and mom," Doke said to her.

She drank, then shook her head. "Terrible." She looked a lot older than twenty-five. She had earrings in her skin that went all the way up the side of her ear. This was the first time I'd ever seen that phenomenon. "I got a baby that's severely retarded. The oxygen wasn't right."

Doke seemed surprised. "You never said she was retarded."

"That's what I said."

She nodded, sadly. She was watching me. "My father took me to Altamont," she said. "I was there. I know Mick Jagger."

"It might be his kid," Doke said, all excited. "Right?"

She seemed to think this over. "No. I don't think so."

"But it could be, though. Right?"

She thought about the question. "No."

"Didn't you —" Doke said, then stopped. He was confused.

"We saw them. We were close, you know. But not that close."

Nobody said anything. I was watching Doke, because I couldn't look at Samantha — the difference between his description of her and the reality was too much. He said, "Well, I thought you said the kid was Jagger's kid."

"I suppose it could be. I had so many lovers back then."

"You mean you might not've noticed that it was Mick Jagger?" I said.

She stared at me. "Why'd he look at me like that?" she asked.

Doke took a drink. He was thinking.

I said something to smooth things over. "I have the kind of face that makes people think I'm being smart with them."

"He's always got that look," Doke said.

"Where is your kid?" I asked her.

She said, "With my mother's family, back east. My father was killed by the government for protesting against them."

"I thought your father killed himself," Doke said.

"He did." And she added, "The government drove him to it."

"Hell," I said.

She nodded importantly. "The government is not legitimate, you know. As long as there are whites living on Indian lands."

"Which Indian lands?" I said.

"The whole country."

"Oh, you mean — like the Constitution and all that. That's not valid."

"Right," she said.

"Not much chance of that going away," I said, meaning to sympathize with her.

"My father was a full-blooded Cherokee," she said. "Doke told you, I'm sure."

"I told him," Doke said. "I told him about that and I told him about the Rolling Stones."

"It wasn't just the Rolling Stones. I traveled a lot. I had three hundred lovers before I was twenty-two."

Doke shook his head.

"Looking for love," I said.

She said, "At least three hundred of them."

"Lovers," I said.

She nodded.

"What was it that interested you about them? If you don't mind my asking."

She looked at me and her face twisted up, as if she smelled something bad. "What?"

"Are you making fun?" Doke asked. His face was a total blank.

"No," I said. I was truly curious. With that many lovers, it was hard to imagine that there wouldn't be some sort of filing system, to keep track of the types anyway. Doke was staring at me, so I put my hand over my mouth, which I had come to think of as the offending part of my face.

He shook his head again, then poured more whiskey. I sat back and pretended to be relaxed and interested, while Samantha talked about herself and her adventures. She was related to Crazy Horse, she said. And on her mother's side there was a distant connection to Mary Lincoln. She had lived in Haight-Ashbury and attended the University of California at Berkeley, majoring in law. She'd had plans to enter the system and ruin it from the inside. The collapse of the American government was the only hope for her and her people. But her father had this thing about rock concerts, and she'd got sidetracked. For years she'd followed the Grateful Dead around from concert to concert. She knew Jerry Garcia well. She'd had a child by him that died, and it was why she left to seek out the Rolling Stones. She liked their names better. Once, when she was only thirteen, she'd met John F. Kennedy. Doke sipped the whiskey, watching me. I was beginning to get sleepy. She droned on. She'd been a member of the Weathermen, and the FBI had crushed them with bombs and fire and infiltrators. Doke was staring at me, waiting for the first sign that I wasn't utterly charmed, but I was actively fighting sleep. He had a big stake in her, and I didn't want to hurt his feelings. Samantha had fixed me with her rodent's eyes. But my eyes were so heavy. I rubbed them, put my hands over a yawn.

"I'm very sensitive to spiritual vibrations," she said. "It's my Indian blood."

This was in reference to something I must have missed in the long monologue, because Doke said, "So that's how you knew he was going to kill himself."

"Yes," she said. "But there wasn't anything I could do. It was his karma." She went on to talk about karma, and how a person's karma caused a glow that she could perceive. "I'm very perceptive," she said. "I can sense what a person is thinking. I get vibes from people."

I was thinking, *Please stop talking.*

"It's uncanny," she went on. "I look in a person's eyes, and I see all their thoughts, their innermost feelings."

Shut the fuck up, please, I was thinking. *Go to bed.*

She seemed never to take a breath. She said, "I learned this when I met Robert Kennedy at his house in McLean, Virginia. I was eighteen, and I think he was interested in me physically, too. It was so odd. I just walked up and knocked on his door and his maid — Eva was her name —"

"Well, I sure am beat," I said. I was desperate now. "Guess I'll turn in."

"I was telling you something," she said.

I said, "You must be awful tired."

"I was in the middle of telling something, and you started talking about turning in." She seemed to pout. I caught myself actually feeling sorry for her.

"We've been keeping you up," I said. "You must be exhausted." I stood, vaguely intending to make polite conversation as I left the room.

"She was telling you something," Doke said.

"Do you have an Indian name?" I asked Samantha.

She shook her head. "My mother insisted that I be given a white woman's name. She knew I would have a terrible time growing up in the white man's world."

I didn't say anything.

She added, "It would have split me in two. And you know how terrible it is to be split down the middle?" She reached over and played with the crown of Doke's hair.

I said I supposed I didn't. I yawned.

She said, "It's much worse than you can imagine. I'm sorry it bores you." She seemed proud to have plumbed my feelings.

"I'm fine," I said. "Just tired."

There didn't seem to be anything else to talk about. She sat. She was biting her nails, taking in the room with those little eyes. I had come to the realization that she was no more of Indian blood than I was the King of Spain. I had an image of her parents — a couple of Italians, probably, holding down an apartment in Brooklyn, wondering where the daughter ran off to. I said, "What's Mick Jagger like?"

"Very grungy and nervous." She was still biting her nails.

I said, "Everything you've told us is a crock, right?"

"You can disbelieve me if you want," she said. "I don't care."

I looked at Doke. "Man," I said. Then I started out of the room. "Bedtime."

But Doke stood suddenly and when I turned, he took me by the front of my shirt. "You think you can treat us like this?"

I said, "Okay, look. I'm sorry. I didn't mean anything."

"Leave him be," Samantha said. "It's his loss."

"Will you excuse us for a few seconds?" Doke said to her.

She got up and went outside. We could join her, she said, when we were through being babies. She closed the door and Doke walked me back against the wall, still holding my shirt in his fists.

"I saw the way you were looking at her."

"What difference does it make what I think?" I said. A mistake.

"Oh," he said. "What do you think?"

"Cut it out," I said. "Come on. Let me go."

"Not till you tell me what you think of Samantha."

"I think she's a liar," I told him. "And she's not even a very good one." I couldn't help myself. "And on top of that I think she's ugly as month-old pizza."

He commenced hitting me. He was swinging wildly, and some of his punches missed, which allowed me to get under the table. Then he started kicking. I was crawling around, trying to get away from him, and Samantha had come back in to stop him. When he stormed out into the dark, she got down on the floor and saw that I was bleeding from a gash on my forehead. I must have hit the edge of the table on my way under it. She was really quite gentle and sweet, getting me a rag for my head, and insisting that Doke would take me down to Dutton, to the emergency room.

As I said, it was while I was in the hospital that I met Hildie. "That's a nasty cut" was the first thing she said to me.

"Yes, ma'am," I said. I thought she was perfect. I wouldn't expect anyone else to think so, necessarily.

"How'd it happen?" she said.

"My brother and I got in a fight."

She shook her head, concentrating on her work, cutting a bandage to size for me. "Two grown boys like you."

"I could tell you about it," I said.

That was all it needed. My mother used to say, when the time is right you don't need to have a committee meeting about it.

When I eventually returned to the cabin, I found that Samantha had gone. She had picked up and headed off into the West, with a few of Doke's records and tapes and most of the money he'd saved. He took it pretty hard. For a while that summer, he had himself convinced that because she'd taken those things she was planning on coming back. But the months turned into the rest of the year, and I stayed on through the next spring and part of that summer, and she was just gone. His drinking got pretty bad, and I started having to look out for the boy a lot on the weekends.

"It's not fair, I know it," Doke said to me. "I can't shake it, though."

"You've got to get ahold of yourself," I told him. I'd been seeing Hildie.

We were married at the end of that next summer, and for a while Doke's boy lived with us while Doke dried out, in rehab. The boy's mother was in some sort of rehab herself. Drugs. Sometimes, back then, it seemed to me that the whole country had gone crazy.

Hildie and I were together almost twenty years. We never had any children. Doke left Montana and lives in Seattle now. He's happy. Some stories do have happy endings, for a while, anyway. He's got a wife, and another boy, and a girl. He probably never thinks about Samantha. I used to imagine the Italian couple in Brooklyn, reunited with their wayward little girl, who pulled up one day, driving a car full of music and money. She was such a bad liar. Doke's son married a nice girl from Catalina, then moved to New York City. Everybody got along fine, really.

Hildie and I lived for a few years in a little three-bedroom rambler on Coronado Street in Sandusky, Illinois. Those first years, we had a lot of fun, usually. Now and then she'd lose her temper, and my old trouble would return: something about my face would cause her to start swinging at me. And I never hit back. But it doesn't, as the saying goes, take two to fight. One person with an urge to hit somebody else is enough. For the person getting knocked out, it might as well be the heavyweight championship.

One night, when we were drinking, I told Hildie about Samantha. I must have been a little careless in how I talked about Samantha's physical qualities, because I upset Hildie. These days, you say something about one woman and you've said it about all of them.

"Is that the way you see us?" she said.

"Us," I said. "What?"

"Is that how you judge women? You see that I'm gaining weight, don't you? And do you see me like this Samantha person?"

I said, "I'm just saying she wasn't what Doke said she was."

"It just kills me that that's how you think."

For about a year things had been going sour. Hildie had ballooned to about two hundred and fifty pounds. I had lost weight. And I was worried about money. So was she, but her worry came out differently. She kept asking me what I thought of her. "You think I'm ugly now," she'd say. "Right? That's how you see me. Why don't you come out and say it?"

"I think you're fine," I'd say.

"Tell me the truth. I'm too big."

"No," I'd say. "Really, hon."

"You're lying. I can see it in your face."

My face again. There was nothing I could say. And, besides, I was about half her size by now.

Once I said, "Do *you* think you're too big?"

"It's not important what I think," she said. "Because, goddamn it, I know how you think. All of you."

We needed extra income, and she hated the idea of nursing anymore, so she got a job serving food at a hospital cafeteria across the river in Missouri. There were nights when we didn't say a thing to each other, and after a few months she started doing things to get shut of me. That was okay. I think I even understood. She made dates with the janitor on her floor, a man fifteen years older than I am and a lot bigger. She told people she was leaving me. She had friends over at all hours of the day and night. When I walked in and someone asked who I was, she'd wave me away. "That's my soon-to-be ex," she'd say. It was always said like a joke, but you could feel the edge to it.

I never answered. I went about my business and tried not to get mad. She was as big as a Buick. She weighed more than my whole family put together, including Doke. I never mentioned that the bed sagged on her side, and that I was having to replace the mattress every six months. I'd watch her settle into her seat in a steak joint, order a porterhouse the size of an infant, and not say a word.

I said nothing about her jeans, which were big enough to throw over a rhinoceros and keep it dry in the rain.

The night she kicked me out, she came home with a friend. A new lover, she told me. She made her lover wait out on the front lawn while she broke the news. "Do you understand me, Ignatius? I want you out. I've decided I don't need a man to tell me who I am. You can stay until you find a place. But sleep on the sofa. Grace is moving in with us."

Grace had walked into the hospital cafeteria several weeks before, after having been bandaged up in the emergency room. She'd been in a traffic accident, and her nose and upper lip were cut. Hildie and she got to talking, and pretty soon they were meeting for drinks after Hildie's shifts. It was just like Hildie and me, in a way, except that now she wanted a woman and not a man. I'd never thought much of myself, but this hurt me. "She's the most interesting person I've ever been around," Hildie said. "And you and I haven't been anything to each other for a long time." This was true. Grace walked up to the door, and Hildie opened it and stepped back for her to come in, acting like this was the grand entrance of her happiness. Grace had a big white bandage over her nose, but we weren't in the same room more than fifteen minutes before I recognized Samantha. Blond this time. A few pounds heavier, a little fuller in the face. But unmistakably her.

"Hello, Grace."

She looked at me with those little black eyes, and then sat on the couch next to Hildie. I went into the bedroom and started packing, throwing shirts in a suitcase, and some slacks and socks and underwear. I wasn't sure what I should take with me. I could hear Samantha/Grace in the next room. She had built her own house, she was saying, and had learned how to play several musical instruments but then forgot how. She had spent the night with Sting during a thunderstorm and power outage in Atlanta. By the time I was back to the living room, she was talking about Mount Saint Helens. She was there when it blew. She almost died.

"Ever been on the reservation?" I asked. I was putting a few of my books into my suitcase.

Both women looked at me as though I had trees growing out of my head.

"Reservation?" Samantha/Grace asked.

I couldn't tell if she recognized me. She stared, and then she smiled. So I smiled back, and resumed packing.

She said, "I've done so much wandering around. I've been in almost every state of the Union, and made love in each one of them, too."

"I always wanted to go to Hawaii," Hildie said, laughing.

"Oh, absolutely. I've been there. I was married and lived there, but I got divorced."

"Must've been a tough week," I put in. It was a nasty thing to say. And it was the wrong time to say it. It made me look bad. I said, "Little joke, girls."

"Oh," Samantha/Grace said. "Haw."

Hildie shook her head. "Men."

"Haw, haw," Samantha/Grace said.

"Ever been to Montana?" I asked her.

"I worked in the emergency room at the hospital in Dutton," Hildie said. "A terrible, lonely job. That's where I had the misfortune of meeting Ignatius."

Samantha/Grace smiled and leaned back in her chair. My name is not one that a person forgets easily. She stared at me with her wolverine's eyes and kept smiling.

Clasping her hands behind her blond head, Samantha/Grace said, "Well, you know, I never was in Montana. That's one of the few places I've never been."

I couldn't help it.

A laugh came up out of me like a sneeze. I laughed and laughed and went on laughing — so hard that Hildie got mad, and the madder she got the more I laughed. Before I had stopped laughing, she'd thrown all my things out on the lawn. This was the last night of my marriage, I knew that, and that was all right with me. I wouldn't want anyone to think I was complaining.

CYNTHIA OZICK

Save My Child!

FROM THE NEW YORKER

RUTH PUTTERMESSER, a white-haired New Yorker in her six-
ties — a retired lawyer, unmarried, cranky in the way of a woman
alone — was as old now as her long-dead father: her father who,
fleeing the brutish Russia of the czars, had left behind parents, sisters, brothers, all swallowed up in the Bolshevik silence, dwindled
now into their archaic names and brittle cardboard-framed photographs. "Do not write anymore," Puttermesser's grandmother had
pleaded more than six decades ago: "My eyes are gone. I am old
and blind. I cannot read." This was the last letter from Moscow; it
lay under the old Russian photos in an envelope blanketed by
coarsely printed stamps. Each stamp displayed the identical profile
of a man with a considerable mustache. Stalin. Puttermesser knew
that the poet Osip Mandelstam had likened that mustache to a
cockroach, whereupon Stalin ordered him murdered. Isaac Babel
was murdered after months of torture and a phony trial. Mikhoels
the Yiddish actor was murdered. All the Russian Yiddish poets were
murdered on a single August night in 1952. Shot in the cellars of
the Lubyanka.

And between Moscow and New York, a steady mute fright. The
hidden warning in Puttermesser's grandmother's plaint was clear:
Stop! We are afraid of a letter from America! They will take us for spies! The
old woman was famous among her children for eyesight so sharp
that she could see the alertly raised ears of a squirrel on a high
branch in a faraway clump of trees. Puttermesser's father, too, had
owned such a pair of eyes. Blue, pale as watery ink. Her poor or-
phaned papa, cut off forever from the ties of his youth: from his

little brother Velvl, ten years old, his head in the photo shaved in the old Russian style, his school uniform high-collared and belted, with a row of metal buttons marching down his short chest. A family sundered for seventy years: the Great War, the Revolution, Stalin's furies, the Second World War, the Cold War — all had intervened. Puttermesser's papa, dying old of stroke, longed for his mother, for Velvl, for his sisters Fanya, Sonya, Reyzl, for his brothers Aaron and Mordecai. Alone in America with no kin. Never again to hear his father's thin, fevered voice. Continents and seas lay between Moscow and New York, and a silence so dense and veiling that in the three decades since her papa's death Puttermesser had almost forgotten she had Russian relations. They were remote in every sense. She never thought of them.

In the midst of that unstable period known as perestroika, when strange acts were beginning to flicker outward from a shadowy Soviet Union into the world at large, Puttermesser received a telephone call from Moscow. More than half a century without a letter; not a syllable; and now, out of the blue, out of the void, out (it felt) of *time,* the telephone rang (prosaically, unmiraculously) in an ordinary New York apartment in the East Seventies — Moscow! Forbidden, locked, sullen Moscow! A woman, panting, high-pitched, overwrought, was speaking in German, and Puttermesser was able to follow most of it; hadn't she, after all, read Schiller's *Maria Stuart* in college? The panicky electric voice belonged to Zhenya, the daughter of the late Sonya — Sonya, the younger sister of Puttermesser's papa. Zhenya was Puttermesser's own first cousin! Tremulous, Zhenya explained that she had no English, that she assumed Puttermesser had no Russian, that Zhenya herself, though now a pensioner, had been a teacher of German, but oh, the danger cannot be named, everything must be understood! *"Rette mein Kind!"* Zhenya wailed.

And so it was arranged: Puttermesser was to save Zhenya's child. She believed she understood from what. The old darknesses were creeping out all over a loosened Soviet Union; who could predict what mean-spirited ghosts of antique hatred were yet to be awakened? Certain newspaper accounts began to jump out at Puttermesser. In Kiev, young men passing under a window are flooded by the passionate sounds of a violin; they crash into the musician's flat and beat him unconscious. In Moscow, brainy students are shut out of the university by a relentless quota. Schoolchildren have their noses bloodied to the taunts of *"Zhid! Zhid!"*

And in New York — in the very hour of perestroika, of glasnost — Puttermesser picks up a joke that is at this moment circulating through Moscow: *Because there is a rumor of a delivery of meat, a long queue forms outside a butcher shop. After a four-hour wait, the manager emerges to address the crowd. "The meat hasn't arrived yet, but there won't be enough for everyone, so all the Jews must leave." Another four hours pass, and out comes the manager: "No delivery yet, but there won't be enough, so all the chronic grumblers against the regime must leave." Another four hours, and finally the manager announces, "Sorry, comrades, but there will be no meat delivery after all. Everyone go home!" And a great moan rises up: "Wouldn't you know it? The Jews are always getting favored!"*

How that poisonous joke with its bitter truths reverberated! How Puttermesser felt for Zhenya's child! She set herself, over several months, the task of letter-writing. She wrote to the State Department, she wrote to her congresswoman, she wrote to her two senators, she wrote to HIAS and NYANA. She visited offices and filled out forms. She emptied a closet and bought extra pillows and sheets and pushed aside chairs and hauled bookcases and made room for a new sofa bed. She listened in the subway for the consonants of Russian — once she grabbed the arm of a startled passenger and asked for the story of his life, but the fellow turned out to be a Pole. She went everywhere for advice, telephoned strangers, was warned against the obduracy of officialdom and the barriers to émigrés. Every day she schemed for the refugee's deliverance; and at night it sometimes seemed to Puttermesser, drained, insomniac, that she could switch on, like a light discovering a hidden stage, any scene from the past.

She saw her papa on a bed, lying on top of the quilt, with his hands under his head, the elbows jutting outward. He did not speak; his pale eyes were open to nothing. He never blinked. It was three o'clock; a big housefly was in the room, slamming itself against the window, the wall, the high mirror above the dresser. In the middle of the afternoon Puttermesser's papa had gone to bed to mourn. His mother was dead — Puttermesser's Moscow grandmother, whom she had never known, except as that dried-out brown photo in the drawer. So many dead: Puttermesser's papa;

her papa's strangely Tatar mother; his shy and scholarly father, also reduced to a cracked old Russian photo (a sick man's face, solemn); all the lost aunts and uncles, the Muscovites, the wartime sufferers; Velvl in his school uniform, with large round pale eyes exactly like her papa's. Distant, oppressed, eclipsed. The scattered graveyards. Puttermesser's papa and mama in Staten Island; and where were all those others, how to imagine the cemeteries of Moscow?

The refugee arrived at one o'clock in the morning in the middle of October, ten months after Zhenya's howl of *"Rette mein Kind!"* In the empty street in front of her building Puttermesser stood waiting for the taxi from Kennedy. Wary, she kept fingering the wallet in the pocket of her cardigan.

The driver, without being asked, carried the refugee's bags — half a dozen of them — into the elevator.

"How much?" Puttermesser said.

"No problem. Fare's all taken care of."

"But she hasn't got any dollars —"

"She gimme *this,*" the driver said, and pulled out a round plastic object. The face of it showed the head of Lenin against a background of the Kremlin, with two red stars in a silvery sky.

"It's a watch. A cheap quartz watch."

"You kiddin'? It's outta Mars, where d'you get to *see* a thing like this?"

Puttermesser was impressed. The driver was right; the watch was a trophy. The barter system had returned to Manhattan.

Her name was Lidia. She had flown on Aeroflot from Moscow to Bucharest to Prague. In Prague she switched to British Airways, which took her to Ireland for a two-hour refueling; after Ireland and before New York she landed in Washington — her ticket was a complication of airports. Her visa was a complication of fibs: she had convinced the American consul in Moscow that she would surely return — she was leaving behind a husband and two children. Sergei was the husband, the children were Yulia and Volodya. But she had no husband. In reality Volodya was her boyfriend. The consul, she reported, was a nasty man. He looked at her as if she were a worm. He thought everyone who applied for a visa was trying to put something over on him; he suspected that all Moscow intended, hook or crook, to pour through the sacred gates of America and vanish behind them.

"You told him you had *children?*" Puttermesser marveled. "You didn't have to say a thing like that."

"I want he give visa."

"When the visa's up we'll get you in legally. I've been working on it. If we need to, we'll get a lawyer," Puttermesser said; the fervor of salvation rose in her. "We'll ask for asylum."

Save my child! But it was no longer Zhenya's voice; it was the voice of Puttermesser's papa. The pathos — the Bolshevik upheavals, the German siege of Moscow, the hunger, the Doctors' Plot, the terror. *Rette mein Kind!*

"I get job," the refugee said. "I clean house for womans."

Puttermesser said doubtfully, "Would Zhenya want you to do something like that?"

"Mama, ha! What mama want!"

Puttermesser was alarmed by such an eruption of mockery. There she stood, the Muscovite cousin, in the middle of Puttermesser's living room, a small space narrowed by the new sofa bed and shrunken still more by these heaps of suitcases and bundles and boxes tied with hairy Russian rope. An ironic beauty of thirty-three, trailing clouds of alien air — or, if not air, some nameless extraterrestrial medium. A Martian. She looked around, fierce and canny; she took things in. Puttermesser felt herself being judged by these sliding satiric eyes the color of Coca-Cola, and by that frail china-thin nose ending in a pair of tiny tremulous nostrils. It was the longish nose of a Mesopotamian princess.

Her full name was Lidia Klavdia Girshengornova. She was a species of biochemist — *eine Sportdoktorin,* Zhenya had said — and traveled all over the Soviet Union with her team: "my guys," she called them, big, coarse country boys, half literate and wild. A B-level track team trying to work itself up to international status. Lidia tested their urine daily for forbidden steroids — or else, Puttermesser speculated, she made sure that her guys were properly dosed. She was careful not to drink with them, but she wrestled and joked around, and she liked going to distant cities, Tbilisi, Kharkov, Vladivostok, Samarkand; especially she liked the trips to the Caucasus, where the hotels had a hint of Europe. She was amazingly up-to-date. Her lipstick was very red, and her hair was almost red, short over the ears, looped over one eyebrow. She wore black tights and

a long turtleneck sweater that fell to the tops of her thighs. Puttermesser had often seen this costume on Lexington Avenue at
lunchtime, and privately wondered at how *normal* her young cousin
seemed: hadn't she been swaddled on a board at birth, like all
infants in backward Russia? Only her shoes were unmistakably foreign. They smelled of a Soviet factory.

In the morning, Puttermesser set out her usual breakfast: toast and
peanut butter. Lidia, suspicious, spread the yellow-brown stuff and
made a horrible face. "What you call thees?"

"You've never had peanut butter?"

"*Nyet*," said Lidia, so Puttermesser took her out to the supermarket. At quarter of nine it was mostly deserted.

"Pick out whatever appeals to you," Puttermesser offered.

But Lidia, oblivious, in a trance, was gaping down the long banks
of freezers with their tall foggy doors, behind which lay mounds
of spinach and broccoli and stringbeans and peppers and peas
in richly bulging plastic bags. Her little nostrils fluttered as she
moved past brilliant boxes of cereals and orderly, shining rows of
bottled olives and pickles and mustards, past gardens of berries
and melons. And when Puttermesser put out her hand to pluck up
a packet of cheese, Lidia whirred out a furtive whisper: "No! Not
to take!"

"What's the matter? It's Jarlsberg, you might like it."

"They will *see!*"

"For God's sake, we're not under surveillance, we're here to buy."

It developed that Lidia Klavdia Girshengornova had supposed
they were visiting an exhibition hall. In Moscow, she explained,
there were occasionally dazzling fairs and expositions: great public
caverns set aside for gargantuan demonstrations of abundance,
mainly foreign goods, strictly guarded. Hundreds came to gaze and
marvel. To steal from a display, Lidia said, even the smallest item,
could land you in prison.

The refugee had other misapprehensions. She thought the telephone was bugged; she was certain there was an official "listener"
always on duty. She was innocent of polyester, and was astonished
that the bedsheets were never ironed. She believed that every trans-
action had to be accompanied by a "gift." Her cases and boxes
were cornucopias of shawls, scarves, colorful swaths of all sizes;
varnished scarlet-and-black ladles and spoons hand carved out of

hardwood, decorated all over with flowers; ugly but clever little plaster ducks and cows; nested hollow dolls shaped like eggs, without arms or legs, each encapsuling a smaller doll, until the last stood alone, a tiny Thumbelina. A circle of red spotted each miniature cheek, and each round head wore a painted babushka. Puttermesser was enchanted by these merry wooden faces redolent of old magical tales: dappled northern forests, silvery birdcalls and fragrant haycocks, a *Baba Yaga*'s dark whim in an out-of-the-way cottage.

But Lidia gave her bundles an instantly entrepreneurial name: Russian folk art, she called it, with a salesman's snap in her voice.

Her voice was shrewd and deep, close to mannish. Puttermesser again felt herself being read by this voice; it took her measure with the speed of an abacus. Lidia, watching Puttermesser watching her unpack, held up one of the painted egglike dolls. "You like?" she asked. "You keep," and handed over the hollow doll with all its interior brood. A businesslike gesture. A payment.

Business was on Lidia's mind. "I tell before, I want clean for womans," she pressed.

"But you can do better than that. Something in a laboratory, something that could get to be permanent —"

"Just like Mama!" Lidia laughed. She drew out a portfolio of photographs, many of them ragged and worn; Zhenya had sent them to show to Puttermesser. And here was Zhenya herself, sorrowing under summer sunlight, a puddle of shade under nose and lower lip. A dowdy plump aging woman in a patterned dress with a big collar. Flat face, eyes with the median Asian lid. Uncomplicated mouth, tightly shut; it made a narrow line. You could not imagine what this mouth thought or desired. But the woman in the snapshot seemed generations removed. She looked old fashioned. She looked . . . Soviet. The others, Puttermesser's papa's brothers and sisters, did not. Fanya, Sonya, Reyzl, Aaron, Mordecai! And Velvl, his school uniform with the metal buttons, the very same picture Puttermesser had known all her life. And what, she asked, had become of Velvl? Run over, Lidia said, killed by a Moscow tramcar in 1951. He left no children, and his widow married a Georgian. There were no happy stories among these photos. So many familiar pale round eyes.

An ache fell over Puttermesser. It was grief for her papa's grief.

*

For emergencies, Lidia had brought along a Russian-English dictionary. She never consulted it. It appeared she understood everything, and in her peculiar fragmented English she could convey almost anything. She had learned these jigsaw phrases in a night class, but had left after only five weeks: there were so many better things to do on winter evenings in Moscow. You could go to someone's room and warm yourself with drink. A party, with strangers, for which you paid an entry fee. She had met her boyfriend in such a room, a communal flat with high old ceilings stippled with grimy plaster roses. Her boyfriend, Lidia said, was really *after* her; he was always pestering her to get married.

"Are you sure he isn't just looking for a chance to get out of the country?" Puttermesser asked.

Lidia beamed; surprisingly, her teeth were magnificent.

"He want go Australia," she said, and slid into laughter.

Sometimes the telephone would ring at four in the morning, and then Lidia leaped up from her sofa bed to catch it before it could wake Puttermesser. But Puttermesser always woke, and it was always Volodya.

"Can't he *count?*" Puttermesser said testily. "Doesn't he know what time zone he's in?"

"He afraid I stay in America," Lidia said. "He afraid I not come back."

"Well, isn't that exactly the point?"

"Just like Mama!"

Mama, Puttermesser was learning, was preposterous. It was not admirable to be just like Mama.

"Please, now we speak business," Lidia urged. "I want clean for womans."

The interviews began. Puttermesser put up a notice in the elevator: "Companionable Russian émigrée, intelligent, charming, lively, willing to clean house, babysit, general light chores. Reasonable. Inquire 3-C from 8 P.M."

Then she blotted out "Russian émigrée" — it was too literary, and smacked of Paris or Berlin in 1920 (she thought of Nabokov) — and wrote instead, "Soviet newcomer." The neighbors streamed in; Puttermesser was acquainted with few of them. A couple arrived carrying a small girl in pajamas and asked for a pot to warm milk in. The child broke into a steady shriek and Lidia dismissed them with a scolding; she didn't want to deal with *that,* she said. The bachelor journalist from 7-G, who occasionally nodded at Puttermesser in the lobby, confessed that he already had perfectly satisfactory help; what he was interested in was a chance to hear a grassroots view of Gorbachev.

"Gorbachev!" Lidia scoffed. "Everybody hate Gorbachev, only stupid peoples in America like Gorbachev," and threw open the substantial valise that occupied her nightly. It was crammed with cosmetics of every kind — eyebrow pencils, rouge, mascara in all colors, a dozen lipsticks, hairnets, brushes, ointments and lacquers in tubes and tubs. Puttermesser could identify few of these emulsions and was helpless before all of them. (But ah, look, so they *did* have such contrivances in the puritanical socialist state!)

The journalist retorted that Gorbachev was certainly an improvement on, say, Brezhnev; but Lidia went on creaming her pointed little chin.

Puttermesser turned all around, like a cat in a cage. There was no place to sit down in her own living room. A pair of young men from the top floor were reclining on Lidia's sofa bed. One of them inquired whether she knew how to use a vacuum cleaner. Lidia laughed her scornful laugh — did they think she was a primitive? — and asked how much they would pay per hour.

It was difficult to tell who was interviewing whom. Lidia was after money, that was the long and the short of it. Day after day Puttermesser tried to lure her cousin out — to a museum, or to the top of the Empire State Building. But Lidia lifted an apathetic shoulder: she liked *things,* not pictures. And she had seen the New York skyline in the movies. She was waiting for evening, when the interviews would resume.

She settled finally on the family in 5-D: a three-bedroom apartment with three children. The husband did something in computers, and four times a week the wife took a bus downtown to Beth Israel Hospital, to work as a volunteer in pediatrics. They were a socially conscious, anti-violence couple; though easy and unrestrained with their children, they banned toy guns, monitored and rationed television, and encouraged reading and chess. Two of the children had piano lessons, the third was learning the violin. "Call me Barbara," the wife told Lidia, and embraced her, and said what a privilege it was for her family to be in a position to provide a job for a refugee. She promised that they were going to be friends, and that Lidia would soon feel at home in 5-D — but if she had any anxieties or complaints she should immediately speak up: there was nothing that could not be negotiated or adjudicated. Lidia was impatient with all this effortful goodness and virtuous heat. She had chosen the Blauschilds because they had offered her more dollars than anyone else.

"Varvara, ha!" Lidia yelped after her first day. "Foolish womans, teacher come for music, children hate!" And another time: "Dirty house! Children room dirty!" She had never in her life seen such disorder: shoes and shirts and toys left in heaps on the floor, every surface sticky, the sink always mountainous with unwashed pans and dishes, papers scattered everywhere. She disapproved of Varvara altogether — why would anyone work for nothing? And leave behind such a vast flat, so many rooms, and all for one family, they lived like commissars! Only dirty!

"You don't have to do this," Puttermesser said. "You didn't come to America to clean houses, after all. Look, we need to go see the people at the agency. To get you past the visa stage. It's about time we took care of it."

Lidia's brown eyes slid cautiously sideways. She lifted her shoulder and dropped it again.

Puttermesser was privately glad of the four hours Lidia spent upstairs in 5-D every afternoon. Sometimes Lidia would talk of God and His angels, sometimes of the splendid old churches the Revolution had destroyed; and now and then she pulled out a certain dream book, which, if read prayerfully, could foretell the future. Lidia was a believer in the world of the sublime. She was moved by icons, by Holy Mother Russia. She told how she often wept at Eastertime, and how Jesus had once appeared to her in a dream, looking exactly like a holy painting on an ancient icon. At such moments poor elderly Puttermesser, with all her flying white hair, saw her Muscovite cousin as some errant Chekhovian character misplaced in a New York living room: *How lovely it is here!" said Olga, crossing herself at the sight of the church.*

"But there's another side to all that, isn't there?" Puttermesser said. "What about the Beilis case?"

Lidia had never heard of the Beilis case.

Puttermesser, a reader of history, explained: "The blood libel.

Pure medieval insanity. A Jew named Mendel Beilis was accused in a Russian court of killing a Christian child in order to drain his blood. Imagine, a thing like that, and in modern times, 1913! The clergy never intervened. So much for Holy Mother Russia."

Lidia sent out her riddling smile, half secretive, half derisive. "Not happen now."

"And the attack on the Writers' Union? That was just this year!"

Puttermesser knew what Lidia was thinking: Just like Mama.

On a rainy night toward the middle of November, they took the subway to the Bronx. Puttermesser had made an appointment with the agency for seven o'clock, so as not to interfere with her cousin's hours at the Blauschilds'. Lidia seemed nervous and reluctant. "We pay?" she asked.

"Not at all. It's a service organization. They hire some staff, but they're mostly volunteers."

"Like Varvara, work for nothing, foolish!"

In the cramped little office Lidia sat morosely in a cul-de-sac of filing cabinets, noiselessly snapping her scarlet fingernails. The woman behind the desk had a doctor's manner: her aim was to make a diagnosis followed by a recommendation. She was, she said, a refugee from the Soviet Union herself. She had arrived five years ago, and had a son in high school; he was currently on the math team at Stuyvesant. Her husband, formerly an engineer, was employed as a salesman in a men's clothing store. The adjustment had been difficult, but now they were settled. They had even joined a synagogue — in Kiev such a thing was inconceivable.

Lidia looked away; all this was for Puttermesser. It had a seasoned professional ring. Except for a mild brush of accent, there was nothing foreign about the interviewer. The woman was stylish, in the way of the boroughs beyond Manhattan — she wore a scarf at her throat, meticulously knotted and draped, held by a silver pin in the shape of a lamb. She drew out several sheets of Cyrillic text and in a rapid cascade of Russian began to question Lidia. Puttermesser observed that her cousin was staring obsessively at the pin on the scarf; she was inattentive, lethargic. In Lidia's darkly unwilling mutter, Puttermesser heard, even in the unaccustomed syllables of Russian, a desultory streak of cynicism.

And then the Muscovite cousin rose up, and a roar of Russian galloped out of the cave of her mouth. The little office was all at once a Colosseum, with the smell of blood in the air.

"Good God! What was *that* all about?" Puttermesser demanded; she had restrained herself until they were nearly home. In the subway Lidia had made herself inaccessible. She pinched up her eyebrows. Her mouth narrowed into a tight line, like Zhenya's mouth in the snapshot. "Commissar!" she said.

They climbed the stairs in a stench of urine at the Seventy-seventh Street station, and nearly stumbled over a homeless man asleep on the concrete. The slanting rain wet his motionless face and neck. An empty bottle rolled past a muddy leg. Lidia hesitated; she was instantly cheerful. "Like in Soviet!" she cried, and Puttermesser understood that her cousin loved mockery best of all.

Lidia threw herself on her sofa bed and crumpled up the papers the interviewer had given her and tossed them on the carpet.

"That woman only wanted to help," Puttermesser said.

"Rules. Much rules."

"Well, they must be worth it. *She* sounds happy enough over here."

"Such womans!" Lidia said. "Commissar!"

The living room was now Lidia's domain entirely. Puttermesser almost never went in there. It was strangely scrambled and unfamiliar, a briar patch behind a barrier of hedgerows — Lidia's boxes and bundles and valises and plastic bags with their contents spilling out. The sofa bed was always open and unmade, a tumble of blankets and pillows. Empty soda cans straggled across the top of the television. Orange sticks and an emery board lay on the edge of a bookshelf. Half-filled cups of coffee languished along the baseboards. Was this the Blauschild influence? Was chaos spawning chaos, 5-D leaching downward into Puttermesser's spare and scholarly 3-C?

But Puttermesser had another theory — the fault was her own. She had been too solicitous of her young cousin, too deferential. *Oh, that's all right, you don't need to think about that. Just leave it, I'll take care of it. Don't worry about it, you really shouldn't, it's fine the way it is.* These were the stanzas of Puttermesser's litany. It was incantation, it was "manners": she had treated Lidia as an honored guest, she had fallen at her feet — because she represented the healing of a great unholy rupture; because it was right that a rush of tender-heartedness, of blood-feeling, should pour into the wilderness of separation. To be blessed with a new cousin overnight!

The first week Lidia had grimly taken the broom — wasn't this

what was expected? as a sort of rent? — and swept up after their
meal. "Oh, please don't trouble," Puttermesser said each time.
Thereafter Lidia didn't. She left the lids of her cream jars on the
bathtub ledge. She left her dirty dishes on the kitchen table. She
left her wet towels on the living room credenza. It soon came to
Puttermesser that her cousin, though spurning atheism, was otherwise a perfect Soviet avatar: she did nothing that was not demanded. Released, she went straight to the television and its mani-
fold enchantments: cars, detergents, toothpaste, cheeseburgers,
cruises. An exhibit more various and abundant than any to be seen
in the great halls of Moscow, and all unnaturally vivid (no green so
green, no red so red, etc.) against an alluring background of meadows, hills, rills, fountains, castles, Ferris wheels. The soda cans on
top of the set multiplied. There was no reciprocity for Puttermesser's
mandarin politesse.

"What did that woman at the agency *say*," Puttermesser pursued,
"that made you explode like that?"

"She say make Lenin go in trash."

"Lenin? You weren't discussing Soviet history, for God's sake,
were you?"

"Medals. I bring much medals."

Lidia spilled them out then: a whole rattling green plastic bag of
little tin effigies of a small boy. The bag had a word printed on it:
фотография.

"Lenin when child, you see? Komsomol prize for children. Junk!
Nobody want! I buy hundred for kopeck." The mocking laugh.
"Woman say not allowed do business, big law for tax. Commissar!"

Every morning Lidia ate black bread and sour cream — she
had chosen these herself from the neighborhood exhibition — followed by strong tea with plenty of sugar. Then she disappeared. She
was always back in time to go up to 5-D to clean for Varvara. She
confessed that she had grown to hate Varvara's children. They were
selfish, wild, indulged; they knew too much, and still they were
common.

Puttermesser never asked about Lidia's absences. The scene at
the agency had shown what questions could lead to. But she noticed that Lidia never went out without carrying one or two of her
many bundles.

At eleven o'clock, when Lidia was gone, Varvara came down to see Puttermesser.

She glanced into the living room: "Mess! Looks like *my* digs! And you don't even have kids."

"Is there a problem?" Puttermesser said. "You don't have to be embarrassed, I mean if things aren't working out with my cousin —"

"Oh, Lidia's a jewel! I wouldn't *dream* of losing her. She's enriched our *lives*," Varvara said. "She just *fascinates* the kids. She tells them Russian fairy stories — they're pretty grisly, the wolf always gets to eat somebody, but the kids love it. And Bill and I don't mind. It's not really mayhem like the stuff they feed them on TV. It's just imagination, it's harmless."

Puttermesser saw her cousin dissecting the limbs of Varvara's children via the surrogacy of lupine fangs.

Varvara peered past the kitchen. "Is Lidia home?"

"She's out for a while."

"Taking in the Big Apple? That's nice. Hey," Varvara said, "I just want to get the two of you to come to a very special party. A private fund-raiser for *Shechinah*. You know *Shechinah*?"

Puttermesser knew it. It was a magazine distinguished only by its advertising: "Politics Against *Motherwit*" — *Motherwit* being a sober old periodical dedicated to rationalist traditions, cautious liberalism, and an impatience with ponytails.

"I told Sky about your cousin," Varvara said. "Sky's a good friend of mine. We worked on the Neighborhood Visionary Project together years ago, when we all lived out in California. And before that we were both on the board of the All-University Free Expression Process, but that was before I met Bill. Bill *hates* Free Expression, he thinks it starts you on the road to violence. Bill's a *real* pacifist."

Puttermesser recalled the Free Expression Process: it had flourished in the age of streaking. The Process specialized in "demonstrations" in which a forbidden word was chanted without pause for exactly two hours ("fuck" and "asshole" were the natural favorites); this was known as "neutering," and the goal was to neuter all the naughty words.

"I remember their slogan," Puttermesser said. "'Everything Comes Up Crystal.'"

"Right! Wasn't that beautiful? And the other one, the one on the T-shirts? 'Dirt Busters.' Cute! Once we did a double Process on 'turd.' Four hours of it. 'Turd, turd, turd, turd.' Well, all that's long ago — B.K., before kids! We take baths with the kids, though. The whole family, two by two, cross-gender."

Varvara looked to be in her forties. Her face was both large and small. Her cheeks and forehead were very wide, her chin was broad and long, but bunched in the middle of all that unused space were the crowded-together eyes, round little nose, round little mouth. A family of features snug in a big tub. You could not tell from such a visage — it was, in fact, a "visage," a bit Dickensian, a touch archaic — that it belonged to an idealist.

Schuyler Hartstein, by contrast — Varvara's old friend — had exactly the sort of head one would expect of a social visionary. Puttermesser had happened on it now and again on television panel shows, a long-skulled baldish rectangle dangling a blond ponytail from its rear and (actually) a curly-ribboned monocle from its front. On such panels Sky — not an abbreviation but a metaphoric allusion to the cloudlessly vivid cerulean of his poet's orbs — always took the idealist position. In him there were no hesitations, reservations, qualifications, impediments. He had a sunny blond face and all the social thinker's certainties. Around his neck hung a gold chain, at the end of which swung the two Hebrew letters that spelled "life."

Puttermesser had subscribed to Sky's magazine, but quit after its first year, partly because she was indifferent to Sky Hartstein's verse — he published his own uplifting poetry in his own pages — but mainly because the radiance of the Divine Presence had begun to dim. He had started advertising in his own Personals columns for a wife, and meanwhile *Shechinah*'s editorial positions were a mist passed off as "spirit," and sometimes as "rage." You knew before you opened the magazine that you would find the nasty anger of the purehearted.

"Wait'll you meet him!" Varvara crowed. "He's got this *mind*."

"But why does he want to meet Lidia?"

"Oh, come *on*," Varvara said. "Isn't it obvious?"

When Lidia returned some hours later, she was not alone — she was pulling along behind her a tall young man.

"Pyotr," Lidia pronounced.

"Hiya," the young man said. He held out his hand. "I'm Pete. Peter Robinson. I manage the Albemarle Sports Shop. Over on Third? Third and Ninety-fourth?"

"Pyotr," Lidia repeated. "Have *clean* eyes."

It was true; Lidia had hit on it exactly. Those were innocent eyes, guileless and unsoiled by wit. Pete Robinson — Pyotr — explained that he was from North Dakota, and was better acquainted with woods and farms than with the New York pavement. He had been in the city — had been transferred from the Seattle branch — less than three months. Back home, and even in a place like Seattle, you would never get to run into someone like Lidia!

The three of them settled around the kitchen table. Pyotr wore a sweater with a V neck and under it a plaid wool shirt. He had a big pale slab of a brow with a lick of shiny hair bouncing down over it like a busy tongue. He seemed as clarified and classified — as simplified — as a figure on a billboard. And Robinson — Puttermesser thought of that radio series of her childhood: Jack Armstrong, the All-American Boy! As quick as you could say Jack Robinson, her cousin had landed his prototype.

Lidia was joyful. "Pyotr help," she said.

And once again she turned the green plastic bag upside down — the one with фотография printed on it. This time not a single medal depicting the child Lenin fell out. Instead, a stream of green bills: all-American money.

"What's going on?" Puttermesser said.

"Ma'am?" said Pyotr. "This young woman's been working in my store all day. I've got to get back there myself pretty soon. She lured me out with that smile."

Puttermesser gave her cousin a skeptical look. "What is it, another job?"

"Ma'am," Pyotr explained, "we were getting ready for Christmas, clearing out the tennis racquets and ski poles from the middle of the floor. Nice big space, it's where we're putting the *tree*. Well, we get the tree up, and in comes this little cutie with this funny way of talking, and next thing you know she's in business. Right in the biggest traffic area."

"Traffic area?" Puttermesser said.

Pyotr nodded. "You bet. If you don't mind my saying so, what you've got in this young woman is free enterprise, the real thing."

Sitting at a card table he had found for her, under a Christmas tree decorated with colored light bulbs in the shape of miniature sneakers and footballs, the Muscovite cousin had sold — in a single morning — her whole stock of Lenin medals. For three dollars each. What lay strewn on Puttermesser's kitchen table were three hundred American dollars. And her cousin still had, in inventory, plenty of scarves and spoons and limbless hollow dolls.

Not to mention an all-American boyfriend.

The *Shechinah* fund-raiser was held in one of those mazy Upper West Side apartments where it is impossible to find the bathrooms. You wander from corridor to corridor, tentatively entering bedrooms still redolent of their night odors. Sometimes there will be a bewildered young child standing fearfully in your path, or else a small animal, but mostly you encounter nothing but the stale smells of an aging building. Such apartments are like demoralized old women shrouded in wrinkles, who, mourning their lost complexions, assert the dignity and importance of their prime. The bathroom sink, if you should happen to locate it in the dark (the light switch will be permanently hidden), is embroidered with the brown grime of its ancient cracks, like the lines of an astrological map; the base of the toilet, when you flush it, will trickle out a niggardly rusty stream. And then you will know how privileged you are: you have been touched by History. Arthur Rubinstein once actually lived here; Einstein attended a meeting in what is now the back pantry; Maria Callas sang, privately, on a summer night, with her palm pressed down hard on that very windowsill; Uta Hagen paid a visit to the famous tenant, whoever it was, before the present tenant.

"Kakoi teatr!" Lidia cried; she was leading Pyotr by the hand. He followed docilely, shyly, dazzled by the doubly exotic: enigmatic New York, where a Muscovite beauty could suddenly swoop you into mysterious rooms! This one was spacious and carpeted: rows of folding chairs, sofas pushed against the walls, and long maroon draperies drawn over two sets of windows, like twin curtained prosceniums. A fresh copy of *Shechinah* had been placed on each chair.

The evening's host, a woman in her middle fifties, dressed in jeans, a creased shirt, and several rings and bracelets, materialized out of the lost rear recesses of the apartment. Puttermesser picked up the magazine she had been sitting on and began to riffle through it, until she came on one of the poems Sky Hartstein liked to sprinkle through each issue:

The unneeded
are needed
for our satisfaction.
We are bloated
with such satisfactions.
Enough!
Let us turn
and satisfy ourselves
with the sublime.

The title was "The Marginalized."

Pyotr was caressing Lidia's raw little hand, each finger with its blood-red hood. Lidia wore her reddest lipstick and her most detached smile; she was fondling the buttons of her new leather coat. The polished leather shone like black glass. She had bought the coat in a shop on First Avenue run by immigrant Koreans — Varvara had told her where to find it — and had paid for it with the profits from her Lenin medals. The label said "Made in China": sewn, for all anyone knew, by eight-year-olds chained to their machines.

The introducer in jeans was just finishing her money pitch — "Remember, Sky's the limit!" — when, in thickening applause, Sky Hartstein ascended out of his chair. It was, he began, "for me personally," an amazing week. His Holiness the Dalai Lama had granted Sky an audience, and what do you suppose they talked about? Those little toy cars you operate by remote control, how they are subject to movement by an invisible force . . . Consider how they stand for the power, from afar, of divine influence drawing on human will . . . Sky Hartstein's speech rushed on, a torrent of sweetness and light. He swept the Beatles into the Psalms and the Prophets into organically grown vegetables. He quoted from Blake and recited the sleep-giving properties of melatonin. Let all borders dissolve, he cried, let the nations vanish away. Let glasnost spread its healing tent over the earth and restore us to classlessness and the end of want — let the poor rise up from their wretchedness according to the verdant primal promise of that genius who once labored long in the British Museum! Karl and Groucho, Lenin and Lennon: Sky ventured this little joke, he didn't care how stale.

Everyone knows, he went on, about the excesses of Stalin, the Gulag, the terror, the KGB, informers, shadows, spies, interrogators, torturers; and yet in an early time, before the betrayal of the noble scheme of universal aspiration, there must have been a little holy seed of human redemption. The Great Experiment failed in its first venue, yes, but is it possible that the seed might be replanted?

"Even for one born into the Experiment," he said, "there must cling some small remnant of its beginnings. The Revolution leaves a trail, a wisp, an aroma of what was *meant.*" He was looking in Lidia's direction, widening his arms.

Lidia, meanwhile, had jumped out of her chair. "You think was in old days clean?" she cried. "Never clean, no! Stupid mans! Stupid womans!"

Someone began to hiss. The host in jeans, worrying about the disruption of her party — a table at the back of the room was stacked with oatmeal cookies and a wholesome pyramid of apples — broke in plaintively: "But wasn't Communism once a beautiful hope? At the start? In principle? With goals that are viable still —"

Lidia laughed.

"Foolish American peoples!" she yelled. "In Soviet stupid peoples more smart! My guys on team more smart!"

Varvara whispered furiously, "Sit down! You're ruining the meeting!"

"Communism!" Lidia yelled. "What Communism? Naïve! Fairy tale always! No Communism, never! Naïve!"

There she stood, her pointed little chin in the air, her elbows firm: A Saint Joan of disillusionment, a commissar of mockery, a perfected Soviet flower. She trusted no one, she trusted nothing. She was no more rooted than a dandelion's head when it has turned into feathers and is ready to fly. For the first time Puttermesser liked her cousin nearly as much as she deplored her.

In the middle of the night the telephone rang. Puttermesser found herself catapulted out of a fierce dream of waves and waves of barbed wire. It crisscrossed the windows, closed off the kitchen, and surrounded Lidia's sofa bed. Thirsty, heading for a drink of water,

Puttermesser leaped over the wire and caught her shin on one of the twisted barbs. Blood was spilling down her ankle . . .

It was Volodya, calling not from Moscow but from Sakhalin. Sakhalin, the czars' penal colony, where Chekhov had gone to investigate prison conditions. A distant island in the inconceivable Sea of Okhotsk, below the Arctic, its southern tip irritably fingering Japan. Talk about Mars! Puttermesser turned in her bed, drove off the bad dream, and listened to the murmur of Russian. Lidia in Russian was a different Lidia: she flew among the rococo gasps and trills of those brilliant syllables as lightly as a gymnast. Her laugh, embedded in Russian, was a different laugh: it was free to do its stunts.

"*Do svidanya*," Lidia breathed out — it was a sly caress — and hung up. "Volodya want do business in Sakhalin," she explained.

"Don't people get arrested for trying that? Isn't it dangerous? Zhenya's grandmother —" Then Puttermesser remembered that Zhenya's grandmother was her own grandmother, too: an old woman in a black babushka skittering across the iron crust of snow again and again, a snatch of movie reel played over and over.

The thirst in her dream had pursued her into the kitchen. She filled the kettle for tea and put out two cups. The windows, cleared of their silver thorns, were black. It was half past three.

"You don't mean *private* business," she said. "Isn't that what they call economic crime —"

Lidia released her amiable shrug. "Perestroika," she said.

"Really? People aren't afraid of breaking the law anymore?"

"Apparatchik rules," Lidia spat out. "*Volodya* not afraid!"

"But I thought you said he was thinking about leaving the country. Going to Australia."

"First get much rubles. First Sakhalin."

"I don't suppose you can buy a leather coat in Sakhalin," Puttermesser said, pouring the water over the leaves and letting it darken to mahogany. She didn't mind that her cousin had converted her away from tea bags.

"I buy coat in America, give Volodya."

"You're out of a job now," Puttermesser said mildly.

They sipped their tea. Lidia produced the half-dozen oatmeal cookies she had been slipping into the pocket of her new coat at the moment Varvara was firing her.

"Foolish Varvara," Lidia said. Nibbling her cookie, she looked almost childlike.

"Well, what did you expect? The woman invites you to the center of her life and you insult everyone in sight. The way you answered Sky Hartstein. *Shechinah*'s getting famouser and famouser."

"*Pravda* also famous," Lidia said.

And in that instant Puttermesser understood her dream. All that barbed wire! It was a platitude of a dream. She had transformed her apartment into the Gulag — it was that simple, so stupidly transparent that it would make Freud yawn. And the eeriness of a call from a former penal colony just as she was bleeding on barbed wire!

"That book you've got?" Puttermesser said. "That dream book?"

Lidia, electrified, dashed through the hedge of her bundles to fetch it. It occurred to Puttermesser that she had finally struck home with her cousin. Until now, she had been a harassment and a bore. How old and irrelevant she must have seemed to a flirt, a foreigner, a beauty!

Lidia returned with the book in her hands as if she were displaying a crown on a cushion. Here was a believer; the cynic had vanished. "What in dream? I look, I find."

Puttermesser waved all around. "Barbed wire. All over the place. Across the windows, everywhere. I got cut on it and blood poured out. I mean *poured*."

Lidia considered; she put her head down to study what appeared to be an index of dream topics.

"Does it list barbed wire?"

"*Nyet.*"

"Prison?"

"Prison not in dream. Dream here, in house." Lidia bent over the pages, turning them so slowly that the ceiling light flashed off each one. "Ah," she said. "*Krov.*"

"What's that?"

An elongated vowel lingered. A ghostly word. "Blooood," Lidia said. "Where blooood come?"

"No, no," Puttermesser said crisply. "It isn't 'blued.' It doesn't rhyme with 'food,' it rhymes with 'mud.' Out of my leg. My foot. My toes."

"*Khorosho,*" Lidia said. "Better from foot. Blooood from head mean you dies." She stopped to study some more; she was uncommonly serious. "Peoples dream blooood from foot, they make holy future. You holy womans. You" — she struggled to translate — "saint."

Puttermesser stared; her ironic cousin was altogether drained of irony. Her cousin was . . . what was she? Anything shoddy, anything that broke at a touch, any part that failed, the switch on the living room wall that suddenly gave out, the leak in the kettle, a crack in the plaster, the bus that was late in coming — all these were occasions for Lidia's satiric call: *Like in Soviet!* Proof of a corrupt and shabby universe. Puttermesser knew what her cousin was — an apparatchik of blemish and smirch, wart and scab, disdain and distrust. *Like in Soviet!* She was either too suspicious or too credulous. She was a skeptic who put her faith in charlatanism.

"I think," Puttermesser said darkly, "you would be a lot better off throwing out such a silly book and getting hold of an English grammar instead."

Lidia's eyes swelled. She slapped the dream book shut. "What for I need English? I go Sakhalin with Volodya! Make big business in Sakhalin!"

"What are you talking about?"

"Volodya say come, get much rubles. Marry, maybe."

A gray blur had begun to brighten the windows. It was still too early for dawn, but the blackest hours of night were receding, and in that morning light that was not quite light, spun together with the sharp cartoonlike brilliance of the ceiling fixture, Lidia had a phosphorescence of her own.

"You came for asylum! You came to escape!" Puttermesser said. "For God's sake, Lidia, what do you think this is? *A vacation?*"

"I come work," Lidia contradicted.

"You're here as a refugee."

"Refugee? What mean refugee?" Her face was a lit stage; every filament of her hair burned red. "Zhenya? Zhenya say this? I am emi-*grant* like you is holy womans," Lidia blazed, and stretched out her long, long laugh, as elongated as the vowel in "blooood," as crucial as inspiration. "What Mama say! What Mama want!"

In the end Pyotr wept. Lidia had been gone only a day; she had managed her ticket — New York to Moscow, a direct flight — all on her own.

"This Korean place on First Avenue?" Pyotr said. "She asked me to go over there with her. To try on this *coat.* That was only the day before yesterday."

"Did she mention that you and her boyfriend are about the same height?" Puttermesser asked.

"I mean, I knew it was a present, but I didn't know who *for.* She said it was for her brother in Moscow. She said she was having it shipped."

"Lidia doesn't have a brother."

"All the time she was planning to leave."

"But not before clearing a profit," Puttermesser said.

"Those dolls went like hotcakes. She must've made around nine hundred dollars off them, never mind what she got for the rest of the stuff. She walked out of my place with maybe two thousand clear."

They were sitting in Puttermesser's living room. It was, in its way, another tea party, but there was booze in the teacups. Pyotr had brought along a bottle of vodka to celebrate with Lidia; it was a month ago to the day that she had revealed herself in the Albemarle Sports Shop.

But Lidia was far above the round earth, heading for the land of perestroika.

Crumpled plastic bags littered the carpet. The sofa bed was an anarchic jumble of cushions and twisted sheets. Ripped pairs of pantyhose sprawled gauzily over a parade of Coke cans. Lidia's various scents — lotions, nail polish, hair spray — wafted like the wake of an apparition.

"She didn't even tell me she was going," Pyotr wailed.

Puttermesser looked into Pyotr's clean, wet North Dakota eyes. Jack Armstrong, the All-American Boy: gulled.

"The Great Experiment," she said, and emptied what was left of the booze into poor Pyotr's innocent cup.

From Tel Aviv, in German (Puttermesser's translation):

Hotel Royale
23. Juni

Liebe Ruth!

As you can see, because of the pressure of circumstances I have emigrated to *das Land, wo die Zitronen blühn* (Goethe). I have been here only two days. Lidia is now living in Sakhalin. She is six months pregnant, and she and Volodya (her boyfriend since last year) will marry very soon. He is very busy setting up a business with other ambitious young men. You probably do not know, because until now it has been kept secret, that a number of paleolithic mammoth tusks have been dug up by farmers in Sakhalin. Volodya has bought the tusks from the locals and plans to resell them in the West. I am told that these tusks are very beautiful and actually resemble fossilized wood. Lidia is somewhat doubtful about their authenticity, but she believes they can easily be passed off as such to potential collectors, since value is as value seems.

I am glad she is safe in Sakhalin, safer than she would be in America. Lidia told me that she was forced to attend an extremely dangerous political meeting in New York. She said she was made to travel to a distant place at night, where a woman official of some unsavory organization tried to dragoon her into signing certain papers — a scheme of indenture, apparently. I am very dismayed to hear of such things in your country.

The night I left Moscow there was a riot in our street. This is because the USSR is falling apart. Some say the death knell has already been sounded. [In the original: *das Totengeläut ist schon verklungen.*] The rioters shouted unpleasant slogans and wore unpleasant uniforms and broke many windows. I thank God that Lidia, who did not wish to accompany me here, is for the time being in quiet Sakhalin. Who knows where fate will finally place her? She confided to me that the baby is regrettably not Volodya's, but assures me that you, dearest Ruth, know who the father is, and that he is a nice boy.

I will write again when I begin to understand this new place. In the meantime, please write *auf Deutsch* to the above address (it is an absorption center for new immigrants) and tell me all you know about the baby's father. Lidia says he has a typically Russian name and sells icons for a living. Where in America could she have unearthed such a person?

Your newfound cousin,
Zhenya

KAREN E. BENDER

Eternal Love

FROM GRANTA

AFTER LENA AND BOB were married in the Chapel of Eternal Love, Ella told them that new husbands and wives were not allowed to share a hotel bedroom. Married couples, she told her retarded daughter, learned to be married slowly, in separate rooms. For the first two days of the honeymoon, Ella shared her room at the El Tropicale with Lena, while her husband, Lou, slept in the other room with Bob. The four of them elbowed their way to the two-fifty, ninety-seven-item buffet table, piling their plates with fat-laced barbecued ribs; they lay, sun-doped, on a sparkling swath of concrete by a pale blue swimming pool. The sounds by the pool echoed, amplified by the water; even the children's shrieks were transformed into the caws of aroused, hysterical birds. Ella could pretend she didn't hear at first when Lena said very softly that she wanted to share a room with Bob.

Ella told Lena about sex in a quiet lounge off El Tropicale's main casino. Her thirty-year-old daughter sat patiently, twirling a pink vinyl coin purse embossed LAS VEGAS: CITY OF LUCK. "You're a wife," Ella began. Her daughter smiled. "There are certain things you can do."

"I'm called Mrs.!" squealed Lena.

A cocktail waitress holding an empty tray strode swiftly across the lounge, her nylon stockings an opalescent orange under the subdued light of the chandelier.

"First," began Ella, then stopped. "Well, how do you feel when Bob kisses you?"

"My mouth feels wet."

"Do you — like it?"

"I like it." Lena paused. "Sometimes he puts his tongue in too much. I don't like that."

A sign by the Canary Room said: EIGHT P.M. TONITE: HILO HATTIE AND THE HAWAIIANS. Loud tourists flowed eagerly through the lounge toward the casino, flashing slabs of sunburnt skin. "Married people — are naked in bed, Lena," Ella said.

"Naked!" Lena said with a tiny shriek.

Ella felt something very tall collapse slowly inside her. "Don't be scared," she said, trying to fit her voice around the immense gentleness that surged inside her. "It's just — skin."

"I liked it when he touched — here," Lena said, reaching up and squeezing her breast.

"Where did he do —"

"In the bathroom. At House of Pancakes." She giggled.

"No," said Ella. "You don't do that in House of Pancakes. You don't do that in any — public place. You do it in your bedroom. Nowhere else."

"In my bedroom," repeated Lena.

"After, you take a shower. You wash your hands with soap."

"It smelt like the ocean."

Ella let go of Lena's hand.

"When he put his hand in my panties. I liked that. He took his hand out and he smelt like me." She clapped her hand over her mouth and giggled, a guilty, thrilled sound.

"Lena," said Ella, "when did Bob do —"

"We came in through the back yard."

"You let him do that in my back yard?"

"I liked it."

"Soap," said Ella, a little desperately. "You use soap."

"Mother," said Lena, "what about when we're naked?"

Ella did not want to continue. Apparently Lena and Bob were doing well enough on their own.

"If he's ever not gentle with you, Lena, tell me."

"Tell what?"

Far away, Ella heard the distant clink of breakfast dishes being washed in the hotel coffee shop, the whir of a vacuum being pushed across the lobby, the gentle sounds of maids and waiters cleaning the guests' messes of the day.

"If he ever does something you don't like."

"Mother," said Lena impatiently, "does everyone married sleep naked in a bedroom? Him?" She pointed to a porter leafing through a newspaper with the headline WAR OF THE BOSOMS CONTINUES. "Him?" A man pushed a rack of pink and peach-feathered costumes toward the Lido de Paris show. "Her?" A tall showgirl, her hair in a rumpled bouffant, sipped a large glass of orange juice and blinked awake. Her feet were swollen in silver sandals, and her eyes were ringed with fatigue.

"They use soap," said Ella. She tried to think of one more crucial rule to tell her daughter, but her mind was filled with only this — in the deep green of her back yard, somewhere amid the walnut and lemon trees, Bob had plunged his hand into Lena's panties. Now everyone flowing through the lounge seemed profoundly tainted. Ella noticed the raw nubbiness of the bandleader's ruby velvet jacket, the too proud grip a tourist had on his white-blond wife, the obsessive way a waitress counted her tips, turning all the green bills in the same direction, before she vanished into the dim, clockless casino again.

Bob had first called six months ago, an April day in 1961. Ella had picked up the phone and heard a male voice whisper, almost plead, "Lena. Lena. Lena there?"

It was a question she rarely heard. "Who may I say is calling?" Ella asked.

"Bob. Goodwill. I drive trucks — Bob —"

She knocked on Lena's door. "Lena. There's a . . . Bob on the phone for you."

Lena burst out of her room with a nakedly joyous expression on her face. "Tell him to wait," she exclaimed.

She was wearing a little rouge and perfume when, five minutes later, she deigned to pick up the phone. At first Ella couldn't figure out why her daughter smelt familiar. Then she knew. Lena had put on some of her Chanel; Lena smelt like her.

Lena had been working at the Van Nuys Goodwill for five years. Her job was to sit at a long table and sort socks and blouses that no one else wanted to own. Ella called Dolores, the coordinator of Goodwill's disabled employees, to check Bob out.

"Bob. Bob," muttered Dolores. "Why?"

"A Bob called Lena on the phone."

"This is so nice!" said Dolores. "We have five Bobs. Bob Winters is considerate, but a drooler. Bob Lanard I wouldn't let in my house, not if you care about your china surviving the night." She paused. "Are you sure it's not a Rob? We have a Rob who's — well — a former convict, but I think he's very nice, too."

"It was Bob. He said he drove trucks."

"Trucks," muttered Dolores. "Bob Silver."

"Tell me about him."

"A sweetie. Short, quiet, brown hair, good driver."

Ella tried to feel relieved but didn't honestly know what she felt. Bob Silver. It was just a name, but it seemed ferocious as a comet, hurtling toward her home to do some new damage.

Bob called again that night. "Is Lena there?"

"Lena who?" Ella said.

She was sorry she said it; she could actually hear the terror mount in his breath. "Lena Rose."

"Who may I say is calling?"

"Bob."

"Why?"

Now he was dying. She heard his breath, everything slow on his end as he struggled not to tell her why he was calling.

"I just want to talk to her," said Bob.

Bob was half an hour early for their first date. He pulled up in an old, candy-apple red Ford that gleamed dully in the afternoon. While Lena sprayed her hair upstairs, Ella and Lou huddled in the sheer-curtained window by the door and watched him come toward them. Bob rushed up the walkway, his hands plunged deep into his pockets, head down as though he was walking into a wind.

Lou opened the door. "Glad to meet you," he boomed.

Bob kept his hands in his pockets, not lifting them to shake with Lou. The part in his hair was crooked.

"Bob, Lena's not ready," Ella lied, touching his arm; she wanted to see how normal he felt. His shoulder was a little damp and surprisingly muscular. Quickly, she removed her hand.

Bob glided deftly past her into the den and plucked up the *TV*

Guide. He flipped wildly through its pages for a moment, then stumbled across the room and clicked the channels until he found *Gunsmoke.*

Bob propped his feet on Lou's green vinyl footstool, sunk down into the couch and thoughtfully eyed the action in *Gunsmoke.* He looked about forty. His short, bristly hair was gray, but his feet, in blue sneakers, bounced on the footstool with the blunt, coarse merriment of a boy. Ella was used to Lena's stubbiness, the way she seemed to bump up unsuccessfully against adulthood. But it seemed strange in Bob, and she could not help thinking that, even though he was taller than she, he resembled an aging dwarf.

Lou sat on the couch and rubbed his palms rapidly against his knees. His face looked as though it had been sculpted hurriedly into an expression of calm — the cheeks were uneven, the smile was off. He surveyed Bob as he did any stranger — as though deciding whether he would hire him. "You like *Gunsmoke?*"

Bob clasped his hands on his lap. "I like the man in the hat," he said.

Lou began to lean into another question; Ella felt he would ask the wrong ones. "How is the job?" Ella asked.

Bob arranged his hands around an invisible steering wheel and twisted it to the right until the wheel came to an abrupt stop. "I drive," he said. "I like to drive."

"Do you like — big trucks or small ones?" Ella asked.

"I just drive big ones," he said, as though insulted.

Cowboys galloped, yelling, across a desert. Ella kept glancing at her aquamarine vase right by his elbow, pretending not to stare at him. There had to be reasons to like him. His fingernails shone. He had tied his shoes neatly. He had blue eyes. And the main point — he wanted Lena. "How long have you worked for Goodwill?" she asked.

"Awhile."

"And you live?"

"On a cot."

"Excuse me?"

"With the Ensons."

"And they are?"

"A man and a wife."

Before she could inquire more, Lena appeared. Ella had helped her match her yellow rhinestone earrings and scarf with a yellow shift, the one she'd worn when she'd gotten the Goodwill job. It seemed lucky. Bob lifted his eyes from the TV. Ella had never looked at Lena the way a man would. Dressing her was like adorning a child — for a specific, decorative purpose, but not for men. Now, creamy lavender eye shadow gleamed iridescent on her eyelids, and her hair was expansive with spray. Bob gazed at her frankly, as though he had a right to her.

Lena whisked past Ella, bumping her with her purse. "I've been talking to your guest," Ella began, "and —"

"Hi, Bob," said Lena.

Bob smiled. "Finish your socks?"

"Shut up!" squealed Lena, clapping her hand over her mouth.

"Excuse me?" asked Ella.

"Learn to park!" Lena said.

"I'm the best parker," Bob said. "I'm the number-one parker. And you know it."

Lena screeched with giggles. "Liar!" She rushed to the door with an exuberant haughtiness. Bob ran after her, as though afraid she would disappear.

"Where are you going?"

"We're going to walk down to House of Pancakes," said Lena.

"House of — it's going to be crowded," said Ella, feeling vaguely hysterical. "There'll be a long wait —"

"I'm hungry," said Bob, tugging Lena.

"Do you have enough money? Let me give you some —"

"Bob has money."

Bob gazed at Lena. His eyes were clear and intelligent with desire. He put his hand on her arm.

"Bye!" Lena said, waving tentatively.

Ella could not speak.

"Bye!" said Lena. "You — you look very pretty."

And they left.

She watched them bound across the lawn. Lena's yellow dress seemed to flutter in slow motion as she ran, as though governed by new physical laws.

Lou sprang back from the window, like a child embarrassed by what he had just seen. He pushed his hand into his glossy gray hair.

"Well," he said, "we're not losing a daughter — we're just gaining another mouth to feed."

Lou had never owned Lena the way she had. For thirty years he had tried hard not to look too closely at their daughter, instead cultivating a relentless optimism that Ella had found incomprehensible, yet also necessary. Now it made her feel alone.

"We're not gaining anything," said Ella. She grabbed her sweater and followed the two figures walking down the street.

She walked briskly, but casually, keeping a block between herself and her daughter. When Lena and Bob turned into a shopping center at the corner, Ella stopped beside a hefty Buick that was parked at one end of the lot.

They walked through the empty parking lot. It spread, like a dark lake, between House of Pancakes and a Hallmark, an ice cream parlor, a laundromat and a pet store. It was Sunday, and all the stores were closed, but Bob and Lena stared hard at the windows as though willing them to open. Ella waited for something to go wrong. Bob went over to cars, rubbed their dusty tops, nodded like an expert, returned to Lena. She put coins into a newspaper rack, removed a paper and handed it to him; he rolled it up and tapped it against his leg.

Lena and Bob walked around the parking lot slowly, once, twice, three times. The orange flanks of House of Pancakes loomed, unreal, candied in the pale light. Customers left the restaurant and walked toward their cars with a casual confidence; Bob and Lena watched them walk. As the two of them finally went through the coffee shop's glass doors, Bob touched Lena's back, just for a moment; his hand reached for the yellow fabric, trying, gently, to hold on.

Bob began to come to the house once a week. Lena was always dressed and ready an hour beforehand; she sat absolutely still on her bed, as though the fact of his imminent arrival was so fragile she had to take care not to disturb even the air. But she always made him wait. One night, while Bob installed himself in the den and waited for Lena to join him, Ella swept in to quiz him about his life. "Where is your cot?" she asked.

"Near the garage."

"Who are the Ensons?"

"A man and a wife."

She dragged out of him the following scintillating facts: he preferred lamb chops to chicken, and peas to potatoes.

Ella ruled that Lena and Bob had to spend part of the date somewhere in the house. They sat on the patio while Ella washed the dishes, observing them through the kitchen window. Toward nine o'clock, when the sky had turned dark, Ella heard a jump and rustle and the sound of running; she looked out a window onto the shining, moon-silver lawn. Lena and Bob were not kissing or touching but just chasing each other, endlessly, like large, slow bears. Their sound was of the purest joy, a soft, hushed giggling as they followed each other through the dark yard.

Dolores told her that Bob lived with the Ensons — a couple — in Sherman Oaks, and had a brother in Chicago, Hugh, who paid them rent. Ella got Hugh's number and called him up.

When she told him that Bob was dating her daughter, there was a silence so hostile she wondered what she had actually said.

"I'm sending money," Hugh said irritably. "I'm sending money."

"I'm not asking —"

"It's not easy, lady. Do you think it's easy sending —"

"Sir," she said, "I'm not asking for money. I just want to know what he's like."

Another silence. "Well, you see what he's like."

"For the last few months. What about before?"

"What is there to know? He's forty-one. Three years older than me."

"Where has he lived?"

"The folks had him at an institution for a while. They didn't know what the hell to do with him. He's been at the Ensons' six years, since the folks died. They got him to Goodwill. He likes driving, I hear."

"What else?"

"You might want to know this. He had a vasectomy."

She pressed the phone more firmly to her ear.

"They did that early. When he was sixteen, seventeen. No little Bobs running around."

Ella did not know how to digest this fact, so she decided to move on. "Anything else? Health problems, disorders, anything?"

"No, he's just real slow."

"And you?" she asked, in spite of herself.

"Me?"

"You, what do you do?"

"I'm in insurance. Life and homes. I just got married two years ago. I've got a son now," he said, his voice suddenly soft and eager to please.

"How nice," she said coolly.

"I hope he and your daughter get along real well," he said, his voice high-pitched with false sincerity. "I'll call back to see how he is —" He hung up. She never heard from him again.

One night, as Ella put on her sweater, preparing for her usual reconnaissance mission to House of Pancakes, she felt Lou's hands on her shoulders. He turned her around.

"I have to go," she said.

"Have dinner with me."

"Dinner?" she asked. "But they're —"

"They're just going to House of Pancakes." He looked away from her. "Who else is going to marry her?" he asked.

He was wearing an undershirt, and his shoulders were thinner now, at sixty-two, almost girlish. She followed him to the kitchen. Lena had recently discovered her own perfume, a chirpy lavender scent from Sav-On, and it floated through the hall. In the kitchen the shiny appliances hummed.

Lou paced around while Ella heated chicken with mushrooms. "What do you think they're doing?" she asked him.

"Eating," he said.

"They'll forget to pay," she said.

"Then they'll get arrested," he said. He folded his arms. They were caramel-colored, dusted with silver hair. His gaze stopped on her, held her. "Let's fool around," he said, a soft huskiness in his voice.

She stopped; she wished she could feel interested. "If you want to," she said, a little hopefully, "then come over here."

She turned away from him and, gently, he wound her long hair into his hands. His after-shave smelt drugstore-blue and sharp. His breath was a hot current against her neck. His hands slid down her bare arms and gently cupped her breasts, and Ella tried to let herself go against him, but she couldn't.

Lou stopped, sensing her resistance. "She's fine," he said.

Delicately Ella disentangled herself from him.

"I need you too," Lou said. He lightly slapped her hip, as though she were a cow, and she heard him walk away from her.

Lena and Bob marched into the kitchen one evening, their fingers wound together tightly, as though they had been assigned to each other as buddies on a school trip. Lena held up their hands. A plastic yellow ring encircled her index finger.

"I'm married!" said Lena.

Bob swiped a bruised pear off the table and took a big, juicy bite.

"You're what?" Ella asked.

"He gave me a ring!"

"You're engaged," said Ella.

"I'm going to have a husband!" screeched Lena. She pulled Bob to her side, like a purse.

Ella slowly laid her dishtowel on the sink. She touched Lena's taut hand, the yellow ring; it was the type that fell, encased in a plastic bubble, out of a gumball machine. Bob's breath was loud and puppyish, and his bristly hair seemed a harder silver than before. Lena giggled. She said to Bob, "Say what I said to —"

"Do I have to?"

"Yes."

Bob slowly got to his knees in front of Ella. He rubbed his hands on the sides of his gray pants and looked at the floor.

"I forget," he said to Lena.

"You know," said Lena. She whispered loudly, "I want to —"

"I want to propose a marriage," Bob said, addressing Ella's knee.

"Lena," Ella said, "honey, he's supposed to kneel in front of you, not me."

"But he's asking you."

Ella looked down at the rosy, bald circle on Bob's scalp. He looked like a gardener sprawled across a patch of lawn, pressing seeds into a plot of dirt. He was inevitable, and perhaps because of that, she felt an unexpected rush of love for him.

"Lou," Ella called carefully. "Lou."

"I'm married!" Lena shrieked as her father came into the room, and then she rushed into his arms. It was something she rarely did; Lou was unsure how to hold her, and his arms curved awkwardly around her. He stepped away and looked at her, blinking.

"Married," Lou said.

"Stand up," Ella said. Bob rocked back onto his feet and stood slowly, grabbing Lena's hip for balance. He was standing up, one of them now.

"We have to have a toast," said Lou.

Ella lifted a pitcher of cranberry juice from the refrigerator and filled the glasses. Lou arranged Lena's and Bob's arms into the gesture of a toast. Lena and Bob clutched their glasses fiercely, as though expecting them to rise to the ceiling, pulling them, legs kicking, off the floor.

"*L'chayim,*" Lou said.

It was Lou's idea that they get married in Las Vegas. They had a nine P.M. appointment at the Chapel of Eternal Love, at the other end of South Fifth, but Bob played the slots too long and almost made them late. Lena played right beside him, a little wobbly in her heels, her veil plopped on top of her machine.

The four of them walked down the Strip to the Chapel of Eternal Love, past the Stardust and the Thunderbird and the Riviera. The streets glowed with the hotels' gaudy pink and orange and white light. Lena wore a polyester puff-sleeved ivory dress, which they had purchased off a mannequin in the window of Treasureland, a discount emporium. The mannequin rose grimly out of a litter of golden ashtrays and inflatable palm trees. Lena had stopped by the window, pointed to the mannequin and said with great assurance, "Her."

Ella held Lena's hand in hers; with the other, she touched Lou's arm. "They do know we're coming?"

"Yes."

"What about flowers? Do they provide them?"

"Relax." He did not look at her. "It's going to be beautiful."

She wanted to ask him if love was truly good, if marriage made you safe, if the right man or woman would make anyone happy. She wanted to ask Lou if she had, in fact, given birth to Lena — if her daughter truly lived outside her body.

Outside the chapel, Ella took Lena to the far corner of the parking lot, drew Red Plum lipstick across her trembling lips.

"Ready?"

Lena nodded.

"Scared?"

Lena shrugged.

Ella took her hand. She wanted to tell her something. Marriage, she thought, was not simply choosing your mate, but the person you wanted to be for the rest of your life. There were other wives Ella could have been. Ella's marriage had shaped her, firmly and precisely, but she could not see the marks of her own evolution; she could not see how the love she gave and took made her what she was.

And here was her daughter with one suitor, one choice.

"Do you understand what this means, Lena?"

"It means that Bob and I will be together and we will be happy."

Ella adjusted Lena's veil with trembling fingers. "Where's your bobby pin?" she asked. "Don't let this fall off. Don't keep touching it."

Lena swatted her hand away. "I want to get married now."

The justice of the peace looked worn down by all the eternal love he'd seen that day. His assistant, wearing a red-sequined dress and a sparkly name tag that said WITNESS, took the wedding fee of twenty dollars from Ella, then flung open the door to a large refrigerator. Rows of cold bouquets were lined up like a silent, aloof audience inside. She shivered. "What color roses, hon? Red, pink, white or silver?"

"I would like silver, please," Lena said.

Lena stood beside Bob, their elbows touching. She tugged her wedding dress straight and nodded obediently at the justice. Her hand gripped the refrigerated spray of silver roses, which were the color of a dull nickel. Her face had the alertness of true happiness.

Ella, the maid of honor, stood beside Lena; Lou removed his navy fedora and held it as he stood beside Bob.

"By the power invested in me by the state of Nevada, I pronounce you man and wife," said the justice. He coughed. He suddenly seemed uncomfortable, as though just realizing he was intruding upon a family gathering.

Lena moved first. She raised her hand to Bob's face with a great tenderness, her fingers spread as though to capture as much of him as she could. Ella stared at Lena's fingers, which looked eerie and remote as a sea animal, and she did not know where Lena had learned to touch someone like that.

The witness hauled over a large, blue-sequined sack of free gifts for the newlyweds. "Something to start off your new home," she said. It was brimming with boxes of detergent, spatulas, colanders. The justice thrust his arm inside and brought out a box of Tide.

"Yuck," Lena said.

"This is your free gift," the assistant said.

"I don't want that one," Lena said, pouting.

"You don't want it?" asked the justice.

"Let them pick," Ella said.

The justice glared at Ella and checked his watch. "Lady, I'd like to stay here all night, but —"

"Let them pick," Ella hissed. She would not let them walk back into the streets of Las Vegas with a bad gift. Lena and Bob plunged their hands into the sack together. They began to bring out another box of Tide, pale detergent flowing out through a crack in the top. Ella pushed in front of Bob and Lena and slapped the box back into the bag. She grabbed hold of a spatula and pushed it into Lena's trembling hand.

"Congratulations," Ella said.

Out by the pool, the Las Vegas sun hammered down on their faces. Ella watched her daughter spread herself on a bright plastic chaise. Lena's eyes were masked by her horn-rimmed sunglasses, and her nipples were visibly erect under her lemon-yellow bathing suit. She lay on the chaise in an aloof silence, as though she were spinning quiet, magnificent thoughts.

"Do you want some lotion?" Ella asked.

Lena did not answer. She stood up regally and walked over to the pool. Standing a little unsteadily on its edge, she looked down at Bob in the water. Bob yanked her leg, and Lena crashed in.

Ella was not the only one who watched while Lena and Bob tumbled and splashed, cheerful, muffled bellows rising from their mouths. Their slick arms smacked the surface and swooped under the water, and their faces butted and kissed, but it was not exactly clear what they were doing to each other, and the crowd around the pool was riveted. Ella felt the backs of her knees tense. She got ready to stand up.

But after a minute Lena swung herself casually out of the pool. She glittered like an unearthly creature, with water shining on her arms, her hair. Lena came right to her chaise and sat beside her.

"I would like to share a room with Bob," Lena said.

That night the four of them stood in El Tropicale's dim hallway. Bob's arm circled Lena's shoulder with a brave attempt at propriety.

"Honey, may I have your key," Ella said.

Lena handed her mother the key. Lou was silent. Bob's fingers fluttered on Lena's shoulder, and Ella tasted fear, metallic, in her throat.

"Lena," Ella started, as her daughter took Bob's hand, "Lena, knock if you need anything." Lena whisked into her room and closed the door.

Lou had assumed a posture of odd, formal politeness. "Do we want to go sit at the piano bar?" he asked.

"I don't feel like it."

"Do we want to play the slots?"

"No," she said, opening the door to their own room next door.

They went inside, twitchy as a couple meeting each other illicitly for the first time. With a sharp, definite motion, Lou shrugged off his wine-colored jacket. His white shirt stuck to his shoulders in the heat.

"Have you noticed the footwear they sell here?" he asked.

"Footwear?"

He tossed his jacket over a chair. "People are on vacation, they lose their shopping sense." He took a deep, sharp breath. "Pink loafers. They take them home and they realize, where the hell am I going to wear pink loafers?"

"They're going to have to live with us," said Ella.

"They probably don't want to."

"She can't cook or clean," said Ella.

"I don't think he'd notice."

She thought she heard the TV's muffled garble start in the other room. "I hear them," she said.

The two of them froze, listening. "No," he said. "You don't hear them."

She put her hands on the wall dividing their room from Lena's. It was strangely cool. She heard only a faint, staticky wave of audience laughter.

"Look!" said Lou. He knocked on the wall sharply, twice. "Hello!" he called. Breathless, they awaited an answer; there was none. "See?" he said. "They can't hear us." He turned abruptly and walked away from the wall. "Come away from there," he said.

She wanted, vaguely, to accuse him of something; she wanted to see pain on Lou's face, a sorrow she could recognize.

"Leave her alone," he said, not sounding entirely convinced. He sank wearily into the sofa and rubbed his hands vigorously over his face. "Let's have a drink."

She couldn't. Instead, Ella pulled the ice tray out of the refrigerator and, in a gesture that felt both normal and alien, shook out cubes of ice and dropped them into a glass. She sat on the bed and crunched the ice cubes slowly and deliberately, trying to listen only to the hard clink they made as they fell back into the glass.

At about one A.M. there was a sharp knocking. Ella opened the door to Lena, who was shivering in her nightgown. Bob was right behind her, naked, holding a white towel across his waist with only middling success.

"What?" Ella demanded. "What's wrong?"

"I'm bleeding, Mother. There's blood —"

Ella yanked Lena into the room. Bob toddled in behind her, wearing the frozen, frightened smile of a child unsure what he was expected to do. Lou stood up. "What's —" he began, and she saw his face melt to alarm.

"I've got her," Ella announced. She pulled Lena into the bathroom. "Sit," she said. Ella wound a long ribbon of toilet paper around her hand. "Show me where."

Lena sat on the toilet and daintily flipped up her nightgown. Ella saw a smear of blood on Lena's large beige panties; she reached up, grapped the elastic and pulled the panties down to the floor. Ella dabbed Lena's vagina with the toilet paper; it came back pale red.

Ella knelt and peered critically between her daughter's legs. She had no idea what she was looking for; there was just a little blood. She held a towel under warm water and gently dabbed Lena's pubic hair.

"Am I okay, Mother?"

Ella didn't speak.

"Am I okay?"

"I don't know." Ella let Lena wonder a moment. "Answer me. Was he nice to you?"

"I think so."

"Does it still hurt?"

"I started bleeding."

"Do you feel better now?"

Lena touched her vagina tenderly, then stood up.

Ella knelt before her daughter and reached for her hands. "You've had" — Ella spoke slowly — "intercourse now, Lena."

Lena slapped Ella's hands away, impatient. "I have to go see my husband."

Bob was waiting in a chair, the towel arranged, like a large white napkin, across his lap. Lou was sitting in a chair on the other side of the room. They each had the alert demeanor of someone trying very hard not to speak.

"I stopped bleeding," Lena said proudly to Bob.

Bob folded the towel around his waist and jumped up; he hurried out of the room. Lena bounded after him, and Ella followed into the hallway. "The TV's still on," he called to Lena.

"Leave it on," said Lena.

As Lena began to follow him into their room, Ella saw Lena's nightgown sticking, indecent, over her hips; she reached forward to tug it down. But Lena pushed grandly past her mother. The pink door shut, and Ella was left standing in the corridor alone.

Back in the room, Lou looked at her. "Is she all right?"

Ella nodded.

He gingerly lifted Lena's beige lace panties off the floor. "She left these," he said.

She remembered when she had bought these panties for Lena — on sale at Henshey's, two for one. Lou folded them gently, barely touching the edges, then handed them to Ella. She was moved by the way he folded them. She went to the bathroom and threw them out.

She opened the refrigerator and took out a perfect, tiny bottle of Dewar's. She unscrewed the cap, swallowed half the bottle and handed it to her husband.

There was only one thing she could think to do.

She went to Lou and kissed him.

They kissed in the strange, clean room, surrounded by lamp-shades and bedspreads and dressers that were not their own.

Ella let her husband kiss her neck, her breasts, her knees, hard enough to erase Lena. Ella had not expected to feel abandoned. She had not expected that Lena's closing the door would make her turn to Lou. The kindest thing he could do was make her forget. And as Lou had been, since Lena's birth, second place to her daughter, Ella sensed, in the muscular trembling of his fingers, how much he wanted to make her forget. She felt the nakedness of their lips in the deep, cooling dark.

Long after Lou had fallen asleep, she sat awake beside him. Then she went to the window and looked down at the street. It was the street Lena had walked down to her wedding, and it burnt with the hotel's twenty-four-hour lights. She watched the lit messages — BINGO and POKER and WIN! — that flashed a brilliant display of pink and orange and yellow into the empty street. Ella believed, suddenly, absolutely, that Lena was also looking out her window. She saw her daughter leaning naked on the ledge, her hair stream-ing over her bare shoulders, gazing at the bright casino lights and their strange, insistent attempts to illuminate the sky.

LEONARD MICHAELS

A Girl with a Monkey

FROM PARTISAN REVIEW

IN THE SPRING of the year following his divorce, while traveling alone in Germany, Beard fell in love with a young prostitute named Inger and canceled his plans for further travel. They spent two days together, mainly in Beard's room. He took her to restaurants for lunch and dinner. The third day Inger told Beard she needed a break. She had had a life before Beard arrived. Now she had only Beard. She reminded him that the city was famous for its cathedral and zoo. "You should go look. There is more to see than Inger Stutz." Besides, she'd neglected her chores, and missed a dental appointment as well as classes in paper restoration at the local museum.

When she mentioned the classes, Beard thought to express interest, ask questions about paper restoration, but he wasn't interested. He said, "You could miss a few more." His tone was glum. He regretted it, but felt justified because she'd hurt his feelings. He'd spent a lot of money on Inger. He deserved better. He wasn't her life, but he'd canceled his plans, and he wouldn't be staying forever. She didn't have to remind him of the cathedral and zoo. Such things had been noted in his travel itinerary by the agent in San Francisco. He also had a travel guide.

Beard had in fact planned to do a lot of sightseeing, but moments after he checked into his hotel there was a knock at the door and he supposed it was a bellhop or chambermaid, and he saw the girl. She was very apologetic and apparently distressed. She'd come to the wrong room. Beard was charmed, not deceived. He invited her in.

Now, the evening of the third day, Beard said, "I don't want to hear about your chores or classes." He would double her fee.

Beard wasn't rich, but he'd inherited money and the court excluded his inheritance from the divorce settlement. It was enough money to let him be expansive, if not extravagant. He'd quit his job in television production in San Francisco, and gone to the travel agent. The trip cost plenty, but having met Inger and fallen in love, he was certainly getting value for his money until she said, "Please don't tell me what I could do or could not do. And it isn't a question of money."

The remark was inconsistent with her profession, even if Inger was still young, only a semi-pro, but it was the way she said "could," exactly as Beard had said it, that bothered him. He detected hostility in her imitation, and he was afraid that he'd underestimated Inger, maybe provoked a distaste for his character that was irredeemable.

He'd merely expressed his feelings, merely been sincere, yet somehow offended her. Her reaction was unfair. He didn't even know what he'd said that was offensive. Worse yet, he was afraid that he'd established with Inger the same relations he'd had with his ex-wife. In twenty-five years of marriage, she'd had many fits of irrational hostility over his most trivial remarks. Beard could never guess what he might say to make her angry. Now in another country, in love with another woman — a prostitute, no less — Beard was caught up in miseries he'd divorced.

The more things change, he thought, they don't.

Inger knew nothing about Beard's marriage, but she'd heard that one's clients sometimes become attached, and it was hard to get free of them. Beard was only her fifth client. What troubled her particularly was that she'd upset Beard more than she might have expected. He sounded deranged, shouting in the crowded restaurant, "I'll pay double," and slapping the table. How embarrassing. What had the waiter thought? She felt slightly fearful. "You are a sweet man," she said. "Very generous. Many women in Germany would be yours for nothing."

"I prefer to pay for you. Can't you understand?"

She understood but shook her head no, astonished and reproachful at once. "I understand that you are self-indulgent. If I were like you, I would soon become dissolute. My life would be irregular. I would feed my monkey table scraps instead of monkey food, because it gives me pleasure. She would then beg every time I sit down at the dinner table. It would be no good for her or for me."

"I'm not your monkey."

"You think you're more complicated."

Beard was about to smile, but realized Inger wasn't making a joke. Her statement was flat and profoundly simple. Beard wasn't sure what she intended. Maybe she was asking a question. But it seemed she really saw in Beard what she saw in her monkey, as if all sentient beings were equivalent. She put him in mind of Saint Francis of Assisi.

As had happened several times during his acquaintance with Inger, he was overcome by a sort of mawkish adoration. His eyes glistened. He'd never felt this way about a woman. Spiritual love. At the same time, he had a powerful desire to ravish her. Of course he'd done that repeatedly in the hotel room, in the bed and on the floor, and each time his desire had been satisfied, yet it remained undiminished, unsatisfied.

"Well, what are you, then?" she asked softly.

Beard, surprising himself, said, "I'm a Jew." With a rush of strong and important feeling, it struck him that he was indeed a Jew.

Inger shrugged. "I might have Jewish blood. Who knows about such things?"

Beard had anticipated a more meaningful, more sensitive response. He saw instead, once again, the essential Inger. She was, in her peculiar way, as innocent as a monkey. She had no particular, cultivated sensibility. No idea of history. She was what she was, as if she'd dropped into the world yesterday. A purely objective angelic being. He had her number, he thought. Having her number didn't make him detached. His feelings were no less intense, no less wonderful, and — no other word for it — unsatisfied. She got to him like certain kinds of music. He thought of unaccompanied cello suites.

"Inger," he whispered, "have pity. I'm in love with you."

"Nonsense. I'm not very pretty."

"Yes, you are."

"If that's how you feel . . ."

"It is."

"You feel this now. Later, who knows?"

"Could you feel something for me?"

"I'm not indifferent."

"That's all?"

"You may love me."

"Thanks."

"You're welcome. But I think . . ."

"I'm self-indulgent."

"It's a burden for me."

"I'll learn to be good."

"I applaud this decision."

"When can I see you again?"

"You will pay me what you promised?"

"Of course."

She studied his face, as if to absorb a new understanding, and then, with no reservations in her voice, said, "I will go home tonight. You may come for me tomorrow night. You may come upstairs and meet my roommate."

"Must you go home?"

"I dislike washing my underwear in a bathroom sink."

"I'll wash your underwear."

"I have chores, things I have to do at home. You are frightening me."

"I'll call a taxi."

"No. My bicycle is still at the hotel."

The next morning Beard went to a barber shop and then shopped for a new jacket. So much time remained before he could see Inger. In the afternoon, he decided to visit the cathedral, a Gothic structure of dark stone. It thrust up suddenly, much taller than the surrounding houses, on a curved, narrow medieval street. Beard walked around the cathedral, looking at saintly figures carved into the stone. Among them he was surprised by a monkey, the small stone face hideously twisted, shrieking. He couldn't imagine what it was doing there, but the whole cathedral was strange, so solemn and alien amid the ordinary houses along the street.

Men in business suits, students in their school uniforms, and housewives carrying sacks of groceries walked by without glancing at the cathedral. None seemed to have any relation to it, but surely they felt otherwise. They lived in this city. The cathedral was an abiding feature of their landscape, stark and austere yet complicated in its carvings. Beard walked inside. As he entered the nave, he felt reduced, awed by the space. Most of all, he felt lonely. He felt a good deal, but it struck him that he could never understand the power and meaning of the Christian religion. With a jealous and angry God, Jews didn't need such space for worship. A plain room would do. It would even be preferable to a cathedral, more appropriate to their intimate, domestic connection to the deity, someone they had been known to defy and even to fight until, like Jonah, they collapsed into personal innerness, in agonies and joys of sacred delirium.

Walking back to the hotel, he remembered that Inger had talked about her monkey. The memory stirred him, as he had been stirred in the restaurant, with sexual desire. Nothing could be more plain, more real. It thrust against the front of his trousers. He went into a coffee shop to sit for a while and pretend to read a newspaper.

That evening in the hotel room, with his fresh haircut and new jacket, he presented himself to the bathroom mirror. He had once been handsome. Qualities of handsomeness remained in his solid, leonine head, but there were dark sacks under his eyes that seemed to carry years of pain and philosophy. They made his expression vaguely lachrymose. "You are growing the face of a hound," he said to his reflection, but he was brave and didn't look away, and he decided he must compensate for his losses. He must buy Inger a present, something new and beautiful, a manifestation of his heart.

In a jewelry store window in the hotel lobby, he noticed a pair of gold earrings set with rubies like tiny globules of blood. Obviously expensive. Much too expensive for his travel budget, but he entered the store and asked what they cost, though he knew it was a mistake to ask. He was right. The price was even higher than he had guessed. It was nearly half of his inheritance. Those earrings plus the cost of the trip would leave him barely enough money to pay his rent in San Francisco, and he didn't have a job waiting for him when he returned.

He left the store and walked about the streets looking in other store windows. Every item that caught his attention was soon diminished by his memory of the swirl of gold and the impassioned red glob within.

Those earrings were too expensive. An infuriating price. It had been determined by a marketing demon, thought Beard, because the earrings now haunted him. He grew increasingly anxious as minutes passed and he continued walking the streets, pointlessly looking into shop windows, unable to forget the earrings.

He was determined not to return to the jewelry store, but then he let himself think: if he returned to the store only to look at the earrings — not to buy them — they would be gone. So it was too late to buy the earrings, he thought, as he hurried back to the store. To his relief, they were still there and more beautiful than he remembered.

The salesperson was a heavily made-up woman in her fifties, who wore a black, finely pleated silk dress and gold-rimmed eyeglasses. She approached and stood opposite Beard at the glass counter. He looked down strictly at a necklace, not the earrings, though only a little while ago he'd asked her the price of the earrings. She wasn't fooled. She knew what he wanted. Without being asked, she withdrew the earrings from their case and put them on the counter. Beard considered this highly impertinent, but he didn't object. As if making a casual observation, she said, "I've never seen earrings like these before. I'm sure I'll never see any like these again."

"They're much too expensive."

"Do you think so?" She looked away toward the street, apparently uninterested in his opinion. It was late afternoon, nearly closing time. Her indifference to Beard's remark annoyed him.

"Too expensive," he said, as if he were inviting her to haggle.

"Should I put them away?" she asked.

Beard didn't answer.

"They are expensive, I suppose," she said. "But prices fluctuate. If you like, I'll keep your business card and phone you if the earrings aren't sold in a few weeks."

Beard heard contempt in her voice, as if she were saying the point of jewelry is to be expensive, even too expensive. He drew his wallet slowly from his jacket pocket, and then, with a thrill of suicidal exultation, he slapped his credit card, not his business card, on the glass beside the earrings. She plucked it up, stepped away, and ran the card through a machine. He signed the receipt quickly to disguise the tremor in his hand.

When he arrived at Inger's apartment house, his heart was beating powerfully. He felt liberated, exceedingly happy, and slightly sick. He planned to take Inger to a fine restaurant. He'd done so before. She'd seemed not the least impressed, but tonight, after dinner, he would give her the earrings. The quality of the light in the restaurant, the delicious food, the wine, the subtle ministrations of the staff — such things matter. The earrings would intensify the occasion. She would be impressed, even if she didn't think precisely like a whore. Besides, it would matter to Beard.

A woman in a short skirt opened the door. She was older than Inger, and had cold violet eyes. Her black hair was cut level with her ears and across into severe, straight bangs, emphasizing her hard, thin-lipped expression. She'd looked somehow damaged and petrified by her beauty. Beard introduced himself. The woman said she was Greta Matti, Inger's roommate, then said, "Inger is gone."

"Impossible."

"It is possible," said Greta, her lips briefly, unpleasantly curled. Beard understood that Greta disliked being contradicted, but he didn't believe her. The woman was malicious.

"She took her monkey," she said. "Please go look for yourself, Mr. Beard. No clothes in her closet, no suitcase, no bicycle."

Greta turned back into the apartment. Beard entered behind her and looked where she gestured toward a room, and then followed her into it. Closets and drawers were empty. There was nothing, no sign of human presence. Stunned by the emptiness, Beard felt he himself had been emptied.

"You never know a person," said Greta. "She seemed so shy and studious, but she must have done something criminal. I was an idiot to let her move in, a girl with a monkey. Half the time it was I who fed the beast. The telephone never stopped ringing."

Beard followed Greta to the kitchen. A teapot had been set on a small table with a cup and saucer.

"Where did she go?" he said. He didn't expect a positive, useful answer. Who would disappear like that and leave an address? But what else could he say?

"You are not the first to ask. I don't know where she comes from or where she went. Would you like a cup of tea?"

Greta sat at the table and turned slightly toward Beard. She crossed her legs. It was clear that she didn't plan to stand up again to get another cup and saucer, and she seemed merely to assume Beard would stay. Her legs, he couldn't not notice, were long, naked, and strikingly attractive in high heels. He glanced at the white flesh of her inner thigh and felt humbled and uncomfortable.

Greta poured tea for herself without waiting for his answer, and took a sip. Did she think her legs gave him enough? He wanted to ask questions, perhaps learn something about Inger. He knew hardly anything about her.

"I'm sorry," said Greta, softening a little. "Her disappearance is very inconvenient for me. Perhaps it is worse for you."

Beard nodded. "Does Inger owe you money?"

"Technically, I owe her money. She paid a month in advance. I can make another cup of tea."

Beard was inclined to say yes. He needed company, but the whiteness of Greta's legs had become unbearable, repulsively carnal. He couldn't not look at them.

"Thank you," he said. "I must go."

Beard found a phone directory in a bar, looked up the address of the museum, and then hailed a taxi. He'd remembered that Inger took classes in paper restoration. They were given in the evening. At the museum, an administrator told him that Inger had quit the program. Beard next went to the restaurants where they had gone together. He didn't expect to find her in any of them. To his painful disappointment, he didn't find her in any of them. He returned to the hotel. Inger's bicycle was no longer in the lobby where it had been propped against a wall for two days. Its absence made him feel the bleakness of the marble floor, the sterility of the potted plants beside the desk, the loneliness of hotel lobbies.

In his room, Beard unwrapped the earrings and set them under the lamp on the night table. He studied the earrings with grim fascination, as if to penetrate their allure, the mystery of value. It came to him that, after creating the universe, God saw it was good. "So what is good about it?" Beard asked himself. He smoked cigarette after cigarette, and felt tired and miserable, a condition long associated with thought.

The earrings, shining on the night table, told him nothing. They looked worthless. But it was value — the value of anything aside from life itself — that Beard thought about. As for life itself, he assumed its value was unquestionable because he hadn't ever wanted to kill himself. Not even this minute when he felt so bad. Before he went to sleep, Beard read a train schedule and set the alarm on his travel clock.

At noon he checked out of his hotel, wearing his new jacket, and went to a restaurant where he ordered a grand lunch. He refused to suffer. He ate the lunch assiduously, though without pleasure, and then he took a taxi to the train station. The ticket he bought was first class, another luxurious expense, but he wanted — angrily — to pamper himself, or, as Inger would say, to be "self-indulgent."

As the train pulled out of the station, Beard slid the compartment door shut and settled beside the window with a collection of colorful, expensive magazines that he'd bought in the station. The magazines were full of advertisements for expensive things. Almost every page flared with brilliant color, and they crackled sensuously. They smelled good, too. He stared at pictures of nearly naked models and tried to feel desire. Exactly for what he couldn't say. It wasn't their bodies. Maybe it was for the future, more experience, more life. Then he reached into his jacket pocket to get his cigarettes and the earrings, intending to look at them again and resume his engagement with deep thought. He felt his cigarettes, but the earrings weren't in his pocket. Nor were they in any other pocket.

Beard knew instantly that he needn't bother to search his pockets, which he did repeatedly, because he remembered putting the earrings on the night table and he had no memory of picking them up. Because he hadn't picked them up. He knew. He knew.

As the train left the city and gained speed, he quit searching his pockets. Oh God, why had he bought the earrings? How could he have been so stupid? In an instant of emotional lunacy, he'd slapped his credit card down in the jewelry store and undone himself. The earrings were a curse, in some way even responsible for Inger's disappearance. He had to get hold of himself, think realistically, practically. He had to figure out what to do about retrieving them.

It was urgent to communicate with the hotel. Perhaps he could send a telegram from the train, or from the next station. He would find a conductor. But really, as he thought further about it, he decided it wasn't urgent to communicate with the hotel. It was a good hotel. This was Germany, not America. Nobody would steal his earrings. They would soon follow him to his destination, another good hotel. They weren't gone forever. He had nothing to worry about. This effort to reassure himself brought him almost to tears. He wanted desperately to retrieve the earrings. He stood up and went to the door. About to slide it open and look for a conductor, he heard a knock. He slid the door open with a delirious expectation. The conductor would be there, grinning, the earrings held forth in his open hand. Beard stared into the face of Inger.

She said, "I'm so sorry. I must have the wrong —" and then she let go of her suitcase and said, "*Gott behüte!*" The suitcase hit the floor with a thud and bumped the side of her leg.

Beard said, "Inger," and he didn't think so much as feel, with an odd little sense of gratification, that she wasn't very pretty. There was a timeless, silent moment in which they stared at each other and his feelings collected. It gave Beard time to see Inger exactly as she was, a slender, pale girl with pensive gray eyes whose posture was exceptionally straight. She made an impression of neatness, correctness, and youth. In this access of plain reality, he felt no anger and no concern for the earrings. As he could now see, they would look absurd on the colorless Inger. He felt only that his heart was breaking, and there was nothing he could do about it.

With a slow, uncertain smile, Inger said, "How are you?"

Beard picked up her suitcase. "You always travel first class?"

"Not always."

"It depends on the gentleman who answers the door."

"I'm very pretty," she said, her tone sweet and tentative and faintly self-mocking.

"Also lucky."

"I don't think so."

"I'm sure of it."

He put her suitcase onto the seat strewn with magazines. Then he took her hand, drew her toward him, and slid the door shut behind her. She said, "Please. Do give me a moment," but she didn't resist when he pressed her to the floor, his knee between her thighs. Her gray eyes were noncommittal and vast as the world. Beard raised up on his knees to undo his trousers and then removed Inger's sandals. He kissed her feet and proceeded to lick her legs, and then he hooked the crotch of her underpants with an index finger and drew them to the side and he licked her until she seized his hair with her fists and pulled him up, needing him inside as much as he needed her. He whispered, "I love you," his mouth against her neck, and he shut his eyes in a trance of pleasure and thrust into her, in her clothes, as the train pressed steadily into a mute and darkening countryside.

LYDIA DAVIS

St. Martin

FROM GRAND STREET

WE WERE CARETAKERS for most of that year, from early fall until summer. We had to look after a house and grounds, two dogs, and two cats. We fed the cats, one white and one calico, who lived outside and ate their meals on the kitchen windowsill, sparring in the sunlight as they waited for their food, but we did not keep the house very clean, or the weeds cut in the yard, and our employers, kind people though they were, probably never quite forgave us for what happened to one of the dogs.

We hardly knew what a clean house should look like. We would begin to think we were quite tidy, and then we would see the dust and clutter of the rooms and the two hearths covered with ash. Sometimes we argued about it, sometimes we cleaned it. The oil stove became badly blocked and we did nothing for days because the telephone was out of order. When we needed help, we went to see the former caretakers, an old couple who lived with their cages of breeding canaries in the nearest village. The old man came by sometimes, and when he saw how the grass had grown so tall around the house, he scythed it without comment.

What our employers needed most from us was simply that we stay in the house. We were not supposed to leave it for more than a few hours, because it had been robbed so often. We left it overnight only once, to celebrate New Year's Eve with a friend many miles away. We took the dogs with us on a mattress in the back of the car. We stopped at village fountains along the way and sprinkled water on their backs. We had too little money, anyway, to go anywhere. Our employers sent us a small amount each month, most of which we spent immediately on postage, cigarettes, and groceries. We brought home whole mackerels, which we cleaned, and whole chickens, which we beheaded and cleaned and prepared to roast, tying their legs together. The kitchen often smelled of garlic. We were told many times that year that garlic would give us strength. Sometimes we wrote letters home asking for money, and sometimes a check was sent for a small sum, but the bank took weeks to cash it.

We could not go much farther than the closest town to shop for food and to a village half an hour away over a small mountain covered with scrub oaks. There we left our sheets, towels, table linen, and other laundry to be washed, as our employers had instructed us to do, and when we picked it up a week later, we sometimes stayed to see a movie. Our mail was delivered to the house by a woman on a motorcycle.

But even if we had had the money, we would not have gone far, since we had chosen to live there in that house, in that isolation, in order to do work of our own, and we often sat inside the house trying to work, not always succeeding. We spent a great deal of time sitting inside one room or another looking down at our work and then up and out the window, though there was not much to see, one bit of landscape or another depending on which room we were in — trees, fields, clouds in the sky, a distant road, distant cars on the road, a village that lay on the horizon to the west of us piled around its square church tower like a mirage, another village on a hilltop to the north of us across the valley, a person walking or working in a field, a bird or a pair of birds walking or flying, the ruined outbuilding not far from the house.

The dogs stayed near us almost all the time, sleeping in tight curls. If we spoke to them, they looked up with the worried eyes of old people. They were purebred yellow Labradors, brother and sister. The male was large, muscular, perfectly formed, of a blond color so light he was nearly white, with a fine head and a lovely broad face. His nature was simple and good. He ran, sniffed, came when we called, ate, and slept. Strong, adept, and willing, he retrieved as long as we asked him to, running down a cliff of sand no matter how steep or how long, plunging into a body of water in pursuit of a stick. Only in villages and towns did he turn shy and fearful, trembling and diving toward the shelter of a café table or a car.

His sister was very different, and as we admired her brother for his simple goodness and beauty, we admired her for her peculiar sense of humor, her reluctance, her cunning, her bad moods, her deviousness. She was calm in villages and cities and would not retrieve at all. She was small, with a rusty brown coat, and not well formed, a barrel of a body on thin legs and a face like a weasel.

Because of the dogs, we went outside the house often in the course of the day. Sometimes one of us would have to leave the warm bed at five in the morning and hurry down the cold stone steps to let them out, and they were so eager that they leaked and left a pattern of drops on the red tiles of the kitchen and the patio. As we waited for them, we would look up at the stars, bright and distinct, the whole sky having shifted from where it was when we last saw it.

In the early fall, as grape pickers came into the neighboring fields to harvest, snails crept up the outside of the windowpanes, their undersides greenish gold. Flies infested the rooms. We swatted them in the wide bands of sunlight that came through the glass doors of the music room. They tormented us while alive, then died in piles on the windowsills, covering our notebooks and papers. They were one of our seven plagues, the others being the fighter jets that thundered suddenly over our roof, the army helicopters that batted their more leisurely way over the treetops, the hunters who roamed close to the house, the thunderstorms, the two thieving cats, and, after a time, the cold.

The guns of the hunters boomed from beyond the hills or under our windows, waking us early in the morning. Men walked alone or in pairs, sometimes a woman trailed by a small child, spaniels loping out of sight and smoke rising from the mouths of the rifles. When we were in the woods, we would find a hunter's mess by the ruins of a stone house where he had settled for lunch — a plastic wine bottle, a glass wine bottle, scraps of paper, a crumpled paper bag, and an empty cartridge box. Or we would come upon a hunter squatting so motionless in the bushes, his gun resting in his arms, that we did not see him until we were on top of him, and even then he did not move, his eyes fixed on us.

In the village café, at the end of the day, the owner's young son, in olive-green pants, would slip around the counter and up the stairs with his two aged, slinking, tangerine-colored dogs, at the same time that women would come in with the mushrooms they had gathered just before dusk. Cartridge cases peppered the ground across a flat field near the house, one of the odd waste patches that lay in this valley of cultivated fields. Its dry autumn grass was strewn with boulders, among them two abandoned cars. Here from one direction came the smell of wild thyme, from the other the smell of sewage from a sewage bed.

We visited almost no one, only a farmer, a butcher, and a rather pompous retired businessman from the city. The farmer lived alone with his dog and his two cats in a large stone house a field or two away. The businessman, whose hyphenated name in fact contained the word *pomp*, lived in a new house in the closest village, to the west of us across the fields. The young butcher lived with his childless wife in town, and we would sometimes encounter him there, moving meat across the street from his van to his shop. Cradling a beef carcass or a lamb in his arms, he would stop to talk to us in the sunlight, a wary smile on his face. When he was finished working for the day, he often went out to take photographs. He had studied photography through a correspondence course and received a degree. He photographed town festivals and processions, fairs and shooting matches. Sometimes he took us with him. Now and then a stranger came to the house by mistake. Once it was a young girl who entered the kitchen suddenly in a gust of wind, pale, thin, and strange, like a stray thought.

Because we had so little money, our amusements were simple. We would go out into the sun that beat down on the white gravel and shone off the leaves of the olive tree and toss pebbles one by one, overhand, from a distance of ten feet or so into a large clay urn that stood among the rosemary plants. We did this as a contest with each other, but also alone when we were finished working or couldn't work. One would be working and hear the dull click, over and over, of a pebble striking the urn and falling back onto the gravel, and the more resonant pock of the pebble landing inside the urn, and would know the other was outside.

When the weather grew too cold, we stayed inside and played gin rummy. By the middle of winter, when only a few rooms in the house were heated, we were playing so much, day and night, that we organized our games into tournaments. Then, for a few weeks, we stopped playing and studied German in the evenings by the fire. In the spring, we went back to our pebble game.

Nearly every afternoon, we took the dogs for a walk. On the coldest days of winter, we went out only long enough to gather kindling wood and pine cones for the fire. On warmer days, we went out for an hour or more at a time, most often into the government forest that spread out for miles on a plateau above and behind the house, sometimes into the fields of vines or lavender in the valley, or into the meadows, or across to the far side of the valley, into old groves of olive trees. We were surrounded for so long by scrub brush, rocks, pine trees, oaks, red earth, fields, that we felt enclosed by them even once we were back inside the house.

We would walk, and return with burrs in our socks and scratches on our legs and arms where we had pushed through the brambles to get up into the forest, and go out again the next day and walk, and the dogs always trusted that we were setting out in a certain direction for a reason, and then returning home for a reason, but in the forest, which seemed so endless, there was hardly a distinguishing feature that could be taken as a destination for a walk, and we were simply walking, watching the sameness pass on both sides, the thorny, scrubby oaks growing densely together along the dusty track that ran quite straight until it came to a gentle bend and perhaps a slight rise and then ran straight again.

If we came home by an unfamiliar route, skirting the forest, avoiding a deeply furrowed, overgrown field, and then stepping into the edge of a reedy marsh, veering close to a farmyard where a farmer in blue and his wife in red were doing chores, trailed by their dog, we felt so changed ourselves that we were surprised nothing about home had changed: for a moment the placidity of the house and yard nearly persuaded us we had not even left.

Between the forest and the fields, in the thickets of underbrush, we would sometimes come upon a farmhouse in ruins, with a curving flight of deep stone steps, worn at the edges, leading to an upper story that was now empty air, brambles and nettles and mint growing up inside and around it, and sometimes, nearby, an ancient, awkward, and shaggy fruit tree, half its branches dead. In the form of this farmhouse we recognized our own house. The animals had lived downstairs in our house, too — our vaulted dining room had once been a sheepfold.

Sometimes, in our walks, we came upon inexplicable things, once — in the cinders of an abandoned fire, two dead jackrabbits. Sometimes we lost our way, and were still lost after the sun had set, when we would start to run, and run without tiring, afraid of the dark, until we saw where we were again.

We had visitors who came from far away to stay with us for several days and sometimes several weeks, sometimes welcome, sometimes less so, as they stayed on and on. One was a young photographer who had worked with our employer and was in the habit of stopping at the house. He would travel through the region on assignments for his magazine, always taking his pictures at dawn or at sunset when the shadows were long. For every night he stayed with us, he paid us the amount he would have paid for a room at a good hotel, since he traveled on a company expense account. He was a small, neat man with a quick, toothy smile. He came alone, or he came with his girlfriend.

He played with the dogs, fondling them, wrestling with them overhead as we sat in the room below trying to work, while we spoke against him angrily to ourselves. Or he and his girlfriend ironed their clothes above us, with noises we did not at first understand, the stiff cord knocking and sliding against the floorboards. It was hard enough for us to work, sometimes.

They were curiously disorganized, and when they went out on an errand, left water coming to a boil on the stove or the sink full of warm, soapy water as though they were still at home. Or when they returned from an errand, they left the doors wide open so that the cold air and the cats came in. They were still at breakfast close to noon, and left crumbs on the table. Late in the evening, sometimes, we would find the girlfriend asleep on the sofa.

But we were lonely, and the photographer and his girlfriend were friendly, and they would sometimes cook dinner for us or take us out to a restaurant. A visit from them meant money in our pockets again.

At the beginning of December, when we began to have the oil stove going full blast in the kitchen all day, the dogs slept next to it while we worked at the dining room table. We watched through the window as two men returned to work in a cultivated field, one on a tractor and one behind a plow that had been sitting for weeks growing rusty, after it had opened perhaps ten furrows. Violent high winds sometimes rose during the night and then continued blowing all day so that the birds had trouble flying and dust sifted down through the floorboards. Sometimes one of us would get up in the night, hearing a shutter bang, and go out in pajamas onto the tiles of the garage roof to tie the shutter back again or remove it from its hinge.

A rainstorm would last hours, soaking the ruined outbuilding nearby, darkening its stones. The air in the morning would be soft and limp. After the constant dripping of the rain or wuthering of the wind, there was sometimes complete silence, minute after minute, and then abruptly the rocky echoes of a plane far away in the sky. The light on the wet gravel outside the house was so white, after a storm, it looked like snow.

By the middle of the month, the trees and bushes had begun to lose their leaves, and in a nearby field a stone shed, its black doorway overgrown by brambles, gradually came into view.

A flock of sheep gathered around the ruined outbuilding, fat, long-tailed, a dirty brown color, with pale scrawny lambs. Jostling one another, they poured up out of the ruin, climbing the tumbledown walls, the little ones crying in high human voices over the dull clamor of the bells. The shepherd, dressed all in brown with a cap pulled low over his eyes, sat eating on the grass by the woodpile, his face glowing and his chin unshaven. When the sheep became too active, he grunted and his small black dog raced once around the side of the flock and the sheep cantered away in a forest of sticklike legs. When they came near again, streaming out between the walls, the dog sent them flying again. When they disappeared into the next field, the shepherd continued to sit for a while, then moved off slowly, in his baggy brown pants, a leather pouch hanging on long straps down his back, a light stick in one hand, his coat flung over his shoulder, the little black dog charging and veering when he whistled.

One afternoon we had almost no money left, and almost no food. Our spirits were low. Hoping to be invited to dinner, we dropped in on the businessman and his wife. They had been upstairs reading, and came down one after the other holding their reading glasses in their hands, looking tired and old. We saw that when they were not expecting company, they had in their living room a blanket and a sleeping bag arranged over the two armchairs in front of the television. They invited us to have dinner with them the next night.

When we went to their house the next night, we were offered

rum cocktails by Monsieur Assiez-de-Pompignan before dinner, and afterward we watched a movie with them. When it ended, we left, hurrying to our car against the wind, through the narrow, shuttered streets, dust flying in our teeth.

The following day, for dinner, we had one sausage. The only money left now was a pile of coins on the living room table, collected from saucers around the house and amounting to 2.97 francs, less than 50 cents but enough to buy something for dinner the next day.

Then we had no money at all anywhere in the house, and almost nothing left to eat. What we found, when we searched the kitchen carefully, were some onions, an old but unopened box of pastry-crust mix, a little fat, and a little dried milk. Out of this, we realized, we could make an onion pie. We made it, baked it, cut ourselves two pieces, and put the rest back in the hot oven to cook a little more while we ate. It was surprisingly good. Our spirits lifted, we talked as we ate and forgot all about the pie as it went on baking. By the time we smelled it, it had burned too badly to be saved.

In the afternoon of that day, we went out onto the gravel, not knowing what to do now. We tossed pebbles for a while, there in the boiling sun and the cool air, saying very little because we had no answer to our problem. Then we heard the sound of an approaching car. Along the bumpy dirt road that led to our house from the main road, past the house of the weekend people, of pink stucco with black ironwork, and then past a vineyard on one side and a field on the other, came the photographer in his neat rented car. By pure chance, or like an angel, he was arriving to rescue us at the very moment we had used up our last resource.

We were not embarrassed to say we had no money, and no food either, and he was pleased to invite us out to dinner. He took us into town to a very good restaurant on the main square where the rows of plantain trees stood. A television crew was also dining there, twelve at the table, including a hunchback. By the large, bright fire on one wall, three old women sat knitting: one with liver spots covering her face and hands, the second pinched and bony, the third younger and merrier but slow-witted. The photographer fed us well on his expense account. He stayed with us that night and a few nights after, leaving us with several 50-franc notes, so we were all right for a while, since a bottle of local wine, for instance, cost no more than 1.50 francs.

When winter set in, we closed one by one the other rooms in the house and confined ourselves to the kitchen with its fat oil-burning stove, the vaulted dining room with its massive oak table where we played cards in the thick heat from the kitchen, the music room with its expensive electric heater burning our legs, and, at the top of the stone stairway, the unheated bedroom with its floor of red tiles so vast there was ample time for it to dip down in the center and rise again on its way to the single small casement window that looked out onto the almond tree and the olive tree below. The house had a different feeling to it when the wind was blowing and parts of it were darkened because we had closed the shutters.

Larks fluttered over the fields in the afternoons, showing silver. The long, straight, deeply rutted road to the village turned to soft mud. In certain lights, the inner walls of the ruined outbuilding were as rosy as a seashell. The dogs sighed heavily as they lay down on the cold tiles, closing their almond-shaped eyes. When they were let out into the sunlight, they fought, panting and scattering gravel. The shadow of the almond tree in the bright, hard sunlight flowed over the gravel like a dark river and lapped up against the wall of the house.

One night, during a heavy rainstorm, we went to the farmer's house for dinner. Nothing grew around his house, not even grass; there was only the massive stone house in a yard of deep mud. The front door was heavy to push open. The entryway was filled with a damp, musty smell from the truffles hanging in a leather pouch from a peg. Sacks full of seed and grain lined the wall.

With the farmer, we went out to the side of the house to collect eggs for dinner. Under the house, in the pens where he had once kept sheep, hens roosted now, their faces sharp in the beam of his flashlight. He gathered the eggs, holding the flashlight in one hand, and gave them to us to carry. The umbrella, as we started back around to the front of the house, turned inside out in the wind.

The kitchen was warm from the heat of a large oil stove. The oven door was open and a cat sat inside looking out. When he was in the house, the farmer spent most of his time in the kitchen. When he had something to throw away, he threw it out the window, burying it later. The table was crowded with bottles — vinegar, oil, his own wine in whiskey bottles that he had brought up from the cellar — and among them cloth napkins and large lumps of sea salt. Behind the table was a couch piled with coats. Two rifles hung in racks against the wall. Taped to the refrigerator was a photograph of the farmer and the truck he used to drive from Paris to Marseilles.

For dinner he gave us leeks with oil and vinegar, bits of hard sausage and bread, black olives like cardboard, and scrambled eggs with truffles. He dried lettuce leaves by shaking them in a dishtowel and gave us a salad full of garlic, and then some Roquefort. He told us that his first breakfast, before he went out to work in the fields, was a piece of bread and garlic. He called himself a Communist and talked about the Resistance, telling us that the people of the area knew just who the collaborators were. The collaborators stayed at home out of sight, did not go to the cafés much, and in fact would be killed immediately if there was trouble, though he did not say what he meant by trouble. He had opinions about many things, even the Koran, in which, he said, lying and stealing were not considered sins, and he had questions for us: he wondered if it was the same year over there, in our country.

To get to his new, clean bathroom, we took the flashlight and lit our way past the head of the stairs and through an empty, high-ceilinged room of which we could see nothing but a great stone fireplace. After dinner, we listened in silence to a record of revolutionary songs that he took from a pile on the floor, while he grew sleepy, yawning and twiddling his thumbs.

When we returned home, we let the dogs out, as we always did, to run around before they were shut in for the night. The hunting season had begun again. We should not have let the dogs out loose, but we did not know that. More than an hour passed, and the female came back but her brother did not. We were afraid right away, because he never stayed out more than an hour or so. We called and called, near the house, and then the next morning, when he had still not returned, we walked through the woods in all directions, calling and searching among the trees.

We knew he would not have stayed away so long unless he had somehow been stopped from coming back. We began to think he had been stolen by a hunter, someone avid for a good-natured, handsome hunting dog, proud to show it off in a smoke-filled café. He could have wandered into the nearest village, lured by the scent of a female in heat. He could have been spotted near the road and taken by a passing motorist. But we believed, first and longest, that he lay in the underbrush, poisoned or caught in a trap or wounded by a bullet.

Day after day passed and he did not come home and we had no news of him. We drove from village to village asking questions, and put up notices with his photograph attached, but we also knew that the people we talked to might lie to us, and that such a beautiful dog would probably not be returned.

People called us who had a yellow dog, or had found a stray, but each time we went to see it, it was not much like our dog. Because we did not know what had happened to him, because it was always possible that he might return, it was hard for us to accept the fact that he was gone. What made it worse was that he was not our dog.

After a month, we still hoped the dog would return, though signs of spring began to appear and other things came along to distract us. The almond tree blossomed with flowers so white that against the soft plowed field beyond them they were almost blue. A pair of magpies came to the scrub oak beside the woodpile, fluttering, squawking, diving obliquely down.

The weekend people returned, and every Sunday they called out to each other as they worked the long strip of earth in the field below us. The dog went to the border of our land and barked at them, tense on her stiff legs.

Once we stopped to talk to a woman at the edge of the village, and she showed us her hand covered with dirt from digging in the ground. Behind her, we could see a man leading another man back into his garden, to give him some herbs.

Drifts of daffodil and narcissus bloomed in the fields. We gathered a vaseful of them and slept with them in the room, waking up drugged and sluggish. Irises bloomed, and then the first roses opened, yellow. The flies became numerous again, and noisy.

We took long walks again, with one dog now. There were bugs in the wiry, stiff grass near the house, small cracks in the dirt, ants. In the field, purple clover grew around our ankles, and large white and yellow daisies at our knees. Blood-red bumble bees landed on buttercups as high as our hands. The long, lush grass in the field rose and fell in waves before the wind, and near us in a thick grove of trees dead branches clacked together. Whenever the wind died, we could hear the trickle of a swollen stream as though it were falling into a stone basin.

In May, we heard the first nightingale. Just as the night fully darkened, it began to sing. Its song was not really unlike the song of a mockingbird, with warbles, and twitters, and trills, warbles, chirps, and warbles again, but it issued in the midst of the silence of the night, in the dark, or in the moonlight, from a spot mysteriously hidden among the black branches.

Perceived Social Values

JUNOT DÍAZ

Fiesta, 1980

FROM STORY

MAMI'S YOUNGEST SISTER — my Tía Yrma — finally made it to
the United States that year. She and Tío Miguel got themselves an
apartment in the Bronx, off the Grand Concourse, and everybody
decided that we should have a party. Actually, my dad decided,
but everybody — meaning Mami, Tía Yrma, Tío Miguel, and their
neighbors — thought it a dope idea. On the Friday of the party
Papi got back from work around six. Right on time. We were all
dressed by then, which was a smart move on our part. If Papi had
walked in and caught us lounging around in our underwear, man,
he would have kicked our asses something serious.

He didn't say nothing to nobody, not even to my moms. He just
pushed past her, held up his hand when she tried to talk to him,
and jumped into the shower. Rafa gave me the look and I gave it
back to him; we both knew Papi had been out with the Puerto Rican
woman he was seeing and wanted to wash off the evidence quick.

Mami looked really nice that day. The United States had finally
put some meat on her; she was no longer the same flaca who had
arrived here three years before. She had cut her hair short and was
wearing tons of cheap-ass jewelry, which on her was kinda attractive. She smelled like herself, which meant she smelled good, like
the wind through a tree. She always waited until the last possible
minute to put on her perfume because she said it was a waste to
spray it on early and then have to spray it on again once you got to
the party.

We — meaning me, my brother, my little sister, and Mami —
waited for Papi to finish his shower. Mami seemed anxious, in her

usual dispassionate way. Her hands adjusted the buckle of her belt over and over again. That morning, when she had gotten us up for school, Mami told us that she wanted to have a good time at the party. I want to dance, she said, but now, with the sun sliding out of the sky like spit off a wall, she seemed ready to just get this over with.

Rafa didn't much want to go to no party either, and me, I never wanted to go anywhere with my family. There was a baseball game in the parking lot outside and we could hear our friends yelling, Hey, and, You suck, to one another. We heard the pop of a ball as it sailed over the cars, the clatter of an aluminum bat dropping to the concrete. Not that me or Rafa loved baseball; we just liked playing with the local kids, thrashing them at anything they were doing. By the sounds of the shouting, we both knew the game was close, either of us could have made a difference. Rafa frowned, and when I frowned back, he put up his fist. Don't you mirror me, he said.

Don't you mirror me, I said.

He punched me — I would have hit him back but right then Papi marched into the living room with his towel around his waist, looking a lot smaller than he did when he was dressed. He had a few strands of hair around his nipples and a surly closed-mouth expression, like maybe he had scalded his tongue or something.

Have they eaten? he asked Mami.

She nodded. I made you something.

You didn't let him eat, did you?

Dios mio, she said, letting her arms fall to her side.

Dios mio is right, Papi said.

I was never supposed to eat before our car trips, but earlier, when she had put out our dinner of rice, beans, and sweet platanos, guess who had been the first one to gobble his meal down? You couldn't blame Mami really, she had been busy — cooking, getting ready, dressing my sister Madai. I should have reminded her not to feed me but I hadn't been thinking. Even if I had, I doubt I would have told her.

Papi turned to me. Why did you eat?

Rafa had already inched away from me. I'd once told him I considered him a low-down chickenshit for moving out of the way every time Papi was going to smack me.

Collateral damage, he said. Ever heard of it?

No.

Look it up.

Chickenshit or not, right then I didn't dare glance at him. Papi was old-fashioned; he expected you to attend him, but not stare into his eyes, while you were getting your ass whupped. I studied Papi's bellybutton, which was perfectly round and immaculate. Papi pulled me to my feet by my ear.

If you throw up —

I won't, I said, tears in my eyes, more out of reflex than pain.

It's not his fault, Mami said. I fed them before I reminded them about the party.

They've known about this party forever. How did they think we were going to get there? Fly?

He finally let go of my ear and I went back to my seat. Madai was too scared to open her eyes. Being around Papi all her life had turned her into a big-time wuss. Anytime Papi raised his voice her lip would start trembling, like it was some sort of specialized tuning fork. Rafa pretended that he had knuckles to crack, and when I shoved him, he gave me a *Don't start* look. But even that little bit of recognition made me feel better.

I was the one who was always in trouble with my dad. It was like my God-given role to piss him off, to do everything the way he hated. It didn't bother me too much, really. I still wanted him to love me, something that never seemed strange or contradictory until years later, when he was out of our lives.

Before I knew it Papi was dressed and Mami was crossing each one of us, solemnly, like we were heading off to war. We said, in turn, Bendición, Mami, and she poked us in our five cardinal spots while saying, Que Dios te bendiga.

This was how we began all our trips, the words that followed me every time I left the house.

None of us said anything else until we were in Papi's Volkswagen van. Brand new, lime green, bought to impress. Oh, we were impressed, considering we couldn't afford no VW van, used or new, but me, each time I got in that VW and Papi went above twenty miles an hour, I vomited. I'd never had trouble with cars before, and that van was like my curse. Mami suspected it was the upholstery. In her mind, American things — appliances, mouthwash, funny-looking upholstery — all seemed to have an intrinsic bad-ness. Papi was careful about taking me anywhere in the VW, but when he did, like that night, I had to ride up front in Mami's usual seat so I could throw up out a window.

You okay? Mami asked over my shoulder as Papi got us onto the turnpike. She had her hand on the small of my neck. One thing about Mami, even when she was nervous, her palms never sweated.

I'm okay, I said, keeping my eyes straight ahead. I definitely didn't want to trade glances with Papi. He had this one look, furious and sharp, that always left me feeling bruised.

Toma. Mami handed me four mentas. She had thrown a few out her window at the beginning of our trip, an offering to Eshú; the rest were for me. Mami considered these candies a cure-all for any disorder.

I took one and sucked it slowly, my tongue knocking it up against my teeth. As always, it helped. We passed Newark Airport without any incident. If Madai had been awake she would have cried because the planes flew so close to the cars.

How's he feeling? Papi asked.

Fine, I said. I glanced back at Rafa and he pretended like he didn't see me. That was the way he was, both at school and at home. When I was in trouble, he didn't know me. Madai was solidly asleep, but even with her face all wrinkled up and drooling she looked cute.

I turned around and concentrated on the candy. Papi even started to joke that we might not have to scrub the van out tonight. He was beginning to loosen up, not checking his watch too much. Maybe he was thinking about that Puerto Rican woman or maybe he was just happy that we were all together. I could never tell. At the toll, he was feeling positive enough to actually get out of the van and search around under the basket for dropped coins. It was something he had once done to amuse Madai, but now it was habit. Cars behind us honked their horns and I slid down in my seat. Rafa didn't care; he just grinned back at the other cars. His actual job was to make sure no cops were coming. Mami shook Madai awake, and as soon as she saw Papi stooping for a couple of quarters she let out this screech of delight that almost took the top of my head off.

That was the end of the good times. Just outside the Washington Bridge, I started feeling woozy. The smell of the upholstery got all up inside my head and I found myself with a mouthful of saliva.

Mami's hand tensed on my shoulder and when I caught Papi's eye, he was like, No way. Don't do it.

The first time I got sick in the van Papi was taking me to the library. Rafa was with us and he couldn't believe I threw up. I was famous for my steel-lined stomach. A third-world childhood could give you that. Papi was worried enough that just as quick as Rafa could drop the books off we were on our way home. Mami fixed me one of her honey-and-onion concoctions and that made my stomach feel better. A week later we tried the library again, and on this go-around I couldn't get the window open in time. When Papi got me home, he went and cleaned out the van himself, an expression of asco on his face. This was a big deal, since Papi almost never cleaned anything himself. He came back inside and found me sitting on the couch; I was feeling like hell.

It's the car, he said to Mami. It's making him sick.

This time the damage was pretty minimal, nothing Papi couldn't wash off the door with a blast of the hose. He was pissed, though; he jammed his finger into my cheek, a nice solid thrust. That was the way he was with his punishments: imaginative. Earlier that year I'd written an essay in school called "My Father the Torturer," but the teacher made me write a new one. She thought I was kidding.

We drove the rest of the way to the Bronx in silence. We only stopped once, so I could brush my teeth. Mami had brought along my toothbrush and a tube of toothpaste and while every car known to man sped by us she stood outside with me so I wouldn't feel alone.

Tío Miguel was about seven feet tall and had his hair combed up and out, into a demi-'fro. He gave me and Rafa big spleen-crushing hugs and then kissed Mami and finally ended up with Madai on his shoulder. The last time I'd seen Tío was at the airport, his first day in the United States. I remembered how he hadn't seemed all that troubled to be in another country.

He looked down at me. Carajo, Yunior, you look horrible!

He threw up, my brother explained.

I pushed Rafa. Thanks a lot, ass-face.

Hey, he said. Tío asked.

Tío clapped a bricklayer's hand on my shoulder. Everybody gets sick sometimes, he said. You should have seen me on the plane over here. Dios mío! He rolled his small Asian-looking eyes for emphasis. I thought we were all going to die.

Everybody could tell he was lying. I smiled like he was making me feel better.

Do you want me to get you a drink? Tío asked. We got beer and rum.

Miguel, Mami said. He's young.

Young? Back in Santo Domingo, he'd be getting laid by now.

Mami thinned her lips, which took some doing.

Well, it's true, Tío said.

So, Mami, I said, when do I get to go visit the D.R.?

That's enough, Yunior.

It's the only pussy you'll ever get, Rafa said to me in English.

Not counting your girlfriend, of course.

Rafa smiled. He had to give me that one.

Papi came in from parking the van. He and Miguel gave each other the sort of handshakes that would have turned my fingers into Wonder bread.

Long time, compa'i, Tío said.

Compa'i, ¿como va todo?

Tía came out then, with an apron on and maybe the longest Lee Press-On Nails I've ever seen in my life. There was this one guru guy I'd seen in the *Guinness Book of World Records* who had longer nails, but I tell you, it was close. She gave everybody kisses, told me and Rafa how guapo we were — Rafa, of course, believed her — told Madai how bella she was, but when she got to Papi, she froze a little, like maybe she'd seen a wasp on the tip of his nose, but then she kissed him all the same. Just a peck really.

Look at that, Rafa whispered to me in English.

Mami told us to join the other kids in the living room. Tío said, Wait a minute, I want to show you the apartment. I was glad Tía said, Hold on, because from what I'd seen so far, the place had been furnished in Contemporary Dominican Tacky. The less I saw, the better. I mean, I liked plastic sofa covers but damn, Tío and Tía had taken it to another level. They had a disco ball hanging in the living room and the type of stucco ceilings that looked like stalactite heaven. The sofas all had golden tassels dangling from their edges.

Tía came out of the kitchen with some people I didn't know and by the time she got done introducing everybody, only Papi and Mami were given the guided tour of the four-room, third-floor apartment. Me and Rafa joined the kids in the living room. Their parents wouldn't be over until late, but the kids had come over anyway. We were hungry, one of the girls explained, a pastelito in hand. The boy was about three years younger than me but the girl who'd spoken, Leti, was my age. She and another girl were on the sofa together and they were cute as hell.

Leti introduced them: the boy was her brother Wilquins and the other girl was her neighbor Mari. Leti had some serious tetas and I could tell that my brother was going to gun for her. His taste in girls was predictable. He sat down right between Leti and Mari, and by the way they were smiling at him I knew he'd do fine. Neither of the girls gave me more than a cursory one-two, which didn't bother me. Sure, I liked girls, but I was always too terrified to speak to them unless we were arguing or I was calling them stupidos, which was one of my favorite words that year. I turned to Wilquins and asked him what there was to do around here. Mari, who had the lowest voice I'd ever heard, said, He can't speak.

What does that mean?

He's mute.

I looked at Wilquins incredulously. He smiled and nodded, as if he'd won a prize or something.

Does he understand? I asked.

Of course he understands, Rafa said. He's not dumb.

I could tell Rafa had said that just to score points with the girls. Both of them nodded. Low-voice Mari said, He's the best student in his grade.

I thought, Not bad for a mute. I sat next to Wilquins. After about two seconds of TV, Wilquins whipped out a bag of dominoes and motioned to me. Did I want to play? Sure. Me and him played Rafa and Leti and we whupped their collective asses twice, which put Rafa in a real bad mood. Leti kept whispering into Rafa's ear, telling him it was okay.

In the kitchen I could hear my parents slipping into their usual modes. Papi's voice was loud and argumentative; you didn't have to be anywhere near him to catch his drift. And Mami, you had to strain your ears to hear her. I went into the kitchen a few times:

once so the tíos could show off how much bullshit I'd been able to cram in my head the last few years, another time for a bucket-sized cup of soda. Mami and Tía were frying tostones and the last of the pastelitos. She appeared happier now, and the way her hands worked on our dinner you would think she had a life somewhere else making rare and precious things. She nudged Tía every now and then, shit they must have been doing all their lives. As soon as Mami saw me, though, she gave me the eye. Don't stay long, that eye said. Don't piss your old man off.

Papi was too busy arguing about Elvis to notice me. Then somebody mentioned Cubans and Papi had plenty to say about them, too.

Maybe I was used to him. His voice — louder than most adults' — didn't bother me none, though the other kids shifted uneasily in their seats. Wilquins got up to raise the volume on the TV, but Rafa said, I wouldn't do that. Muteboy had some balls. He did it anyway and then sat down. Wilquins's pop came into the living room a second later, a bottle of Presidente in hand. That dude must have had Spider-senses or something. Did you raise that? he asked Wilquins, and Wilquins nodded.

Is this your house? Pa Wilquins asked. He looked ready to kick Wilquins's ass but he lowered the volume instead.

See, Rafa said. You nearly got your ass *kicked*.

I met the Puerto Rican woman right after Papi had gotten the van. He was taking me on short trips, trying to cure me of my vomiting. It wasn't really working but I looked forward to our trips, even though at the end of each one I'd be sick. These were the only times me and Papi did anything together. When we were alone he treated me much better, like maybe I was his son or something.

Before each drive Mami always crossed me.

Bendición, Mami, I would say.

She would kiss my forehead. Que Dios te bendiga. And then she would give me a handful of mentas because she wanted me to be okay. Mami didn't think these excursions would cure me, but the one time she had brought it up to Papi, he had told her to shut up and what did she know about anything anyway?

Me and Papi didn't talk much. We just drove around our neighborhood. Occasionally he would ask, How is it?

And I would nod, no matter how I felt.

One day I got sick outside of Perth Amboy. Instead of taking me home like he usually did, he went the other way on Industrial Avenue, stopping a few minutes later in front of a light blue house I didn't recognize. It reminded me of the Easter eggs we colored at school, the ones we threw out the bus windows at other cars.

The Puerto Rican woman was there and she helped me clean up. She had dry papery hands and when she rubbed the towel on my chest, she did it hard, like I was a bumper she was waxing. She was very thin and had a cloud of brown hair rising above her narrow face and the sharpest, blackest eyes you've ever seen.

He's cute, she said to Papi. What's your name? she asked me. Are you Rafa?

I shook my head.

Then it's Yunior, right?

I nodded.

You're the smart one, she said, suddenly happy with herself. Maybe you want to see my books?

They weren't hers. I recognized them as ones my father must have left in her house. Papi was a voracious reader, couldn't even go cheating without a paperback in his pocket.

Why don't you go watch TV? Papi suggested. He already had his hand on her ass and didn't care that I was watching. He was looking at her like she was the last piece of chicken on earth.

We got plenty of channels, she said. Use the remote if you want.

The two of them went upstairs and I was too scared of what was happening to poke around. I just sat there, ashamed, expecting something big and fiery to crash down on all our heads. I watched a whole hour of the news before Papi came downstairs and said, Let's go.

About two hours later the women laid out the food and like always nobody but the kids thanked them. It must have been some Dominican tradition or something. There was everything I liked — chicharrónes, fried chicken, tostones, sancocho, rice, fried cheese, yucca, avocado, potato salad, a meteor-sized hunk of pernil, even a tossed salad, which I could do without — but when I joined the other kids around the serving table, Papi said, Oh, no you don't, and took the paper plate out of my hand. His fingers weren't gentle.

What's wrong now? Tía asked, handing me another plate.

He ain't eating, Papi said. Mami pretended to help Rafa with the pernil.

Why can't he eat?

Because I said so.

The adults who didn't know us made like they hadn't heard a thing and Tío just smiled sheepishly and told everybody to go ahead and eat. All the kids — about ten of them now — trooped back into the living room with their plates aheaping, and all the adults ducked into the kitchen and the dining room, where the radio was playing loud-ass bachatas. I was the only one without a plate. Papi stopped me before I could get away from him. He kept his voice nice and low so nobody else could hear him.

If you eat anything, I'm going to beat you. ¿Entiendes?

I nodded.

And if your brother gives you any food, I'll beat him, too. Right here in front of everybody. ¿Entiendes?

I nodded again. I wanted to kill him, and he must have sensed it because he gave my head a little shove.

All the kids watched me come in and sit down in front of the TV.

What's wrong with your dad? Leti asked.

He's a dick, I said.

Rafa shook his head. Don't say that shit in front of people.

Easy for you to be nice when you're eating, I said.

Hey, if I was a pukey little baby, I wouldn't get no food either.

I almost said something back but I concentrated on the TV. I wasn't going to start it. No fucking way. So I watched Bruce Lee beat Chuck Norris into the floor of the Coliseum and tried to pretend that there was no food anywhere in the house. It was Tía who finally saved me. She came into the living room and said, Since you ain't eating, Yunior, you can at least help me get some ice.

I didn't want to, but she mistook my reluctance for something else.

I already asked your father.

She held my hand while we walked; Tía didn't have any kids but I could tell she wanted them. She was the sort of relative who always remembered your birthday but who you only went to visit because you had to. We didn't get past the first-floor landing before she opened her pocketbook and handed me the first of three pastelitos she had smuggled out of the apartment.

Go ahead, she said. And as soon as you get inside, make sure you brush your teeth.

Thanks a lot, Tía, I said.

Those pastelitos didn't stand a chance.

She sat next to me on the stairs and smoked her cigarette. All the way down on the first floor we could hear the music and the adults and the television. Tía looked a ton like Mami; the two of them were both short and light-skinned. Tía smiled a lot and that was what set them the most apart.

How is it at home, Yunior?

What do you mean?

How's it going in the apartment? Are you kids okay?

I knew an interrogation when I heard one, no matter how sugar-coated or oblique it was. I didn't say anything. Don't get me wrong, I loved my tía, but something told me to keep my mouth shut. Maybe it was family loyalty, maybe I just wanted to protect Mami or I was afraid that Papi would find out — it could have been anything really.

Is your mom all right?

I shrugged.

Have there been lots of fights?

None, I said. Too many shrugs would have been just as bad as an answer. Papi's at work too much.

Work, Tía said, like it was somebody's name she didn't like.

Me and Rafa, we didn't talk much about the Puerto Rican woman. When we ate dinner at her house, the few times Papi had taken us over there, we still acted like nothing was out of the ordinary. Pass the ketchup, man. No sweat, bro. The affair was like a hole in our living room floor, one we'd gotten so used to circumnavigating that we sometimes forgot it was there.

By midnight all the adults were getting crazy on the dance floor. I was sitting outside Tía's bedroom, where Madai was sleeping, trying not to attract attention. Rafa had me guarding the door; he and Leti were in there, too, with some of the other kids, getting busy no doubt. Wilquins had gone across the hall to bed, so I had only the roaches to mess around with.

Whenever I peered into the main room I saw about twenty moms and dads dancing and drinking beers. Every now and then some-body yelled, Quisqueya! And then everybody else would yell and stomp their feet. From what I could see, my parents seemed to be enjoying themselves.

Mami and Tía spent a lot of time side by side, whispering, and I kept expecting something to come of this, a brawl maybe. I'd never once been out with my family when it hadn't turned to shit. We were a Doomsday on wheels. We weren't even theatrical or straight crazy like other families. We fought like sixth graders, without any real dignity. I guess the whole night I'd been waiting for a blow-up, something between Papi and Mami. This was how I always fig-ured Papi would be exposed, out in public, where everybody would know.

You're a cheater!

But everything was calmer than usual. And Mami didn't look like she was about to say anything to Papi. The two of them danced every now and then, but they never lasted more than a song before Mami rejoined Tía in whatever conversation they were having.

I tried to imagine Mami before Papi. Maybe I was tired, or just sad, thinking about the way my family was. Maybe I already knew how it would all end up in a few years, Mami without Papi, and that was why I did it. Picturing her alone wasn't easy. It seemed like Papi had always been with her, even when we were waiting in Santo Domingo for him to send for us.

The only photograph our family had of Mami as a young woman, before she married Papi, was the one that somebody took of her at an election party, which I found one day while rummaging for money to go to the arcade. Mami had it tucked into her immigra-tion papers. In the photo, she's surrounded by laughing cousins I will never meet who are all shiny from dancing, whose clothes are rumpled and loose. You can tell it's night and hot and that the mosquitoes have been biting. She sits straight, and even in a crowd she stands out, smiling quietly like maybe she's the one every-body's celebrating. You can't see her hands but I imagined they're knotting a straw or a bit of thread. This was the woman my father met a year later on the Malecón, the woman Mami thought she'd always be.

Mami must have caught me studying her because she stopped what she was doing and gave me a smile, maybe her first one of the night. Suddenly I wanted to go over and hug her, for no other reason than I loved her, but there were about eleven fat jiggling bodies between us. So I sat down on the tiled floor and waited.

I must have fallen asleep, because the next thing I knew Rafa was kicking me and saying, Let's go. He looked like he'd been hitting off those girls; he was all smiles. I got to my feet in time to kiss Tía and Tío goodbye. Mami was holding the serving dish she had brought with her.

Where's Papi? I asked.

He's downstairs, bringing the van around. Mami leaned down to kiss me.

You were good today, she said.

And then Papi burst in and told us to get the hell downstairs before some pendejo cop gave him a ticket. More kisses, more handshakes, and then we were gone.

I don't remember being out of sorts after I met the Puerto Rican woman, but I must have been, because Mami only asked me questions when she thought something was wrong in my life. It took her about ten passes but finally she cornered me one afternoon when we were alone in the apartment. Our upstairs neighbors were beating the crap out of their kids, and me and her had been listening to it all afternoon. She put her hand on mine and said, Is everything okay, Yunior? Have you been fighting with your brother?

Me and Rafa had already talked. We'd been in the basement, where our parents couldn't hear us. He told me that yeah, he knew about her.

Papi's taken me there twice now.

Why didn't you tell me? I asked.

What the hell was I going to say?

I didn't say anything to Mami either. She watched me, very, very closely. Later I would think, maybe if I had told her, she would have confronted him, would have done something, but who can know these things? I said I'd been having trouble in school, and like that everything was back to normal between us. She put her hand on my shoulder and squeezed, and that was that.

We were on the turnpike, just past Exit 11, when I started feeling it again. I sat up from leaning against Rafa. His fingers smelled and he'd gone to sleep almost as soon as he got into the van. Madai was out, too, but at least she wasn't snoring.

In the darkness, I saw that Papi had a hand on Mami's knee and that the two of them were quiet and still. They weren't slumped back or anything; they were both wide awake, buckled into their seats. I couldn't see either of their faces and no matter how hard I tried I could not imagine their expressions. Every now and then the van was filled with the bright rush of somebody else's headlights. Finally I said, Mami, and they both looked back, already knowing what was happening.

DONALD HALL

From Willow Temple

FROM THE ATLANTIC MONTHLY

WE LIVED ON A FARM outside Abigail, Michigan, when I was a girl in the 1930s. My father was a Latin teacher, which was how I came to be called Camilla. I cannot say that I have lived up to the name of Virgil's warrior. My father served as the principal of Abigail High School, and we kept chickens and horses on our flat and scrubby land near the Ohio line. My father's schoolwork kept him busy, so we employed a succession of hired hands for chores around the farm. Many were drunks. A weekly rite, when I was small, was for my father to pay a fine on Monday morning — 6:00 A.M., before school — and drive the befuddled, thirsty, shamefaced hired man back home. When the advances for fines grew monstrous, so that our man was indentured a month ahead, he hopped a freight west. In hard times the quality of help increased, even as my father's salary and the price of eggs went down; he hired strong young men for three dollars a week, some of them sober. The poverty of those years touched everyone, including a protected child. I remember tramps coming to the back door; I remember men with gray faces whom my mother succored with milk and buttered bread. I can see one of them now, preserved among the rest because he addressed me rather than my mother. "It's hard, little girl. Could you spare a crust, little girl?"

The house was my mother's house. She was Ella, the bright face of our family, beautiful and lively — a lover of horses, poetry, and jokes. People said, lightly, that she married my father to hold herself down. I grew up loving my quiet father with a love that was equally quiet; I desperately loved my serene, passionate mother.

What a beauty she was. When I see reproduced a *Saturday Evening Post* cover from the 1930s, I see my mother's face: regular features, not large but strong, bold cheekbones with good coloring; dark short hair; fullish lips, deeply red without lipstick; large blue eyes, staring outward with a look both shy and erotic. When my mother walked into a group of strangers, the room hushed.

She had grown up with four sisters, isolated on a backcountry farm in Washtenaw County. The Great War was only a distant rumor. Her childhood was a clutch of girls, a female conspiracy on a remote, patchy forty acres, in a domain of one-room schools where half the pupils belonged to her own family. They made one another clothespin dolls for Christmas; they sewed and did fancywork in competition for their stepmother's praise; they passed their dreams and their dresses on to one another. How I wanted a little sister to pass my dresses and dolls on to! When my mother told me stories from her childhood, I heard themes repeated: the family was self-sufficient (I grew up reading and rereading *The Swiss Family Robinson*) and "got by on little." When she spoke of their genuine simplicity, she spoke with wonder, not with bitterness; she didn't make me feel guilty over my relative comfort. The Hulze farm never prospered as the Battells' — my father's family's — did for decades. The land was poor, but to survive by your own labor on your own land was triumph enough. Another theme was death, for she had lost a baby sister to a fever at eighteen months; and her mother, Patience, died of diabetes, not long before insulin was discovered, when my mother was nine. Two years later she acquired a stepmother, my grandmother Huldah, who was kindly but fierce, with a Christianity modeled on that of Massachusetts Bay in the seventeenth century. Like my father, my mother was an eldest child; she mothered her younger sisters even after Huldah's access, since Huldah quickly bore Herman Hulze two more daughters.

Life on the Hulze farm was hard — Monday washing, Tuesday ironing, Wednesday baking — but as my mother remembered it for me, it mustered grave satisfactions. Everyone worked equally, according to age and ability; everyone was clothed, warm, and well fed; in a venture of equal labor no one was dependent on another's largesse. Weekdays were half school, half work; the children, who rose at five, *after* their parents, did housework before school and darning or fancywork before bed. Saturday's chores finished the

week, and the family looked forward to a workless Sunday. Yet
Huldah's Sabbath was strenuous. Her church was two hours of
hellfire in the morning, with Christian Endeavor (hymns, visiting
speakers) at night. Sometimes Huldah searched out a Sunday afternoon church meeting, to occupy her family for an otherwise idle
moment.

An exception to my mother's largely female nation was a dear male
cousin whose story she told me as I grew older. Rudolph Howells
was her first cousin, two years older, her father's sister's boy, who
lived three miles down the road. Even at ages when boys and girls
avoid each other, Rudy and Ella played together. They hiked to
each other's houses, or barebacked a workhorse on a rare workless
weekday; or they met under a great willow beside a creek halfway
between them. Its shelter was their hideout, and they came to call
it Willow Temple. In the absence of telephones they exchanged
penny postcards to arrange their meetings. For my mother, isolated
among sisters in that flat countryside, the boy's friendship was
redemptive; Rudolph was the male of my mother's early life —
after her father, who was alternately working and asleep. For Rudy,
who was an only child, my mother provided the sole companionship close to his age. As she described him, Rudy sounded unnaturally solemn; it was Ella's childhood joy to bring out the child in
Rudolph, to set him giggling or dreaming. Rudy was a reader. He
brought books to my mother, who became a reader herself in order
to please him. In Willow Temple they recited for each other the
poems they had memorized at school and performed for Prize
Speaking — works by Whittier, Longfellow, Joaquin Miller, Edgar
Allan Poe, James Whitcomb Riley. My mother could say "Telling the
Bees" right through, without a mistake, when she was eighty.

Rudolph was a "scholar," as Michigan country people called a
serious student. In 1900 few from the farmland went to college.
After the Great War people began to think about college, and to
assume that Rudolph would attend the University of Michigan. As
my mother late in her life told stories about Rudolph, I understood
that for all his studiousness he felt some diffidence about his capaci-
ties. He worried that he would not do well at college. My mother
not only made him laugh but encouraged him to leave the countryside and enroll in Ann Arbor's domestic Athens. He would *excel*, she

told him. Then, doubtless, he would become a minister. What else did one go to college for? Doctor, lawyer, teacher, pastor. Rudy in his solemnity found a way to combine the romance of his reading — the South Seas, piracy, jungles of Africa — with his dark Christianity. Some speakers at Christian Endeavor were missionaries returned from outlandish places, where they had won souls to Christ, ministering to the pigtailed hordes of China and the naked savages of the Congo. Now they traveled the Protestant Midwest to raise money for hospitals that would treat leprosy and pellagra.

When he was fourteen, Rudy left his one-room school to attend an academy in the mill town of Trieste, eleven miles away. He endured his semi-exile — boarding weekdays and coming home for weekends — until he was sixteen. For two years my mother saw him at church every Sunday morning, and rarely at other moments except in summer. They wrote each other a midweek postcard. They remained so close that people teased them about being sweethearts, even about marrying — first cousins or not. My mother assured me that it would never have happened: they were too much brother and sister. One Sunday in the May when my mother turned fifteen, the church members packed picnics and lunched together in a field beside Goosewater Creek, not far from Willow Temple. Ella remembered Rudy at the picnic playing with a new baby, another cousin, by trundling her carriage fast and slow, making the baby Agnes jerk and laugh with abrupt stops and accelerations. After eating deviled eggs and pork sandwiches and rhubarb pie, Ella and Rudy took a long walk together, talking about their futures, continually brushing away mosquitoes. They tramped happily among the weed trees that grew along the creek, my mother remembered, and sat inside the green dome of Willow Temple. They spoke of the university and Ella's high school, where she took Latin because Rudy had recommended it. Ella told him jokes she had saved for him. Mostly they began, "A minister, a priest, and a Christian Science practitioner . . ." One story made him laugh until he wept; she could never remember which one. When she was terribly old, and dying, Ella still recalled the small yellow butterflies that had been abundant in the fields like migrant buttercups; she remembered the blue dress she wore, embroidered with red tulips.

That night, when Rudolph's ride came to take him back to Trieste, no one could find him. He was not in his room; he did not respond to his mother's "Yoo-hoo!" After half an hour his ride went off without him. His father and the hired man took lanterns from the barn and searched for him in the darkness among the outbuildings. Then they climbed the small pasture hill. I remember seeing that hill when I was a child. In my mind I can watch the yellow lanterns rise in the black evening, and hear the men's voices calling for him: "Rudolph! Ru-dee!" His parents were frightened; maybe Rudy had fallen taking a walk after five o'clock supper; maybe he had hit his head on a rock and lay somewhere unconscious. They summoned neighbor cousins to help.

Three miles away, asleep in bed, my mother knew nothing.

After an hour searching outside the house the men came back, thinking to look in the root cellar. It was Agnes's young father, cousin Michael, who found Rudolph where he had hanged himself in the attic. As Michael walked up the steep stairs with his lantern low, his face brushed against the boots. The impact pushed the boots away, and they swung back to hit him.

As long as any of his contemporaries lived, Rudolph's suicide was the subject of speculation. Rudolph — everyone repeated — was a sensible and lovable boy, affectionate if a little serious, "old for his age" but capable of playfulness. He loved his mother and father and his cousin Ella; he was a *happy* child. Ella's family reconstructed, by gradual accumulation of detail, the days and weeks before the tragedy occurred. No one could find anything that hinted of despair or violence. Why did a bright, cheerful, beloved seventeen-year-old boy hang himself in his attic? *Why? Why? Why?* Could it have been an accident? How could he tie a noose and slip it over his head by accident? People said, *It must have been something he read in a book.* They decided at the end of every discussion that reading stories caused Rudolph's death.

That Sunday night began the infection that throbbed and festered at the center of my mother's life. Although she was warm-hearted, charming, and funny, although most of her life she appeared serene or even content, I believe that a fever always burned inside her. What happened was so savage, and so inexplicable, that it never let her go. Over fifty and sixty and seventy years her incredulity remained intact. She wept when she told me this story, or made reference to it. "Oh, Camilla," she said, "why did it happen?"

In my sexually obsessed youth I tried out the notion that something had occurred or almost occurred inside Willow Temple. But my mother's continual, enormous astonishment — and her absence of guilt — convinced me that nothing untoward, or even unusual, had happened in Willow Temple on that Sunday afternoon. For Rudolph and Ella the erotic life concealed itself under hymns and petticoats.

Part of the story was how my mother first heard the news. Monday morning, ignorant of what had happened (ten years would pass before the Hulzes had a telephone), my mother took the seven o'clock train for Bosworth and its high school. Every school day of the year she and her sister Betty took the milk train. When they sat down and the locomotive jerked forward, behind them were two men who had boarded three miles north, at the depot near Rudolph's house. My mother heard Mr. Peabody say to Mr. Gross what a terrible thing it was when his own father, just last night, had had to cut Rudolph Howells down from a beam in the attic. Why would a fine boy like Rudy go and kill himself?

My fifteen-year-old mother alighted at the first stop, took the next train back, and went to bed. (Betty went on to school. It was part of the story, always, that Betty continued to school.) Ella vomited and for three days would not eat. She stayed home the rest of the school year, four weeks. She turned pale and lost weight; Dr. Fowles said that she was anemic. Once a week a Trieste butcher sent two quarts of steer's blood for Huldah to store in the icebox. My mother drank a tumbler of blood every day; it nauseated her, but mostly she kept it down. Once, she left her bed and slipped from the house for half a day — terrifying her father and Huldah — to walk by the creek until she came to Willow Temple, where she crept inside and howled hysterical tears. ("I thought he would be there," she told me when she was old. "*Camilla*, I thought he was *there*.") Thereafter her family contrived to keep her in bed. She failed all summer, eating little, until one evening she heard Huldah's harsh voice in the garden beyond her window telling a visitor, "We're going to lose our big girl."

This overhearing or eavesdropping appeared to startle my mother back to life. By the time school opened in September, she had become bright and energetic again — brighter and more energetic than before. After her mourning she turned from a shy fifteen-year-old into the creature who caused the intake of breath.

As her beauty became obvious for the first time, her youthful life began. She took part in high school literary and theatrical groups, as much as commuting allowed. A year later, in her senior year, she boarded in Bosworth weekdays. If a hayride or a square dance occurred on a Saturday night, she stayed over in town for the weekend, despite Huldah's disapproval. The summer after graduation, when she was seventeen, she took a job at Muehlig's department store in Ann Arbor, boarding with a family related to her mother.

It was clear, when my mother recollected, that Ann Arbor raised a pleasant devil in her. When another boarder arranged a blind date for her with a university student, she entered into a new life, and its excitement still reverberated when she was eighty and remembered those years. She became *popular,* a powerful word in the vocabulary of the time, and dated many young men. One fraternity (my father never belonged to one; to join would have been unthinkable) elected Ella Hulze its sweetheart, granting her an honor normally reserved for a sorority girl. She would have joined a sorority if she had been a student. (When I attended the university, I joined one and quit after a year.) My mother dated someone every night of the week, she told me, and her engagement book was full a month ahead. She made me laugh with her stories of boys she dated — a collateral Ford who drove a Stutz, a broker-to-be who waxed his red mustache into points, a fainting swain who sent long-stemmed roses to Muehlig's. "It was innocent," she told me when I was seventeen. Ten years later I reminded her of that word, when she stayed with me after my daughter's birth. She laughed. "It was *mostly* innocent, Camilla." She told me about driving to Chicago for a weekend in a roadster with two fraternity boys. They visited a speakeasy; having taken a room at the YWCA, she had to ring a bell to be let in at 3:00 A.M., and covered her mouth to disguise her breath. She returned to Ann Arbor on Monday at 7:00 A.M., to drink coffee and attend her counter at Muehlig's. A week later both boys died at dawn in the same roadster, careering off the road into a maple tree near Walled Lake after a night of Prohibition gin and jazz. When she met my father, as he shopped for Christmas presents for his family, my mother was ready to settle down. They were engaged by Easter. My mother was eighteen then, my father twenty-six.

She clerked in a department store; he was a graduate student in classical languages. People speak of the attraction of opposites. Opposites are attracted when each is anxious about its own character. (And I am their product, in old age still a woman anxious about the conflicts in her character.) I think of my father as he must have appeared in 1925. He came from country people, as she did, but he wore eyeglasses and lived for books — particularly books in ancient languages. My mother had taken Latin for two years of high school, but she stopped after Rudy died. How did my father find the courage to approach the beautiful Ella Hulze? I suppose his innocence was his courage; eight years older, bound to his library carrel, he would not have known that she was *popular.* Billy, or William, had reached the moment in his life, halfway through his last year of study, with a high school teaching job waiting for him, when he was ready for courtship and marriage. Through a legacy from his godmother, who had married into Flint's auto industry, he had $1,500, which would provide the down payment on a house with a mortgage at two and a half percent. Possibly his studies contributed to his infatuation: I laughed when I learned, not long before he died, that his final seminar at Michigan had examined Ovid's *Art of Love.* Like Ella, my father jolted himself into looking for an opposite. Then he met a beautiful girl, from a Michigan farm, selling scarves at Muehlig's.

Maybe William was not quite so opposite as he appeared to be. After all, he grew up outside Abigail on a hog farm — prosperous for many decades — that his parents and his bachelor brother worked until foreclosure in 1937. Billy became the Latinist — "William Hammersmith Battell," as his diplomas read, and "foremost scholar in the history of Abigail High," the *Abigail Journal* called him — who majored in classics at the University of Michigan. He was the first in his family to finish high school, and, of course, college. After he made Phi Beta Kappa, in 1922, he returned to raise pigs with his father and his brother. He did this on principle, full of Roman republican notions; he enjoyed tales of colonial American blacksmiths who read forty lines of Hebrew before dawn. A pig farmer who translated Latin poetry seemed no anomaly to my father.

But my father was not a skillful farmer. When pig raising did not take his full attention, he felt inadequate or hypocritical; in

his absentmindedness he failed his agrarian ideals. The Latin language, and only the Latin language, enthralled him. Exhausted
after a day among hogs, he sat by the oil lamp placed on a central
table in the small living room, reading Tacitus while his mother
darned and his brother studied baseball scores and his father
drifted into sleep. In Virgil's *Georgics* the Michigan farm crossed
paths with the study of Latin. As a young man my father dreamed of
translating the *Georgics,* adapting them to southern Michigan, but
the farming tired him out; he never completed the first book.

By 1925 the family realized that the Battell farm could not support four adults. The agricultural depression had started a decade
before the rest of the country crashed, and the once rich farm
began to fail. Somebody had to leave the place and get a job. Then
came the disaster, as my father always called it. One of his chores
was to feed the piglets once they were weaned from their great
mothers, carrying buckets of corn from the Battell cribs. The
stored feed nourished a guerrilla army of rats. One morning my
young father, weary after staying up with Virgil half the night, fed
rat poison to sixty-seven young pigs. The whole family wept, even
his hard father and stolid brother, as they dug a long trench on a
rainy day and buried their hopes for a prosperous or even a toler-
able year. When he was an old man, he still shook his head in
melancholy guilt as he spoke of his lethal error. "The bags were
different colors and sizes. The pellets were gray. How could I have
done it?" I remember him at seventy-four, still lamenting his terrible mistake; he could see the pale young bodies in the rain, and
puddles gathering in the trench. My mother, the family wit and
teaser, knew better than to joke about the disaster. But once, when
my father was soaring high in self-confident absentmindedness,
and made tea by pouring hot coffee over tea leaves, she called him
"the Great Poisoner." He laughed, I remember, but looked abashed
and sorrowful.

After the disaster the Battell family took out a mortgage to provide capital for my father's M.A. at the university. Back in Ann
Arbor, my father undertook courses in education as well as Greek
and Latin, so that he might become a high school teacher. Two
months after he returned to his studies, he met my mother in
Muehlig's. The elderly Miss Wuestefeld, of Abigail High, who had
taught Billy, had told him that she would hold on until William was

finished with graduate school. Thus my father revisited, ten years afterward, the classroom where he had learned to chant *amo, amas, amat,* eagerly leading new students to recite *amo, amas, amat.* It was a secure position, as everyone knew: "There'll always be work for a Latin teacher." A monthly check would repay his family's bank loan and help to repair his conscience, mourning after the poisoned piglets. In Abigail his old schoolmates would breed him pupils and call him "professor" without irony. My parents had been married three years, and I was a baby, when the position of principal opened. My father was chosen not because of his administrative ability but because of his sex. Most teachers were women, but principals were men; only men could deal with unruly boys. Maybe my mother was unruly too.

My early life was happy — or at least it was *even,* like a plain as it steadily upthrust a crop of corn. The radio and the automobile were our wonders, and I measure my childhood by the names of products: the Crosley, the Emerson, the Philco; the Model T, the brief blue Chevrolet, the Model A, which never broke down as we took rides every warm-weather Sunday afternoon, adventurously speeding at forty miles an hour over Michigan backcountry roads, knowing where we were headed without being sure how we would get there. My parents sat together in the front seat and I sat in the back, scooting from side to side in my Sunday dress as the landscape drew me. Having clear access to both sides was a luxury of only-child-hood. On these Sunday drives my parents spoke little. I watched my father's mild, bespectacled eyes take in an Angus herd; I gazed at my mother's poised, beautiful profile as her face turned from side to side, calm or complacent, accepting what the route offered. Every Sunday we rode two or three hours over southern Michigan and northern Ohio, looking at cattle, chickens, turkeys, pigs, and horses. When we had driven as far as we would go, and started back, my father would search out an ice cream parlor and treat us to a sundae.

Always we returned in order to ride our horses for an hour before Sunday night supper, which was sandwiches around the radio. I cannot remember when the Jack Benny show began broadcasting, but in my old age Jack Benny's running gags, remembered, taste of cream cheese and crushed pineapple. My mother and I rode together after school in good weather. On Saturdays as well

as Sundays all three of us saddled up: my father's horse, the roan
stallion, Bigboy, unruly like a high school boy; my mother's Morgan
mare, Benita; and my multicolor pony, Skylark, who was large
enough to carry my slight figure until I was sixteen. These handsome creatures were the enduring quotidian romance of my girl-
hood. After school I curried Skylark's flanks until my mother was
ready for our amble along a stony road at the side of a hayfield.
Both my parents grew up with workhorses, and would have missed
equine company were it not for these three, stabled in the barn
adjacent to our chickens. I'm not sure why we kept chickens, except
that my father considered farming a *good thing* — and he no longer
cared to raise pigs. Selling eggs and broilers paid for the hired men
and the horses.

When my mother sat on a horse, she looked not like a Michigan
farmgirl but like the Honorable Lady Something; she wore a horse
the way a model wears clothes. My father was unpredictably impetuous, an excellent rider on a capricious, powerful horse. Bigboy
liked to run, and would have run away if my father had not been so
masterful; they galloped ahead of us and galloped back, pulling up
in a froth of high spirits. One of my mother's teasing names for my
father was Billy Cowboy.

In my earliest recollections my parents acted like lovers, if not quite
like a pastoral shepherd and his shepherdess. They were polite, in
the old-fashioned way, but they took every opportunity to touch
each other. When they didn't want me to understand something,
they talked in Latin, or something Latinish enough to confuse me.
My father delighted, in his mild, fussy way, in their domestic classi-
cism. *Equus* was an early word, not to mention *amor.* Before I was
seven, I knew that *via* meant both "road" and that we would take a
ride in the Model A. Horses were every day and the Model A was
Sundays. I cherished those afternoons in the back seat. I cherish
them still, as I approach my seventies. In my life, when I have been
especially troubled — my daughter died in childhood; I divorced
my husband — I have found myself for comfort playing back mental films of those afternoons in the back seat of a Ford, exploring
the flat country roads.

Driving the car, my father, I imagine, daydreamed Latin. I have
no notion what my mother dreamed. Maybe she thought of my

father, or of Rudolph. Because Rudolph was the source of my mother's Latin, and because he and my father were both serious, even solemn, I came to think of Rudolph as an antecedent to my father. I considered that my mother made up for losing Rudolph when she married William. I was too shy to advance this theory to her until she was well into her eighties. "Perhaps," she said, but my notion clearly annoyed her. "They did not look alike at all," she said, and a moment later she wiped her eyes.

My mother learned to drive — a fairly advanced idea for a small-town housewife in 1933 — in order to go to the library, so that she and I could stock up on books. I progressed from dog-and-cat books to a wonderful poetry anthology called *Silver Pennies*. Next I found novels, from *Rebecca of Sunnybrook Farm* to *Black Beauty*, with excursions into the Nancy Drew series, and started to inhabit the house of stories, in love with the improbable and the heroic. My mother enjoyed novels and biographies but cared more for poetry. She deserted Whittier for Wordsworth, and Longfellow for Keats, but she also admired the moderns: Sara Teasdale, Edna St. Vincent Millay, John Masefield, Elinor Wylie, Edwin Arlington Robinson. She wore out a copy of *Tristram*. Later she found Robert Frost — my father admired Frost, the classical side — and the young Stephen Vincent Benét. It would have been too much for her to admire T. S. Eliot or Wallace Stevens; later, when I tried them on her (I was at college), she shook her head regretfully.

My father reread Virgil, Horace, and Catullus; he preferred Cicero's letters to his orations; he worked away at Thucydides, read journals of classical studies — and increasingly took part in a battle over the place of classical studies in the American high school curriculum. Voices in the 1930s proclaimed that learning Latin was impractical, that our youth, rather than waste valuable time on dead languages, should concentrate on arithmetic, mechanical drawing, and business letters. To my father, the suggestion was retrograde. In Abigail he tried to institute at least one year of Latin for all students, with four years for those few students aiming toward college. Two years of Latin were required for admission to the University of Michigan.

He gave speeches after lunch at the Rotary Club; he wrote letters to the *Abigail Journal*. Although principal, he still taught Latin, and because he taught with enthusiasm, Abigail's Latin courses were well subscribed. Elsewhere the walls were falling. When an old Detroit high school chose to remove "Classical Academy" from its name, he wrote a letter to the *Detroit News,* ending, "If our civilization is to survive encroaching darkness, Latin and Greek must keep alight the fires of learning, shining beacons that keep us to the path." He signed it "William Hammersmith Battell, Principal, Abigail High School." If I let him sound pompous, remember that he pursued a passion.

With his duties as chairman of the Michigan Classical Association, and as secretary of the Great Lakes Latin Society, he paid less attention to our farm, haphazardly preserved by the succession of hired men. The first I remember is Herbert Ganke, an old man who talked to himself while he worked. He was courtly to me and my mother, and worked slowly but steadily. Once a month he got into trouble. Finally he passed out in a back yard after stealing clothes from the family's clothesline. Later we hired boys who worked a week or two and vanished; a sweet hobo named Tom lasted a whole winter, sleeping under the eaves in the hired man's room. He disappeared after one payday, around the time the snowdrops poked up. A shy, handsome local boy named Raymond was marvelous with horses, and could even control the volatile Bigboy. Raymond was illiterate, my mother discovered, and she taught him to read.

Late afternoons, when my father came home from school, and my mother and I were back from our ride, he changed into overalls, consulted with the latest hand, and checked out the hens while my mother cooked supper. I attended the one-room school a quarter of a mile away, and sometimes brought a friend, Caroline or Rebecca, back to play; but on rainy days, or when I played alone with my dollhouse or read stories, I interrupted myself to visit the barn and the outbuildings with Herbert or Raymond or Miller, to curry Skylark and feed apples to Skylark, Benita, and (carefully) Bigboy. Some hands were grumpy, possibly not fond of small girls, as I followed them around; others took the opportunity to smoke cigarettes and tell the stories of their lives. With Raymond, I was in love; after school I liked it when Raymond sat at the kitchen table doing his ABCs under my mother's supervision, reading my dog-and-cat books, moving on to *Silver Pennies.*

*

When I was eight or nine, my father's advocacy of classical studies
became his unrelenting obsession. In memory his passion seems to
have occupied most of my childhood; in reality it probably took two
years. Every night he read bulletins from the Department of Education, or a mimeographed sheet from the university's classics department, or *The American Classicist*. Every day the mail brought letters,
bulletins, and notices. William Hammersmith Battell founded the
Southeastern Michigan Secondary School Classical Studies Association. When he came home from school and went to his desk, he
studied not Horace but statistics about the classroom study of Horace's language. My father ignored my mother and me in order to
defend Cicero in the senate of popular opinion. My mother and I
still took our afternoon rides on Skylark and Benita, sometimes
with Raymond on Bigboy, who needed the exercise, but no longer
did the family go on Sunday afternoon joyrides in the Model A.
Sometimes my father brought me with him on a Saturday afternoon in the car to visit someone engaged in the same struggle; they
had long, urgent conversations while I tried talking with strange
children or knitting mittens or reading my book. My mother stayed
home. She read her poets; she kept up with darning and the prodi-
gious canning of summer. She again took up quilting, which she
had learned as a girl, to occupy her hours while my father spent
himself elsewhere. He approved of quilting — it was classic if not
Latin — but his enthusiasm was principled. Ella lacked theoretical
passions. When her spectacular patchwork took a red ribbon at the
Michigan State Fair in 1937, it was clear that the Idea of Quilthood
— not this extravagant bright assemblage — exalted my father's
soul. "*Splendidissimus,*" he said.

Often my mother and I remained alone together on weekends, quiet in the living room, or riding over dusty fields, while my
father drove overnight up to Mackinac Island to chair an emergency meeting called by Michigan Concerned Latinists. No longer
did my parents touch each other when they passed in the hallway. My father's eyes behind rimless glasses gazed into the distance, shiny with urgency. My mother's beautiful eyes looked low at
hooked rugs and waxed floors, and I heard her sighing, sighing,
sighing. I knew she was unhappy, and I sighed as I heard her sigh.

For my tenth birthday, in March of 1938, my parents gave me
the sheepdog I had begged for. Memory of Dido as a puppy allows

me to date events of that spring, because I recollect her with a love purer than any other; Skylark was a dear, but did not follow me to school and to bed. At the library I discovered Albert Payson Terhune's *Lad: A Dog* and its siblings. With my mother I trained Dido; I slept with her; I grew up with her — and when she died of old age at the farm (I was in graduate school, in a female co-op that forbade animals), a part of me died with her.

A month or two after my birthday I woke to hear my parents quarreling. I slept lightly that spring, for Dido wriggled under the covers or sometimes signaled that she needed to go out. It wasn't an argument that I heard first; it was the sound of my father crying unmitigated tears — a sound I had never before heard. He was not an unemotional man, as men went in those days, and I had heard him weep over a friend's death; but that night I heard a terrible sound — my father's wail of utter misery, as he gagged and coughed and spluttered. My heart pounded and I left my bed in order to run to their room, but then my mother's soft, continual murmur — controlled, persistent — held me back and calmed me, as it was intended to calm my father. I had no notion of the reason for his tears. I heard no words from him except "Ella" among the cries, and "Ella" repeated. When I made out her words, I heard her say that she loved him — but the words carried a cadence of withholding, like "anyway" or "still" or "despite everything." She was trying to console him, but in her tone I heard something I had never heard before, as chilly as a wheat field in January.

For some nights — a week? a month? — I stayed awake deliberately in order to listen. I could not hear everything they said, and maybe I slept through a night or two, though I doubt it. I heard enough. With Dido's wriggling help, I conspired to hear my new parents, my parents as I had never known them. After years of our daily routine — farm, school, horses, chickens, canning, quilting, Sunday rides, radio, Virgil — I entered a moonless darkness of conspiracy as frigid as the stars. Everywhere I went, I carried with me this enormous debilitating secret, something I could not speak of to anyone — not to Rebecca in the hayloft, not to my teacher at school, not to my cousins.

Night after night, when they thought I was asleep, I heard them quarrel. Sometimes they attacked each other. My mother's voice rose and I heard her use the word "divorce," a notion I scarcely understood. I heard my father say, "I'll take the child," and I realized they were talking about me. Increasingly now they mentioned "him," and I became aware that my mother loved someone other than my father. I hugged Dido so hard that she made a squeaking noise and then licked my face. Lying in bed with my dog, my heart pounding, I knew whom my mother loved. Only a short time before, just after my birthday, I had come home from school to find my mother agitated, not looking at me, running back and forth to tidy or do small chores. She told me that Raymond — the boy she had taught to read — no longer worked for us and that old Ferdinand was back, to fill in for a while. I had never liked Ferdinand, who didn't like children or perhaps girls, and I adored Raymond, so I burst into tears. My mother turned on me in a rage (something she never did, not even when I broke a cup of wedding china) and shouted, "Go to your room!"

It was Raymond whom my mother loved instead of my father. That Raymond was ten years younger than she was — feckless though sweet, illiterate, diffident, from a family that lived in a shack, with a father often in jail — did not then occur to me. Later I put things in their places: my father had raised himself up, become learned, dedicated himself to the finer things, become "professor" in Abigail; how it must have pummeled him, along with profounder jealousy, that my mother picked *Raymond* to love — Raymond who had never graduated from grammar school. Doubtless my mother loved Raymond at least partly because he was so pitiable, so unlike my distinguished father. Something about Raymond was pathetic or beaten, even hangdog. A combination of prettiness and need made him so attractive.

Listening to my stranger-parents, in their hurts and deliberations, I felt terror and misery. But I also felt exalted: I was a romantic figure, like a child in a book, like the match girl in the snow, a wistful, pathetic product of adult abandonment or deceit. In my conspiracy or secret knowledge, in my separation from my parents and the rest of my world — friends and school and house, everyone but Dido, who listened to my complaints ecstatic with adoration — I felt myself the locus of an extraordinary fate. I thrilled myself with the vision of my despair. I felt ennobled by self-pity and by awareness of, and admiration for, my mother's recklessness, beauty, abandon, and sin.

One night I heard my father say "Damn you to hell!" — he never swore — and laugh when my mother took offense. I seemed to have been stolen by gypsies. My parents had been gypsies always, disguising themselves as ordinary Michigan people. During the day — I was sleepy, of course; my mother was puzzled when I dozed in my school dress on the hearthrug after school — my parents tried to carry on as they always had. I was impressed by the aplomb with which they behaved, "for the child's sake." Their ability to deceive, to be utterly different by day and by night, carved itself into my soul. My father came home from school, put on his overalls, did a few chores with Ferdinand, spoke politely with my mother over dinner, and asked Camilla about her schoolwork. We were a conspiracy of three, a play for three characters. I pretended or dissembled as much as they did, and rejoiced in the skill of my deceit. I pretended ignorance or innocence while I knew for certain that my parents were cruel enemies inside the appearance of their marriage. Although they continued as if they cared for me, I was alien and an encumbrance. We were three strangers, as only I was aware.

Officially I did not know the facts of life, as we called sex in those years, because parents waited to tell a daughter until she was ready to menstruate. But as a farm child I had watched barnyard copulation. Already I was attempting to read novels written for adults in which men and women — when they loved each other, whether they were married or not — disappeared into the privacy of a blank page to do something that confirmed their love and made for mayhem. I knew what they did; it was wicked and it was wonderful, the most extreme of pleasures and the worst. I knew that my mother and Raymond — while my father and I were at school, or on weekends when my father and I visited someone — did what the rooster did with the hens; what the stallion Bigboy attempted with the neutered mare Benita.

One night, as my parents spoke in bed, I understood that they were approaching a crisis. The next night at nine o'clock Raymond would come to the house and the three of them would talk. From what was said I gathered that they would decide about divorce and about "the child." The next night, after dinner, my father proposed that we ride in the car. It was unheard of that I stay up after seven on a school night; they wanted to tire me out so that I would sleep soundly. Disingenuously I remarked on my late bedtime, and in a single voice my parents said that it didn't matter, that I could sleep in and be late for school. They seemed unaware how unprecedented their behavior was.

That night I did not need to struggle to stay awake; I set my bedroom door ajar and crouched on the floor with my ear at the opening, hugging Dido, so that I would miss nothing. I heard Raymond — he had an unusual gait — walk up the path. I heard him enter; I heard perfunctory, conventional exchanges. How frightened Raymond must have been. I could imagine his drawn, white, lean, weak, handsome face. I heard my father's level voice, grave and formal; I heard my mother weeping; I heard a new sound that I could identify as Raymond's tears. Later I heard my father weeping also — three grownups crying in the living room at the foot of the long stairs.

Maybe I dropped off to sleep, leaning between the doorjamb and Dido, because the next sound I heard was a shout of rage or despair, and then came hurried steps and the door slamming and steps running outside. Raymond had run away. I pushed my face around the jamb of the door and saw that my father and mother stood side by side. Suddenly I heard my father scream, "Bitch!" The front door hurtled open, my father shouted, "I'll never be back!" — and I heard the door slam again. I crept to the top of the stairs. My mother stood in the doorway as the Model A started and my father drove away. When she turned back to enter the living room, I stood halfway down the stairs in my white nightgown, a fierce Virgilian warrior who had read Victorian romances. "I have known all," I said.

Within two months my father quit all his associations and societies. In a year his subscriptions had run out. He dismissed Ferdinand, came home earlier from school, and did long weekend chores, farming without help. Later he canceled his annual order for three hundred chicks and let his poultry venture dwindle to eggs for our household. He traded Bigboy for an older, more tractable gelding called Rusty, and we three rode together again.

The night of the confrontation my father could not have stayed away for long. We ate breakfast together the next morning; I remember because we had pancakes, a rarity usually saved for birthdays. In my ten-year-old cynicism I made note of our treat. My mother never looked me in the eye; my father praised the pancakes and left quickly, but behaved toward me with his competent affectation of ordinariness, which let me understand that my mother had not spoken of my eavesdropping.

When she saw me on the stairs, as she turned back from the door, her face went dead white. After I made my rehearsed announcement, she struggled quickly to recover herself, and asked questions to find out what I knew. At once I dissembled; her aspect terrified me, and in order to bring blood back into her face I lied or played innocent. When she asked me what I had known, I answered only that my father was not coming back. My mother assured me, grasping for an appearance of calm, that he didn't mean it. Forcing a frail smile, she said, "He'll be back soon, Camilla." They had quarreled about the horses; she wanted him to sell Bigboy . . . When I kept my silence then, my secrecy resumed itself forever. My secrecy dug itself a lightless castle inside the hill. My secrecy bricked up a dungeon door behind which something still languishes.

Our lives restored themselves — at least theirs did, or seemed to. I doubt that my mother saw Raymond again. Four or five years later he was killed in the war; I know that much only because his name with its gold star ornaments the scroll by the Abigail Town Hall. If anyone else came into my mother's life, later or earlier, I never knew it. My father went back to his Latin classes and his school administration. Every day after chores he sat down to his books, Lucretius more than Virgil, Tacitus more than Livy, some Horace but never Ovid. In the evenings he studied while my mother quilted or revisited her poets, or read novels aloud to my father and me: Dickens, Mark Twain, early Steinbeck. After a while they were touching each other again; I watched with careful, secretive eyes. Two years later my mother had a hysterectomy and told me I would remain an only child.

Surely I was changed forever. Life at the farm was calm, but I lived elsewhere in my fancy. I absented myself by reading stories, imagining myself a reckless heroine or a pathetic victim. Outside the house of fiction I was chronically restless. Nothing in life, I knew, was what it appeared to be. When I read a story by Nathaniel Hawthorne, I recognized the minister and his pious congregation who met at midnight in the woods to celebrate Mass for the devil. I knew that by universal conspiracy we agreed to deny the secret wickedness of every human being. We needed, every hour, to understand that the fabric of routine covered unseen deceptions and enormities. We also needed to remember that the cloth must show no rips or tears, and that this covering was as real as anything. I admired the fabrics my father and mother wove, whatever might throb or coil underneath the cloth.

When I left home, at eighteen, to attend the University of Michigan, I contrived to continue the life of fiction. I delighted in keeping two or three boyfriends at the same time; my schemes provided opportunity for plot-making. Majoring in English, I found Henry James, and wrote an honors thesis on *What Maisie Knew* — and I knew what Maisie knew better than my teachers did. My parents were pleased with my academic success. My father offered to finance a Ph.D. if I wished to enter his profession as a college teacher, but I wanted to write rather than to talk about the writing of others. I won a Hopwood in fiction, took an M.A. in library science, and spent many years working in the library at Barnaby Academy in Grosse Arbor, south of Detroit — a servant in the house of fiction, and in the houses of history, poetry, and biography. I found it less necessary to dissemble in my private life as I plotted and published my own literary fictions. Critics sometimes wondered at the violence in my stories, not aware of my provenance as a warrior.

My history is not especially interesting; nor was my parents' history, so far as I can tell, after the incident of Raymond. They lived the even life of the cornfields, with their horses and Chevrolets, with their quilts and classical studies. I visited sometimes for weekends. Sometimes we met in Detroit or Ann Arbor for a play or a concert. When I married, they approved of my husband, and when Valerie was born, my mother spent two weeks with us, sleeping on the sofa, to help me out. We lived in a dormitory then, because my husband taught French at the academy, and my mother's aging beauty did not escape the attention of the sixteen-year-olds on our hall. During the long illness of my daughter — she contracted leukemia at five, when medicine seldom cured leukemic children — my parents tendered comfort and support. They took a new mortgage after paying off the old, to help with expenses; more important, they supplied their presence, their grief, and their abundant tears.

Our marriage could not survive Valerie's death. My husband and I could scarcely look at each other, and both of us found comfort elsewhere. I fell in love with a student, as it happens, and caused considerable suffering. When my ex-husband, Emil, suddenly flew off to teach at the American School in Beirut, the football coach's ex-wife went with him. Emil subsequently achieved fame, if that's the word: three and a half years as a hostage; freedom; talk shows; a book, in which "an early marriage" received mention.

I remained for two decades in the Barnaby library; the school authorities never acknowledged my escapade — if they ever knew. I settled down among the books and the bookish boys. My fiction enjoyed some success, so the English department borrowed me to teach a writing class. When I was forty-five, I married a widower retired from Ford, a rare executive who loved theater and literature, and we led a good life together until he died, nine years later. I found relative comfort in middle age, as I suppose my parents did.

But I need to say: even through the worst times — torments and disasters; losses; gains that were worse than losses — I kept on loving my parents. Whatever they did in the dark of the moon, they performed as well as they could in daylight. I honored their brave, sad endeavor. When I sought calm, waiting for electroshock during depression in the worst years, I thought of Sunday rides in the Model A — the back of my mother's neck and my father's trim haircut.

When Latin went down to defeat after the war, my father withdrew from teaching but remained principal of Abigail High until he retired, at sixty-five, the subject of farewell banquets and testimonials. He lived for eleven more years, pruning fruit trees and raising berries on the farm he had brought his bride to. Occasionally he worked at translating Lucretius into blank verse, a project with which my mother helped; her ear for iambic pentameter was more secure than my father's. I keep the unfinished manuscript, with its fussy Victorian diction. When he died, my mother remained on the old place; I moved there when she was eighty, about five years after my second husband died. I read *Tristram* aloud to her, along with *Rabbit, Run*. We walked every day in the pine woods that grew where hayfields had been. We drove to Ann Arbor for the bookstores, and visited Muehlig's, which appeared to have shrunk. We drove to Detroit to see the Rivera murals again. In desultory fashion I finished a quilt she had started, and I held my mother's hand when she died, last year, at eighty-seven. I board my horse at a neighbor's farm; my latest sheepdog is another Dido; I live in the house where everything happened.

Or almost everything. In her last years my mother kept returning in her mind to her cousin Rudolph, and told me much of what I recounted earlier. I listened hard to understand her, Ella still beautiful in the noble bones of her lean ninth-decade face. When I heard her speak of Rudy's young pedantry, expressed in bookishness and missionary Christianity, I thought of my father, although my father was never troubled by diffidence. Then I made the association that annoyed her. Once, as she spoke of Rudy, she revealed something else, or two things at once: Rudolph's eyes, she said, were a blue-gray one could never forget — light and mild, yet so piercing that they were painful to look at. She remembered such eyes in one other face only — that of a farmhand named Raymond, she said, whom I had probably forgotten.

Her mind remained sharp, although she sometimes wandered among episodes of the past. "Nothing happened," she told me during the last month of her life, "in Willow Temple that day." I knew what day she meant. "But maybe he felt something," she said, and stopped speaking.

"Maybe he wanted something to happen?" I said.

"I've thought so," she said. "Maybe he felt something in his trousers. I've wondered so." I held her hand. "It could have been something as small as that." Then her old humor asserted itself: "Not that I had *witnessed* his dimensions!" She laughed her trim laugh. "It was so long ago," she said. "He wanted so much to go to China. What if something *had* happened in Willow Temple? Sometimes I think he never died." She shook her head to deny dementia. "Sometimes I think he never lived — or that I never lived, or your father. How preposterous we are. Jokes and disasters, that's all there are. Is." Her tone suggested that she spoke without consequence. "The world is *arbitrary*," she went on. "Why did I work at Muehlig's? Why did the pigs die? Why do poets write poems? If insulin had been discovered, I would never have known Huldah; I might have been a Christian. Why did Raymond put a noose over his head?"

Some mistakes you don't point out. Some mistakes lack great implication, though I suspect that nothing is wholly arbitrary — not mistaken names or poisoned pigs or leukemia or a kidnapping in Beirut. The latest Dido let me understand that she wanted to go outside, and I took her walking past fallen outbuildings into the new wood.

Killing Babies

FROM THE NEW YORKER

WHEN I GOT OUT of rehab for the second time, there were some legal complications, and the judge — an old jerk who looked like they'd just kicked him out of the Politburo — decided I needed a sponsor. There was a problem with some checks I'd been writing for a while there when all my resources were going up the glass tube, and since I didn't have a record except for traffic infractions and a juvenile possession when I was fifteen, the court felt inclined to mercy. Was there anybody who could speak up for me, my attorney wondered, anybody financially responsible? Philip, I said, my brother Philip. He's a doctor.

So Philip. He lived in Detroit, a place I'd never been to, a place where it gets cold in winter and the only palm trees are under glass in the botanical gardens. It would be a change, a real change. But a change is what I needed, and the judge liked the idea that he wouldn't have to see me in Pasadena anymore and that I'd have a room in Philip's house with Philip's wife and my nephews, Josh and Jeff, and that I would be gainfully employed doing lab work at Philip's obstetrical clinic for the princely sum of six dollars and twenty-five cents an hour.

So Philip. He met me at the airport, his thirty-eight-year-old face as trenched with anal-retentive misery as our father's was in the year before he died. His hair was going, I saw that right away, and his glasses were too big for his head. And his shoes — he was wearing a pair of brown suede boatlike things that would have had people running for the exits at the Rainbow Club. I hadn't seen him in six years, not since the funeral, that is, and I wouldn't have even recognized him if it wasn't for his eyes — they were just like mine, as blue and icy as a bottle of Aqua Velva. "Little brother," he said, and he tried to gather a smile around the thin flaps of his lips while he stood there gaping at me like somebody who hadn't come to the airport specifically to fetch his down-on-his-luck brother and was bewildered to discover him there.

"Philip," I said, and I set down my two carry-on bags to pull him to me in a full-body, back-thumping, chest-to-chest embrace, as if I was glad to see him. But I wasn't glad to see him. Not particularly. Philip was ten years older than me, and ten years is a lot when you're a kid. By the time I knew his name he was in college, and when I was expressing myself with my father's vintage Mustang, a Ziploc baggie of marijuana, and a can of high-gloss spray paint he was in medical school. I'd never much liked him and he felt about the same toward me, and as I embraced him there in the Detroit airport I wondered how that was going to play out over the course of the six months the judge had given me to stay out of trouble and make full restitution or serve the next six in jail.

"Have a good flight?" Philip asked when I was done embracing him.

I stood back from him a moment, the bags at my feet, and couldn't help being honest with him; that's just the way I am. "You look like shit, Philip," I said. "You look like Dad just before he died — or maybe after he died."

A woman with a big shining planetoid of a face stopped to give me a look, then hitched up her skirt and stamped on by in her heels. The carpeting smelled of chemicals. Outside the dirt-splotched windows was snow, a substance I'd had precious little experience of. "Don't start, Rick," Philip said. "I'm in no mood. Believe me."

I shouldered my bags, stooped over a cigarette, and lit it just to irritate him. I was hoping he'd tell me there was a county ordinance against smoking in public places and that smoking was slow suicide, from a physician's point of view, but he didn't rise to the bait. He just stood there, looking harassed. "I'm not starting," I said. "I'm just . . . I don't know. I'm just concerned, that's all. I mean, you look like shit. I'm your brother. Shouldn't I be concerned?"

I thought he was going to start wondering aloud why *I* should be concerned about *him*, since I was the one on the run from

an exasperated judicial system and twelve thousand and some-
odd dollars in outstanding checks, but he surprised me. He just
shrugged and shifted that lipless smile around a bit and said,
"Maybe I've been working too hard."

Philip lived on Washtenaw Street, in an upscale housing development called Washtenaw Acres, big houses set back from the street
and clustered around a lake glistening with black ice under a weak
sky and weaker sun. The trees were stripped and ugly, like dead
sticks rammed into the ground, and the snow wasn't what I'd expected. Somehow I'd thought it would be fluffy and soft, movie
snow, big pillows of it cushioning the ground while kids whooshed
through it on their sleds, but it wasn't like that at all. It lay on the
ground like a scab, clots of dirt and yellow weed showing through in
mangy patches. Bleak, that's what it was, but I told myself it was
better than the Honor Rancho, a whole lot better, and as we pulled
into the long sweeping driveway to Philip's house I put everything I
had into feeling optimistic.

Denise had put on weight. She was waiting for us inside the door
that led from the three-car garage into the kitchen. I didn't know
her well enough to embrace her the way I'd embraced Philip, and
I have to admit I was taken aback by the change in her — she was
fat, there was nothing else to say about it — so I just filtered out
the squeals of welcome and shook her hand as if it was something
I'd found in the street. Besides which, the smell of dinner hit me
square in the face, so overpowering it almost brought me to my
knees. I hadn't been in a real kitchen with a real dinner in the oven
since I was a kid and my mother was alive, because after she died,
and with Philip away, it was just my father and me and we tended to
go out a lot, especially on Sundays.

"You hungry?" Denise asked while we did an awkward little dance
around the gleaming island of stainless steel and tile in the middle
of the kitchen. "I'll bet you're starved," she said, "after all that
bachelor cooking and the airplane food. And look at you — you're
shivering. He's shivering, Philip."

I was, and no denying it.

"You can't run around in a T-shirt and leather jacket and expect
to survive a Michigan winter — it might be all right for L.A. maybe,
but not here." She turned to Philip, who'd been standing there as if

someone had crept up on him and nailed his shoes to the floor. "Philip, haven't you got a parka for Rick? How about that blue one with the red lining you never wear anymore? And a pair of gloves, for God's sake. Get him a pair of gloves, will you?" She came back to me then, all smiles: "We can't have our California boy getting frostbite, now, can we?"

Philip agreed that we couldn't, and we all stood there smiling at one another till I said, "Isn't anybody going to offer me a drink?"

Then it was my nephews — red-faced howling babies in dirty yellow diapers the last time I'd seen them, at the funeral that had left me an orphan at twenty-three, little fists glomming onto the cold cuts while drool descended toward the dip — but here they were, eight and six, edging up to me in high-tops and oversized sweatshirts while I threw back my brother's Scotch. "Hey," I said, grinning till I thought my head would burst, "remember me? I'm your Uncle Rick."

They didn't remember me — how could they? — but they brightened at the sight of the two yellow bags of M&M peanut candies I'd thought to pick up at the airport newsstand. Josh, the eight-year-old, took the candy gingerly from my hand, while his brother looked on to see if I was going to sprout fangs and start puking up black vomit. We were all sitting around the living room, very clean, very *Home & Garden,* getting acquainted. Philip and Denise held on to their drinks as if they were afraid somebody was going to steal them. We were all grinning. "What's that on your eyebrow?" Josh said.

I reached up and fingered the thin gold loop. "It's a ring," I said. "You know, like an earring, only it's in my eyebrow."

No one said anything for a moment. Jeff, the younger one, looked as if he was going to start crying. "Why?" Josh said finally, and Philip laughed and I couldn't help myself — I laughed, too. It was all right. Everything was all right. Philip was my brother and Denise was my sister-in-law and these kids with their wide-open faces and miniature Guess jeans were my nephews. I shrugged, laughing still. "Because it's cool," I said, and I didn't even mind the look Philip gave me.

Later, after I'd actually crawled into the top bunk and read the kids a Dr. Seuss story that set off all sorts of bells in my head, Philip and Denise and I discussed my future over coffee and homemade cinnamon rolls. My immediate future, that is — as in tomorrow morning, 8 A.M., at the clinic. I was going to be an entry-level drudge despite my three years of college, my musical background and family connections, rinsing out test tubes and sweeping the floors and disposing of whatever was left in the stainless-steel trays when my brother and his colleagues finished with their "procedures."

"All right," I said. "Fine. I've got no problem with that."

Denise had tucked her legs up under her on the couch. She was wearing a striped caftan that could have sheltered armies. "Philip had a black man on full time, just till a week ago, nicest man you'd ever want to meet — and bright, too, very bright — but he, uh, didn't feel . . ."

Philip's voice came out of the shadows at the end of the couch, picking up where she'd left off. "He went on to something better," he said, regarding me steadily through the clear walls of his glasses. "I'm afraid the work isn't all that mentally demanding — or stimulating, for that matter — but, you know, little brother, it's a start, and, well —"

"Yeah, I know," I said, "beggars can't be choosers." I wanted to add to that, to maybe soften it a bit — I didn't want him to get the idea I wasn't grateful, because I was — but I never got the opportunity. Just then the phone rang. I looked up at the sound — it wasn't a ring exactly, more like a bleat, *eh-eh-eh-eh-eh* — and saw that my brother and his wife were staring into each other's eyes in shock, as if a bomb had just gone off. Nobody moved. I counted two more rings before Denise said, "I wonder who that could be at this hour?" and Philip, my brother with the receding hairline and the too big glasses and his own eponymous clinic in suburban Detroit, said, "Forget it, ignore it, it's nobody."

And that was strange, because we sat there in silence and listened to that phone ring over and over — twenty times, twenty times at least — until whoever it was on the other end finally gave up. Another minute ticked by, the silence howling in our ears, and then Philip stood, looking at his watch, and said, "What do you think — time to turn in?"

I wasn't stupid, not particularly — no stupider than anybody else, anyway — and I was no criminal, either. I'd just drifted into a kind of thick sludge of hopelessness after I dropped out of school for a band I put my whole being into, a band that disintegrated within the year, and one thing led to another. Jobs came and went. I spent a lot of time on the couch, channel-surfing and thumbing through books that used to mean something to me. I found women and lost them. And I learned that a line up your nose is a dilettante's thing, wasteful and extravagant. I started smoking, two or three nights a week, and then it was five or six nights a week and then it was every day, all day, and why not? That was how I felt. Sure. And now I was in Michigan, starting over.

Anyway, it wouldn't have taken a genius to understand why my brother and his wife had let that phone ring — not after Philip and I swung into the parking lot behind the clinic at seven forty-five the next morning. I wasn't even awake, really — it was four forty-five West Coast time, an hour that gave me a headache even to imagine, much less live through. Beyond the misted-up windows, everything was gloom, a kind of frozen fog hanging in air the color of lemon ice. The trees, I saw, hadn't sprouted leaves overnight. Every curb was a repository of frozen trash.

Philip and I had been making small talk on the way into town, very small talk, out of consideration for the way I was feeling. Denise had given me coffee, which was about all I could take at that hour, but Philip had gobbled a big bowl of bran flakes and sunflower seeds with skim milk, and the boys, shy around me all over again, spooned up Lucky Charms and Frosted Flakes in silence. I came out of my daze the minute the tires hit the concrete apron separating the private property of the lot from the public space of the street: there were people there, a whole shadowy mass of shoulders and hats and steaming faces that converged on us with a shout. At first I didn't know what was going on — I thought I was trapped in a bad movie, *Night of the Living Dead* or *Zombies on Parade*. The faces were barking at us, teeth bared, eyes sunk back in their heads, hot breath boiling from their throats. "Murderers!" they were shouting. "Nazis!" "Baby-killers!"

We inched our way across the sidewalk and into the lot, working through the mass of them as if we were on a narrow lane in a dense forest, and Philip gave me a look that explained it all, from the lines in his face to Denise's fat to the phone that rang in the middle of the night no matter how many times he changed the number. This was war. I climbed out of the car with my heart hammering, and as the cold knife of the air cut into me I looked back to where they stood clustered at the gate, lumpish and solid, people you'd see anywhere. They were singing now. Some hymn, some self-righteous churchy Jesus-thumping hymn that bludgeoned the traffic noise and the deep-frozen air with the force of a weapon. I didn't have time to sort it out, but I could feel the slow burn of anger and humiliation coming up on me. Philip's hand was on my arm. "Come on," he said. "We've got work to do, little brother."

That day, the first day, was a real trial. Yes, I was turning over a new leaf, and yes, I was determined to succeed and thankful to my brother and the judge and the great giving, forgiving society I belonged to, but this was more than I'd bargained for. I had no illusions about the job — I knew it would be dull and diminishing, and I knew life with Philip and Denise would be one long snooze, but I wasn't used to being called a baby-killer. Liar, thief, crackhead — those were names I'd answered to at one time or another. Murderer was something else.

My brother wouldn't talk about it. He was busy. Wired. Hurtling around the clinic like a gymnast on the parallel bars. By nine I'd met his two associates (another doctor and a counselor, both female, both unattractive), his receptionist, Nurses Tsing and Hempfield, and Fred. Fred was a big rabbity-looking guy in his early thirties with a pale reddish mustache and hair of the same color climbing up out of his head in all directions. He had the official title of "technician," though the most technical things I saw him do were drawing blood and divining urine for signs of pregnancy, clap, or worse. None of them — not my brother, the nurses, the counselor, or even Fred — wanted to discuss what was going on at the far end of the parking lot and on the sidewalk out front. The zombies with the signs — yes, signs, I could see them out the window, "Abortion Kills" and "Save the Preborns" and "I Will Adopt Your Baby" — were of no more concern to them than mosquitoes in June or a sniffle in December. Or at least that was how they acted.

I tried to draw Fred out on the subject as we sat together at lunch in the back room. We were surrounded by shadowy things in jars of formalin, gleaming stainless-steel sinks, racks of test tubes, reference books, cardboard boxes full of drug samples and syringes and gauze pads and all the rest of the clinic's paraphernalia. "So what do you think of all this, Fred?" I said, gesturing toward the window with the ham-and-Swiss on rye Denise had made me in the dark hours of the morning.

Fred was hunched over a newspaper, doing the acrostic puzzle and sucking on his teeth. His lunch consisted of a microwave chili-and-cheese burrito and a quart of root beer. He gave me a quizzical look.

"The protesters, I mean. The Jesus-thumpers out there. Is it like this all the time?" And then I added a little joke, so he wouldn't think I was intimidated: "Or did I just get lucky?"

"Who, them?" Fred did something with his nose and his upper teeth, something rabbity, as if he were tasting the air. "They're nobody. They're nothing."

"Yeah?" I said, hoping for more, hoping for some details, some explanation, something to assuage the creeping sense of guilt and shame that had been building in me all morning. Those people had pigeonholed me before I'd even set foot in the door, and that hurt. They were wrong. I was no baby-killer — I was just the little brother of a big brother, trying to make a new start. And Philip was no baby-killer, either — he was a guy doing his job, that was all. Shit, somebody had to do it. Up to this point, I guess I'd never really given the issue much thought — my girlfriends, when there were girlfriends, had taken care of the preventative end of things on their own and we never really discussed it — but my feeling was that there were too many babies in the world already, too many adults, too many suet-faced Jesus-thumping jerks ready to point the finger, and didn't any of these people have better things to do? Like a job, for instance? But Fred wasn't much help. He just sighed, nibbled at the wilted stem of his burrito, and said, "You get used to it."

I wondered about that as the afternoon crept by, and then my mind went numb from jet lag and the general wash of misery and I let my body take over. I scrubbed out empty jars and test tubes with Clorox, labeled and filed the full ones on the racks that lined the walls, stood at Fred's elbow and watched as he squeezed drops of urine onto strips of litmus paper and made notations in a ledger. My white lab coat got progressively dirtier. Every once in a while I'd come to and catch a glimpse of myself in the mirror over the sinks, the mad scientist exposed, the baby-killer, the rinser of test tubes and secreter of urine, and have an ironic little laugh at my own expense. And then it started to get dark, Fred vanished, and I was introduced to mop and squeegee. It was around then, when I just happened to be taking a cigarette break by the only window in the room, that I caught a glimpse of one of our last tardy patients of the day hurrying up the sidewalk elbow to elbow with a grim middle-aged woman whose face screamed *I am her mother!*

The girl was sixteen, seventeen maybe, a pale face, pale as a bulb, and nothing showing on her, at least not with the big white dough-boy parka she was wearing. She looked scared, her little mouth clamped tight, her eyes fixed on her feet. She was wearing black leggings that seemed to sprout from the folds of the parka and a pair of furry white ankle boots that were like house slippers. I watched her glide through the dead world on the flowing stalks of her legs, a spoiled pouty chalk-cheeked sweetness to her face, and it moved something in me, something long buried beneath a moun-tain of grainy little yellow-white rocks. Maybe she was just coming in for an examination, I thought, maybe that was it. Or she'd just become sexually active — or was thinking of it — and her mother was one step ahead of her. Either way, that was what I wanted to believe. With this girl, with her quick fluid step and downcast eyes and all the hope and misery they implied, I didn't want to think of "procedures."

They'd almost reached the building when the zombies began to stir. From where I was standing I couldn't see the front of the building, and the Jesus-thumpers had already begun to fade out of my consciousness, dim as it was. But they came crashing back into the picture now, right there at the corner of the building, shoulders and heads and placards, and one in particular. A shadow that sepa-rated itself from the mass and was instantly transformed into a hulking bearded zealot with snapping teeth and eyes like hard-boiled eggs. He came right up to the girl and her mother, rush-ing at them like a torpedo, and you could see how they shied away from him and how his head raged back on his shoulders, and then they ducked past the corner of the building and out of my line of sight.

I was stunned. This wasn't right. I was thinking, and I didn't want to get angry or depressed or emotional — keep on an even keel, that's what they tell you in rehab — but I couldn't help snuffing the cigarette and stepping quietly out into the hallway that ran the length of the building and gave me an unobstructed view of the front door. I moved forward almost against my will, my feet like toy cars on a track, and I hadn't got halfway down the hall before the door opened on the dwindling day and the dead sticks of the trees, and suddenly there she was, pale in a pale coat and her face two shades paler. We exchanged a look. I don't know what she saw in my eyes — weakness, hunger, fear — but I know what I saw in hers, and it was so poignant and so everlastingly sad I knew I'd never have another moment's rest till I took hold of it.

In the car on the way home Philip was so relaxed I wondered if he wasn't prescribing something for himself. Here was the antithesis of the ice man who'd picked me up at the airport, watched me eat pork chops, read to his children, and brush my teeth in the guest bathroom, and then thrown me to the wolves at the clinic. "Sorry about all that commotion this morning," he said, glancing at me in the glowing cubicle of the car. "I would have warned you, but you can never tell when they're going to pull something like that."

"So it gets better, is that what you're saying?"

"Not much," he said. "There's always a couple of them out there, the real hard-core nuts. But the whole crew of the walking dead like you saw today, that's maybe only once a week. Unless they go on one of their campaigns, and I can't figure out what provokes them — the weather, the tides in the lake, the phases of the moon — but then they go all out, theater in the street, schoolchildren, the works. They throw themselves under the wheels, handcuff themselves to the front door — it's a real zoo."

"But what about the cops? Can't you get a restraining order or something?"

He shrugged, fiddled with the tape player — opera, he was listening to opera, a thin screech of it in the night — and turned to me again, his gloved hands rigid on the wheel. "The cops are a bunch of pro-lifers, and they have no objection to those people out there harassing my patients and abridging their civil rights, and even the women just coming in for an exam have to walk the gauntlet. It's hell on business, believe me. And it's dangerous, too. They scare me, the real crazies, the ones that shoot people. You've heard of John Britton? David Gunn? George Tiller?"

"I don't know," I said. "Maybe. You've got to realize I've been out of touch for a while."

"Shot down by people like the ones you saw out there today. Two of them died."

I didn't like hearing that. The thought of one of those nutballs attacking my brother, attacking me, was like throwing gasoline on a bed of hot coals. I'd never been one to turn the other cheek, and I didn't feature martyrdom, not at all. I looked out on a blur of brake lights and the crust of ice that seemed to narrow the road into a funnel ahead of us. "Why don't you shoot them first?" I said.

My brother's voice was hard. "Sometimes I wish I could."

We stopped to pick up a few things at the market and then we were home, dinner stabbing at my salivary glands, the whole house warm and sugary with it, and Philip sat down to watch the news and have a Scotch with me. Denise was right there at the door when we came in — and now we embraced, no problem, sister- and brother-in-law, one big happy family. She wanted to know how my day was, and before I could open my mouth she was answering for me: "Not much of a challenge, huh? Pretty dull, right? Except for the crazies — they never fail to liven things up, do they? What Philip goes through, huh, Philip? Philip?"

I was beat, but the Scotch smoked through my veins, the kids came and sat beside me on the couch with their comics and coloring books, and I felt good, felt like part of the family and no complaints. Denise served a beef brisket with oven-roasted potatoes, carrots, and onions, a fresh green salad, and coconut cream pie for dessert. I was planning on turning in early, but I drifted into the boys' room and took over the *Winnie-the-Pooh* chores from my brother because it was something I wanted to do. Later, it must have been about ten, I was stretched out on my own bed — and again I had to hand it to Denise, because the room was homey and private, done up with little knickknacks and embroidery work and whatnot — when my brother poked his head in the door. "So," he said, mellow with the Scotch and whatever else, "you feeling okay about everything?"

That touched me. It did. Here I'd come into the airport with a chip on my shoulder — I'd always been jealous of Philip, the great shining success my father measured me against — thinking my big brother was going to be an asshole and that assholery would rule the day, but it wasn't like that at all. He was reaching out. He was a doctor. He knew about human foibles and addictions and he knew about his little brother, and he cared, he actually cared. "Yeah" was all I could manage, but I hoped the quality of my voice conveyed a whole lot more than that.

"Good," he said, framed in the light from the hallway, his sunken orbits and rucked face and flat shining eyes giving him a look of wisdom and calm that reminded me of our father on his good days.

"That girl," I said, inspired by the intimacy of the moment, "the last one that came in today?"

His expression changed. Now it was quizzical, distant, as if he were looking at me through the wrong end of a telescope. "What girl? What are you talking about?"

"The young-looking one in the white parka and furry boots? The last one. The last one in. I was just wondering if, uh, I mean, what her problem was — if she was, you know, coming in for a procedure or whatever."

"Listen, Rick," he said then, and his voice was back in the deep freeze, "I'm willing to give you a chance here, not only for Dad's sake but for your own sake, too. But there's one thing I ask — stay away from the patients. And I'm not really asking."

It was raining the next morning, a cold rain that congealed on the hood of the car and made a cold pudding of the sidewalk out front of the house. I wondered if the weather would discourage the Jesus-thumpers, but they were there, all right, in yellow rain slickers and green gum boots, sunk into their suffering with gratitude. Nobody rushed the car when we turned into the lot. They just stood there, eight of them, five men and three women, and looked hate at us. As we got out of the car, the frozen rain pelting us, I locked eyes across the lot with the bearded jerk who'd gone after the girl in the white parka. I waited till I was good and certain I had his attention, waited till he was about to shout out some hoarse Jesus-thumping accusation, and then I gave him the finger.

We were the first ones at the clinic, what with the icy roads, and as soon as my brother disappeared into the sanctum of his office I went straight to the receptionist's desk and flipped back the page of the appointment book. The last entry, under four-thirty the previous day, was staring me in the face, neat block letters in blue metalpoint: "Sally Strunt," it read, and there was a phone number jotted beneath the name. It took me exactly ten seconds, and then

I was in the back room, innocently slipping into my lab coat. Sally Strunt, I whispered to myself, Sally Strunt, over and over. I'd never known anyone named Sally — it was an old-fashioned name, a hokey name, Dick and Jane and Sally, and because it was old-fashioned and because it was hokey it seemed perfect for a teenager in trouble in the grim sleety washed-out navel of the Midwest. This was no downtown Amber, no Crystal or Shanna — this was Detroit Sally, and that really appealed to me. I'd seen the face attached to the name, and the mother of that face. *Sally, Sally, Sally.* Her name sang through my head as I schmoozed with Fred and the nurses and went through the motions of the job that already felt as circumscribed and deadening as a prison sentence.

That night, after dinner, I excused myself and strolled six cold wintry blocks to the convenience store. I bought M&M's for the boys, some white chocolate for Denise, and a liter of Black Cat malt liquor for myself. Then I dialed Sally's number from the phone booth out front of the store.

A man answered, impatient, harassed. "Yeah?"

"Sally there?" I said.

"Who's this?"

I took a stab at it: "Chris Ryan. From school?"

Static. Televised dialogue. The roar of Sally's name and the sound of approaching feet and Sally's approaching voice: "Who is it?" And then, into the receiver: "Hello?"

"Sally?" I said.

"Yes?" There was hope in that voice, eagerness. She wanted to hear from me — or from whoever. This wasn't the voice of a girl concealing things. It was open, frank, friendly. I felt expansive suddenly, connected, felt as if everything was going to be all right, not only for me but for Sally, too.

"You don't know me," I said quickly, "but I really admire you. I mean, your courage. I admire what you're doing."

"Who is this?"

"Chris," I said. "Chris Ryan. I saw you yesterday, at the clinic, and I really admire you, but I just wanted to know if, uh, if you need anything."

Her voice narrowed, thin as wire. "What are you talking about?"

"Sally," I said, and I didn't know what I was doing or what I was feeling but I couldn't help myself, "Sally, can I ask you something? Are you pregnant, or are you — ?"

Click. She hung up on me. Just like that.

I was frozen through by the time I got back with the kids' M&M's and Denise's white chocolate, and I'd finished off the beer on the way and flung the empty bottle up under a squat artificial-looking spruce on the neighbor's lawn. I'd tried Sally twice more, after an interval of fifteen or twenty minutes, but her father answered the first time and when I dialed again the phone just rang and kept on ringing.

A week went by. I scrubbed out test tubes and jars that smelled powerfully of the urine of strange women and learned that Fred didn't much care for Afro-Americans, Mexicans, Haitians, Cubans, Poles, or Hmong tribesmen. I tried Sally's number three more times, and each time I was rebuffed — threatened, actually — and I began to realize I was maybe just a bit out of line. Sally didn't need me — she had her father and mother and maybe a gangling big-footed slam-dunking brother into the bargain — and every time I glanced through the blinds in the back room I saw another girl just like her. Still, I was feeling itchy and out of sorts despite all Denise and Philip and my nephews were doing for me, and I needed some sort of focus, a plan, something to make me feel good about myself. They'd warned me about this in rehab, and I knew this was the trickiest stage, the time when the backsliders start looking up their old friends and hanging out on the street corner. But I didn't have any old friends, not in Detroit, anyway, and the street corner was about as inviting as the polar ice cap. On Saturday night I went out to a bar that looked as if it had been preserved under Plexiglas in a museum somewhere, and I came on to a couple of girls and drank too much and woke up the next morning with a headache.

Then it was Monday and I was sitting at the breakfast table with my brother and my two nephews and it was raining again. Sleeting, actually. I wanted to go back to bed. I toyed with the idea of telling Philip I was sick, but he'd probably insist on inserting the rectal thermometer himself. He sat across from me, expressionless, crunching away at his bran flakes and sunflower seeds, the newspaper spread out before him. Denise bustled around the kitchen brewing coffee and shoving things into the microwave while the boys and I smeared Eggo waffles with butter and syrup. "So," I said, addressing my nephews over the pitcher of pure Grade A maple syrup, "you know why the California kids have it all over the mid-western kids when it comes to baseball?"

Josh looked up from his waffles; Jeff was still on dreamtime.

"Because of this," I said, gesturing toward the dark windows and the drooling panes. "In L.A. now it's probably seventy degrees, and when the kids wake up they can go straight out and play ball."

"After school," Josh corrected.

"Yeah," I said. "Whatever. But that's the reason your California and Arizona players dominate the big leagues."

"The Tigers suck," Josh said, and his brother glanced up to add his two cents. "They *really* suck," he said.

It was then that I became aware of the background noise, a thin droning mewl from beyond the windows as if someone were drowning kittens in the street. Philip heard it then, too, and the boys and Denise, and in the next moment we were all at the window. "Oh, shit," Philip hissed. "Not again. Not today, of all days."

"What?" I said. "What is it?" And then I saw, while my nephews melted away and Denise gritted her teeth and my brother swore: the zombies were out there at the edge of the lawn, a hundred of them at least. They were singing, locked arm in arm and swaying to the beat, stretched across the mouth of the driveway in a human chain.

Philip's face was drawn tight. He told Denise to call the police, and then he turned to me. "Now you're going to see something, little brother," he said. "Now you're going to see why I keep asking myself if I shouldn't just close down the clinic and let the lunatics take over the asylum."

The kitchen was gray, a weak played-out light pasted on every surface. Sleet rattled the windows and the conjoined voices mewled away in praise of mercy and forgiveness. I was about to ask him why he didn't do just that — close up and move someplace friendlier, someplace like California, for instance — but I already knew the answer. They could harass all the chalk-faced Sallys and thump all the Bibles they wanted, but my brother wasn't going to bow down to them — and neither was I. I knew whose team I was on and I knew what I had to do.

It took the police half an hour to show up. There were three squad cars and a bus with wire mesh over the windows, and the cops knew the routine. They'd been here before — how many times you

could guess from the deadness in their eyes — and they'd arrested
these very people, knew them by name. Philip and I waited in the
house, watching the *Today* show at an uncomfortable volume, and
the boys stayed in their room, already late for school. Finally, at
quarter past eight, Philip and I shuffled out to the garage and
climbed into the car. Philip's face was like an old paper sack with
eyes poked in it. I watched him hit the remote for the garage door
and watched the door lift slowly on the scene.

There they were, right there on the street, the whole bug-eyed
crew from the clinic, and ninety more. I saw squat, brooding mothers with babies, kids who should have been in school, old people
who should have known better. They jerked their signs up and
down and let out with a howl when the door cranked open, and
though the cops had cleared them from the mouth of the drive
they surged in now to fill the gap, the big Jesus-thumper with the
board right in front. The cops couldn't hold them back, and before
we'd got halfway down the drive they were all over us, pounding on
the windows and throwing themselves down in the path of the car.
My brother, like a jerk, like the holy fool who automatically turns
the other cheek, stepped on the brake.

"Run them over," I said, and all my breath was gone. "Run the
fuckers over."

Philip just sat there, hanging his head in frustration. The cops
peeled them away, one by one, zipped on the plastic cuffs and
hauled them off, but for every one they lifted out of the way another dove in to take his place. We couldn't go forward, we couldn't
back up. "Your neighbor kills babies!" they were shouting. "Dr.
Beaudry is a murderer!" "Kill the butchers, not the babies!" I tried
to stay calm, tried to think about rehab and jail and the larger
problems of my life, but I couldn't. I couldn't take this. I couldn't.

Before I knew what I was doing I was out of the car. The first face
I saw belonged to a kid of eighteen maybe, a tough guy with veins
standing out in his neck and his leather jacket open to the sleet to
show off a white T-shirt and a gold cross on a gold chain. He was
right there, right in my face, shouting "Jesus! Jesus!" and he looked
genuinely surprised when I pitched into him with everything I had
and shoved him back into a pair of dumpy women in matching
scarves and earmuffs. I went right for the next guy — a little toad-
stool who looked as if he'd been locked in a closet for the last forty

years — and flung him away from the car. I heard shouts, saw the cops wading through the crowd, and then I was staring into the face of the big guy, the king yahoo himself — Mr. Beard — and he was so close I knew what he'd had for breakfast. In all that chaos he just stood there rigid at the bumper of the car, giving me a big rich phony Jesus-loving smile that was as full of hate as anything I'd ever seen, and then he ducked down on one knee and handcuffed himself to the bumper.

That put me over the line. I wanted to make a martyr out of him, wanted to kick him to death right there, right in the driveway and with the whole world looking on, and who knows what would have happened if Philip hadn't grabbed me from behind. "Rick!" he kept shouting. "Rick! Rick!" And then he wrestled me up the walk and into the house, Denise's scared white face in the door, the mob howling for blood and then lurching right into another weepy, churchy song as if they were in a cathedral somewhere.

In the safety of the hallway, the door closed and locked behind us, my brother turned on me. "Are you crazy?" he shouted, and you would have thought *I* was the enemy. "You want to go back to jail? You want lawsuits? What were you thinking, anyway — are you stoned on something, is that it?"

I looked away from him, but I wanted to kill him, too. It was beating in my veins, along with the Desoxyn I'd stolen from the clinic. I saw my nephews peeking out of their room down the hall. "You can't let these people push you around," I said.

"Look at me, Rick," he said. "Look at me."

I was dodging around on my feet, right with it, and I lifted my eyes grudgingly. I felt like a kid all over again, Rick the shoplifter, the pothead, the fuckup.

"You're just playing into their hands, don't you see that? They want to provoke you, they want you to go after them. Then they put you back in jail and they get the headlines." His voice broke. Denise tried to say something, but he shut her up with a wave of his hand. "You're back on the drugs, aren't you? What is it — cocaine? Pot? Something you lifted from the clinic?"

Outside I could hear them, "We Shall Overcome," and it was a cruel parody — this wasn't liberation, it was fascism. I said nothing.

"Listen, Rick, you're an ex-con and you've got to remember that, every step you take. I mean, what did you think, you were protecting me out there?"

"Ex-con?" I said, amazed. "Is that what you think of me? I can't believe you. I'm no ex-con. You're thinking of somebody in the movies, some documentary you saw on PBS. I'm a guy who made a mistake, a little mistake, and I never hurt anybody. I'm your brother, remember?"

That was when Denise chimed in. "Philip," she said, "come on, Philip. You're just upset. We're all upset."

"You keep out of this," he said, and he didn't even turn to look at her. He just kept his Aqua Velva eyes on me. "Yeah," he said finally, "you're my brother, but you're going to have to prove it to me."

I can see now the Desoxyn was a mistake. It was exactly the sort of thing they'd warned us about. But it wasn't coke and I just needed a lift, a buzz to work behind, and if he didn't want me to be tempted, then why had he left the key to the drug cabinet right there in the conch-shell ashtray on the corner of his desk? *Ex-con.* I was hurt and I was angry and I stayed in my room till Philip knocked at the door an hour later to tell me the police had cleared the mob away. We drove to work in silence, Philip's opera chewing away at my nerves like a hundred little sets of teeth.

Philip didn't notice it, but there was something different about me when I climbed back into that car, something nobody could notice unless they had x-ray vision. I was armed. Tucked inside the waistband of my gray Levi's, underneath the flap of my shirt where you couldn't see it, was the hard black stump of a gun I'd bought from a girl named Corinne at a time when I was feeling especially paranoiac. I had money lying around the apartment then and people coming and going — nobody desperate, nobody I didn't know or at least know through a friend — but it made me a little crazy. Corinne used to drop by once in a while with my roommate's girlfriend, and she sold me the thing — a .38 Special — for three hundred bucks. She didn't need it anymore, she said, and I didn't want to know what that meant, so I bought it and kept it under my pillow. I'd only fired it once, up a canyon in Tujunga, but it made me feel better just to have it around. I'd forgotten all about it, actually, but when I got my things out of storage and shipped them to Philip's house, there it was, hidden away in a box of CDs like some poisonous thing crouching under a rock.

What I was feeling is hard to explain. It had to do with Philip, sure — ex-con, that really hurt — and with Sally and the clinic and the whole Jesus-thumping circus. I didn't know what I was going to do — nothing, I hoped — but I knew I wasn't going to take any shit from anybody, and I knew Philip didn't have it in him to protect himself, let alone Denise and the kids and all the knocked-up grieving teenage Sallys of the world. That was all. That was it. The extent of my thinking. I walked into the clinic that morning just as I had for the past week and a half, and nobody knew the difference.

I cleaned the toilets, washed the windows, took out the trash. Some blood work came back from an outside lab — we only did urine — and Fred showed me how to read the results. I discussed the baseball strike with Nurse Tsing and the prospects of an early spring with Nurse Hempfield. At noon I went out to a deli and had a meatball wedge, two beers, and a breath mint. I debated dialing Sally just once more — maybe she was home from school, headachy, nauseous, morning sickness, whatever, and I could get past the brick wall she'd put up between us and talk to her, really talk to her for the first time — but when I got inside the phone booth I just didn't feel like it. As I walked back to the clinic I was wondering if she had a boyfriend or if it was just one of those casual encounters, blind date, back seat of the car — or rape, even. Or incest. Her father's voice could have been the voice of a child abuser, easily — or who even knew if he was her father? Maybe he was the stepfather. Maybe he was a Humbert Humbert type. Maybe anything.

There were no protesters out front when I got back — they were all in jail — and that lightened my mood a bit. I even joked with Fred and caught myself whistling over my work. I forgot the morning, forgot the gun, forgot Pasadena and the life that was. Coffee kept me awake, coffee and Diet Coke, and I stayed away from the other stuff just to prove something to myself — and to Philip, too. For a while there I even began to suffer from the delusion that everything was going to work out.

Then it was late, getting dark, and the day was almost done. I pictured the evening ahead — Denise's cooking, *Winnie-the-Pooh*, my brother's Scotch, six windblown blocks to the store for a liter of Black Cat — and suddenly I felt like pulling out the gun and shooting myself right then and there. Uncle Rick, little brother, ex-con: who was I kidding? I would have been better off in jail.

I needed a cigarette. Badly. The need took me past the waiting room — four scared-looking women, one angry-looking man

— through the lab, and into the back corner. The fluorescent lights hissed softly overhead. Fred was already gone. I stood at the window, staring into the nullity of the drawn blinds till the cigarette was a nub. My hands were trembling as I lit another from the butt end of the first, and I didn't think about the raw-looking leftovers in the stainless-steel trays that were like nothing so much as skinned frogs, and I didn't think about Sally or the fat-faced bearded son of a bitch shackling himself to the bumper, either. I tried hard to think nothing, to make it all a blank, and I was succeeding, I was, when for some reason — idle curiosity, boredom, fate — I separated two of the slats and peered out into the lot.

And there she was, just like that: Sally.

Sally in her virginal parka and fluffy boots, locked in her mother's grip and fighting her way up the walk against a tide of chanting zombies — and I recognized them, too, every one of them, the very ones who'd been dragged away from my brother's door in the dark of the morning. Sally wasn't coming in for an exam — there weren't going to be any more exams. No, Sally meant business. You could see that in the set of her jaw and in the way she lowered her head and jabbed out her eyes like swords, and you could see it in every screaming line of her mother's screaming face.

The light was fading. The sky hung low, like smoke. And then, in that instant, as if some god had snapped his fingers, the streetlights went on, a sudden artificial burst of illumination exploding in the sky above them. All at once I felt myself moving, the switch turned on in me, too, all the lights flaring in my head, burning bright, and I was out the door, up the corridor, and pushing through the double glass doors at the front entrance.

Something was blocking the doors — bodies, deadweight, the zombies piled up on the steps like corpses — and I had to force my way out. There were bodies everywhere, a minefield of flesh, people stretched out across the steps, obliterating the sidewalk and the curb in front of the clinic, immobilizing the cars in the street. I saw the punk from this morning, the teenage tough guy in his leather jacket, his back right up against the door, and beside him one of the dumpy women I'd flung him into. They didn't learn, these people, they didn't know. It was a game. A big joke. Call people baby-killers, sing about Jesus, pocketful of posies, and then the nice policeman carries you off to jail and Mommy and Daddy bail you out. I tried to kick them aside, lashing out with the steel toes of my boots till my breath was coming in gasps. "Sally!" I cried. "Sally, I'm coming!"

She was stalled at the corner of the building, standing rigid with her mother before the sea of bodies. "Jesus loves you!" somebody cried out and they all took it up till my voice was lost in the clamor, erased in the everlasting hiss of Jesus. "We're going to come looking for you, brother," the tough guy said then, looking up at me out of a pair of seething blue eyes. "You better watch your back."

Sally was there. Jesus was there. Hands grabbed at me, snaked round my legs till I couldn't move, till I was mired in flesh. The big man came out of nowhere, lithe on his feet, vaulting through the inert bodies like the shadow of something moving swiftly overhead, and he didn't so much as graze me as he went by. I was on the third step down, held fast, the voices chanting, the signs waving, and I turned to watch him handcuff himself to the door and flash me a tight little smile of triumph.

"Sally!" I shouted. "Sally!" But she was already turning around, already turning her back to me, already lost in the crowd.

I looked down at my feet. A woman was clutching my right leg to her as if she'd given birth to it, her eyes as loopy as any crackhead's. My left leg was in the grip of a balding guy who might have been a clerk in a hardware store, and he was looking up at me like a toad I'd just squashed. "Jesus," they hissed. "Jesus!"

The light was burning in my head, and it was all I needed. I reached into my pants and pulled out the gun. I could have anointed any one of them, but the woman was first. I bent to her where she lay on the unyielding concrete of the steps and touched that snub-nose to her ear as tenderly as any man of healing. The noise of it shut down Jesus, shut him down cold. Into the silence, and it was the hardware man next. Then I swung round on Mr. Beard.

It was easy. It was nothing. Just like killing babies.

CLYDE EDGERTON

Send Me to the Electric Chair

FROM THE OXFORD AMERICAN

TWO OTHER EVENTS happened that same summer Mrs. Toomey
killed her son Paul's kitty, Inky, with a baseball bat to put him out of
his misery. One of the other two big events started a few weeks later,
when Mrs. Toomey was putting on lipstick, getting ready to take
Paul up to see the electric chair for the first time. She thought
about Terry Daniels. Terry was about Paul's age — six. She would
take him along too. The Danielses lived two houses down, and Mrs.
Daniels had started going to church some. They were poorer than
the Toomeys, but Mrs. Toomey told herself that shouldn't make a
difference.

When Mrs. Toomey and Paul stopped by to get Terry, Terry's
mother squinted through the door screen like she might be afraid,
but as Mrs. Toomey explained the purpose of the trip, Mrs. Daniels
considered the dress Mrs. Toomey was wearing, a white dress with
big blue flowers. And Mrs. Toomey's hair had nice waves in it, and
little Paul was so neat, his hair pushed back in front with what,
water? or maybe some of that Jew gel that pushed up a crew cut in
front. As Mrs. Toomey talked, Mrs. Daniels began to take it in, to
understand, that what Mrs. Toomey was about to do was exactly
right for Terry at that time in his life. She said, "Terry, go get on
some pants and shoes."

"We'll just wait out here in the swing," said Mrs. Toomey.

In the swing, Paul held his mother's hand. His legs didn't reach
the porch floor. He looked over at the gas station across the road.
There was a man drinking a beer, turning up a dark bottle with a
long swelled neck. He knew to take his eyes away. If he kept looking,

his mother might ask him what he was looking at. Inside the Danielses' house — through the window screen near his elbow — he saw
the foot of a bed, a rumpled sheet. He'd never seen an unmade bed
in the daytime. It made the room seem wild.

Inside, Mrs. Daniels, following Terry into the room, said,
"Where's 'at other sock?"

"I 'on' know."

"Didn't you have it on yesterday?"

"No."

"Do you want me to whip you?"

"No."

"You say no ma'am."

"No ma'am."

"You say no ma'am to Mrs. Toomey, you hear?"

"Yes ma'am."

"She's taking you to see the electric chair, and if you don't behave, when you grow up that's where you'll end up. Just like she
said."

Mrs. Toomey let Paul and Terry sit in the back seat together. That
way they could kind of talk and she could kind of hear what they
talked about.

"Did you know Mr. Riggs has a electric paddle?" Terry asked Paul.

Mrs. Toomey said, "Honey, I don't think that's true about a electric paddle. I think somebody made that up."

"That's what Leland said. Said he had one in his office."

"Well, I know, but I don't believe that's true. That's a rumor."

Paul rolled a little red metal car up and down his leg.

"Can I play with that?" asked Terry.

Mrs. Toomey stretched her neck, looked in the rearview mirror.

The strong, acrid odor from the fertilizer factory came in
through the open windows.

"Paul. Let Terry play with the car."

Paul handed the car to Terry and said, "I got about five more."

"I got a wood one that's bigger."

They drove past the Dairy DeeLight, where Mrs. Odum, the
Toomeys' next-door neighbor, worked part time. Mrs. Toomey decided they might stop by on the way back from the prison for a little
reward if Paul and Terry behaved. She wasn't above getting a little

reward for herself, either. "Now, the reason we're doing this," she said, "is so you-all can see what will happen if you ever let the devil lead you into a bad sin. If you commit a bad crime they'll put you in the electric chair and electrocute you. And little crimes can lead up to big crimes."

"Leland said it burns your tongue out," said Terry. "He said he knew a man went to the electric chair."

"I don't know about that," said Mrs. Toomey. "I think somebody made that up."

They drove past red clay roadbanks, past green pastures with cows, wood outbuildings, fishing ponds, some pastures holding a line or two of thick, dark cedar trees.

When they parked, Mrs. Toomey said, "See how big the building is? That's because there's so many prisoners."

Along the walkway, Paul reached for his mother's hand.

"See up there?" said Mrs. Toomey. "If they try to escape, that guard will shoot them. That's a shotgun he's got."

The guard at the gate said, "Yes ma'am. What can I do for you? Hey boys."

"I called ahead to see about showing these boys the electric chair."

"Oh, yeah. We got a note about that." He opened one gate, then another. "There's a door buzzer at that second door over there. Just push it and they'll let you in." As the boys walked by, the guard said, "How old are you boys?"

"Seven," said Terry.

"Six," said Paul.

"This one's mine," said Mrs. Toomey.

A man in a gray guard outfit let them in the building.

"What'd she say?" the guard on the tower asked the gate guard.

"Show them boys the electric chair." He shook a Lucky Strike up out of a pack, lit it with a flip-top lighter that had a rising sun on the side. "They won't but six and se'em year old."

"I wish I'd brought Buck up here once a year or so from the time he was six or seven. Maybe he'd a stayed in school and made something out of hisself."

"You can't ever tell. When did he drop out?"

"Eleventh . . . tenth. Somewhere in there."

Inside, a guard led Mrs. Toomey and the boys through a jail door, several other doors, and finally to a small room with a large metal door. The door had an eye-level window about the size of a saltine cracker box.

"You boys come over here and I'll show you the switch first. My name's Floyd. Here it is. There's the white, which is off. The green means ready. And the red is zap. You see, the executioner can't see the prisoner. Here, let me get you boys a stool. Mrs. Toomey, you can look through that little window there, if you want to, to see it."

Mrs. Toomey looked. Paul went next. He saw a chair made of dark shiny wood, not as big as he thought it would be, on a low platform. Straps hung to the chair arms and legs, and a light-colored canvas bag hung from the top of the chair back.

"What's that bag?"

"That's what you put over his head so you don't see his face when the charge hits him. That's something you don't want to see."

"Let me see," said Terry.

"Let's let Terry see," said Mrs. Toomey. She placed her hands under her son's arms, lifted him and set him on the floor. Terry stepped up.

"Where's the paddle?" said Terry. "The electric paddle."

"Oh, they just got them at school," said Floyd. He looked at Mrs. Toomey and winked. "Now, this chair though. Our bad people up here use this chair twiced — first time and last time." He winked at Mrs. Toomey again.

"I don't think you can teach them too soon," said Mrs. Toomey.

Mrs. Odum stood waiting behind the small open serving window at the Dairy DeeLight. It seemed to Paul as if her large, sad, moon-shaped face with the dark eye circles filled up the entire little window. "Hi y'all," Mrs. Odum said, very slowly. Her whole body seemed sloped downward somehow — lines out from her eyes, her mouth, her shoulders, all sloped downward.

"Just fine, Mrs. Odum, how you doing today?" Mrs. Toomey placed her purse on the counter.

"Oh, I'm doing all right, I reckon."

"We want to order three banana splits. These boys have been real good today."

Mrs. Odum pulled three bananas from a bunch in a fruit bowl and turned to begin her work. She picked up her lit Pall Mall from a Miami, Florida, ashtray and took a deep draw. The cigarette tip was orange, then gray. She moved slowly, as if she were underwater. "Where y'all been?"

"We been up to see the electric chair."

"Oh?"

"I don't think you can start teaching them too young."

"About . . . electricity?"

"Right and wrong. About right and wrong."

"Oh yes. Well, one thing is for sure — you just can't beat the electric chair for putting a mean man to death."

"I guess that's right."

The boys seated themselves at a table. Terry watched Paul roll his car up his arm. Mrs. Toomey stood at the order window, waiting, talking to Mrs. Odum.

Mrs. Odum smoked and worked, and in a few minutes she placed three banana splits on the counter at the window.

"Oh, my," said Mrs. Toomey.

At the table, Paul asked his mother, "What do prisoners get to eat?" A glob of whipped cream stuck to his lower lip. Mrs. Toomey wiped it off with her napkin.

"They eat bread and water. Maybe a few vegetables."

The last big event that summer started when Paul stood holding a grocery sack of loaf bread and a quart of milk, watching Terry Daniels and Leland Pendergrass dig for fishing worms out behind Mr. Pendergrass's auto shop. Leland dug up a hunk of black dirt and Terry shook it apart for worms.

Paul understood something, he wasn't sure what, about the difference between Terry and Leland. Leland was mean and Terry was mostly scared. Terry was back in there somewhere. When you looked at him or when he talked, it seemed like the real him was back in there somewhere, usually not saying what he was thinking. Leland, on the other hand, was always outside himself, doing something bad, saying exactly what he wanted to say, doing something to a dog or cat or somebody littler than him.

The hoe blade was sharpened until it shined — sharp as a razor. Leland hoed up a clump of black dirt, Terry picked it up and shook it, checked it for worms. Paul was just standing there watching. Leland and Terry were working well together — hoe up dirt, can the worm, hoe up dirt, no worm, hoe up dirt, no worm, hoe up dirt, can the worm, hoe up dirt — when half a worm dropped out of a clump of dirt and landed wriggling. Paul saw it and Terry must have seen it because he reached for it. Leland didn't see. The hoe commenced its powerful arc downward, razor edge glinting in the sun, the blade cutting down so fast it made a swish sound, a sound like a burning rag through the air, and the angle of strike was a full ninety degrees at the meeting place of the hoe blade and the thumb — just on the outside of the thumb's big joint. Terry drew his hand back as if he'd touched fire, as if he could get the hand back to his breast quickly enough to undo the violence, as if he could save it — as he drew it back he realized something was horribly wrong. He stopped his hand in midair and the thumb swung back and forth, dangling, and Paul's refusing-to-believe eyes saw hanging there, not a severed thumb, but instead a greatly enlarged worm, bunched into a little sausage, running blood all over itself. A bloodworm. And the news that Terry's thumb was cut off came to the boys in a terrible silent two seconds — thousand one, thousand two.

Terry's scream, threaded with hysteria, got the attention of all people within hearing distance. He started running toward his house, toward his mama and daddy.

It was a Saturday, the day his daddy would be home drinking because it was by God the end of the week and he deserved a little relaxation and relief from his business of bringing in money to support a wife and daughter and a boy who got on his nerves awful because he couldn't learn things as quick as — my God Almighty, what the hell was that God-awful screaming about? Gotdamn.

Paul and Leland, walking, followed Terry. Paul looked at the hoe propped on Leland's shoulder, like a soldier carries a rifle. Leland stopped, held out the hoe and looked at it himself, dropped it. "I got to go to the bathroom," he said.

Terry, holding his thumb to his shirt, had disappeared around the back corner of the auto shop.

Paul wondered if maybe he had to go to the bathroom, too. But the lure of the chopped thumb drew him toward the Danielses' house, and as he rounded the corner he saw Mr. Daniels walk unsteadily to meet Terry, ask him something, and before Terry could answer, hit him with his open hand on the butt hard enough to propel Terry forward toward the house. Terry had placed the thumb back and was holding it there, thinking it would maybe stick back and hold, that the blood would work like the glue in school, and dry, and in so doing fasten the thumb back the way it had been — with nothing to show but a thin red line.

Inside the house, Mr. Daniels hollered something, and Mrs. Daniels screamed.

Paul thought of Terry's presence, his being, the way he was — always far back inside himself, looking out as if he were afraid. And in a sweat, in a heat that suddenly covered his head and ears, Paul wanted somebody to rescue Terry, somebody to go in there and get him out and take him to the hospital. He would run tell his mother.

A man over at the service station called out, "What happened, son?"

"Terry cut his thumb just about off. It's just hanging by a little piece of skin."

And with that, two men sitting on the bench over there stood.

Paul felt compelled to stand there and watch as the first man crossed the road, walked up the steps, and knocked on the Danielses' door.

Cheryl, Terry's sister, rode up on her bicycle, leaned it against the steps, and walked into the house, past the man waiting on the porch.

Paul stood there in the narrow front yard of the Danielses' house, the porch pretty high up off the ground, as Mr. Reddings, the man who owned the service station, drove his black '39 Ford sedan into that little yard, and the two or three men from the gas station bench now stood by the porch to get a better look at the thumb as the Daniels family came down the steps. Terry had stopped crying, and his right hand was wrapped in a pillowcase, bloodied. He looked a little pale.

Around the side of the house came the entire Pendergrass family — Leland and his mama and daddy. Mrs. Pendergrass had gotten the word and sort of put two and two together and figured she needed to do the right thing by getting on over there with Leland. She'd asked her husband to come along in case Mr. Daniels was drunk.

Mr. Daniels held Terry's elbow as they came down the high front-porch steps. When Mr. Daniels saw Leland he stopped, still holding to Terry. "What happened, Leland?" he said. He stared at Leland with hard eyes.

"I didn't do nothing," said Leland. He pointed — pointed past everybody — at Paul. "Paul done it," he said.

Heads turned. The service-station man nearest Paul stepped back a step to give the world room enough to look on him, and then the attention of all the people swung back to Terry, standing with his free hand holding the bloody pillowcase wrapped around his other hand.

Paul felt something collapsing, imploding in his chest like those old buildings that blow up from the inside, collapsing into themselves. He knew, in spite of his scant experience in the world, what was coming.

Terry raised both hands, one holding the other, and pointed his index finger. "Paul done it," he said.

The electric chair floated up into Paul's view, the shiny wood, the straps, the white, green, and red paint beneath the switch.

He turned, ran home, and in the kitchen told his mother what had happened, all of it, as fast as he could, crying, trying to get his breath. She led him to the front door, knelt down, put her hands on his shoulders, and told him that there were times in life when you had to do the right thing. He had to go back down there by himself and tell those people the truth. All those people. Jesus would go with him. She stood and pushed him on out the door.

In the yard he slowed down, stopped, looked back. Mrs. Toomey walked out to him, knelt down again, placed her hands on his shoulders. "You got to do the right thing," she said. "You can't let people lie and you not do nothing. Jesus will be with you. And God, too. Now, go on like I told you."

Paul felt as if he were walking toward a firestorm. When he passed the hedgerow and saw the Danielses' porch and yard empty except for Cheryl sitting on the steps, he decided with lifted spirits to go on down and tell Cheryl the truth.

As they sat on the steps together, Cheryl listened, nodding her head, agreeing, understanding, believing him. Then they talked about her bicycle, about the difference between a girl's bike and a boy's bike, and then for a while she talked about the atomic bomb, about all the people it killed, and how America had called Japan on the telephone before they dropped it, so they could get all the little children out of town.

JUNE SPENCE

Missing Women

FROM THE SOUTHERN REVIEW

THREE WOMEN HAVE VANISHED, a mother, her teenage daughter, and the daughter's friend — purses and cars left behind, TV
on, door unlocked. The daughter had plans to spend the day at the
lake with friends and never showed. The phone has rung and rung
all morning, unanswered. Puzzled friends walk through the interrupted house, sweep up broken glass from a porch light before
calling the police. Broom bristles, shoe soles, finger pads smearing,
tamping down, obscuring possibilities. Neighbors come forward,
vague. It was late, they say. A green van, a white truck seen in the
area, trolling. A man with longish brown hair, army jacket, slight to
medium build. Down by the train tracks, panties. A single canvas
sneaker.

Details are not clues. What happened? Police conjecture an in-
truder or intruders intended only to deal with the mother, to rob or
to rape. The girls' arrival was unexpected. Panicking, the perpetra-
tor(s) abducted all three. Haste should have made the abductor(s)
sloppy, dribbling evidence all the way to some lair. But little is
found: a single drop of blood in the foyer, but it belongs to a friend
— she nicked her finger while sweeping glass. We're aghast at all
the friends who tidied up. No alarm in broken glass? Those purses;
women don't leave their purses.

There is truth and there is rumor. The missing daughter, Vicki,
has not been particularly close to the missing friend, Adelle, since
junior high. They went in different directions — the stocky, glossy
Vicki somewhat of a party girl, her hair bleached yellow-white
against iodine skin; Adelle the more academic and wholesomely

cheerleaderish one, willowy and fine-boned. Graduation party nostalgia brought them back together that night, where they let bygones be bygones, forgiving the small betrayals. Adelle called home to say she'd be spending the night at Vicki's, the first time in almost four years. Her shiny compact car blocks the driveway to show she made it as far as that.

In her abandoned purse is medicine Adelle must take every day. Early on, this is what worries her parents most. They circle the town doggedly, their station wagon filled with fliers, her face emblazoned on their sweatshirts. *Please. If you know anything, anything at all.* In a video they lend to the TV stations, she is modeling gauzy, diaphanous wedding gowns for a local dressmaker. With her skirts and hair swirling, her perfect pearly teeth, we feel that she is innocent and doomed.

Of the missing mother Kay and daughter Vicki, we are not so sure. Their estranged husband/father cannot immediately be located. Vicki once had a restraining order against her ex-boyfriend, and he is taken in for questioning. He is at first sullen and uncooperative with investigators. With grim confidence we await his confession, but he foils us: a punched timecard and security video corroborate his third-shift presence in the chicken-parts processing plant that night. The husband/father likewise disappoints. He is not on the lam but simply lives out of state. Someone calls him and he comes, and the son/brother too. They are briefly suspected, then cleared. But there is another shady matter. Kay ran a beauty parlor with increasingly disreputable ties. Some say she laundered money for drug dealers and got greedy, funneling too large a share for herself. The police deny all that, but we note her expensive tastes, the leather in her daughter's wardrobe, and conclude the worst.

Still, each of the three might have her own reasons for wanting to disappear. Kay had maxed out her credit cards and was falling behind in her mortgage payments. Was Vicki pregnant? Some say police found an unopened urine-test kit in her bureau. Adelle the consummate perfectionist was failing precalculus. Running off might have been easier to contemplate as a group: the girls plotting new looks in better towns; Kay mulling the practical details of bus tickets and low-profile jobs. We cannot rule out anything, but the strongest current is foul play, not the gentle fantasy of escape that we all have entertained.

Seventy-two hours pass without a trace, and the search kicks into high gear. Divers slick in neoprene suits bob the shallow lake as if for apples, rake the algaed muck along the bottom. City workers sonar the reservoir. The waters yield nothing, but the surrounding woods still swarm promisingly with hunters and hounds. We admire those who have volunteered to don orange caps and peer through binoculars, their dogs fanning out ahead and weaving through trees, loyal noses snuffling the ground. We admire the highway patrolmen in their thin summer khakis, poised in the roadside gravel, persistent but polite at the roadblocks checking licenses. The churchwomen bring pies and fried chicken and cold cans of soda to everyone tired and hungry from searching, and we admire them too.

All of us admirable, the way we rally together. We say, "We." We say, "Our community," "Our women," basking in the evidence of so many heroes lured out by tragedy: storefronts papered by high school kids with fliers provided free by local print shops, reward donations quietly accruing, information streaming through the phone lines, the cards and letters of commiseration. Surely this abundance of goodwill, mercy, and selfless volunteerism will prevail over the darker elements that abide here. For there are certain haggard people on the street, there are certain pockets of immigrants who will not master our grammar, whose children are insolent and fearless. There are people who look and sound uncannily like the rest of us, but if you shine a light in their crawlspaces, you might find the difference. Any might have stared with longing and hatred into the bright windows of pretty blondes.

There are leads. A reporter gets an anonymous call about a box, hidden in the park, containing information about the missing women. The caller will not disclose the nature of this information, will not linger on the line. Police are dispatched to the park, locate said box nestled amid gazebo shrubbery, examine it for explosives, dust it for prints, pry it open to find: a map, hastily sketched, of a floor plan. A park official recognizes the U shape of the building, the tiny hexagonal kitchen and bathroom appendages flanking individual units. Police converge on the apartment building. Excited tenants cluster in the halls as rooms are searched. Nothing. WILD GOOSE CHASE, read the headlines. POLICE VEXED BY FRUITLESS SEARCH. Again Adelle's parents appear on television.

Their anguish chastens other would-be pranksters, but was it just a prankster? Someone who could snatch three women away without a trace might then goad the searchers. No person of authority will come right out and say so, but there it is. We feel it, huddled indoors, or venturing out in twos and threes.

A Waffle Hut waitress comes forward. She is fairly certain she served the three women omelets, french toast, and coffee around two A.M. on the day of the disappearance. They seemed quietly anxious, not like the raucous post-bar crowd she usually waits on around that time. The cheerleader type asked for boysenberry syrup and, told there was none, sank into a sullen lassitude.

A SuperDairy QuikMart clerk comes forward. Around two that same morning, a woman resembling the missing mother burst into the store, asked if he had seen two teenage girls, and stormed out when he said he hadn't. She sometimes bought cigarettes there, and milk in single-serving containers.

The graduation party attendees are questioned further. The girls were spotted leaving the party together at one, two, and three A.M. The hostess thought she heard them arguing in the bathroom, something about a borrowed necklace. The hostess's parents said both girls were polite and charming but seemed troubled. The hostess's boyfriend saw them hugging on the lawn. Others said the lawn embrace was a brawl; Vicki had Adelle in a chokehold. Or Adelle held Vicki while she vomited malt liquor onto the zinnias. Unless it wasn't those two at all. The salutatorian has his doubts. Around one-thirty, he says, he was sitting alone on the back patio. He had turned down a joint only to have the smoke blown into his ear, leaving him giddy and fretful and confused. He is going to Yale in the fall, and the prospect was then lying heavily on his mind. Now he feels relief and a delightful anticipation of leaving, but that night he brooded while the full moon silhouetted two figures dancing together on the lawn. The salutatorian watched in darkness two moving bodies he could identify as female by their shapes, the pitch of the laughter. It's possible they kissed or only whispered. He is pale and stammering in recall. Police seize his journals but return them the next day, almost dejected. His nervous intelligence seemed so promising — a budding sociopath? — but his journals hold only the sex-obsessed ramblings of run-of-the-mill adolescence: "May 5 — Would absolutely rut Bethany R. given half a

chance. Tits like grapefruit, and she smells like bubble-gum-fla-
vored suntan lotion and sex."

The time is ripe for confessions, so people start to confess, as if in
fits of misguided volunteerism. Some march right into the police
station or the newspaper editor's office. Some hold press confer-
ences. A man calling himself a freelance private eye and soldier of
fortune says he helped the women conceal their identities and
relocate, to where he is forbidden to disclose, but rest assured they
are alive and well, enjoying lucrative careers in finance. A youth
generally regarded as troubled leads police and reporters to an
empty culvert, an empty railcar, and on a hike through acres of
empty field. A woman claiming to be one of the missing women
comes forward but will not specify which one she is — she resembles none — and is vague about the other two, saying only that they
ditched her. Her parents persuade her to recant. A group calling
itself the Urban Tide says they have taken the women hostage in
belated protest of the U.S. invasion of Grenada. They are revealed
to be performance artists living off college fellowships. They say
their intention was to "tweak the media and thereby tweak collective perceptions." There is talk of dismantling the university's theater arts program altogether, which is hotly debated until the diver-
sion of Vicki's ex-boyfriend's appearance in a television interview.

He reaffirms his innocence and describes their first date: they
had agreed to meet at the football game. She had not permitted
him to kiss her that night. The first thing he admired about her was
how she blew smoke rings "like she was forty years old or something." They dated for two years and got pre-engaged. She loved
redhots and for him to knead her shoulders after a long day of
school and sweeping up her mother's shop. The restraining order
grew out of a misunderstanding, he explains. He was a jealous guy,
he admits. She could be sort of a flirt, but no more than that, he is
careful to emphasize. No speaking ill of the missing. He has grown
up a lot since then, he swears, and his former guidance counselor
agrees in a pre-taped clip. What's next for this wrongly accused
young fellow who has stolen all our hearts? He's studying for his
General Equivalency Diploma and plans to enter technical school.
Weekends he fishes with Dad and brothers.

Lovely Adelle had (*has?* we must be careful with what tenses
imply) no boyfriend. She seemed unapproachable, schoolmates

say. Boys were intimidated by her height and her perfect smile. She carried herself as if maybe she thought she was a little better than everyone else. We detect the trace of a smirk in her wedding-dress video. Her parents start to seem a little *too* perfect in their televised worry, forever circling the town, meeting with the police chief, presiding over candlelight vigils. We can't help but wonder: don't they have to work? The friendly wood panels on their station wagon begin to come across as less than sincere. When Adelle's face appears alone on a billboard and a separate award fund is established from her college savings, we say they are elitist. Someone rents a billboard featuring only the faces of the other two, and passers-through unfamiliar with the case think they are unrelated disappearances.

The paper still presents them as a united front, the Missing Women, and prints their photos side by side in equal rectangles. The rectangles have shrunk, though, and are relegated to the B section, except on Sundays, when a summary appears on the front page featuring the best of the tip cards and the psychic *du jour.* In the absence of verifiable fact, reporters track the psychics' emanations and contribute wispy, artful meditations on the nature of truth. One suggests that the women never existed at all except as modern local archetypes: Kay the divorced mom, Vicki the short-skirted slattern, Adelle the model child from a better neighborhood. Cruise any strip mall in town, muses the reporter, and you will see several of their ilk. Subscriptions to the paper take a nose-dive until the reporter resigns and a larger-format, full-color TV schedule is introduced.

How we are holding up: Summer presses on, August flares. As the phones' ringing wanes, crime-line volunteers drop off reluctantly, like rose petals. Friends and relatives of the missing women who have flocked here must return to their towns, jobs, more immediate families. There is no such thing as indefinite leave unless you are the missing women. Fliers in windows start to flap at the edges, tape losing its tack. Still, church attendance remains up. Moonlight strolls are kept to a minimum. Locksmiths can't install deadbolts quickly enough. Neighborhoods stay illuminated by floodlights and seething with attack dogs. Psychologists from the university advise us, in these prolonged times of stress, to be absolutely forthright with one another and to get plenty of rest and light to moderate exercise. Sixty-four percent of residents polled believe there will be more disappearances. Seventy-nine percent say the missing women are dead. Eleven percent believe the supernatural was involved. Two percent suggest they know something about the disappearance that the rest of us don't, and they aren't telling. The poll has a two percent margin of error.

Our police chief is often spotted raking a hand through his thin, whitening hair, loosening his collar. He has gained thirty pounds. We worry that the ordeal will force him into early retirement. For the most part we appreciate what he has done for the town, keeping both the leftist fringe and the religious zealots at bay to preserve our moderate sensibilities. Whereas our mayor is perceived to be an ineffectual weasel, the apprehended drunk drivers, college rowdies, neo-Nazis, drug dealers, and other riffraff can attest that our police chief has kept the peace. But even he cannot collar this invisible threat, this thief who whisks our women into the night, leaving only their plaintive, flat faces pressed against yellowing planes of paper, asking everyone: *Have you seen us?*

August simmering down, the newspaper finally succumbs to investigative inertia. No news is no news; they've been carrying the missing women for weeks now without a new development. Journalism must prevail; the women's photos are sponged from the B pages. Without the newspaper's resolve, we let the fair distract us, then a strike at the chicken-parts processing plant, then the college students' return to town. There's talk of rebuilding the stadium. We have our hands full.

The mayor orates, finally. This tragedy has torn at the heart of our community, he says. We are shocked, saddened, and bewildered, he says. Grappling for clues. Desperate for answers. Neighbor pitted against neighbor in suspicion and fear. We are momentarily stirred by the drama of his speech, but he is voicing sentiments of weeks ago. A belated coda. We've gotten on with it. That's his problem: no finger on the pulse. He's slow to evaluate, even slower to act. We resent his jowly, bow-tied demeanor. He proposes a monument in the square, a small gas torch that will stay lit, eternally vigilant, until the women return. Donations trickle in, guiltily.

From this, the newspaper enjoys a brief second wind of missing-women coverage. After the press conference, there are additional quotes to be gleaned from the mayor, the locally available friends and family of the missing, and the major contributors to the gas torch. There is even a statement from the fire marshal attesting to the relative safety of the proposed monument. The newspaper's cartoonist, known for her acid social commentary, draws bums and bag ladies toasting skewered rats over the torch's flame — to call attention to the downtown homeless. This is generally derided as tasteless, and the editor prints what amounts to an apology under CORRECTIONS, saying the paper "regrets the error." The cartoonist resigns under pressure and files suit. She donates part of her settlement to the torch fund, part to the soup kitchen. There will be other occasional flare-ups. Adelle's parents will reemerge woefully from time to time, but in retrospect we will see that it was here the story's last traces turned to ash.

And what of the missing women? They do turn up, but only in dreams. We're at a party, and though the dream seems intended only to air private anxieties (we find ourselves naked in a room full of people), there are the three of them, lingering over the bean dip. Or we walk into an alcove filled with light and see Adelle in her wedding dress, spinning, spinning, her face aging with each rotation, the smile lined and straining, G forces undulating her cheeks. Or from the reception area of her beauty shop we watch Kay cutting hair that drops in soft heaps, the yellow-blond hair of her daughter, black at the root. Or the girls are wearing graduation caps and robes and clutching scrolls. The scrolls are not diplomas but maps of their whereabouts. They offer us a peek, but when we lean in to look, they pull away, snickering with teenage disdain, and vanish. Or, in the one we don't speak of, we are running down a familiar forest path, hunted, and we sense them beneath the pads of our feet, planted deep in the dark, green woods, bones cooling, and we wake, knowing they've been here all along.

JEFFREY EUGENIDES

Air Mail

FROM THE YALE REVIEW

THROUGH THE BAMBOO Mitchell watched the German woman, his fellow invalid, making another trip to the outhouse. She came out onto the porch of her hut, holding a hand over her eyes — it was murderously sunny out — while her other, somnambulistic hand searched for the beach towel hanging over the railing. Finding it, she draped the towel loosely, only just extenuatingly, over her otherwise unclothed body and staggered out into the sun. She came right by Mitchell's hut. Through the slats her skin looked a sickly, chicken-soup color. She was wearing only one flip-flop. Every few steps she had to stop and lift her bare foot out of the blazing sand. Then she rested, flamingo style, breathing hard. She looked as if she might collapse. But she didn't. She made it across the sand to the edge of the scrubby jungle. When she reached the outhouse, she opened the door and peered into the darkness. Then she consigned herself to it.

Mitchell dropped his head back to the floor. He was lying on a straw mat, with a plaid L. L. Bean bathing suit for a pillow. It was cool in the hut and he didn't want to get up himself. Unfortunately, his stomach was erupting. All night his insides had been quiet, but that morning Larry had persuaded him to eat an egg, and now the amoebas had something to feed on. "I told you I didn't want an egg," he said now, and only then remembered that Larry wasn't there. Larry was off down the beach, partying with the Australians.

So as not to get angry, Mitchell closed his eyes and took a series of deep breaths. After only a few, the ringing started up. He listened, breathing in and out, trying to pay attention to nothing else. When the ringing got even louder, he rose on one elbow and searched for the letter he was writing to his parents. The most recent letter. He found it tucked into Ephesians, in his pocket New Testament. The front of the aerogram was already covered with handwriting. Without bothering to reread what he'd written, he grabbed the ballpoint pen — wedged at the ready in the bamboo — and began:

Do you remember my old English teacher, Mr. Dudar? When I was in tenth grade, he came down with cancer of the esophagus. It turned out he was a Christian Scientist, which we never knew. He refused to have chemotherapy even. And guess what happened? Absolute and total remission.

The tin door of the outhouse rattled shut and the German woman emerged into the sun again. Her towel had a wet stain. Mitchell put down his letter and crawled to the door of his hut. As soon as he stuck out his head, he could feel the heat. The sky was the filtered blue of a souvenir postcard, the ocean one shade darker. The white sand was like a tanning reflector. He squinted at the silhouette hobbling toward him.

"How are you feeling?"

The German woman didn't answer until she reached a stripe of shade between the huts. She lifted her foot and scowled at it. "When I go, it is just brown water."

"It'll go away. Just keep fasting."

"I am fasting three days now."

"You have to starve the amoebas out."

"*Ja*, but I think the amoebas are maybe starving me out." Except for the towel she was still naked, but naked like a sick person. Mitchell didn't feel anything. She waved and started walking away.

When she was gone, he crawled back into his hut and lay on the mat again. He picked up the pen and wrote, *Mohandas K. Gandhi used to sleep with his grandnieces, one on either side, to test his vow of chastity — i.e., saints are always fanatics.*

He laid his head on the bathing suit and closed his eyes. In a moment, the ringing started again.

It was interrupted some time later by the floor shaking. The bamboo bounced under Mitchell's head and he sat up. In the doorway his traveling companion's face hung like a harvest moon. Larry was wearing a Burmese lungi and an Indian silk scarf. His chest, hairier than you expected on a little guy, was bare, and sunburned as pink as his face. His scarf had metallic gold and silver threads and was thrown dramatically over one shoulder. He was smoking a bidi, half bent over, looking at Mitchell.

"Diarrhea update," he said.

"I'm fine."

"You're fine?"

"I'm okay."

Larry seemed disappointed. The new pink skin on his forehead wrinkled. He held up a small glass bottle. "I brought you some pills. For the shits."

"Pills plug you up," Mitchell said. "Then the amoebas stay in you."

"Gwendolyn gave them to me. You should try them. Fasting would have worked by now. It's been what? Almost a week?"

"Fasting doesn't include being force-fed eggs."

"One egg," said Larry, waving this away.

"I was all right before I ate that egg. Now my stomach hurts."

"I thought you said you were fine."

"I am fine," said Mitchell, and his stomach erupted. He felt a series of pops in his lower abdomen, followed by an easing, as of liquid being siphoned off; then from his bowels came the familiar insistent pressure. He turned his head away, closing his eyes, and began to breathe deeply again.

Larry took a few more drags on the bidi and said, "You don't look so good to me."

"You," said Mitchell, still with his eyes closed, "are stoned."

"You betcha," was Larry's response. "Which reminds me. We ran out of papers." He stepped over Mitchell, and the array of aerograms, finished and unfinished, and the tiny New Testament, into his — that is, Larry's — half of the hut. He crouched and began searching through his bag. Larry's bag was made of rainbow-colored burlap. So far, it had never passed through customs without being exhaustively searched. It was the kind of bag that announced, "I am carrying drugs." Larry found his chillum, removed the stone bowl, and knocked out the ashes.

"Don't do that on the floor."

"Relax. They fall right through." He rubbed his fingers back and forth. "See? All tidy."

He put the chillum to his mouth to make sure that it was drawing.

As he did so he looked sideways at Mitchell. "Do you think you'll be able to travel soon?"

"I think so."

"Because we should probably be getting back to Bangkok. I mean, eventually. I'm up for Bali. You up?"

"As soon as I'm up," said Mitchell.

Larry nodded, once, as though satisfied. He removed the chillum from his mouth and reinserted the bidi. He stood up, hunching over beneath the roof, and paused again, staring at the floor.

"The mail boat comes tomorrow."

"What?"

"The mail boat. For your letters." Larry pushed a few around with his foot. "You want me to mail them for you? You have to go down to the beach."

"I can do it. I'll be up tomorrow."

Larry raised one eyebrow but said nothing. Then he started for the door. "I'll leave these pills in case you change your mind."

As soon as he was gone, Mitchell got up. There was no putting it off any longer. He retied his lungi and stepped out on the porch, covering his eyes. He kicked around for his flip-flops. Beyond, he was aware of the beach and the shuffling waves. He came down the steps and started walking. He didn't look up. He saw only his feet and the sand rolling past. The German woman's footprints were still visible, along with pieces of litter, shredded packages of Nescafé or balled-up paper napkins that blew from the cook tent. He could smell fish grilling. It didn't make him hungry.

The outhouse was a shack of corrugated tin. Outside sat a rusted oil drum of water and a small plastic bucket. Mitchell filled the bucket and took it inside. Before closing the door, while there was still light to see, he positioned his feet on the platform to either side of the hole. Then he closed the door and everything became dark. He undid his lungi and pulled it up, hanging the fabric around his neck. Using Asian toilets had made him limber: he could squat for ten minutes without strain. As for the smell, he hardly noticed it anymore. He held the door closed so that no one would barge in on him.

The sheer volume of liquid that rushed out of him still surprised him, but it always came as a relief. He imagined the amoebas being swept away in the flood, swirling down the drain of himself and out of his body. The dysentery had made him intimate with his insides; he had a clear sense of his stomach, of his colon; he felt the smooth muscular piping that constituted him. The combustion began high in his intestines. Then it worked its way along, like an egg swallowed by a snake, expanding, stretching the tissue, until, with a series of shudders, it dropped, and he exploded into water.

He'd been sick not for a week but for thirteen days. He hadn't said anything to Larry at first. One morning in a guesthouse in Bang-kok, Mitchell had awoken with a queasy stomach. Once up and out of his mosquito netting, though, he'd felt better. Then that night after dinner, there'd come a series of taps, like fingers drumming on the inside of his abdomen. The next morning the diarrhea started. That was no big deal. He'd had it before in India, but it had gone away after a few days. This didn't. Instead, it got worse, send-ing him to the bathroom a few times after every meal. Soon he started to feel fatigued. He got dizzy when he stood up. His stom-ach burned after eating. But he kept on traveling. He didn't think it was anything serious. From Bangkok, he and Larry took a bus to the coast, where they boarded a ferry to the island. The boat put-tered into the small cove, shutting off its engine in the shallow water. They had to wade to shore. Just that — jumping in — had confirmed things. The sloshing of the sea mimicked the sloshing in Mitchell's gut. As soon as they got settled, Mitchell had begun to fast. For a week now he'd consumed nothing but black tea, leaving the hut only for the outhouse. Coming out one day, he'd run into the German woman and had persuaded her to start fasting, too. Otherwise, he lay on his mat, thinking and writing letters home.

Greetings from paradise. Larry and I are currently staying on a tropical island in the Gulf of Siam (check the world atlas). We have our own hut right on the beach, for which we pay the princely sum of five dollars per night. This island hasn't been discovered yet so there's almost nobody here. He went on, describing the island (or as much as he could glimpse through the bamboo), but soon returned to more important pre-occupations. *Eastern religion teaches that all matter is illusory. That includes everything, our house, every one of Dad's suits, even Mom's plant hangers — all* maya, *according to the Buddha. That category also in-cludes, of course, the body. One of the reasons I decided to take this Grand Tour was that our frame of reference back in Detroit seemed a little cramped.*

And there are a few things I've come to believe in. And to test. One of which is that we can control our bodies with our minds. They have monks in Tibet who can mentally regulate their physiologies. They play a game called "melting snowballs." They put a snowball in one hand and then meditate, sending all their internal heat to that hand. The one who melts the snowball fastest wins.

From time to time, he stopped writing to sit with his eyes closed, as though waiting for inspiration. And that was exactly how he'd been sitting two months earlier — eyes closed, spine straight, head lifted, nose somehow alert — when the ringing started. It had happened in a pale green Indian hotel room in Mahalibalipuram. Mitchell had been sitting on his bed, in the half-lotus position. His inflexible left, western knee stuck way up in the air. Larry was off exploring the streets. Mitchell was all alone. He hadn't even been waiting for anything to happen. He was just sitting there, trying to meditate, his mind wandering to all sorts of things. For instance, he was thinking about his old girlfriend, Christine Woodhouse, and her amazing red pubic hair that he'd never get to see again. He was thinking about food. He was hoping they had something in this town besides *idli sambar.* Every so often he'd become aware of how much his mind was wandering, and then he'd try to direct it back to his breathing. Then sometime in the middle of all this, when he least expected it, when he'd stopped even trying or waiting for anything to happen (which was exactly when all the mystics said it would happen), Mitchell's ears had begun to ring. Very softly. It wasn't an unfamiliar ringing. In fact, he recognized it. He could remember standing in the front yard one day as a little kid and suddenly hearing this ringing in his ears, and asking his older brothers, "Do you hear that ringing?" They said they didn't but knew what he was talking about. In the pale green hotel room, after almost twenty years, Mitchell heard it again. He thought maybe this ringing was what they meant by the Cosmic Om. Or the music of the spheres. He kept trying to hear it after that. Wherever he went, he listened for the ringing, and after a while he got pretty good at hearing it. He heard it in the middle of Sudder Street in Calcutta, with cabs honking and street urchins shouting for baksheesh. He heard it on the train up to Chiang Mai. It was the sound of the universal energy, of all the atoms linking up to create the colors before his eyes. It had been right there the whole time. All he had to do was wake up and listen to it.

He wrote home, at first tentatively, then with growing confidence, about what was happening to him. *The energy flow of the universe is capable of being perceived. We are, each of us, finely tuned radios. We just have to blow the dust off our tubes.* He sent his parents a few letters each week. He sent letters to his brothers, too. And to his friends. Whatever he was thinking, he wrote down. He didn't consider people's reactions. He was seized by a need to analyze his intuitions, to describe what he saw and felt. *Dear Mom and Dad, I saw a woman being cremated this afternoon. You can tell if it's a woman by the color of the shroud. Hers was red. It burned off first. Then her skin did. While I was watching, her intestines filled up with hot gas, like a great big balloon. They got bigger and bigger until they finally popped. Then all this fluid came out. I tried to find something similar on a postcard for you but no such luck.*

Or else: *Dear Petie, Does it ever occur to you that this world of earwax remover and embarrassing jock itch might not be the whole megillah? Sometimes it looks that way to me. Blake believed in angelic recitation. And who knows? His poems back him up. Except for that one about the lamb, which I've always hated. Sometimes at night, though, when the moon gets that very pale thing going, I swear I feel a flutter against the three-day growth on my cheeks.*

Mitchell had called home only once, from Calcutta. The connection had been bad. It was the first time Mitchell and his parents had experienced the transatlantic delay. His father answered. Mitchell said hello, hearing nothing until his last syllable, the *o*, echoed in his ears. After that, the static changed registers, and his father's voice came through. Traveling over half the globe, it lost some of its characteristic force. "Now listen, your mother and I want you to get on a plane and get yourself back home."

"I just got to India."

"You've been gone six months. That's long enough. We don't care what it costs. Use that credit card we gave you and buy yourself a ticket back home."

"I'll be home in two months or so."

"What the hell are you doing over there?" his father shouted, as best he could, against the satellite. "What is this about dead bodies in the Ganges? You're liable to come down with some disease."

"No, I won't. I feel fine."

"Well, your mother doesn't feel fine. She's worried half to death."

"Dad, this is the best part of the trip so far. Europe was great and everything, but it's still the West."

"And what's wrong with the West?"

"Nothing. Only it's more exciting to get away from your own culture."

"Speak to your mother," his father said.

And then his mother's voice, almost a whimper, had come over the line. "Mitchell, are you okay?"

"I'm fine."

"We're worried about you."

"Don't worry. I'm *fine*."

"You don't sound right in your letters. What's going on with you?"

Mitchell wondered if he could tell her. But there was no way to say it. You couldn't say, I've found the truth. People didn't like that.

"You sound like one of those Hare Krishnas."

"I haven't joined up yet, Mom. So far, all I've done is shave my head."

"You shaved your head, Mitchell!"

"No," he told her, though in fact it was true: he had shaved his head.

Then his father was back on the line. His voice was strictly business now, a gutter voice Mitchell hadn't heard before. "Listen, stop cocking around over there in India and get your butt back home. Six months is enough traveling. We gave you that credit card for emergencies and we want you . . ." Just then, a divine stroke, the line had gone dead. Mitchell had been left holding the receiver, with a queue of Bengalis waiting behind him. He'd decided to let them have their turns. He hung up the receiver, thinking that he shouldn't call home again. They couldn't possibly understand what he was going through or what this marvelous place had taught him. He'd tone down his letters, too. From now on, he'd stick to scenery.

But, of course, he hadn't. No more than five days had passed before he was writing home again, describing the incorruptible body of Saint Francis Xavier and how it had been carried through the streets of Goa for four hundred years until an overzealous pilgrim had bitten off the saint's finger. Mitchell couldn't help himself. Everything he saw — the fantastical banyan trees, the painted cows — made him start writing, and after he described the sights, he talked about their effect on him, and from the colors of the visible world he moved straightaway into the darkness and ringing of the invisible. When he got sick, he'd written home about that, too. *Dear Mom and Dad, I think I have a touch of amoebic dysentery.* He'd gone on to describe the symptoms, the remedies the other travelers used. *Everybody gets it sooner or later. I'm just going to fast and meditate until I get better. I've lost a little weight, but not much. Soon as I'm better, Larry and I are off to Bali.*

He was right about one thing: sooner or later, everybody did get it. Besides his German neighbor, two other travelers on the island had been suffering from stomach complaints. One, a Frenchman, laid low by a salad, had taken to his hut, from which he'd groaned and called for help like a dying emperor. But just yesterday Mitchell had seen him restored to health, rising out of the shallow bay with a parrotfish impaled on the end of his spear gun. The other victim had been a Swedish woman. Mitchell had last seen her being carried out, limp and exhausted, to the ferry. The Thai boatmen had pulled her aboard with the empty soda bottles and fuel containers. They were used to the sight of languishing foreigners. As soon as they'd stowed the woman on deck, they'd started smiling and waving. Then the boat had kicked into reverse, taking the woman back to the clinic on the mainland.

If it came to that, Mitchell knew he could always be evacuated. He didn't, however, expect it to come to that. Once he'd gotten the egg out of his system, he felt better. The pain in his stomach went away. Four or five times a day he had Larry bring him black tea. He refused to give the amoebas so much as a drop of milk to feed on. Contrary to what he would've expected, his mental energy didn't diminish but actually increased. *It's incredible how much energy is taken up with the act of digestion. Rather than being some weird penance, fasting is actually a very sane and scientific method of quieting the body, of turning the body off. And when the body turns off, the mind turns on. The Sanskrit for this is* moksa, *which means total liberation from the body.*

The strange thing was that here, in the hut, verifiably sick, Mitchell had never felt so good, so tranquil, or so brilliant in his life. He felt secure and watched over in a way he couldn't explain. He felt *happy.* Not so the German woman. She looked worse and worse. She hardly spoke when they passed now. Her skin looked even paler, splotchier. After a while Mitchell stopped encouraging her to keep fasting. He lay on his back, with the bathing suit over his eyes now, and paid no attention to her trips to the outhouse. He listened instead to the sounds of the island, people swimming and shouting on the beach, somebody learning to play a wooden flute a few huts down. Waves lapped, and occasionally a dead palm leaf or coconut fell to the ground. At night, the wild dogs began howling in the jungle. When he went to the outhouse, Mitchell could hear them moving around outside, coming up and sniffing him, the flow of his waste, through the holes in the walls. Most people banged flashlights against the tin door to scare the dogs away. Mitchell didn't even bring a flashlight along. He stood listening to the dogs gather in the vegetation. With sharp muzzles they pushed stalks aside until their red eyes appeared in the moonlight. Mitchell faced them down, serenely. He spread out his arms, offering himself, and when they didn't attack, turned and walked back to his hut.

One night as he was coming back, he heard an Australian voice say, "Here comes the patient now." He looked up to see Larry and an older woman sitting on the porch of the hut. Larry was rolling a joint on his *Let's Go: Asia*. The woman was smoking a cigarette and looking straight at Mitchell. "Hello, Mitchell, I'm Gwendolyn," she said. "I hear you've been sick."

"Somewhat."

"Larry says you haven't been taking the pills I sent over."

Mitchell didn't answer right away. He hadn't talked to another human being all day. Or for a couple of days. He had to get reacclimated. Solitude had sensitized him to the roughness of other people, too. Gwendolyn's loud whiskey baritone, for instance, seemed to rake right across his chest. She was wearing some kind of batik headdress that looked like a bandage. Lots of tribal jewelry, too, bones and shells, hanging around her neck and from her wrists. In the middle of all this was her pinched, oversunned face, with the red coil of the cigarette in the center blinking on and off. Larry was just a halo of blond hair in the moonlight.

"I had a terrible case of the trots myself," Gwendolyn continued. "Truly epic. In Irian Jaya. Those pills were a godsend."

Larry gave a finishing lick to the joint and lit it. He inhaled, looking up at Mitchell, then said in a smoke-tightened voice, "We're here to make you take your medicine."

"That's right. Fasting is all well and good, but after — what has it been?"

"Two weeks almost."

"After two weeks, it's time to stop." She looked stern, but then the joint came her way, and she said, "Oh, lovely." She took a hit, held it, smiled at both of them, and then launched into a fit of coughing. It went on for about thirty seconds. Finally she drank some beer, holding her hand over her chest. Then she resumed smoking her cigarette.

Mitchell was looking at a big stripe of moon on the ocean. Suddenly he said, "You just got divorced. Is that why you're taking this trip?"

Gwendolyn stiffened. "Almost right. Not divorced but separated. Is it that obvious?"

"You're a hairdresser," Mitchell said, still looking out to sea.

"You didn't tell me your friend was a clairvoyant, Larry."

"I must have told him. Did I tell you?"

Mitchell didn't answer.

"Well, Mr. Nostradamus, I have a prediction for you. If you don't take those pills right now, you are going to be hauled away on the ferry *one very sick boy*. You don't want that, do you?"

Mitchell looked into Gwendolyn's eyes for the first time. He was struck by the irony: she thought he was the sick one. Whereas it looked to him the other way around. Already she was lighting another cigarette. She was forty-three years old, getting stoned on an island off the coast of Thailand while wearing pieces of a coral reef from each earlobe. Her unhappiness rose off her like a wind. It wasn't that he was clairvoyant. It was just obvious.

She looked away. "Larry, where are my pills now?"

"Inside the hut."

"Could you get them for me?"

Larry turned on his flashlight and bent through the doorway. The flashlight raked the floor. "You still haven't mailed your letters."

"I forgot. Soon as I finish them, I feel like I've sent them already."

Larry reappeared with the bottle of pills and announced, "It's starting to smell in there." He handed the bottle to Gwendolyn.

"All right, you stubborn man, open up."

She held out a pill.

"That's okay. Really. I'm fine."

"Take your medicine," Gwendolyn said.

"Come on, Mitch, you look like shit. Do it. Take a goddamn pill."

For a moment there was silence, as they stared at him. Mitchell wanted to explain his position, but it was pretty obvious that no amount of explanation would convince them that what he was doing made any sense. Everything he thought to say didn't quite cover it. Everything he thought to say cheapened how he felt. So he decided on the course of least resistance. He opened his mouth.

"Your tongue is bright yellow," Gwendolyn said. "I've never seen such a yellow except on a parrot. Go on. Wash it down with a little beer." She handed him her bottle.

"Bravo. Now take these four times a day for a week. Larry, I'm leaving you in charge of seeing that he does it."

"I think I need to go to sleep now," Mitchell said.

"All right," said Gwendolyn. "We'll move the party down to my hut."

When they were gone, Mitchell crawled back inside and lay down. Without otherwise moving, he spit out the pill, which he'd kept under his tongue. It clattered against the bamboo, then fell through to the sand underneath. Just like Jack Nicholson in *Cuckoo's Nest*, he thought, smiling to himself, but was too genuinely exhausted to write down.

With the bathing suit over his eyes, the days were more perfect, more obliterated. He slept in snatches, whenever he felt like it, and stopped paying attention to time. The rhythms of the island reached him: the sleep-thickened voices of people breakfasting on banana pancakes and coffee; later, shouts on the beach; and in the evenings, the grill smoking, and the Chinese cook scraping her wok with a long metal spatula. Beer bottles popped open; the cook tent filled with voices; then the various small parties bloomed in neighboring huts. At some point Larry would come back, smelling of beer, smoke, and suntan lotion. Mitchell would pretend to be asleep. Sometimes he was awake all night while Larry slept. Through his back, he could feel the floor, then the island itself, then the circulation of the ocean. The moon became full and, on rising, lit up the hut. Mitchell got up and walked down to the silver edge of the water. He waded out and floated on his back, staring up at the moon and stars. The bay was a warm bath; the island floated in it, too. He closed his eyes and concentrated on his breathing. After a while, he felt all sense of outside and inside disappearing. He wasn't breathing so much as *being* breathed. The state would last only a few seconds, then he'd come out, then he'd get it again.

His skin began to taste of salt. The wind carried it through the bamboo, coating him as he lay on his back, or blew over him as he made his way to the outhouse. While he squatted, he sucked the salt from his bare shoulders. It was his only food. Sometimes he had an urge to go into the cook tent and order an entire grilled fish or a stack of pancakes. But stabs of hunger were rare, and in their wake he felt only a deeper, more complete peace. The floods continued to rush out of him, with less violence now but rawly, as though from a wound. He opened the drum and filled the water bucket, washed himself with his left hand. A few times he fell asleep, crouching over the hole, and came awake only when someone knocked on the metal door.

He wrote more letters. *Did I ever tell you about the leper mother and son I saw in Bangalore? I was coming down this street and there they were, crouching by the curb. I was pretty used to seeing lepers by this point, but not ones like this. They were almost all the way gone. Their fingers weren't even stubs anymore. Their hands were just balls at the ends of their arms. And their faces were sliding off. It was like they were made of wax and were melting. The mother's left eye was all filmy and gray and stared up at the sky. But when I gave her 50 paise she looked at me with her good eye and it was really keen and intelligent looking. It was sort of* warm. *She touched her arm-knobs together, to thank me. And right then my coin hit the cup, and her son, who maybe couldn't see, said, "Atcha." He said it in a very pleased sort of way, almost smiling, though it was hard to tell if he was smiling because of the way his face was melting off. But what happened right then was this: I saw that they were people, not beggars or terribly unfortunate bad-karma types or anything like that — but just a mother and her kid. I could sort of see them back before they got leprosy or whatever, back when they used to just go out for a walk. And then I had another kind of revelation. I had a hunch that that kid was a nut for mango lassis. And this seemed a very profound revelation to me at the time. It was as big a revelation as I think I ever need or deserve. When my coin hit the cup and the boy said, "Atcha," I just knew that he was thinking about a nice cold mango lassi.* Mitchell put down his pen, remembering. Then he went outside to watch the sunset.

He sat down on the porch cross-legged. His left knee no longer stuck up. When he closed his eyes, the ringing began at once, louder, more intimate, more ravishing than ever.

So much seemed funny viewed from this distance. His worries about choosing a major. The way he used to not even leave the house when afflicted with glaring facial pimples. Even the searing despair of the time he'd called Christine Woodhouse's room and she hadn't come in all night was sort of funny now. You could waste your life. He had, pretty much, until the day he'd boarded that airplane with Larry, inoculated against typhus and cholera, and had escaped. Only now, with no one watching, could Mitchell find out who he was. It was as though riding in all those buses, over all those bumps, his old self had become dislodged bit by bit, so that it just rose up one day and vaporized into the Indian air. He didn't want to go back to the world of college and clove cigarettes. He was lying on his back, waiting for the moment when the body touched against enlightenment, or when nothing happened at all, which would be the same thing.

Meanwhile, next door, the German woman was on the move again. Mitchell heard her rustling around. She came down her steps, but instead of heading for the outhouse, she climbed the steps to Mitchell's hut. He removed the bathing suit from his eyes.

"I am going to the clinic. In the boat."

"I figured you might."

"I am going to get an injection. Stay one night. Then come back." She paused a moment. "You want to come with me? Get an injection?"

"No, thanks."

"Why not?"

"Because I'm better. I'm feeling a lot better."

"Come to the clinic. To be safe. We go together."

"I'm fine." He stood up, smiling, to indicate this. Out in the bay, the boat blew its horn.

Mitchell came out onto the porch to send her off. "I'll keep the home fires burning," he said. The German woman waded out to the boat and climbed aboard. She stood on deck, not waving, but looking in his direction. Mitchell watched her recede, growing smaller and smaller. When she disappeared at last, he realized that he'd been telling the truth: he *was* better.

His stomach was quiet. He put a hand over his belly, as though to register what was inside. His stomach felt hollowed out. And he wasn't dizzy anymore. He had to find a whole new aerogram, and in the light from the sunset he wrote, *On this day in I think November, I would like to announce that the gastrointestinal system of Mitchell B. Carambelis has hereby been cured by purely spiritual means. I want especially to thank my greatest supporter, who stuck with me through it all, Mary Baker Eddy. The next solid shit I take is really for her.* He was still writing when Larry came in.

"Wow. You're awake."

"I'm better."

"You are?"

"And guess what else?"

"What?"

Mitchell put down his pen and gave Larry a big smile. "I'm really hungry."

Everyone on the island had heard about Mitchell's Gandhian fast by this point. His arrival in the cook tent brought applause and cheers. Also gasps from some of the women, who couldn't bear to see how skinny he was. They got all maternal and made him sit down and felt his forehead for lingering fever. The tent was full of pineapples and watermelons, when he came in, also beans, onions, potatoes, lettuce. Long blue fish lay out on chopping blocks. Coffee thermoses lined one wall, full of hot water or tea, and in the back was another room containing a crib and the Chinese cook's baby. The baby looked sort of blue itself. Mitchell sat down and looked around at all the new faces. The dirt under the picnic table felt surprisingly cool against his bare feet.

The medical advice started up right away. Most people had fasted for a day or two during their Asian travels, after which they'd gone back to eating full meals. But Mitchell's fast had been so prolonged that this one American, a former medical student, said it was dangerous for Mitchell to eat too much too quickly. He advised having only liquids at first. The Chinese cook scoffed at this idea. After taking one look at Mitchell, she sent out a sea bass, a plate of fried rice, and an onion omelet. Most everybody else was for pure gluttony, too. Mitchell struck a compromise. First he drank a nice big glass of papaya juice. He waited a few minutes, then began, slowly, to eat the fried rice. After that, still feeling fine, he moved cau-

tiously, bite by bite, to the sea bass. Every so often, the former
medical student would say, "Okay, that's enough," but this would be
greeted by a chorus of other people saying, "Look at him. He's a
skeleton. Go on, eat. Eat!"

It was actually sort of nice to be with people again. He hadn't
become as ascetic as he'd thought. He missed people. All the girls
were wearing sarongs. They had truly accomplished tans and fetch-
ing accents. They kept coming up to encircle his wrists with their
thumbs and forefingers. "I'd die for cheekbones like yours," one
girl said. Then she made him eat some fried bananas.

Night fell. Somebody announced a party in hut number six.
Before Mitchell knew what was happening, he was being escorted
by two Dutch girls down the beach. They waitressed in Amsterdam
five months of the year and spent the rest traveling. Apparently,
Mitchell looked exactly like a van Hanthorst Christ in the Rijks-
museum. The Dutch girls found the resemblance both awe inspir-
ing and hilarious. Mostly hilarious. Mitchell started wondering if
he'd made a mistake by staying in the hut. Some kind of tribal life
had started up here on the island. No wonder Larry'd been having such a good time. Everybody was so friendly. It wasn't even
sexual so much as just warm and intimate. One of the Dutch girls
had a nasty rash on her back she turned around to show him.

The moon was already rising over the bay, casting a long swath of
light in to shore. It lit up the trunks of palm trees and gave the sand
a lunar phosphorescence. Everything was blue except for the orange, glowing huts. Mitchell felt the air rinsing his face and flowing
through his legs as he walked. There was a lightness inside him, a
helium balloon around his heart. There was nothing a person
needed beyond this beach.

He called out, "Hey, Larry." Larry was just up ahead.

"What?"

"We've gone everywhere, man."

"Not everywhere. Next stop Bali."

"Then home. After Bali, home. Before my parents have a nervous breakdown."

He stopped suddenly, holding the Dutch girls back. He thought
he heard the ringing — louder than ever — but then realized that
it was just the music coming from hut number six. Right out front,
people were sitting in a circle in the sand. They made room for
Mitchell and the new arrivals.

"What do you say, doctor? Can we give him a beer?"

"Very funny," the medical student said. "I suggest one. No more."

In due course, the beer was passed along the fire brigade and into Mitchell's hands. Then the person to Mitchell's right put her hand on his knee. It was Gwendolyn. He hadn't recognized her in the darkness. She took a long drag on her cigarette. She turned her face away, to exhale primarily, but also with the suggestion of hurt feelings, and said, "You haven't thanked me."

"For what?"

"For the pills."

"Oh, right. That was really thoughtful of you and everything."

She smiled for about four seconds and then started coughing. It was a smoker's cough, with gravel shifting around inside. She tried to suppress it by leaning forward and covering her mouth, but it didn't help. The coughs just echoed inside her chest cavity. Finally they stopped, and she wiped her eyes. "Oh, I'm dying." She looked around the circle of people. Everyone was talking and laughing. "Nobody cares."

All this time Mitchell had been examining Gwendolyn closely. It seemed clear to him that if she didn't have lung cancer already, she was going to get it soon. "Do you want to know how I knew you were separated?" he said.

"Well, I think I might."

"It's because of this glow you have. Women who get divorced or separated always have this glow. I've noticed it before. It's like they get younger or something."

"Really?"

"Yes, indeed," said Mitchell.

Gwendolyn smiled. "I am feeling rather restored."

Mitchell held out his beer and they clinked bottles.

"Cheers," she said.

"Cheers." He took a sip of beer. It was the best beer he'd ever tasted. Suddenly he felt ecstatically happy. There wasn't a campfire in the center, warming everyone, but it felt like that. Mitchell squinted at all the different faces and then just looked out at the bay. He thought about his trip. He tried to remember all the places he and Larry had gone, all the smelly pensions, the baroque cities, the hill stations. If he didn't think about any single place, he could sort of feel them all, kaleidoscopically shifting around inside his head. He felt complete and satisfied. At some point the ringing had started up again, and he was concentrating on that, too, so that at first he didn't notice the twinge in his intestines. Then, from far off, piercing his consciousness, came another twinge, still so delicate that he might have imagined it. In a moment it came again, more insistently. He felt a valve open inside him, and a trickle of hot liquid, like acid, begin burning its way toward the outside. He wasn't alarmed. He felt too good. He just stood up again and said, "I'm going down to the water a minute."

"I'll go with you," said Larry.

The moon was higher now. As they approached, the bay was lit up like a mirror. Away from the music, Mitchell could hear the wild dogs barking in the jungle. He led Larry straight down to the water's edge. Then, without pausing, he let his lungi drop and stepped out of it. He waded out.

"Skinny-dip?"

Mitchell didn't answer.

"What's the water temp?"

"Cold," said Mitchell, though this wasn't true: the water was warm. It was only that he wanted to be alone in it for some reason. He waded out until the water was waist deep. Cupping both hands, he sprinkled water over his face. Then he dropped into the water and began to float on his back.

His ears plugged up. He heard water rushing, then the silence of the sea, then the ringing again. It was clearer than ever. It wasn't a ringing so much as a beacon penetrating his body.

He lifted his head and said, "Larry."

"What?"

"Thanks for taking care of me."

"No problem."

Now that he was in the water, he felt better again. He sensed the pull of the tide out in the bay, retreating with the night wind and the rising moon. A small hot stream came out of him, and he paddled away from it and continued to float. He stared up at the sky. He didn't have his pen or aerograms with him, so he began to dictate silently: *Dear Mom and Dad, The earth itself is all the evidence we need. Its rhythms, its perpetual regeneration, the rising and falling of the moon, the tide flowing in to land and out again to sea, all this is a lesson for that very slow learner, the human race. The earth keeps repeating the drill, over and over, until we get it right.*

"Nobody would believe this place," Larry said on the beach. "It's a total fucking paradise."

The ringing grew louder. A minute passed, or a few minutes. Finally he heard Larry say, "Hey, Mitch, I'm going back to the party now. You okay?" He sounded far away.

Mitchell stretched out his arms, which allowed him to float a little higher in the water. He couldn't tell if Larry had gone or not. He was looking at the moon. He'd begun to notice something about the moon that he'd never noticed before. He could make out the wavelengths of the moonlight. He'd managed to slow his mind down enough to perceive that. The moonlight would speed up a second, growing brighter, then it would slow down, becoming dim. It *pulsed*. The moonlight was a kind of ringing itself. He lay undulating in the warm water, observing the correspondence of moonlight and ringing, how they increased together, diminished together. After a while, he began to be aware that he, too, was like that. His blood pulsed with the moonlight, with the ringing. Something was coming out of him, far away. He felt his insides emptying out. The sensation of water leaving him was no longer painful or explosive; it had become a steady flow of his essence into nature. In the next second, Mitchell felt as though he were dropping through the water, and then he had no sense of himself at all. He wasn't the one looking at the moon or hearing the ringing. And yet he was aware of them. For a moment, he thought he should send word to his parents, to tell them not to worry. He'd found the paradise beyond the island. He was trying to gather himself to dictate this last message, but soon he realized that there was nothing left of him to do it — nothing at all — no person left to hold a pen or to send word to the people he loved, who would never understand.

Soon

FROM THE SOUTHERN REVIEW

1

MARTHA'S MOTHER, Elizabeth Long Crawford, had been born with a lazy eye, and one morning when she was twelve her father and the doctor sat her down in the dining room at Marlcrest, the Longs' place near Augusta, Georgia, and told her they were going to fix her so that a man would want to marry her someday. Her father held her on his lap while the doctor pressed a handkerchief soaked with chloroform over her nose and mouth, and she went under, dreaming of the beauty she would be. But the doctor's hand slipped, and when Elizabeth came to, she was blind in her right eye. For the rest of her life what she remembered of that morning were the last sights she'd seen through two eyes: the shadows of leaves on the sunny floor, the hair on the backs of her father's hands, the stripe on the doctor's trousers, the handkerchief coming down. Then blindness. The rise and the downfall of hope, one complete revolution of the wheel that turned the world, that's what she'd lived through.

Marlcrest was a hard name to pronounce. The first syllable sprawled, it wouldn't be hurried; the last climbed a height and looked down on the rest of the world the way Martha's mother had done all her life. It had been a hard place to live, too. One hundred acres of level, sandy land on a bluff above the Savannah River, and a house raised high on brick pillars to offer the people of the house a view of the river, a chance at the river breezes. When Elizabeth married Perry Crawford, he agreed to live there, too. *She* wasn't leaving. In the family cemetery on the bluff stood the Long tomb and the graves of the children who'd died at birth, who had fallen or been trampled by horses or killed by cholera or yellow fever during the two hundred years the Longs had lived at Marlcrest. Before the Civil War, slaves hauled muck up from the river — the *marl* of which the *crest* was made — to spread on the fields. Many died there: smothered in the mud, collapsed in the heat, snakebit, drowned. They were buried in a corner of a distant field that the pine woods had taken back years before Martha was born, though even in Martha's time a person could still find pieces of broken dishes, shells, empty brown medicine bottles under the pine needles, as if the people buried there had been carried out and lowered down by others who believed that the dead could be quieted and fed.

After the botched operation, Martha's mother lived where the wheel had stopped and she'd stepped off. The blind eye that the doctor had closed gave her a proud, divided look, as though half her face slept while the other stayed fiercely alert, on the lookout for the next betrayal. It was how she'd looked at seventy-five — disfigured and ferocious — when she'd summoned Martha and her brother, Perry Jr., to the nursing home in Augusta where they'd put her after a series of small strokes had made it dangerous for her to live alone at Marlcrest any longer. For six months before they'd put her in the home, there'd been trouble after trouble. She'd stopped payment on every check she wrote. The doors of the house, inside and out, had filled up with locks. Every night her calls to her children were packed with complaint. The woman they'd hired to stay with her was a thief, a drunk. Someone was downstairs picking the locks. It was that Herbert Long from up the road. He and his family, descendants of the slaves who'd once lived on the place. For a hundred years they'd bided their time; now they'd come to steal from her.

At the nursing home that day, Martha and Perry Jr. found their mother in her wheelchair in the sun by the window. She was dressed in beige linen, her best earrings, heirloom pearls. Her hair had been freshly restored to a cresting silver wave, and she was draped in Arpège perfume, as she had been in all her finest hours. "Well, don't you look nice, Mother. What's the occasion?" Martha asked, kissing her mother's sweet, powdered cheek.

Some papers their mother had in her purse, that was the occasion. Notarized contracts. Smiling brilliantly, she handed over the documents, one by one, to Martha and Perry Jr. She'd sold Marlcrest — the whole kit and caboodle — to a developer who planned to bulldoze the house, clear the land, build a subdivision there. Plantation Oaks, he'd call it. "Here is a copy of the title deed," she said, passing it to Perry Jr. "As you will see, it is properly signed and notarized." He turned it over, held it up to the light, looking for the error that would void the contract. As for the family records and belongings — the *contents* of the house, she said, leaning toward them from her wheelchair with her hands folded in her lap and high color in her cheeks, savoring (Martha saw) the vengeful triumph of this theft — she'd sold them all to a young man from a southern history museum in Atlanta. *Smack*, she struck the wheelchair's armrest. *Done.* He'd been coming to visit her in the nursing home since Martha and Perry Jr. had put her there — it had been almost exactly one year now. He'd even driven her out to Marlcrest a time or two to pick up something she'd forgotten. The Long family had many possessions of historical interest; already the museum people were calling their belongings the most important collection of southern artifacts ever acquired in Georgia. Fine linen shirts and baby gowns sewn by slave seamstresses. Diaries and ledgers and sharecropper contracts. Tools, portraits. A complete record of plantation life. The young man had been so sweet to her. He had all the time in the world to sit and talk. He never sneaked looks at his watch or found some excuse to jump up and rush off five minutes after he'd sat down.

Not that Martha and Perry Jr. hadn't been expecting it somehow. What has been lived will be handed on. Throughout their childhoods their mother had told them she lived by *high ideals*, which meant that everything had to be right — but since nothing ever was right, she was constantly, deeply, and bitterly disappointed by every person and every circumstance. *Horsy* had been her word for Martha, and in it were catalogued all of Martha's lacks. A long face, big teeth, lank hair, eyes that shone with dark, equine clarity. Yes, and Martha was also too *big*, too meaty. She sweated in the summer heat, and in winter her fingertips stayed cold. Perry Jr. was never more than an adequate student, a lukewarm son. Even her husband, Perry Sr., had failed her. When Martha was sixteen and Perry Jr. eighteen, their father sneaked off early one October morning to go duck hunting alone in the swamp below the old slave burying ground and was struck dead by a heart attack. After dark the sheriff found him up in the duck blind, still seated on his camp stool with his gun across his knees, looking out the little window hole in the sidewall of the blind, as though he were watching the mallards flash and preen in the dark water below.

His death made their mother furious; afterward she widened her search for the thief who'd robbed her. And yet, though Martha and Perry Jr. had both expected that someday their mother would get to their names on her long list of suspects in the crimes against her, neither was prepared for it. Is anyone *prepared* for the actuality of life, which is always more surprising or horrifying or sweet than we could ever have imagined? Not at all. We dream and wish and plan, but something more subtle, more generous and devious, arranges reality for us.

After they'd heard all their mother had to say about what she'd taken from them, after she'd leaned back, satisfied, and looked from one to the other of them with that brilliant and terrible *any questions?* look on her face, Martha had closed her eyes. She saw the bulldozer push the house. It swayed, cracked, fell, carrying beds, tables, chairs, the smell of closets, her grandmother's round hat-boxes and furs, the river's wide curve that she could see from her bedroom window in winter when the leaves had fallen and the trees along the banks were bare. Carrying even the slave cemetery, where, in the spring just past, Martha had found weeded ground, plastic lilies in a Mason jar. In the nursing home that day, Martha felt the world fail and move away from her for the first time; fail and move away the way her mother had taught her it would, not with words exactly, though Elizabeth had certainly given her children enough of those, but with her footsteps walking away from them, her closed face, her fury.

Their mother died within a year of that day. A stroke, of a magnitude even *she* would have approved — maybe — as the cause of death of a person of her stature, knocked her out of her wheelchair in the nursing home dining room one Saturday evening and killed her before the first hand touched her. In her coffin, Martha was startled to discover, her mother looked different than she had in life. The perfect wave of silver hair was intact, as were the long, elegant fingers, and yet, lacking the ferocious hauteur that had been its life, her face looked wasted and starved, as if under the rage a ravenous sadness had been at work. Not even the undertaker's crafted composure, the small rueful smile he'd shaped on her mouth, or the benign glow of the pink light bulbs in the funeral home lamps could soften the face she would wear now into eternity.

2

What do you do with what you've been handed? Martha would not have her children saying *poor Mother* over her coffin. She went back to the life she wanted, a calm and common life, firmly planted. As Martha saw it, her mother's bitterness and rage were exactly as large and violent as her hopes and her longings, and so it was these longings that Martha would uproot in herself. That's why she'd married Raymond Maitland in the first place (against her mother's wishes), a decent man from a decent family, a big, careful, sober man with jug ears who wanted what she wanted. They lived in the country outside Augusta, and Raymond, a salesman, traveled up and down the coast, only he called it the *eastern seaboard*, because he believed the high-minded sound of those words gave him a competitive edge over his coarser peers. His territory stretched from Myrtle Beach, South Carolina, to Jacksonville, Florida, and at one time or another, he sold insurance, encyclopedias, building materials, pharmaceuticals, vending machine snacks, and office supplies. The drawers in their kitchen and den filled up with pencils, ballpoint pens, rulers, rubber jar-lid openers, key chains, thermometers, and spatulas, all printed with the names and slogans of companies he'd represented.

In the spring, summer, and early fall, he drove with the windows rolled down (this was in the fifties, before air conditioners were standard in most cars), his left arm resting on the window ledge, so that arm was always sunburned when he returned from a sales trip. At home, it was one of their pleasures for him to shower, lie on their bed in his undershorts, and doze, with the fan blowing across him and the radio tuned to the light classics station, while she rubbed Solarcaine on his sunburned arm as gently and patiently as if his skin were her skin, so that he imagined sometimes that the spreading cool relief came from her fingertips, their delicate, swirling touch.

Then one day in late July, the summer he was fifty-eight and
Martha had just turned fifty-six, the summer Raymond Jr. finished
graduate school at Georgia Tech and their daughter, Louise, had
her second baby, Raymond returned from a week-long trip up the
coast. He traveled for Tom's Peanut Company then. He threw
his car keys onto the kitchen counter and fell into her arms, groaning about the six hundred miles he'd just driven through the *goddamn* heat, and at his age, too. He smelled of fry grease and cigarette smoke overlaid subtly with sweat and metal, the smell of the
road. Someday they'd find him dead of a heart attack, slumped
over the steering wheel on the shoulder of some sweltering back
road in the Pee Dee swamp. A desk job, that's what he wanted now.
To keep him closer to home, closer to *her,* that was the ticket. "Take
a shower," she said. "Come lie down."

While she rubbed the cream into his arm, she felt the silky slack-
ness of aging flesh under her hands; she saw that his muscles were
starting to droop, go ropy. His chest had begun to sag, too. And as
she tenderly catalogued the marks of time on her husband's body,
she noticed that his left arm was as pale as the rest of him. She
looked at the small, pleased, and peaceful smile on his mouth. She
sat on the edge of the bed with the fan blowing across them, the
Solarcaine squeezed onto her fingers, and a picture rose up to meet
her as though his skin had released it, like a smell: a woman in
green shorts lounging in a white wicker chair, her big tanned legs
crossed, smoking a cigarette and laughing.

She rubbed the Solarcaine into his pale arm. Next day she went
through the phone bills for the last six months, found call after call
to a number in Little River, South Carolina. The voice that answered when Martha called matched the thick legs, the cigarettes,
the indolence of the woman whose image had wormed its way into
her mind. That night, when she showed him the phone bills, Raymond put his hands over his face and cried. It was true, he said, it
was true, he'd gotten in over his head. He would break off with her,
her name was — "Don't you dare speak her name in my house,"
Martha shouted — if Martha would just be patient and give him
time. If she would just forgive him.

Patience she had, and time. Plenty of both, and also the will to
forgive. For six months they tried, but it had gone too far with the
other woman. The story came out in pieces: the things he'd given

her — jewelry and cash, a semester's tuition for her son at the University of South Carolina — the promises he'd made. She was a widow, twenty years younger than Martha. It almost drove Martha crazy. Just when she thought she'd heard the whole story, he'd choke out more until it seemed there was no end to the future he'd planned with this woman.

When Raymond left to go live with his big-legged woman in Little River, Martha told him she wanted two things — no, three, she wanted three things: she wanted the house in Augusta, and she wanted the house in Scaly Mountain. Louise and Raymond Jr. had been in grade school when Raymond and Martha had bought a beat-up old white clapboard house two stories tall and one room wide, roofed with tin, that sat on a foundation of stacked stones in a valley at the foot of Scaly Mountain, North Carolina; they went there every summer and at Thanksgiving, too, if they could manage it. Always, when they got there, Raymond had to be first out of the car. "Let Daddy have his minute," she'd say to the children, holding them back. He'd make a big show of stretching and breathing, as if he couldn't get enough of that air. Then he'd stand with his hands on his hips, his chest thrown out, king of the hill. Next he'd lean his elbows on the car door, push his wide, smiling face through the open window, squeeze her arm and say, "We're fifty-cent million-aires, Martha, sure enough," as if this discovery were new to him every time, meaning it didn't take much to make him feel rich. Meaning that what he had was all of what he wanted. Then he'd kiss her richly on the mouth, and they had arrived.

The last thing she wanted from Raymond was never to hear from him again. She meant it, too, about cutting him out of her life for good. She knew the way to the cold, bare space inside herself where she could live by the absolutes she declared. Goodbye, Raymond. "I thank my mother for the strength she instilled in me," she told Louise during the divorce. "No, really. She's the one who gave me the backbone for this." Finishing cleanly, she meant, cutting the cord.

3

Five years after the divorce, Martha announced that she was moving to the house in Scaly Mountain. "My thermostat must be broken, I can't take this heat any longer," she told Louise, who was frantic about her mother's moving so far away, and all alone, too. "What if you fall?" Louise asked. "What if you have a stroke or a heart attack?"

"Friend, come up higher," Martha joked with her friends from the Episcopal church when they asked her if she'd thought through what she was doing. She told others that she was retiring. From what? they demanded to know. From what? From canasta on Monday and bridge on Tuesday (she did not say), from standing in the vestibule before Sunday morning services, alert for a new face. ("Welcome to All Saints'. Are you visiting with us this morning? Would you please fill out this card and drop it in the collection basket? We're glad to have you.") From taping books for the blind and pushing the book cart around the hospital corridors, intruding on the desperately ill, challenging them with her smile to cheer up. From muffins and casseroles and sympathy calls and notes of congratulation or consolation. From rushing to church every time the doors swung open or having to explain her absence to some anxious friend. Goodbye to all that.

She did not speak to anyone of the solitude she craved: to be alone, with new vistas in front of her eyes and unfamiliar, rocky ground below her feet. She did not tell anyone how she wanted to be rid of Raymond, whose cigarette smoke clung to the paneling in the den and lingered in the closets of the Augusta house. The week before she decided to move, she'd come across a moldy package of Tom's cheese crackers way in the back of a kitchen drawer, and she'd known then that this house would always push reminders of Raymond up to the surface, no matter how hard she scrubbed and bleached and aired. He rested more lightly on the mountain house. There she would lift Raymond's few T-shirts out of the bottom drawer of the dresser in their bedroom and tear them into rags; she would take down his coffee mug from a kitchen shelf, tear his meticulous handwritten instructions off the wall between the hot-water heater and furnace and be finished with him for good. Then he would be gone the way her mother was gone. The mother whose grave she still visited dutifully twice a year, carrying a poinsettia at Christmas, a lily at Eastertime, standing with head bowed, her heart empty of any longing to see her mother, of any wish to speak.

But a person can't just do *nothing*, can she? Can't sit all day with her hands folded or a game of solitaire spread out on the kitchen table. Can't not talk to other people without beginning to hear strange echoes in the conversation she's carrying on with herself. So she went to work. She had the pasture behind the house cleared, she put in a pond. She added two rooms and a porch onto the back of the house, and she lengthened the kitchen until the house looked like a white, wooden shirt with outstretched arms. Over the mountain, to Highlands, twice a week she drove her white Dodge Dart to the senior citizens' center for canasta and talk.

Every week she wrote to her children, letters full of questions and advice. "Have Sarah Lynn's teeth shown any signs of straightening?" she asked her daughter. "If not, do *please* take her to the orthodontist." And "Those old linen napkins I gave you are to be used as *tea towels*," she wrote after she'd visited Louise and found the napkins balled up in the rag basket under the kitchen sink. Her daughter's letters were long and chatty, with fabric swatches stapled to them or pictures of the children enclosed. Raymond Jr. wrote his full-speed-ahead notes on "Memo from Raymond Maitland Jr." paper. He was big in Coca-Cola down in Atlanta, she told her friends over the canasta table. Very big, she'd repeat, arching her eyebrows to show that words simply could not map the circumference of his orbit.

Without fail she wrote a weekly letter to her brother, Perry Jr. After his wife died, he'd drifted into mysticism, joined the Rosicrucians. His letters were about the migration of souls, the power of the spirit to transcend time and space, to enter that place where there was no death, no beginning or end, only a current that carried you up and up, endlessly spiraling toward fulfillment, completion, bliss. He wanted to join his wife, he wrote. He could hardly wait for that day.

Martha sat in her bedroom in the mountain house she had made her own — no trace left of her traitor husband or her bitter black wind of a mother, not so much as a photograph of either of them — a plain, tall woman in a sleeveless blouse and a full cotton skirt made of a coarse woven material like burlap. Her braids were crossed and pinned over the top of her head; she wore orthopedic sandals with wool socks and sat with her ankles crossed, her back very straight in a high-backed chair pulled up to a white wooden table. One must be *realistic,* she wrote to her brother, apply the styptic pencil to one's scratches, pour iodine into the deeper wounds, get on with life in *this* world. Reality (she underlined it twice) was a constant and trustworthy companion who, once befriended, never let one down or walked away and loved someone else. A person must not wear himself out with wanting what it is impossible to have. What was finished must be done with and put away. "False hopes are cruel, Perry," she wrote. "We must not exhaust ourselves waiting for what will never happen. I speak from experience when I say this. As you well know, I have suffered indignities at the hands of life, we all have, but the longer I live the surer I become that the consolations of life — if any — must be sought and found in facing life squarely, as it is. The mind must not be allowed to wander where it wants, else it might end up lost in a wilderness of longing and regret. This I believe."

And then, late one September afternoon, when she'd lived in Scaly Mountain for a year, when the pond was full, the meadow fenced, the hay rolled and drying in the field she leased to a neighbor, as she sat on the porch after supper, watching the evening light flood into her valley and spread across the foot of her meadow, something changed in her. She felt it catch and roll over the way tumblers move inside a big lock. Maybe it was the gold light slanting across the fat rolls of hay that invited the change. Maybe it was the chore she'd finished — writing her mother's name and the date of her death in the Long family Bible — or the way she sat with the book open on her lap, watching the ink dry on the page.

Now this was no modest Sunday school Bible with a white pebbled cover and gold-leaf pages, a tiny gold cross dangling from a red-ribbon marker. It was the original family Bible in which the record of Long births, weddings, and deaths had been written since 1825. A serious and heavy book with a tooled leather cover, a lock and key. It smelled of the smoke of many fires, and its registry pages were stained and soft as cloth. When her father had opened it for family devotions, Martha used to imagine thunder rolling off its pages. She had gone to Marlcrest after her mother had sold everything; without hesitation and without guilt, she'd lifted the Bible off the carved wooden stand next to the fireplace in the downstairs parlor, where it had rested throughout her life and her mother's life and her mother's and her mother's lives, and taken it home. For a year, the museum wrote to her about the Bible. They were tentative, respectful letters at first. Later, letters from lawyers began to arrive. She'd ignored them all. Now, looking from her mother's name out to the hay drying in her meadow, she felt herself lifted, carried, and then set down one place closer to the head of the line her mother had vacated.

That's when the idea of the reunion came to her. She would gather what was left of the Long clan around her, here, in this place. The next morning she drove into Highlands and ordered stationery printed up with *Long Family Reunion* embossed across the top. She set the date for the following summer: July 6–9, 1969. All winter she wrote letters and logged in the answers, then sent back diagrams of the house with rooms and beds assigned.

Give Martha time, her brother used to say, and she could plan anything. Perry Jr. had landed with the Allies on D-Day; he always said that Martha could have planned the Normandy landing. She'd certainly planned *this.* Collected promises from twenty-five far-flung Longs, then stood in the parking lot she'd leveled in her meadow and waved them to their designated spaces with a flashlight, like a state trooper at a football game. She carried their suitcases and marched them up to the house and directed them to their rooms.

For the children there were relay races and treasure hunts and nature hikes down the valley with Martha at the head of the column, like the Scout leader she'd been when Louise was growing up, a walking catalogue of the lore of trees, reptiles, and stones. The girls in her troop had nicknamed her Skink, the lizard, for her bright-eyed, darting restlessness. For the grownups there was plenty of food, plenty of talk; the family Bible and photographs traveled from hand to hand. There was the Long family tree, a scroll as big as a blueprint, on which their genealogist had mapped every twig and root. At night there were games and prizes. A prize for the oldest Long, a dim old uncle, ninety-three that summer, who sat patiently wherever he was put until someone came back for him. And for the youngest, a son born in June to Lamar Long, who'd been promoted that summer to foreman of the weave room at the Bibb Mill in Porterdale, Georgia. A blue baby, they called him, born with a defective valve in his heart. A good baby, all eyes, who lay quietly in his basket studying the faces that followed each other like clouds across his sky.

Bossiest woman in the world, they whispered among themselves. Exactly like her mother, poor soul, some of the other ones said. Even her own brother had butted heads with her in the kitchen over something silly, over cream. One morning he came whistling into the kitchen, intending to skim a dollop of cream for his coffee from the top of one of the bottles of raw milk that Martha had bought from a neighbor. Right behind him came Martha, who plucked the bottle out of his hand before he could shut the refrigerator door. "I am saving this, Perry," she told him, "to go on top of the blackberry pie I shall make for the farewell dinner."

"Oh, come on, Martha, I only want a teaspoon," he said.

"No, I cannot spare that much." For half an hour it went on this way.

Then Perry tried for the last word. "I want some of that cream, Martha," he said, holding out his cup to her. It trembled in his hand. "Just a smidgen to put in my damn coffee."

"Well, you can't have it, Perry," she said. "I told you, it's for the pie. I need it all." She held the bottle out to show him — not the thick yellow clot in the neck of the bottle, but the cream, the *cream* whipped into high, stiff points and her pie, warm and rich beneath that sweet, smothering layer. Couldn't he see it? She could, and the thought of that cream-to-be made tears stand in her eyes. Then the thought of herself crying over *whipped cream* made her furious. She who'd written to her brother about dignity and the pitfalls of looking too far into future or past for happiness or consolation, who had thrown all the force of her considerable will into living in the world as it *is*. Finally Perry Jr. slammed his coffee cup down onto the kitchen counter and walked out. That night he said to one of the other men, "I had to lock horns with Martha today." And a child who overheard the remark and the laughter that followed pictured two warring moose in a mountain meadow, their enormous racks locked, shoving each other until they fell from exhaustion and died. Then the passing seasons, then the bones covered with hide, the bleached antlers still entangled.

On the last day of the reunion, as she'd planned, Martha climbed the rickety wooden stepladder, shooed away helpers, and strung Japanese paper lanterns between the big silver maple beside the road and the cedar nearest the house. At six-fifteen they would eat, followed at seven by speeches, testimonials, recollections, a song or two, and a final word from the genealogist, who'd traced the family back to England and tonight would name for them the place from which the first Longs had set out for the New World hundreds of years before. Exactly at six, Martha struck a small silver bell with a silver fork and waited until its clear note had died away, then invited everyone to line up, which they did, oldest to youngest, as she'd planned. Then they filed past the tables made of sawhorses and planks and covered with white cloths and filled their plates. Chicken and corn and beans — they heaped it on — banana pudding and coconut cake and, of course, Martha's blackberry pie topped with a mountain range of whipped cream.

They'd just settled down to eat when she heard Abel Rankin coming down the road. He was her neighbor, the one who sold her the raw milk out of cans that he carried in the back of his wagon, that wholesome milk from his own cows from which she'd salvaged *all* the cream. When she heard the clink of the cans, the jolting rattle of the wagon, the jingle of Sawdust the mule's bridle and the stumbling crack of his hooves on the rocky road, she dished up a plate — chicken and beans and coconut cake — and walked out to the edge of the yard to wait for him. When Abel Rankin saw her, he reined in the dun-colored mule and said, "Evening" (never quite meeting her eyes), touched the brim of his brown felt hat, and took the plate of food she held up to him. "Eat this, Mr. Rankin," she said.

He ate quickly, hunched over on the wagon seat as though eating were a chore he had to finish before nightfall, while she held Sawdust's bridle, patted his face, felt the bony plank of his nose, his breath on her hands. When the children came running to pat the mule, she took charge. She made them line up and listen to her. "Now, stroke his nose lightly," she said. "You must stroke an animal as lightly as you'd stroke a hummingbird. You want him to remember you?" she asked. "Blow into his nostrils. Gently, gently, like this, you hear me talking to you?"

Those were her mother's teachings, her mother's actual *words*. As soon as they'd left her mouth, she felt her mother walk up and stand behind her, listening, to hear if she'd gotten it right, how to treat an animal. Her mother had always kept a reservoir of tenderness toward animals unpolluted by her general disappointment and bitterness. No animal had ever betrayed her. Oh, no. When Martha was a child, there had always been a pack of half-starved stray dogs skulking around the back steps at Marlcrest, waiting for her mother to feed them. There had always been a shoebox on top of the stove full of baby squirrels rescued from a fallen pine, tenderly wrapped in flannel and bottle-fed into independence.

Her mother had owned a Tennessee walking horse, a flashy bay named Jimbo, whose black mane and tail she'd braided with red ribbons before she rode him in shows. She used to nuzzle, stroke, pat the horse, bury her face in his mane, while Martha hung on the paddock fence, listening to the dark-gold and fluid warmth that filled her mother's voice when she talked to him, waiting for that warm and liquid love to overflow the dam in her mother's heart and pour over her. Waiting, still waiting. And now her mother had come and stood so close that Martha imagined she heard her mother's breath whistling down the bony narrows of her imperial nose. Her mother, who'd traveled this long way to find Martha and withhold her love again, just to remind her daughter, as a good mother should, that her love might still be won if Martha would just be patient and not lose heart, if she would just get it right for once.

Martha held her breath, then shook her head to clear it and turned to see if anyone had noticed her standing there like a fool with her eyes squeezed shut and her fists clenched at her sides, swept away in a fit of hope. Up on the wagon seat, Abel Rankin worked steadily at his supper; the children cooed and stroked Sawdust's nose and laid their cheeks against his whiskery muzzle. Back in the yard, people sat on the green grass and on the porch, enjoying their food. They circled the table and filled their plates a second time, a third; they lifted thick slabs from her beautiful pie. What a ridiculous old woman you are, she thought. Standing there waiting for your dead mother to touch you. But there it was again, percolating up through the layers of years, bubbling out at Martha's feet like a perverse spring. This sly and relentless force that moved through the world, this patient and brutal something that people called hope, which would not be stopped, ever, in its work of knitting and piecing and binding, recovering, reclaiming, making whole. Which formed from the stuff of your present life a future where you would be healed or loved and sent you running forward while it dissolved and remade itself ahead of you, so that you lived always with the feeling, so necessary to survival in this world, that you were not just trudging along but moving *toward* something.

She guessed that if you could just give up hope, your time on earth would be free of longing and its disfigurements. God knows she'd tried. But you couldn't. Not even her mother had done that, finally. Even after she'd sold Marlcrest out from under them and momentarily righted the wrong of her life by taking from someone else what she felt had been taken from her, she hadn't been satisfied. Instead, she'd begun to pine and grieve over her old poodle.

Rowdy was his name, Martha's only inheritance. She'd taken him to her house when she and Perry Jr. had put their mother in the nursing home. He was thirteen years old then, morose and incontinent, a trembler, a fear-biter. Nothing left of him but gluey old eyes, a curly coat, and bones. On a Saturday morning soon after he came to live with her, he turned over her garbage while she was at the grocery store and ate rancid bacon drippings out of a small Crisco can. She found him on her kitchen floor, greasy and struggling to breathe, and rushed him to the vet's, where he died two hours later, his blood so clogged with fat his old heart just choked on it.

Until her dying day their mother had been greedy for news of Rowdy, details of his diet, the consistency of his stools, and Martha and Perry Jr. had given them to her. They'd even pretended to be passing Rowdy back and forth between them, sharing the wealth. On one visit, Perry Jr. would tell their mother how on cool fall mornings Rowdy had enough spark to chase squirrels around Perry's back yard. On the next visit, Martha would continue the story, say that Rowdy still enjoyed his dog biscuits even though he gummed them now and it took him forever to eat one. He's a little constipated, she would say, but he's fine. "Well, then, you're not feeding him enough roughage," their mother would say. "Feed him apples. I must have told you that a thousand times, don't you listen when I talk to you?" she would say, the old fierceness darkening her good eye. Then she would smile. Toward the end, when she smiled at them, it was her skull that smiled; then the weeping would begin, the longing, the sorrow. "Why don't you bring my little dog to see me?" she would sob. "Soon, Mother," they would promise, patting her hand, smoothing back her hair. "Next time."

4

Now it is August, twenty-five years past the summer of the reunion. Olivia Hudson, one of Martha's grandnieces, is driving through the mountains with her husband and small son when they pass a road that runs up a narrow valley, and she says, "That looks like the road to my great-aunt Martha's house, the one where we had the family reunion, remember my telling you about that?" She had been seven that summer, the blue baby was her brother; in photographs she stands protectively close, her hand always resting near him, on the side of bed or blanket. Now they turn back and head up the valley, and as they drive Olivia studies the landscape, looking for clues. She cannot imagine that the house is still standing, but she hopes that some arrangement of trees and pastures and fences will rebuild it in her mind's eye and set it down on its lost foundation. She hopes for sheets of roofing tin, a standing chimney, steps leading up to an overgrown field. Anything.

Instead, they drive around a curve and she sees the house, the *house* itself, rising out of a jungle of saplings and shaggy cedars. Silver maple saplings, hundreds of them, Olivia sees as they drive closer. The leaves flash and flutter in the breeze. A realtor's sign lies on its side in the grass, near the stump of the big silver maple that has spawned the little trees, the one that threw its wide shade across the front lawn the summer of the reunion. And what Olivia feels as they wade and push toward the house through the thick grass and saplings is an emotion so quick and powerful it takes her by surprise. It is as potent as love *recovered*, the feeling itself, not the memory of the feeling — an urge to laugh out loud and also a dragging sadness, and a longing for no particular person or thing, a longing to *know* what the longing is for.

And Olivia thinks that if the house had been sold, had become someone else's house, unpainted, the screens kicked out, the yard full of junk cars, if a picket fence had been thrown around it, a straw hat with flowers in the band hung on the door, its power to move her would have dissolved into its new life. As it is, its power is original, strong. She feels as if she could look in and find them all at dinner, Martha circling the long table, pouring raw milk into the children's glasses, and the mothers following her, pouring it out, refilling their children's glasses with the store-bought, pasteurized kind.

Of course, what she sees when they've waded through the grass and stepped over the rotten place on the porch and looked in through the cloudy glass of the narrow window beside the door is the front room of an abandoned and neglected house. Bloated chairs, scattered papers, white droppings everywhere, a cardboard box packed with blue bottles. She *has* to get inside.

Down the mountain they find the realtor. Billie is her name. She has diamonds on the wings of her glasses, jewels on her long black T-shirt, ragged black hair and Cherokee-dark eyes, Cherokee cheekbones. She is so heavy and short of breath that Olivia's husband has to boost her up the broken front steps, but when they get inside the house, she turns brisk, businesslike. Martha's children still own the place, but they're so busy they never come here. That's why they've put it up for sale. Someone is about to buy this place and turn it into a bed-and-breakfast inn, take advantage of the business from the new ski slope over at Scaly Mountain. Since Olivia is kin (now that she's been around Olivia for a while, Billie can see the resemblance, yes: "You favor your aunt Martha," she says), wouldn't she be interested in buying it? Of course, Olivia would have to make an offer right away, today in fact. Billie checks her watch. She's expecting an offer any minute from the bed-and-breakfast people.

Books lie scattered on the floor of every room; faded curtains sag from bowed rods; blackberry vines tap against the glass in the kitchen door. "You know, people around here say this place is haunted," Billie calls to Olivia as Olivia starts up the stairs to the second floor. "Your great-aunt Martha died in this house, and they say she came back as a cat to haunt it."

Olivia laughs. "If anyone would haunt a place, it would be Martha," she calls down the stairs, thinking of the grizzled tabby with the shredded ear and stony face that had been sitting on the porch when they'd driven up, that had dissolved like smoke between the foundation stones when they'd stepped out of the car. Thinking of Martha's tenacity. The famous struggle with her brother over the cream. She thinks of Martha fighting battles, righting wrongs, the clean, bleached smell of her clothes. Martha had wanted something out of life that couldn't be found in one lifetime, no doubt about it. Naturally, her spirit would go on poking and probing and quarreling here, striding, big nose first, into a room.

Remembering all that, Olivia comes into the long room under the eaves where the women and girls slept during the reunion. Now it is full of rusty file cabinets and busted-open suitcases and, strangest of all, in a closet, a wedding dress and veil, vacuum packed in a white box under a clear plastic window, without a date to place it in time or a name to connect it with anyone's life. Outside the window that's set so low in the wall she has to stoop to look through it, she sees her husband following their son through the tall grass behind the house, and beyond him, a dip in the overgrown meadow where Martha's pond once lay, that shallow, cold, muddy pond that never cleared except where it ran over the spillway.

Olivia opens a drawer in one of the file cabinets — she has to yank it because of the rust — and flips through crumbling file folders stuffed with brown and brittle papers. Real estate forms, a Rosicrucian newsletter, yellowed stationery with *Long Family Reunion* printed across the top. She thinks of the week she spent in this room, The Henhouse, the men had named it. All that clucking, fussing, preening, a bunch of broody hens. Her father, who loved jokes, had lettered the name on a piece of cardboard, along with a drawing of a plump hen with a big behind and long eyelashes looking coyly over her shoulder, and tacked it onto the door. Olivia had never before been included among the women nor surrounded by so many of them. They slept under starched sheets and thin blankets on old camp beds set in rows. She'd pulled her bed over near the window, next to her mother's bed and the baby's basket. From there she'd watched the moon rise, the constellations wheel up from behind the mountain, the morning light fill the valley. The month before she died, so Olivia has heard, Martha added a sunroom onto the south side of the house. And now this house and all its rooms have been died out of, left and locked away, abandoned, begun again and never finished.

"Your aunt Martha really knew her way around these mountains," Billie calls up from the bottom of the stairs. "One time she went to a neighbor's funeral at the Church of God up the road there and another woman went with her who wasn't from around here either. But that other woman, she dressed up in high heels, a nice navy dress, a mink stole, and a hat. You know those Church of God people are *strict.* They don't allow any fancy show in their churches. They say that when that woman came in dressed in her finery and took a seat, everybody turned and stared until she got up and left their church. But your aunt Martha now, she wore a plain black cardigan sweater over a dark dress. She wore low-heeled shoes. She came in and sat in a back pew, quiet as a mouse. They accepted her just like she was one of their own kind."

Olivia is pleased to hear about Martha's dignity for a change.

Billie's story restores height and luster to the foolish and shopworn figure her aunt has become over time, handed down through the family. All over that part of the mountains, Billie says, people had talked about Martha at the funeral as though she'd done something remarkable by going there properly dressed. But when the story got back to Martha, she didn't see what all the fuss was about. It didn't surprise her that she'd done the right thing. Dressing for the funeral that morning, she hadn't given a thought to what she should wear: everyone knows what to wear to a *funeral*. She'd just reached into her closet and pulled out a black dress. Since it was a cool fall morning, she'd added a black sweater. At the last minute she'd even slipped off her wristwatch and left it in a dresser drawer to keep its gold band from offending the eye of any member of that stern congregation. The watch had been a birthday gift from her children one year, and looking at it reminded her of their faces — small and clear and full of light — when they were young and the days ahead seemed numberless.

She'd gone into the crowded, chilly church and sat in the back pew and listened to the congregation sing a hymn. Harsh, unaccompanied, the singing had reminded her of a creekbed in a drought with the sun beating down on dry stones, but that dry creek had carried her anyway, back to the summer of the reunion and the walk she'd taken with her grandchildren to see the orchard. The haunted orchard, the children had called it, where a blight had killed the trees and withered apples had clung to the branches through a whole year of seasons. Standing there with the children, she'd turned to her daughter's oldest boy. "And what do you intend to make of yourself when you grow up, Mr. Albert Redmond?" she'd asked.

He'd look up at her out of pale blue eyes as he pivoted on his heels, inscribing circles in the dirt of the road. He was ten, beginning to fizz. He wore red high-tops, a whistle on a lumpy purple-and-orange lanyard that he'd made at Boy Scout camp earlier that summer. "A fifty-cent millionaire," he'd answered her, grinning.

Hearing Raymond's words in the child's mouth had made her heart pound, her cheeks flush. And just like that, Raymond had joined them. Uninvited, unwelcome, he'd come back with his gosh-and-golly face, his pale traitor's arm, all the things she'd made herself cold and deaf and blind to years ago. "Well, son-of-a-gun," she'd heard him whisper warmly in her ear, insinuating more, "how about them apples?"

"Well, I hope you won't waste too much of your valuable time pursuing that course," she'd said to the boy that day, staring at the orchard, dizzy, suddenly, as though she'd waked up to the earth's circling, the endless motion of return that had brought her here, where it had seemed for a moment that the stubborn and contradictory truths of those trees had merged with the warring truths of her own life: the trees had died, but the fruit would not fall. Hope could cling to nothing, and a shriveled apple was all it took to coax love to come slinking back into this world. Inside the fruit she saw seeds; inside the seeds, more fruit. In this motion she saw the turning shadow that eternity throws across this world and also the current that carries us there. She had not forgotten.

When the hymn was done, the preacher told the story of the narrow gate, the strict accounting, the raked, leveled, and weeded ground of the promised land toward which they traveled in sure and certain hope of the resurrection. And when the service was over, she stood outside the church and greeted those harsh and unblinking souls as if they were kin.

Rites of Passage

MICHAEL BYERS

Shipmates Down Under

FROM AMERICAN SHORT FICTION

MY DAUGHTER, Nadia, was sitting up in bed; she looked per-
turbed, as if someone had told her a joke she hadn't understood.
She had books arrayed around her like brochures, but she wasn't
reading. This was my youngest child, six years old and smart as a
firecracker. Her room smelled thick, a musty fog of feet and dirty
pajamas; and her plastic dolls lay dismembered here and there on
the carpet, arms missing, plastic heads scattered like nuts.

"Looks like a war zone," I said.

She squinted at me. "Bluh."

"Tranh says you're sick," I said. My wife had hired Tranh, our
housekeeper, a year ago.

"Bluh."

I put a palm on her forehead. "Ooh, jeez, Najee, you're really
hot."

"I have a fever."

"You sure do." I hugged her, gently; she was wet and limp as a
weed.

"Tranh kept giving me apple juice."

"You feel all right?"

"No." She scowled at me. "I feel sick."

"Feel like you're about to yurk?"

"Maybe."

"You haven't yurked yet, have you?"

"I almost did at school," she said. "Then I fell asleep in class and
I had these weird dreams."

"I bet you did."

"There were all these lines," she said. She wiggled her fat fingers and squinted. "And I had to keep track of all the lines going back and forth, and then they kept cutting in half, and I couldn't wake up. Then Tranh had to pick me up and I almost yurked in the car."

There were crusts in the corners of her eyes, and she plucked at them.

"Tranh drove?"

"Yes."

I sighed.

"It was okay," Nadia said.

"I really don't like Tranh's driving," I said.

"I think it's fun."

"It gives me nightmares," I said.

"Well, we almost ran over a dog," Nadia said, judiciously.

For six years Nadia had been a perfect pink baby, blessed with a preternatural happiness that I had occasionally found unnerving. Who should be so happy as this? At times I thought she was putting on a baby's determined act for us, ignoring her brother, Ted, who had thrown dead beetles in her crib (Harriet and I had read about these things) and then later made Nadia his personal slave — *get me oranges, get me raisin bread, get me dried peaches* — while he watched basketball games or built his tremulous towers of blocks. Nadia no longer did these things for Ted, thank God — it makes you nervous, watching your kids naturally reenacting the grimmest parts of history — but neither did she hold a grudge against him; she was *happy to be here,* it seemed, and as if in reward for this, she was beautiful, very much resembling my wife with her pale snowy skin and dark wavy hair, and, like Harriet, she had a thick spray of freckles beneath her eyes and over the fine bridge of her nose. You sat her on her rump on the counter like sculpture and she beamed, pushing her hair out of her eyes.

Ted — my young man, my acolyte — had been different, a difficult baby, small and wormy. He'd squirm out of our hands when we picked him up and then he'd lie bawling, loud and alarming in his crib, screaming like a seagull. Now, at nine, he was suddenly serious about being my son — he'd recently decided to be a doctor, too, a geneticist, like me: *I want to help people,* he'd say, carefully, watching me; and he wanted to know all about genetics, so in the evenings we'd take out the yellow pad and go AGCTCGGT, TCGAGCCA, amino acids, ionic bonding, mRNA, on and on. We were conspirators, men together. He never let on when he was confused — he was too proud for that — but I'd see his green eyes glaze over and I'd want to pull back from him, stop inflicting myself upon him. But he insisted, and we went on with it — maybe out of pride on my part, or fear of embarrassing him, and we sat elbow to elbow in the bright kitchen and worked it through, mutations, chromosomal breakages, Turner's, cri du chat, this basic damage done so easily, unintended.

I was cooking when Harriet came home from work that night. Harriet is a larger version of my daughter, but unlike my daughter, my wife is sometimes tense and snappish. She had the *Seattle Times* rolled up like a weapon in her hand, and she waved it at me, once, then sat at the dining room table, her long pink skirt settling around her like a parachute.

"Well hello," I said.

She rattled the newspaper. "Mumph," she said.

"Mumph yourself," I said.

My wife saw dying kids every day, kids with cancer or cystic fibrosis, and she often had to inspect the bodies of stillborn babies, dead collodion babies whose yellow skin had cracked like parchment, or anencephalic babies born flat-headed, their hair thick and medieval. She had flat boxes of rubber gloves in her office cupboards, snap on, snap off; this was her specialty, pediatric genetics, a grim business, and she saw every week in a clinic a series of freakish, broken babies, the old products of witchcraft and comets, of horrible sins and longings, though sometimes I think our explanations these days don't make much more sense: cosmic rays? pesticides? genetic disposition? Occasionally I found Harriet staring off over dinner, her eyes fixed in the mirror behind the table, entranced by us all, by our hands and arms equal in number and nimble, by our foreheads fine and high and clear.

So I stayed in the kitchen, stirring the chili with a long wooden spoon.

When she came back in I said, "Nadia's got a fever."

"How high?"

"I haven't checked," I said.

Harriet took her wine glass and started for the stairs. She glared at me. "Jesus, Alvin, you know that fucking *Tranh* never calls me, I'd think at least *you'd* tell me."

"I just did," I said, but she was gone.

Often lately I had been unable to predict Harriet's moods, something I'd always been good at — in fact, I'd once been so good at predicting them that it used to surprise me — mild precognitions that had felt very much like dreaming, in which I'd known, as in a dream, what Harriet would be feeling. I'd have baths ready for her, and I'd call her at odd hours during the day: *How did you know?* And this prescience made her fall for me, I think, when we were both interns, both haggard and sleep-deprived, tossing on thin blue cots in big bright rooms.

But now Harriet's moods seemed to me volatile and dangerous, not so much changing, really, as crushing one another in succession, and it made me nervous and precarious; I felt as if one imprecise word would enrage her, irrationally. She cursed me, I cursed her; we threw words at each other. How had we come to this? She was of course under great strain at work, and she needed a break; and, in fact, in ten days we were all going to Australia, to Perth, the city where I'd spent the first ten years of my life. I hadn't been back since then, so I was quite excited, a long-awaited vacation, two weeks at the big Normandy Hotel, renovated now, according to the brochures, rid of its sailors and prostitutes.

When Harriet came back downstairs her wine glass was empty. "A hundred and three," she said.

"That's awfully high."

"I'm very pissed off, Alvin."

"I know." I turned off the burner.

"I specifically asked her to call us when the kids get sick."

"Yes, I know you did. We both did."

"I'm thinking we should take her in."

"I don't think it's *that* bad."

"A hundred and three's really high. We can't take her to Australia like that."

"No, I know that."

"I don't think you're even worried about her." Harriet peered at me, her long Irish nose aimed like a saber.

"Of course I am," I said. "But kids get sick."

*

But awake in bed that night, with Harriet slim and silent under the quilt next to me, I spun out a series of fantasies, an old gray spider sick with worry: Nadia's fever did not break, and she grew sicker and sicker, and lost weight; she fainted, red-faced and delirious, and then she fell down the stairs, her head banging like a wooden shoe. Then the fever became a speckle of chickenpox, and then viral meningitis, and then the first gray augur of leukemia. Jets passed over the house, blinking across the fiberglass skylight, and my mind moved relentlessly into a number of congested futures: she had cancer, diabetes, Tay-Sachs. Why do we torture ourselves with these things? It's not pleasant. We're intrigued by pain, I think by the possibilities of submission it offers. Sickness was once a red demon we let in, willingly — which meant that the sick were sick willingly, by their own hands, punishing themselves; and this is at least a little bit true, I think.

So I got out of bed and put on my robe. The room extended in darkness, the sloped walls. Our big bedroom was at the peaked top of the house — we had the whole third floor to ourselves — and tonight the windows rattled and little individual gusts went tossing along the floor like loose paper. Our big old house sits back in the trees; we have a view of the lake through the tall window. Of course the house sucks up a great deal of money, but it's absolutely worth it. On the way downstairs I touched the hard plaster walls with my palms. It was ten minutes to midnight.

I went to Nadia's room and creaked the door open. She was asleep on top of the sheets. The room was dark, but around the edges of the room I could sense the bumpy shapes of stuffed animals; and then, as I approached her bed, she turned and stared straight at me, and she frightened me — the whites of her eyes glowed like eggs, and her hair was wet and plastered against her head. I turned on the lamp and she rolled away like a dog. Harriet had left the thermometer on the windowsill, on a Kleenex; I shook it and slipped it under Nadia's tongue and held her round, wet head in my hands. She rolled her cheek against my palm. She was hot and shivering, and I imagined the long, senseless, wiry lines dividing, halving and multiplying, relentless.

Her fever was a hundred and two. I got her a glass of water, which she drank, slowly, and then I took a washcloth from the bathroom rack, wet it in the sink, and wiped her face and ears, and her little round forehead, and the hollow in her neck, gently, as if I were preparing a surface for further work. She smelled sour, and she was mumbling to herself. "Yodey yode," she said, scowling.

"Yodey yodey," I said, dabbing at her eyes.

"Rings in reedoreed," she said.

"Yes indeedy deed," I said. She winced when I rubbed her nose.

She was still shivering, so I tucked her beneath the jungle sheet, and then pulled the blankets up over her shoulders. She said, "Finish time."

For a while I sat with her, listening to the house — it creaked and popped in the wind as if loosing its hawsers — then I said, "If you need anything, just yell, and I'll come down for you." She nodded weakly, and I kissed her hot, salty cheek and left the room. I left her door open so we could hear her, but now she was deep in the blankets, calm, her face away from the door, her black hair flying behind her on the pillow like a small, dark flag.

Next door, Ted's light was on. I knocked once. "Ted?"

"What?"

"You up?"

"Yes," he said.

"Can I come in?"

There was a rustle of bedclothes. "Sure."

He was sitting up in bed, reading; his long, pale arms reached hairless and smooth across the blankets. His room was spare and clean; an empty white desk stood by the windows, and his books were aligned perfectly in the shelves; he was neat as always, tidy as a curate, a penitent. He had folded tomorrow's clothes on the desktop.

"How's Nadia?" he asked.

"Still feverish."

"Mom said she has to go to the hospital."

"Well, maybe tomorrow, if she doesn't get better." And now I felt the house warm a little, felt us inhabiting it as a family — how else can I describe the feeling I have with my son? If I know anything about love, it's his doing. I said, "You should be asleep."

"I don't have school tomorrow."

"Yeah, it's late, though."

"Ten minutes," he said.

"What're you reading?"

He tipped the book, a ratty paperback: *Danny Dunn and the Voice from Space.*

"Seems like you've read that before."

"Yes, many times," Ted said.

"What's it about?"

He said, "Well, there's these two boys, and this girl, and they have a professor friend, and they make contact with an alien race with a radio telescope. It's fairly interesting."

"Ah."

"It's sort of science fiction."

"What do the aliens have to say?"

"Well, actually they just send a picture of themselves, and then they send more, at the end, but that's where the book ends, unfortunately."

This depressed me; Nadia had read that book, too. I didn't want Ted to fall behind. "Let me recommend something," I said. I walked to Ted's bookshelf. "It's about Australia."

"Are you in it?"

"No," I said, scanning the shelves. "But I used to read it over and over."

"What's it called?"

"It's called *Shipmates Down Under.* It's got a green cover."

Ted sat up straighter in bed.

I found it, pulled it out, and sat at the foot of his bed. "You should read this before we go."

"What's it about?" He shrugged in his pajamas.

I said, "Well, it's about this boy, whose name is Lionel, and his friend, Ewing, and they stow away on a pirate ship that's going to India or someplace, and then they go to this emir's castle, this big old castle in the jungle, and that's where they have their adventures."

Ted rubbed his nose. He was listening as he always listened to me: intentionally, seriously, as if studying for a role.

I opened the book to the middle and read aloud, whispering. "*At long last, night fell upon the weary boys, and they slept deep in the hold, huddled close to one another for the warmth their bodies gave, while above them the splendid ship creaked and shuddered, crashing through the salty main. The sea splashed against the bulwarks of the mighty ship, and spray hissed past their heads.* See? They're stowing away," I said.

"Mm-hm."

"*Late at night Lionel woke believing he felt something climbing over his legs and he shouted out, 'Get off!' and shook his legs with all his might. But he felt nothing more and thought perhaps he had been dreaming. In the darkness of the hold he could see only the colours of black and grey, and these melted into one another a few feet from his eyes. Perhaps it had been a rat. He knew rats lived in the holds of ships, eating the stores of grain and whatever else they could find. Slowly the ship rocked him back to sleep."*

"They're going to India?"

"Yep."

"Do they have any money?"

"No," I said. "I don't think so."

"How're they going to eat?"

"Well, it's an adventure. They don't know how it's going to turn out."

"Sounds like they're pretty stupid to me."

"Well, maybe so."

"They should plan things better," he said. "What if they starved?"

"I guess so," I said. "But I liked it because they lived in Perth, so I could pretend it was about me."

"Oh." He nodded.

"Actually I had a friend in Perth named Lionel, but I don't think he ever read it."

"Why not?"

"I don't know," I said.

He looked at me levelly. "I'll read it after this," he said, and put it neatly beside him, by his clock radio. He listened to talk stations and oldies, and as I left his room he turned the radio back on, very low, a little measured murmur. Of course I love my children, and I love Ted and his little eccentricities, his fierce, perverse maturity, and I loathe parents who condescend to their children, or who think any ill of them at all. But I do find Ted a little strange. He is so level and principled and controlled. He had already packed for Australia; he had a journal and a pencil tucked in the side pocket of his suitcase, and I imagined he would be recording our travel times, and dates, and meals, and mileage. It is, I think, one of the many discoveries of parenthood that you can love your children differently — not more or less, but differently.

Upstairs in our sloped room Harriet was sleeping on her back, as if contemplating the sky through the skylight; and now, in bed, I did feel calm again, more certain of a single, easy future. I believed Nadia would be better tomorrow, and when we flew out next Saturday I would sit beside her and she'd stare out the airplane window in astonishment as the earth dropped away. In bed I too stared up, out through the skylight at the blinking jets, and I heard our old house creak, and I imagined it tipping just a little, like a ship, or maybe just like an old house sailing into the night, its four stowaways tucked safely in.

I woke alone on Saturday morning. Through the skylight I saw blue sky, high white clouds, a cold, windy winter day. Harriet was gone. Her side of the bed was already made. I went downstairs; I could smell pancakes. I passed Nadia's room and glanced in — Harriet and Ted were crouched in their robes on Nadia's bed, and Harriet was whipping the thermometer back and forth with her wrist. "A hundred and four," she said.

"Uh-oh."

Nadia was asleep with her head lolling on the pillow. I felt her forehead: papery and rough and raspy, as if her skin were being cured. Her mouth was open.

"I can't get her to drink anything."

"Oh, hell."

"She's been throwing up." In the bottom of the red bowl — Harriet passed it to me — was a pool of what looked like thick, stringy water; it smelled sour and strong, an alchemist's condensation of sickness. "Nice," I said. Harriet swirled the vomit once, slowly, as if reading a fortune.

Ted said, "She doesn't look too good."

"No, she doesn't."

Harriet said, "We should take her in."

"You want to?"

"Well, Jesus, Alvin, she hasn't kept anything down in almost a day. I think we have to if she doesn't wake up and start drinking something." She fluffed her hair and stood; then she moved briskly to rinse out the bowl, her heels thumping away down the hall. She poured the vomit into the toilet and flushed it down.

Nadia didn't wake up for another hour — Ted sat by her, reading his book on his lap and feeling her forehead with his pale, narrow palms — and when she woke up she vomited a thin green fluid on the carpet, as if she'd been eating grass. "Dad!" Ted called, still in his pajamas, and of course we came running up the stairs; and with a gathering sense of dread, a sense of *This is real, this is no dream,* I wiped her white face and lifted her gently against my shoulder and walked downstairs. She was soft and pliant against my shoulder; she seemed to have no bones at all; her head rolled back and forth as I stepped carefully down, down, down, past the pictures, past the coat rack, out into the world.

At the curb I buckled her into the back seat, pulling the belt tight over her hips. She put her head back and began talking. "Over in the end," she said, sighing delicately. "Tall and tall and tall. And the mag's around."

"She's delirious," Harriet said, calmly. She reached back and petted Nadia's hair.

I started the car. "You don't seem too concerned," I said.

"No, neither do you."

"Well." I shrugged. "I am."

Nadia said, "Ohzy ohzy ohz."

Harriet took a breath and said, "I had a kid last week who was babbling like that. Not a fever, just a drug reaction, but I couldn't understand what he was saying."

"Oh?"

"Turns out his parents were Irish."

"Ah," I said. I whipped the car around a corner, clipping bushes. "An accent."

"No, the kid was speaking Irish. Gaelic."

"No kidding." I reached my hand back and felt for Nadia's head. It felt loose, dry, inhuman.

"It was his crib language. They said he was telling a story to himself."

"Was he all right?"

"Oh, sure." She smiled. "We just switched his medicine."

The university hospital is a huge white sprawling building set back in trees by the lake. In the marble lobby, under a huge dry ficus, Harriet clipped her black name tag to her shirt. "I'll check her in," she said, and disappeared around a corner. Nadia babbled softly into my ear, telling me insensate secrets, a string of letters random and tangled. "Bobido medee," she said. "Winda beena." The lobby was bright with Christmas music, and a huge tree loomed in the corner, and there were gifts spread beneath it.

Patients parted and hobbled along, a little veterans' parade; there were two boys in aluminum wheelchairs and a man with a ball of gauze where his eye should have been and a bald woman walking out slowly to see the parking lot. A gold fountain sprayed softly in the middle of the lobby. I shifted Nadia's weight on my shoulder and smiled, uneasily. Now she was sleeping again, it seemed. I checked her back to be sure she was breathing, and she was, deeply and evenly, her round, warm back rising like a loaf of bread in my hand. "Najee," I said. And if I'd just turned around, taken her out from this harmful place, walked out into the sunny, windy parking lot? Hell to pay, of course; unforgivable.

Nadia's room had sky-blue walls and reading lamps by the beds. It wasn't bad, as hospital rooms go; the windows looked down from a great height on Portage Bay and the marina and the university. "Nice view," I said. There was a boy in the other bed, a fat boy with a crew cut, and he turned and looked at the view for a long time, as if he hadn't noticed it before. I lay Nadia down softly on the white narrow bed; she was half asleep, mostly incoherent.

"There'll be a nurse in a minute," Harriet said.

I tucked Nadia's legs beneath the sheet.

"I'm just going to run her blood down to the lab," she said. "Make sure there's nothing really wrong with her."

"Like?" I said.

"Like I think you know."

"Sure," I said.

She said nothing. From the wall cabinet she took a blood vial, tore the flat paper off a needle, and fitted the two together; then she gently arranged Nadia's arm, turning it upside down as she would a piece of chicken. "You never know," she said, and then she pierced Nadia's arm, delicately; Nadia didn't seem to notice. Harriet drew blood, the needle in and out in a second, no mark on Nadia's arm at all. Then she snapped off the needle and threw it away and held the little vial to the light like a jewel, a red, dark charm. "The nurse'll get an IV going." And then she charged out the door, holding the vial in her fist.

Nadia sighed once and rolled over onto her stomach; she was wincing into the thin pillow, and she looked as if she were pleading, as if she hadn't yet learned that there were no negotiations with sickness, no arguing with a replicating virus, *Please, it'd make us all feel better if you'd just go away; if she dies, you die, too.* She lay on her face as if crushed.

"What's wrong with her?" the fat boy asked. His leg was elevated on a frame beneath the sheet.

"Ssh," I said. "Don't wake her up."

"Sorry."

"That's all right." I walked to his bed. His big body mounded up beneath the sheets like a balloon. "What happened to your leg?"

"I broke it falling off a horse."

"Ouch."

"Yeah. Then the horse rolled over on me."

"Oof." I lifted the sheet. The knee was soft and purple, a big, fleshy eggplant. The shin was encased in a plaster cast.

"I got four pins put in."

"Congratulations."

"It hurts," the fat boy said.

"I bet it does."

"Are you my new doctor?"

"No, but I'm *a* doctor," I said. "Sort of. I do research. That's my daughter, Nadia. She'll probably be here a couple days."

"What's wrong with her?"

"She's got a fever that won't go down."

He snorted.

"A fever can be very dangerous if it doesn't go down by itself. She can't keep anything in her stomach. She keeps throwing up."

"Oh."

"What's your name?"

"Dustin."

"She's Nadia."

Then Harriet came in again and said, "There isn't a nurse on this whole goddamn floor."

"This soldier over here's got a busted leg," I said. "Horse rolled on him when he was charging the enemy bunker."

Harriet smiled wanly. "I'm going to go find someone," she said, and disappeared.

"Is *that* the doctor?" Dustin asked.

"That is the doctor," I answered, as the door sighed shut.

*

I drove home alone. There I found Ted in the kitchen in my big wicker chair, still wearing his blue pajamas. He was drinking a cup of coffee and reading *Shipmates Down Under.* "Hey!" I said. "Good book."

"Where's Mom?"

"Taking care of business," I said.

"How's Nadia?"

"The same. She'll be fine." And it seemed right to say that; I didn't feel as if I were lying — a fever? Really, we were taking extreme measures, precautions — more to make sure we could all go to Australia on time than anything else, more for us than for her. Six days? Surely she'd be better in six days. Discount the vial of blood, the phrases that might be found spinning there.

"I like this book," Ted said. He scratched his armpit. "I like their school."

"Ah, that's a real school, you know, in Perth, the Palmer School."

"Did you go there?"

"No. It was for rich kids."

"*You* were rich."

"We were definitely *not* rich," I said.

He felt his hair, oily and thick, and said, "Did people really talk like this?"

"Like what?" I bent over the book, put my hands on his shoulders.

"Like 'This is a gosh-awful bore.'" He was on page eight.

"Oh, no way. At least no one *I* knew did. I didn't."

"What'd you talk like?"

"Me? I don't know. We used to say things were *shorey.*"

"Shorey?"

"It meant sort of like *cool.*"

"Where'd that come from?"

"I don't know. We also used to say *decent.* If something was really great, we called it decent."

"Mm." Ted turned back to the book.

I made myself a cup of coffee and went upstairs. I made my half of the bed, then sat down at my desk. She'd be fine; of course she'd be fine. Harriet would call. From my desk I could see the lake, gray and cold; and here and there in the neighborhood I could see red Christmas lights strung on porches, and swinging in the breeze;

and across the lake I could see the soft, mounded hills of Bellevue, the huge waterfront houses, the yachts, the long, precarious docks.

I keep my journal reading for the weekends, so it's usually quick and perfunctory, but sometimes something catches my eye, wedges itself into my attention — recently, *National Genetics Review* had published a paper on Fatal Familial Insomnia, a syndrome in which patients, around the age of forty, slowly and irrevocably lost the ability to sleep. The patients could take years to finally die, losing ground gradually to madness; and as the end approached they exhibited an array of bizarre symptoms — ataxia, amnesia, temporal disorientation, forgetting who and where and when they were — and then at the very end of the course of this illness they told long, fabulous lies: they were spies for unimaginably powerful kings, or they had designed machines that could cure cancer, or end hunger, or destroy the world — and they insisted on these ideas as madmen do, with utter sincerity. *Confabulation* was the author's word for it, a pleasant-sounding word that suggested to me rainbows, and flying unicorns, and staircases spiraling into the clouds, a complete fanciful realm where the world could be told and retold. Of course, after reading it I'd tossed in bed, uncomfortable, imagining the first advance scouts of age and dementia; I'd imagined my own mind leaking slowly away out my ears, and then I'd imagined myself pacing sick and doomed through the windy house and coming to know the very remotest corners of the night. It was a frightening thought, and by coincidence I was then nearing the typical age of onset. But of course it was very rare, and inherited to boot.

I read at my desk until noon — I pored over this article again carefully, and resolved to write a letter to the author — then I went back downstairs. I found Ted still sitting at the kitchen table in his pajamas. "You haven't moved," I said.

"Still reading," he said.

"You like it?"

"Yeah. They're in Ceylon now."

"Uh-huh."

"Which I couldn't figure out where they were, but then I looked it up and figured out it's Sri Lanka."

"Have you gotten to the emir's palace?"

"Ah, just about, I guess. They're still walking around the town."

"The palace is my favorite part," I said.

"They're still talking weird," he said, smiling down at the table.

"Like I used to."

"You still talk weird."

"Ha ha."

"You do," he said. "Leever. Rahther."

"Listen, smart guy. I've been talking since before you were born."

He laughed.

"At least I don't talk like those guys. If we'd known anyone who talked like that we'd have beat the crap out of him."

He laughed again.

The phone rang. I picked it up. "Hello?"

"Alvin. She spiked at a hundred and four, two hours ago, and now she's back down to a hundred and two. First of all," she said, "it's not leukemia." She was breathing hard, as if she'd run up stairs.

I sighed. "Good." But how could I have ever thought that, imagined such a betrayal?

"It *looks* like it's just some sort of throat infection, but it's weird. It's not in her tonsils. It's sort of in her tongue and in her palate. She might need to have her adenoids taken out."

"Her palate's infected?"

"Well, maybe. It's weird."

"Weird how?"

"I've just never seen it before," she said. "She still can't keep anything down."

"She awake?"

"Sometimes."

"She scared?"

"A little bit. She doesn't know exactly where she is yet."

"You coming home?"

"Maybe. Maybe tonight. I want to see how she is. I might end up staying."

"Well. Say hello for me," I said. I said this gently.

"I will." She cleared her throat. "She'll be okay," she said, and she was gentle too, unusually so.

When I hung up, Ted asked, "When's she coming home?" He was hopeful, honest; we were here together, and he liked that, he liked having me to himself, and I liked it too.

I said, "Well, we don't know. Couple days, probably. The infection's in her tongue and up here, in her palate," I said, and pressed my thumb against the roof of my mouth. "Very strange."

"I'm excited about Australia now," he said.

"Really? Well, good," I said.

"We might not go, though, right?" he said. He examined his hands. "If Nadia doesn't get better."

"That's right," I said. "We might not."

"I figured."

"We'll *probably* go," I said.

"I'd like to see your house."

"You would?"

"You think it's still there?"

"Oh," I said, beaming, "it's probably still around."

"Can we go see it?"

"Well, sure."

"What'd it look like?"

I sighed. "Ah — well, it was white when we lived in it, and it had a little concrete porch, and a little walled-in yard. It was pretty tiny. I had a little bedroom in back that I shared with my sister."

"Did you have any friends?"

"Oh, sure. Australian friends, you mean?"

"Yeah."

"Sure. I was telling you about that guy Lionel. We didn't go to any special school or anything. It was just the elementary school. Primary school." I smiled. "I'm excited too, if you can't tell."

"Yeah." Ted gave a small, wry smirk.

"You think I'm being silly?"

"No."

"Did I ever tell you about the streetcars?"

"Just about a billion times."

"We used to have a picnic on Christmas morning," I said. "The seasons are reversed down there, you know. We used to have turkey sandwiches and go out to the beach."

"You told me that, too," Ted said.

So I left my son alone, reading, in the kitchen; then, as I walked back upstairs, I called out, laughing, "I want a book report on my desk by tomorrow!" — and I remembered the rotten old white palace, deep in the jungle, where, through a tangle of vines, the boys had spied a lost golden pool, and where they had slept,

soundly, then woken to find that the palace monkeys had gathered
for them heaps of gleaming fruit, papayas and bananas and thick,
rich breadfruit, and I remembered the monkeys sitting at a respectful distance, off in the high white niches and alcoves of the walls.

When Harriet clomped up the stairs that night I was already in bed.
     "You look cozy," she said, and threw down her backpack.
     "How's the kid?"
     She sighed. "Okay. She had another spike this afternoon at a
hundred and four, but when I left she was at a hundred and two. It's
normal, more or less. Stubborn."
     "You came home, though."
     "She's okay. I told her I'd be back in the morning. She likes the
nurse."
     "That fat kid talk to her? Dustin?"
     "Ugh."
     "Seemed nice enough," I said.
     "He was reading a pornographic comic book."
     "No he wasn't," I said.
     "Oh yes he was, Alvin."
     "Batwoman's pretty hot these days."
     "Batwoman doesn't wear garters and walk around naked on a
glass table."
     "Well. No, not usually."
     "So I gave him the evil eye," Harriet said.
     "I know the feeling."
     "I should've taken it away from him."
     "Oh, Harriet." I sighed. "It's none of your business."
     "What if he decides to limp over and practice on Nadia?"
     I closed my eyes and got deeper under the quilt. "Christ, Harriet.
Don't say that."
     "I bet you used all the bath water."
     "No," I said.
     "You're always inconsiderate with the water," she said.
     "Oh, shit," I said. "I am not."
     She ran the tub, and I began to fall asleep; then she said, "Alvin?"
     "Hm."
     "Did you ever go out to the outback?"
     "Mm."

"Yes or no?"

I sighed. "Once, when I was in second form."

"Goddamn it, Alvin," she said.

"What?"

"You know, you use those fucking Australian *terms* like I'm supposed to understand them, but you *know* I don't, and it's like you're trying to *exclude* me from something."

"First grade," I said, patiently. I was awake now.

She splashed around in the tub.

"What's it like?"

"What?"

"The outback."

"Oh . . ." There'd been a bus trip, but I hardly remembered it. I didn't particularly feel like remembering it at the moment, or talking to her about it. "Like Nevada, sort of, but prettier."

"Can we go? Is it a day trip sort of arrangement?"

"Maybe a couple days."

"Would you want to do that?"

"Sure."

She splashed away for a minute. Then she said, "Nadia says hello."

"Hello," I said, and smiled in the dark.

When we arrived at the hospital the next morning Nadia had a horrible rash below her nostrils, like red silt spilling from a river's mouth. She was breathing shallowly and her skin was gray; the plastic IV tube snaked away, a second umbilicus.

"What the hell," I said. I touched her rash. She was still asleep.

"I don't know," Harriet said. "That's very strange."

"She was talking last night," Dustin said.

"I'm going to find somebody," Harriet said, and left.

"She wasn't making any sense," Dustin said.

I adjusted her blankets; the sheet by her head was stained orange.

"She was all like *talkative*. Sounded like she was having a conversation."

I propped her up with pillows; her head rolled, frighteningly loose. "She was delirious," I said. "She didn't know where she was. That happens a lot when people have fevers."

"Sounded like she was crazy," Dustin said.

"She's not crazy."

"Pretty annoying if you ask me."

"How about you just quiet down over there, kiddo," I said.

"Why?"

"Because," I said.

"You think she's going to die?"

"Watch your mouth," I said.

"Huh," he said.

Nadia's lips were chapped and broken; I sat at her bedside and watched her roll her dry lips against each other; there were words in there, I thought; but she said nothing, nothing I could hear.

After work Monday night I walked back down through the dark wintertime campus to the hospital — there were Christmas lights hung in the fir trees up and down Rainier Vista, and it was sprinkling a little, and there were students hurrying off to exams — and then I went upstairs to Nadia's room, ducking past the hairy-armed attendants pushing their shiny carts full of dinner. Nadia was asleep and looked a little better — her hair had been combed and washed — but the rash had spread to her nose and cheeks and had started around her eyes, like a raccoon's mask. I touched it: it was resilient, raised, tender. She winced in her sleep and turned away. I pulled up a chair.

"That girl's looking weird," Dustin said. He was watching television — a stock car race — and holding the remote in front of him like an offering. "She'd better not be contagious, that's all I've got to say."

"She's not contagious," I said, though I wasn't sure. Harriet was around somewhere; her pink backpack was on the side table.

"She woke up today around lunchtime," Dustin said.

"Really? Good."

"Yeah, for like six minutes. She didn't want to watch TV."

"Well, she's not feeling so good."

"The doctor was in here a lot, too. That weird lady."

"That's my wife."

"That's your *wife*?"

"Yes it is."

"Oh. She said I was a pervert for my comic book."

"I heard about your comic book."

"My brother gave it to me the first day," he said.

"Your parents don't know about it, I bet."

"No way," he said.

I glanced at his nightstand; just flowers.

"It's in my cast," he said.

"Ah-ha."

"You know what?"

"What?"

"I heard the doctors talking about making me an experimental case. They want to replace me bit by bit."

"Yeah, I bet they do."

"Pretty soon I'm going to be like Robocop."

"No kidding."

"No, for real they might have to replace my knee with a steel one," he said. "It's all twisted up."

"Sorry to hear that," I said.

Then Nadia turned over again. I put my hand on the back of her head and smoothed her hair — the rash had spread there, too, to the back of her ears, scaly and moist, the cracks glistening with lymph.

And she stayed sick. At home we packed, perfunctorily. The red Qantas envelopes sat in their places on the banister. But nothing changed with Nadia; she didn't get better, she didn't get worse, her fever never went below a hundred and one. I visited her before and after work all week; her IV bag emptied and was replaced, the back of her hand around the needle was bruised black as an Oreo. She would wake up occasionally and say hello, her voice hoarse, her palate swollen and red when I peered to look; and I would say hello back, and touch her face. Ted came after school and read aloud from his book, sitting with his legs crossed, his big dark head bent over the pages. Every day he bought an orange soda in a paper cup for sixty-five cents. Nurses came by in red fur hats, sang "Jingle Bells," "O Christmas Tree." And the rash traveled over her body like a scabby raft: it left her face and traveled down over her neck and back, then across to her stomach, drifting, and I imagined something about the size of my palm moving under her skin, some unformed thing lost, looking for a place to moor itself. Harriet rubbed it with salves and balms till it was shiny as a playing card; but it traveled on.

On Thursday evening, with Dustin asleep in his bed and rain nittering against the dark windows, I said, "We should call about the tickets."

"Sure," Harriet said. She was reading *Gene*.

"She shouldn't have taken this long," I said.

"She's getting better," Harriet said. "It's just taking a while."

"We could push the trip back a week."

"Oh, Alvin. You don't want a week there. It's two days' travel just getting there and getting back."

"I know."

"So we'll cash in the tickets."

"Ted'll be disappointed," I said.

"And you won't."

"Well, I will be too," I said. "But I'm worried about what he'll think."

"Well," she said, "I'm sorry. There's next year."

"I know."

"He'll understand," she said, wiping Nadia's lips. "It's not like they're not refundable."

"No, I know."

"So. Maybe this spring I'll have some time," she said.

"I doubt it," I said.

She laughed, and her magazine slid off her lap. "You're so pissy."

"No I'm not."

"You are. It's not like we haven't gone anywhere together."

"I haven't been there in thirty-five years."

"So what's another year?" she said; and I didn't want to nod at the bed and say, *What if I'm like that, or what if I'm dead, or what if you decide to leave?* Things were precarious enough already, I felt.

After Harriet left that night, I read to Nadia. She was snuggled small against me, tired and weak — she hadn't opened her eyes all day, but she wasn't quite so hot as she'd been. We followed the boys through the emir's palace, abandoned now a hundred years, a messy, complicated place: Satin pillows had turned to dust in dusty chambers, vines spiraled down the walls, and big, unidentifiable fruit dropped rotting on the floor. Tigers roamed lax and supple down the halls, sleek and pettable, the tame descendants of the emir's old clowder. Marble statues had fallen to the stone floors, so arms and legs lay here and there, alabaster and perfectly formed. The boys stood mystified in the open courtyard while bright red birds flashed through the air. *This certainly isn't Perth, Ewing said, staring;* and then, in that little blue room, my daughter shrugged against my chest, and I stopped reading. I put the book down, and I imagined a long view of my city, as if from the air, and from slightly out to sea — a charitable view from a distance, a scene of white walls and stone bridges and wharves, my bright childhood city — and then I made it go away; I forgot about it, or resolved to do so; there would be other times.

Dustin stirred and opened his eyes and said, "Keep going."

"Later," I said.

Friday evening at home (it was raining again, and we had a fire going), Ted and I put up a Christmas tree, halfheartedly, in the corner of the living room. We got our hands pitchy, and I barked at him a few times for letting it fall over; but it stayed up eventually. Then into the basement for the ornaments, the red balls, the pink, glittering acorns, the angels, the star. We were two men laboring together, and that felt good; he liked helping, of course, and he played along, trying not to smile. I turned on the stereo: choral music, tenors in a huge stone church. I had a beer and read the paper in the living room, the tree winking gaudily in the corner. Ted brought down his gifts, three square boxes meticulously wrapped and tagged, and arranged them under the tree. It was the twentieth of December; Tranh wouldn't be back till after the new year, and messes were already beginning to gather in the corners.

Ted disappeared, then came back with a huge fold-out map of Australia — it was four feet square and had an inset of New Zealand in the upper right-hand corner. I recognized it: we'd got it from the travel agent, and I had dropped it in the bathtub, so it was dry and crispy now. "Going somewhere?" I asked.

Ted opened a blue spiral notebook. "Nope."

I got down on my knees beside him; I was conscious of my beery breath, my adult bulk. "What're you doing?"

"I'm writing a sequel to that book."

"You are?"

"I've got a good plot."

"What?"

"I think I'm going to have them get kidnapped," he said. "It's going to be an Australian adventure."

"Neat," I said. "You finished the book?"

"I finished it at school today."

"Liked it?"

"I thought the ending was pretty stupid."

"Mm." With my finger, I traced the border of New South Wales: desert, mountains. "I actually forget what happens at the end."

"It was stupid. They just went home and nobody's noticed they were gone."

"Oh, yeah," I said.

"And they'd been gone like a year or something."

"I remember that. That *was* stupid."

"So I'm going to write a sequel."

"You'd better have a better ending."

"I haven't figured that part out yet," he said. "I'm just determining their route. I know how I'm going to start it, though."

"How?"

"Well, I think they're going to get kidnapped by a guy who needs little kids for a burglary because they can fit through some bars that he can't fit through."

"Not bad."

"Then they're going to go rob this museum for him, except they take something they're not supposed to take, and then they get in trouble for some reason."

"Uh-huh."

"After that I don't know."

"Sounds better than the first book," I said. I leaned into him, bumping him with my shoulder. "Will I get to read it?"

"I guess so."

"Good." Then I said, "I hope you're not mad about not going this year."

"No, I'm not mad. I'm disappointed," Ted said. He wouldn't look at me. "I wanted to do some research."

"Sure."

"Also, I wanted *you* to go."

"Oh you did."

"I think you'd have had a really good time."

"Well, I do too," I said.

"I think it'd have been good for Mom, too."

"Well, probably."

"She's been pretty cranky lately," he said.

"She's got a tough job," I said.

"I think she needs a vacation."

"Me too," I said.

"You should take her somewhere," he said.

"Huh. Where?"

"Take her to Idaho or something. Someplace weird."

"Yeah. I've been cranky too, though," I said. "I don't know if she'd want to go with me."

"Mm. Maybe not."

I got back up on the sofa and finished my beer. "I liked how you came and read to your sister," I said. "Her fever's getting better."

"That Dustin kid gives me the creeps," he said.

"Why?"

"He was like making faces at me the whole time."

"You see his leg?"

"Yeah. Gross. Also he kept trying to interrupt me."

"I think he's probably pretty bored."

"No excuse to be rude," Ted said. Then he laughed. "Mom wants to throw him out the window."

"I know."

"Aaaaah!" Ted splatted himself comically on the carpet. "I'm dayuhd," he said.

Saturday, when the boys meet the emir, he is locked in a bottle. Nadia, who seems a little better, brushes my chin with her hand. She is beginning to see things clearly again, and she's staring: at my pores, my stubble, the pointy end of my nose. She says, Your nose is all *sharp*. *Ssh ssh,* I say, putting her hand back down. *Listen:* Lionel turns the bottle this way and that, holds it up to the torch, held aloft by his shoulder, a rag torch burning in this dark, wet room. A man is sitting inside the bottle, shrunken and asleep, in white robes, with a white headdress; he is curled around something secret, something shining he holds at the center of his belly, even in sleep. And the boys think, What spells do they know? What words do they know to set him free? The boys rub the bottle as if affectionately, but nothing happens. Dustin leans on his elbow and watches us. *Spells,* Lionel says, *are usually quite complicated, at least from what I've read.* Can the emir grant wishes? Can he tell them the safe way home? They set the bottle carefully on the ground, consider stomping on it, decide not to, then pick it up again and see the emir awake and gazing at them, serene, distant, his dark eyes tiny but triumphant. Ted is writing in the corner, smiling to himself, his paper cup beside him on the desk. Nadia is staring at her fingers, entranced, as if they're about to speak.

When the fever finally relented three days later — gone without reason, without explanation, her illness never having been quite diagnosed, her drugs never having quite taken hold — we brought her home. She awoke while I carried her upstairs and tucked her into bed; she poked curiously at the black spot on the back of her hand as if it were a button, as if some slot would slide open in her chest. For a few minutes she sat and looked out her window at the back yard, her familiar view. Then she slept and slept, still weak, still tired. What exactly had she had? A stubborn strep, Harriet decided, though it hadn't acted like strep; it hadn't acted like anything.

In bed that night — our plane had gone off that afternoon, and we'd have been on it still, only halfway to Guam — with Harriet beside me, I said, "Ted thinks we should take a vacation. You and me, I mean."

She said nothing. The dark multiplied around us, came in waves, a cloudy night, orange through the skylight.

I laughed. "He said we should go to Idaho."

"No thanks."

"No, I think he was kidding. But," I said, "sounds nice, though. Be sort of nice to one another for a while?"

"I think I'm fairly nice," she said.

"Well," I said. "Sometimes."

"And then there's you, Mister Distant, Mister Nowhere." She snorted. "Mister Say Nothing."

"That's what I mean," I said. "I don't know why you say things like that."

"Well, no — you, Alvin, you think I'm an idiot, don't you?" She propped herself up on an elbow and poked me. "You think I don't know what you're thinking all the time, like I don't know what goes on with you, your little fancy ideas about me and having Ted all to yourself, this little thing where you're off in your own little fucking world with Ted and with Nadia and you're just pretending I don't even exist, and you just don't give a shit about whether I might want to have any *part* of it, and you're always just avoiding me because you think I'll bite your head off, and you know *what,* Alvin?" She began to cry. "I think they're afraid of me *too* now, they think I'm some sort of *monster* because of the way you *avoid* me so much." She said, "Oh, *shit,*" and wiped her eyes and flung herself back down on the bed. "Fucking telling your own kids all these lies about me."

"I don't tell them lies," I said. "I don't know what you're talking about."

"Well you may as well with the way you act around me."

"I think sometimes you do scare them," I said. "You do yell a lot."

"Oh, *shit,* Alvin. No more than you do."

"Maybe not," I said. "But I don't scare them."

"Oh, shit, you do too," she said. "God, Ted's scared to death of you. He cringes when you walk upstairs."

"Oh, for chrissake, Harriet, he does not."

"He does too! You should *see* him when you're not around! He's just like this normal *kid* who has this normal sort of life and then you come around and he's all *serious* again, like he's in training or something for the fucking master class."

"He likes it."

"He only likes it because you do. It's nothing he'd like on his own. Everything else is just some little fantasy you've invented."

"Well," I said. I thought of his dazed eyes, his persistence. "Maybe."

"It's true," she said.

"He asks me to do it with him, though," I said. "I'm supposed to say no, you can't ask me these things? I can't do that."

"Just don't be so fucking *promotional* about it all the time. It's like you're selling chocolate bars or something." Then she mimicked me: "Hey, Ted, wanna do some chromosomes?"

I said nothing. What could be said to that? We stared through the skylight together for a long time, silent. No wind tonight, no rain.

"We'll go next year," she said, finally. And then, to my surprise, she huddled against me, her breathing deep and even and directly into my ear, as if imparting secrets without words, without secrecy.

It was decided we would send Ted to San Diego to see my mother. I told him the next morning; he was unpacking — he had quietly refused to unpack before our plane had taken off, and now, this morning, he was unzipping his bags, settling his clothes carefully back in their drawers. "A week in San Diego," I said. "A consolation prize."

"When would I leave?"

"You could leave right after Christmas, if you wanted." I sat at his desk. "Next weekend."

Ted stopped unpacking.

"I know it's not the same," I said. I put my hand on my son's notebook.

Ted put his suitcase back on the bed, began packing again.

"Your grandma'd really like to see you," I said. Idly, I opened his notebook.

"That'd be fun," Ted said, quietly, taking a handful of socks.

I glanced secretly down and read Ted's first precise sentence: *My father and I live in Perth in a tiny white house with a wall around the garden,* it read; and a little bloom of secretive joy burst open in my heart.

Nadia and I finished the book that week. She was sitting up now, her eyes quite bright, her hair orderly, her nightgown cinched around her neck. She could enjoy it now: Dad reading to her, soup in bed, all the television she wanted, Christmas almost here. The boys found the magic words written on the wall, the emir exploded out of his bottle, he showed them how to follow the orange vines toward the exit, he gave them gold in leather bags for saving him. *Are they rich?* she asked, and I said, *You bet they're rich.* Then they took a spice ship home, and the captain let them jump into the spice holds, where cloves were piled like tiny teeth and cinnamon bark curled like letters; and one morning, from far out to sea, they could see Perth, and I imagined they recognized the Normandy Hotel, towering on the shore. So let's say Harriet and I make it; let's say I apologize, and she apologizes, and let's say we make it with one another in whatever final way people do, settling on certain things.

Let's say this happens. If that happens, then I'm certain we'll eventually go to Perth, and we'll be careful — we won't swim after eating, and we'll heed the shark warnings, beware the traffic, avoid the bad parts of the city; the Normandy will stand shining in the holiday sun — there'll be a crowded pool, and thin white towels, but the kids'll love it, the free soap, the other children, strange, accented, the little attractions and peeks they get around corners, and years later they'll both remember happily that hotel, running down the carpeted halls, the leathery tropical trees reaching to our balcony, the bellhops wheeling breakfast to the door, the way the hotel stood out against the water, strong, precise, unchanging, the solid keeper of my precious cargo, these two damaged packages of my detailed dreams.

TOBIAS WOLFF

Powder

FROM FISH STORIES

JUST BEFORE CHRISTMAS my father took me skiing at Mount
Baker. He'd had to fight for the privilege of my company, because
my mother was still angry with him for sneaking me into a night-
club during our last visit, to see Thelonious Monk.

He wouldn't give up. He promised, hand on heart, to take good
care of me and have me home for dinner on Christmas Eve, and
she relented. But as we were checking out of the lodge that morning it began to snow, and in this snow he observed some quality that
made it necessary for us to get in one last run. We got in several last
runs. He was indifferent to my fretting. Snow whirled around us in
bitter, blinding squalls, hissing like sand, and still we skied. As the
lift bore us to the peak yet again, my father looked at his watch and
said, "Criminey. This'll have to be a fast one."

By now I couldn't see the trail. There was no point in trying. I
stuck to him like white on rice and did what he did and somehow
made it to the bottom without sailing off a cliff. We returned our
skis and my father put chains on the Austin-Healy while I swayed
from foot to foot, clapping my mittens and wishing I were home. I
could see everything. The green tablecloth, the plates with the
holly pattern, the red candles waiting to be lit.

We passed a diner on our way out. "You want some soup?" my
father asked. I shook my head. "Buck up," he said. "I'll get you
there. Right, doctor?"

I was supposed to say, "Right, doctor," but I didn't say anything.

A state trooper waved us down outside the resort. A pair of
sawhorses were blocking the road. The trooper came up to our car

and bent down to my father's window. His face was bleached by the cold. Snowflakes clung to his eyebrows and to the fur trim of his jacket and cap.

"Don't tell me," my father said.

The trooper told him. The road was closed. It might get cleared, it might not. Storm took everyone by surprise. So much, so fast. Hard to get people moving. Christmas Eve. What can you do?

My father said, "Look. We're talking about four, five inches. I've taken this car through worse than that."

The trooper straightened up, boots creaking. His face was out of sight but I could hear him. "The road is closed."

My father sat with both hands on the wheel, rubbing the wood with his thumbs. He looked at the barricade for a long time. He seemed to be trying to master the idea of it. Then he thanked the trooper, and with a weird, old-maidy show of caution turned the car around. "Your mother will never forgive me for this," he said.

"We should have left before," I said. "Doctor."

He didn't speak to me again until we were both in a booth at the diner, waiting for our burgers. "She won't forgive me," he said. "Do you understand? Never."

"I guess," I said, but no guesswork was required; she wouldn't forgive him.

"I can't let that happen." He bent toward me. "I'll tell you what I want. I want us to be together again. Is that what you want?"

I wasn't sure, but I said, "Yes, sir."

He bumped my chin with his knuckles. "That's all I needed to hear."

When we finished eating he went to the pay phone in the back of the diner, then joined me in the booth again. I figured he'd called my mother, but he didn't give a report. He sipped at his coffee and stared out the window at the empty road. "Come on!" When the trooper's car went past, lights flashing, he got up and dropped some money on the check. "Okay. *Vamanos*."

The wind had died. The snow was falling straight down, less of it now; lighter. We drove away from the resort, right up to the barricade. "Move it," my father told me. When I looked at him he said, "What are you waiting for?" I got out and dragged one of the sawhorses aside, then pushed it back after he drove through. When I got inside the car he said, "Now you're an accomplice. We go down together." He put the car in gear and looked at me. "Joke, doctor."

"Funny, doctor."

Down the first long stretch I watched the road behind us, to see if the trooper was on our tail. The barricade vanished. Then there was nothing but snow: snow on the road, snow kicking up from the chains, snow on the trees, snow in the sky; and our trail in the snow. I faced around and had a shock. The lie of the road behind us had been marked by our own tracks, but there were no tracks ahead of us. My father was breaking virgin snow between a line of tall trees. He was humming "Stars Fell on Alabama." I felt snow brush along the floorboards under my feet. To keep my hands from shaking I clamped them between my knees.

My father grunted in a thoughtful way and said, "Don't ever try this yourself."

"I won't."

"That's what you say now, but someday you'll get your license and then you'll think you can do anything. Only you won't be able to do this. You need, I don't know — a certain instinct."

"Maybe I have it."

"You don't. You have your strong points, but not . . . you know. I only mention it because I don't want you to get the idea this is something just anybody can do. I'm a great driver. That's not a virtue, okay? It's just a fact, and one you should be aware of. Of course you have to give the old heap some credit, too — there aren't many cars I'd try this with. Listen!"

I listened. I heard the slap of the chains, the stiff, jerky rasp of the wipers, the purr of the engine. It really did purr. The car was almost new. My father couldn't afford it, and kept promising to sell it, but here it was.

I said, "Where do you think that policeman went to?"

"Are you warm enough?" He reached over and cranked up the blower. Then he turned off the wipers. We didn't need them. The clouds had brightened. A few sparse, feathery flakes drifted into our slipstream and were swept away. We left the trees and entered a broad field of snow that ran level for a while and then tilted sharply downward. Orange stakes had been planted at intervals in two parallel lines and my father ran a course between them, though they were far enough apart to leave considerable doubt in my mind as to where exactly the road lay. He was humming again, doing little scat riffs around the melody.

"Okay then. What are my strong points?"

"Don't get me started," he said. "It'd take all day."

"Oh, right. Name one."

"Easy. You always think ahead."

True. I always thought ahead. I was a boy who kept his clothes on numbered hangers to ensure proper rotation. I bothered my teachers for homework assignments far ahead of their due dates so I could make up schedules. I thought ahead, and that was why I knew that there would be other troopers waiting for us at the end of our ride, if we got there. What I did not know was that my father would wheedle and plead his way past them — he didn't sing "O Tannenbaum" but just about — and get me home for dinner, buying a little more time before my mother decided to make the split final. I knew we'd get caught; I was resigned to it. And maybe for this reason I stopped moping and began to enjoy myself.

Why not? This was one for the books. Like being in a speedboat, only better. You can't go downhill in a boat. And it was all ours. And it kept coming, the laden trees, the unbroken surface of snow, the sudden white vistas. Here and there I saw hints of the road, ditches, fences, stakes, but not so many that I could have found my way. But then I didn't have to. My father in his forty-eighth year, rumpled, kind, bankrupt of honor, flushed with certainty. He was a great driver. All persuasion, no coercion. Such subtlety at the wheel, such tactful pedalwork. I actually trusted him. And the best was yet to come — switchbacks and hairpins impossible to describe. Except maybe to say this: If you haven't driven fresh powder, you haven't driven.

ALYSON HAGY

Search Bay

FROM PLOUGHSHARES

AT NIGHT the wind sometimes woke him as it sliced across the tin roof of the cabin, and he would open his eyes in darkness to find his hands gripping the bedframe. Thirty-five knots, forty knots — it was impossible not to gauge the speed of the gusts in his mind. He felt, too, the chastened shudder of a hull and the inevitable way his bones prepared themselves for a hard roll to port. The lake was a quarter mile away, beyond two ridges feathered with birch and spruce, yet he could hear her, feel her. The wind might eventually shift to the south, or it might blow itself out. Still, he never again found sleep on those nights — a cruel, honest fact of his body. He lay alert on his thin mattress, boots and slicker hanging so close he could smell them, completing his watch as he must.

November. A month of chance, a time of vigil. The last of the leaves flared and fell away, scouring the withdrawn horizon. Winter almost always broke over the bay like a green sea this time of year, this far north. It happened quickly, without much warning even to him, and he'd lived on this stretch of the eastern peninsula all of his life except when he'd been on the lakes, or tramping the Atlantic. He cut wood. He laid in kerosene and dry goods, reorganizing supplies on the shelves of the cold porch until they made sense only to him. He repaired the roof, suffered a bitter night's rain, repaired the roof again. He visited his sister in town, took her a face cord of mixed hardwood even though she hadn't asked for it. He turned back the deer hunters who wandered east from the state forest. He studied the patterns of the crews from the power company as they did their last work of the year in his territory. It was a season of reckoning and recognition, one he liked to mull over. He was old. Preparation was the only rule left to live by.

On most days he walked down to the shore. It was the one aimless routine he allowed himself, and it was far better, he thought, than being part of the union flotsam that washed up on waves of coffee or worse along the gangways of the Soo locks. Those were the men who couldn't break their habits, or didn't know they had them to begin with. Not that he avoided every laker he ran into. He did not. He'd taken his nephews to the locks once or twice, shared some stories with the jaw gang there. And he saw the old pissers in the Indian casinos when he went, former oilers and bosuns and mates exchanging their pension cash for lightweight tokens, their dark deck clothes replaced with golf shirts that made no sense on their bodies. He had little need for their sort of commerce. It was enough to come to the edge of the bay. Sniff at the nearly odorless water, utter the old names that gave character to its waves and the ranging grays of its skies. Mackinac, the queen island, stood some miles offshore, her bluffs a charcoal slash of shadow and spume. Often there would be a ship clearing the straits as well, and he would eye her as carefully as he dared, knowing there was a good chance he'd recognize her, that she'd been plying her trade when he'd been scrambling at his. Seven hundred feet long, a thousand feet long, riding high on ballast or filled with grain, phosphates, maybe ore. There was a great deal he could tell from a glance. Yet all he really found himself studying was her silhouette and her motion, knowing she held desperate men. November, and the ice was not here yet, the gales were still howling their chorus to the north. A walk to the rocky, wind-whisked shore of the bay. A savored cigarette. The rest of the day for the simpler, bracing tasks he now asked of himself.

He had the bulldozer out of the shed the day the boy came. He was lubing the blade lifts and half tinkering with the engine, which was how he explained his unreadiness when it needed to be explained. There was a locked gate between his place and the state road two miles west. No one was supposed to bother him except the Sandhursts, who used his track to get to their cottage, and maybe the Mahans, who owned a few acres along the shore to the southeast.

Even his brother, Otto, didn't come out here. Too far from town, Otto said. They could talk at the shop if they needed to talk, or at their sister's. Then the boy appeared, on foot, moving like he knew where he was going and why. He was startled and felt surprise flutter across his face like a dusky wing just before he went spiteful.

If the boy said hello, he never heard it. But the boy did stop walking, waiting for a moment on the wet leaves of the path, which allowed him to cut the grind of the bulldozer's diesel to silence. It was as though the afternoon went dead when he did that — no noise, no heat or vital stink from the engine. The boy was dressed in a red plaid wool coat, jeans, a beaten felt hat, no gloves. He looked warm enough, though he wasn't wearing any blaze orange, which made him a damn fool. Dark eyes and skin, flattish nose, wide jaw. Chippewa, maybe, though it wasn't a face he recognized. If the boy was poaching, he'd gotten half smart and stashed his gun. If he was just wandering, he'd made a considerable mistake.

He laid his crescent wrench in the toolbox bolted behind the seat of the dozer. It was the boy's place to get nervous and speak.

"Came for the beaver." The voice was quick and casual, though deep enough to make him believe the boy was older than he looked.

"Don't look like you came ready for much of anything." He waved at the boy's empty hands and began a controlled laugh, wondering if the boy had heard any bad stories about him and the lonely way he lived in the woods. He hoped he had. "You shouldn't be here."

"I got the permission." The boy swung an arm down the track past the cabin. "Man called from Lansing, having trouble with too many beaver."

He understood then, enough of it. A portion of Sandhurst's land had been flooded all spring and summer; they'd had a helluva time with the road. He'd been over there a time or two himself to clear the dammed culverts. Once he'd spent part of a morning taking potshots at the animals as they swam across their new pond, but he hadn't hit anything. Beaver learned fast. He'd told Sandhurst he'd trap them out if he wanted. Sandhurst, it looked like, had decided to do it right. Indians had unrestricted rights to trap beaver. The boy was definitely Indian.

"You know what you're doing, go on."

"I know what I'm doing." The boy shrugged his wrists up into the sleeves of his plaid coat. "My uncle said to come out here and look it over. He also said to come to you, let you know. His legs are bad today."

"You walk in from the gate?"

The boy nodded.

"Sandhurst plan to send you a key?"

A shrug again like that didn't really matter. The boy lifted one foot, then the other, restless. The boots he wore were too large for him and cracked along the soles. They'd be wet and awkward in the bogs.

"Who's your uncle? He know me from somewhere?"

The boy stepped back like he'd been cut loose by the question. "He didn't say to talk about it." A straight look, black-eyed. "Just said to tell you I had the job. If you knew that, he said, I'd probably be all right."

It made his chest burn in the old way to watch the boy walk off like he did, easy, preoccupied. He'd be a better man, he thought, if he didn't want to bust everybody like they were on his crew. Yet it was the truth that he sometimes lost his taste for people for weeks at a time. It always came back to him, a doglike understanding of companionship. But as warm and viscous as the feeling was on its return, this desire to tolerate others, to congregate with them, it remained fickle within him. It made him a disappointment, too — he knew that — but he hadn't decided to live any other way.

The boy's face came back to him when the day was done. He hadn't left by the road, choosing to hack through the undergrowth instead, or to follow the rocky hip of the lake. That was how he imagined it, anyway — the boy's evasion. But as he fried his potatoes and onions in a skillet, the broad face with the angled, assessing eyes came back to him. The boy reminded him a little of Henderson, that was the only connection he could make. Henderson was an Indian, too, from somewhere up in New York State, and he'd been a cook on the *Pontiac* for a while. Reasonable cook, reasonable man. Not much remarkable about him, though he never ran short of coffee, ever, which was a good trait in a galley man. Most of his people walked steel in Pittsburgh or New York City, that's what he said, but he'd signed onto a freighter out of Buffalo after his

stint in the army and never looked back. Henderson told some
good stories, as most cooks did — he remembered that. The man
kept his hair braided; he told stories while he worked both messes,
officers' and crew's; he stayed out of people's business. It was funny
he even recalled Henderson; he'd worked with hundreds of men
on a long line of ships. But this was the *Pontiac,* old and cranky
even when he hadn't been, running coal up the dark spine of Lake
Erie, her every inch, he remembered, stinking of black dust and
hurry. Henderson had never been able to cook a meal that didn't
taste of it.

Later, when he was on his bunk with the radio turned low, a
hockey game from endless Canada, he believed Henderson hadn't
been on the *Pontiac* at all. It had been the bad luck *McCurdy.* Memories lagged and heeled, and he understood he'd hoped to fool
himself. Yet even as he closed his eyes, he found he could clarify
little more than the smell of burnt anthracite and onion. Henderson would have laughed to hear it. No ship's cook he knew had ever
been so bad he ruined onions.

He turned off the radio and lay square on the bunk. It seemed as
though he ought to prepare himself for something that was as yet
out of sight, beyond guessing. The thing he called his storm sense
was tracking a disturbance; he felt the fine tingle in his skull. A low
pressure system, maybe. Illness. Maybe ghosts. He'd have to bide
his time before he knew.

The snow came. Not enough to plow but enough to blanket the
ground, quilt its mineral smells, leave him to feel like his season
had begun. Most of the years he'd sailed on the lakes, they'd made
it into December, the ice of Superior would hold off that long, so he
wasn't home to see the tatted crystals begin to fringe the bay or to
taste the air's last flavor of earth. He returned to a world already
insulated and hard. There were the years he'd bunked in Toledo, of
course. Not so cold there, or easy. That was when he'd been married, had a house, aimed to study his way off deck and onto the
bridge, a foolishness he'd undertaken for Mary and her sad, pleading face, though it had been a good thing in the end. Officers
served two months on, two off. Able-bodied seamen worked as
many voyages as they could hustle. Mary believed she wanted him
home in that gum-green cottage above the scudding Maumee. So

he studied when he could and parlayed his long years aboard into favors. Made himself into a third mate from nothing in the days when such a thing could still be done. Then he lost Mary.

He gathered half a sack of Idas from the cold porch and set off down the track, his head soon clear in the still, dry air. He took the apples up on a knoll he knew, one that had the black trickle of a spring at its base. The deer would find the shriveled fruit by sundown. He fed them most of the winter if he could — carrots, apples, acorns — not so he could hunt them, but so he could know they were there and that they would stay there, in his woods, because of him. He hadn't taken a buck on his own property in several years. Foolishness, no doubt, but it was a foolishness he could afford. His family had owned this land above the bay for more than a hundred years. They'd logged it, fished it, trapped it, hunted it, tried to sell it to rich people from downstate who didn't stick. Now they held it because it was easy to hold and righteous to claim. He stayed there because his brother and sister didn't care if he did otherwise, and because it was good for him to be planted, safer. It made him pay attention to himself — this place that expected little of him, which needed even less than he gave. The lakes had not been like that.

He'd nearly ruined the memory because he'd dragged it out so much, the one about how he got his start on water. He'd been young and crazy and skittish, enraged by his father in all the usual ways. So he hitched rides on mail boats and farm trucks, made his way to Leeland, where there was damn near nothing to do, and lied himself onto a leaky, jury-rigged vessel named the *Alma L.* They wanted him on the black gang shoveling coal, but when he convinced them he halfway knew how to navigate and that he'd skidded his share of logs in his life, they put him on the deck crew instead. It was merciless work, yet he loved it in ways it took him years to understand. Weather and exasperation, water and breakdown — he went at it all.

The captain was an arrogant drunk who used his instruments and charts when he felt like it. The mate, soon satisfied that he couldn't buffalo the new boy, gave him half of his own job to do, and he lasted at it as long as the *Alma L.* did. The captain ran her across a bar near the Manitous in a spunky summer storm; the mean pounding they took there snapped the chain to her rudder.

Another vessel answered the captain's obscene distress call and was
able to put a line across *Alma*'s bow, but it was clear they'd need to
jettison cargo if they hoped to be pulled free. The old man went
into a blind rage when he heard that, calling for barges to take on
his pulpwood, then for a breeches buoy rescue, though they were
too far from shore for that and no one but the captain himself was
old enough to have ever seen such a thing. He helped the mate cut
loose a level of logs, but the captain ordered them to stop and
struck them both across the face with a leather lanyard. It was the
first act of shipboard madness he'd seen.

Since they weren't allowed to rebalance her load, the *Alma L.*
listed starboard and eventually heeled over in the waves. He later
heard that she was salvaged and that she and her captain made hell
and money in those waters for many years after. He, however, disappeared as quietly as he'd come, heading south until he found deck
passage across Lake Michigan to Wisconsin. He'd been told that
the place he needed to be was Duluth. Freighters reigned both the
Iron Range and the big waters up there, and there was a belief
within him, even at sixteen, that some men were meant to labor
their way toward extremes of their own choosing.

He walked until he couldn't think about that version of himself
anymore, then he turned back. He skirted the thicket of the cedar
bog, passed close to a bear's den he knew about, eyed the empty
trees. On his way to the cabin, he saw a speckled scatter of feathers
near the splintered stump of a pine and realized that there was a
thing he would miss until spring, the sky occupation of the loons on
the bay, the full sound of their inhuman laughter.

Some days later the boy left him a note on the ground near his
door. *Set 3 traps,* it said. *Uncle still sick.* The note was written in pencil
on a large, silvery square of birch bark. Its letters were careful and
upright. The boy had even signed his name. Frank Andrews. When
he walked out to the track, he could see the muddy, bowlegged
wells made by the boy's misfit boots as he labored under the weight
of his traps. A stagger coming and going, and that was all.

That night he awoke in his chair near the stove only to realize
that his deck crew had not run short of paint and primer, that his
boiling anxiety about a young wheelman was phantom vapor and
heat. He thought about taking a drink. He thought about going

beyond solitude toward something dark and squatting entirely. He believed he'd been talking in his sleep, though to whom he couldn't say.

His sister, Frieda, liked him to come for Sunday dinner, so he went when he felt like it or guessed she could use a little money or help around the house. Cecil, her husband, was a long-haul trucker who did what he could when he had the time. Frieda had been talking for years now about how good things would be when Cecil finally got a job at the prison. But prison jobs were hard to come by; they paid damn well. People waited a long time.

Frieda never said much about the money he slipped her when he visited. He told her to consider it rent, since he was living on property that belonged to all three of them. She kept the books for a gift shop in town and made a few things to sell there herself — wood-burnt plaques and Snow Island table runners — but she mostly stayed home with the boys. She'd take the money from him, her big brother, and thank him for something else, firewood or a door he'd rehung. They both knew if they stooped to talking about money, they'd end up discussing the years he'd traded most of his for liquor.

This Sunday they had sauerbraten that Frieda had marinated, and mashed potatoes, and a salad thrown together by the boys. He was in the kitchen smoking the one cigarette his sister allowed; his nephews were watching football on the TV in the den. Somehow it came about that he told Frieda of the boy's visit to the beaver ponds. Nothing else had happened to him in the last few weeks, unless he counted finding a gut-shot doe near the north edge of the bog a piece of news, and Frieda didn't like to hear about things like that. Ravens had led him to the doe, the heavy way they croaked and gathered in the treetops attracting his attention more than usual, and he'd cut the doe's throat with his knife, though she was nearly dead anyway. Frieda wouldn't want to hear about the ravens, either, or the raucous bald eagles, or the chipmunk that desperately wanted to hibernate on his porch. His sister liked to hear about the human leftovers, snapped saw blades or rusted drag chains, implements that proved the Hansens had broken their backs and spilled their sweat out there in the woods like any other family with an honest history. She also liked him to talk about how things were along the western shallows of the bay where they'd built teepees of birch saplings and bark when they were children, the three of them, and their father took them camping. She loved that place, she said, how the yellow sun fell off behind the spiked fence of the pines, the way grilling fish smelled, and she would never forget it. She wished Cecil would take the boys there, just pitch a tent and forget about the motorboat for one damn day. But she never suggested he take his nephews instead, as though it would not be the right favor to ask, as though his choice to live the way he did now, just like his choice to sign onto a steamer thirty-some years before, was the wrong combination of impulsiveness and love.

"You say his name is Andrews?" Frieda scraped hard at a crusted pot. "Paula Andrews's got a son still in school, and I know you know who Paula is."

Frieda didn't bother to turn away from the sink after she spoke, but he understood he was about to be punished. "Chad," she shouted, "get your butt in here."

There were groans and the padded sounds of a scuffle before his oldest nephew appeared in the doorway with his forearms folded across his black T-shirt. He felt Chad look at him neutrally, the one houseguest he didn't have to behave for. They'd had a short conversation at dinner about his Venezuelan tattoo and how much it had hurt, and they'd talked about the Lake State hockey team. It had been enough for both of them.

"Frank Andrews go to school with you?"

"Not no more. Dropped out." Chad lifted his arms above his head and mimed a jump shot. "Chip kid. You know how it is."

"I know it's tough for everybody." Frieda dried her palms on her skirt, looked at him, then away. "Take the garbage out, will you, then go on back and behave. Leave your brother alone."

Chad headed toward where his boots were sprawled on a rug by the door. "His mom's the one works at the bar."

"I know that," Frieda snapped. "I better not find out you've been over there."

Chad clomped out the door without his coat, and his sister turned on him. "Get what you came for, Johnny? I could have hooked you up with Paula without feeding you a good dinner."

He spun his glazed coffee mug between his hands. There were lots of Andrewses between here and the Soo. He hadn't really thought about the boy belonging to Paula. "I haven't been in there in a long time," he said. "Not since before I retired."

Frieda sat opposite him at the table. Her fair skin was smooth and pretty, flushed with the anger she'd stirred up, but still pretty. He was more than ten years older than she was, and there'd been times he'd taken care of her as well as any parent could. "I guess I'd be the first to hear otherwise, since the place is still packed with tat-tlers and assholes. I'd like to keep Chad out of there. He takes after Cecil's side, too slow to stay out of trouble. Not like his uncle."

He listened to her voice, careful and parched with forgiveness. Cecil ought to be around more, he thought, or somebody should. "Paula Andrews just poured the drinks I ordered," he said. "And it's all over, anyhow. I don't have time to drink."

Frieda laughed then, raising her chin and flexing her shoulders just as their father had when things were right with him. "You got time to do nothing *but* drink, so you give it up like a stubborn bastard. John Hansen, always cutting his own trail."

He stood, the trill of her chuckle running through him. Frieda closed things up between them; she always had. She flattened her hand as he slipped a fifty-dollar bill from his pocket. "Take the leftovers with you, do that much," she said. "And thank you for the wood. Chad and C.J. stacked it like you taught them. It's worked out good."

He drove like he was in a hurry until he reached the blinking yellow light across from the grocery, where he turned toward the water. He drifted past the house of a childhood friend who was on disability from his job with the road commission. Two doors down was the brown, asbestos-shingled bungalow his own family had lived in during a good stretch. The lake was in front of him, broken up by the gaunt reach of a few docks and the frosted cluster of Les Cheneaux Islands. The water here looked black, but common, polished into a series of pathways that led from shelter to shelter.

He parked, but it wasn't until he was out of the truck, his fingers working at the large horn buttons of his jacket, that he realized he was just up the block from the Chinook. He'd been thinking about Otto and how he was going to drop by the shop to say hello, and his fidgeting had driven everything else from his head. Everything except muscle memory. He walked across the damp, deserted street and looked in the storefront window of the bar. Closed until four.

Chairs upended on the tables like spindly carcasses. Pool table in the same naked place. There were plastic garlands strung with Christmas lights nailed inside the windowframe, though the lights weren't plugged in, and he could see a pall of fine dust on the sprigs of false holly and cedar. There was a tiny crèche nestled in cotton wadding on the varnished windowsill as well. Touches of Paula. Sweet. Well-meaning. Incomplete. He reopened the top button of his coat and began to search for his gloves. He'd lived a piece of his life in the Chinook, fighting, paring down love, filling his core with the false heat of bourbon. Then he'd moved on. The building felt no different in his mind now than the small dog-brown bungalow hunkered just out of sight on this same hill. He would swear to that.

He knew Otto would be working, even with the marina shut until spring, because that's what Otto did. His brother had repainted the building that fall, and he'd put in double-paned windows and new barn-red awnings. But he hadn't changed the name of their father's business. It was the same. *Hansen and Sons. Boat Builders. Docks. Storage.*

He knocked on the bolted front door, though he had a key to the lock on his own key ring. Otto had never been one for surprises. He waited, then heard a motor fire up just as he was setting his face to meet his brother's. The engine sounded muted and sluggish in the cold. He stepped around the corner of the shop, across the old launch ramp that was now boarded up, and toward the quay. His brother was casting off in the Chris-Craft, his face a putty-colored mask above his coveralls and the thick, speckled scarf done up for him by his wife, Marge. The gunwales and windshield of the boat were glazed with ice, and the inlet was curdled with slush. Boxes and bags crowded the floor of the boat behind where Otto stood at the wheel, his movements stiff but sure as he throttled into the channel. He was running groceries to widows and shut-ins out among the islands, stern and charitable with his yellow Labrador braced against his legs, her nose raised in the slapping air. That was his younger brother, as able and Lutheran as they came. He watched Otto take the chill breath of the lake across his face, watched him handle himself as any good wheelman might as his wake spooled and crimped the dark water. Something about the sight made his neck feel bowstrung, but he conquered it. Then he worked his way back to his still warm truck and the narrow, patchy roads to the bay.

The boy came when the girl got hurt, and it later seemed to him that the boy, Frank Andrews, had guessed that they'd be shut up in a room together one day, that he was somehow prepared for it. He was patching the wall behind his wood stove with metal cut from a wrecked panel truck because it's what he had for the job. There'd been a wet five-inch snow the night before; he didn't feel like plowing his way toward town. Besides, he liked an ugly repair that called on him to be resourceful.

The cabin door was open a crack for fresh air, but the boy knocked on the jamb anyway. The noise of the knock pivoted him against the stove, crouching. Then he saw it was the boy from the brownish slash of face, the drained color of his hat. "Yeah," he said, standing with the hammer still in his hand.

"It's Frank Andrews." The boy laid out each syllable like it was stolen. "Got my beaver, but had a accident with a trap and wondered if you had a bandage. Just till I can get to my car."

He went to the door with purpose then, knowing that cold and shock could make a bad thing seem not so bad at first. A man could break an arm in one of those traps. The low, marbled sky was spitting snow which had begun to dust the boy's sturdy shoulders with flakes. He took in the boy's eyes first, which were black and even and undeluded by pain, then he saw the sleek carcass of a beaver cast into a pocket drift near a corner of the shack. It was bloodless as it ought to be, since the traps were made to drown a beaver and never tear its pelt. It took him a moment to register the girl standing half shielded by the boy. She was the one who'd been hurt. One of her hands was cupped beneath the other like a bowl, collecting the run of blood.

"Get in here," he said, "get on in," and he didn't take time to say what he wanted to say about the cramped way he lived. The blood he'd seen was bright red, but there wasn't much of it. There'd be more in the heat of the cabin, but if she hadn't nicked an artery he supposed he could handle it. Otherwise, it would be compresses and blankets and a damn crazy dozer ride out to the road. Neither kid did anything more than cross the threshold, though the boy reached for the girl's elbow, as if to offer her rivuleted skin as

evidence of some sort of sincerity. "I got a first-aid kit," he said
before either of them could start with an explanation. "Sit her in
my chair and lay that hand where I can see it."

Coat and cap off, hands washed, kit opened on the table, which
was scoured smooth and clean because he kept it that way. He'd
never served as purser onboard, but he'd cleaned up his share of
sailors after fights or mishaps with winches and snapped lines. He'd
doctored himself plenty, too. He placed a towel under the girl's
blood-mapped wrist. Her eyes were a shiny tannin brown, contracted some with pain and worry, though her cold-flushed mouth
flitted with a smile that was part embarrassment, part apology.
Indian, too, he decided, though not as full-blooded as the boy. Her
hair was pulled off her face and hung down her back in a smooth,
water-beaded hank. It was easy for him to see that she was pretty. Of
course any son of Paula's would be used to that, fine looks in a
woman, though whether he'd come to expect it, to search for it, was
maybe another matter. He laid his own toughened fingertips at the
base of her hand, felt it quiver, yet coaxed her without words to
open her fingers. She shivered all over then, and he remembered
what little he'd seen of her when she'd been standing on his door-
step. She was wet to the waist, soaking wet, like anybody might
be who went after beaver dressed in jeans and cheap stay-in-town
boots. He nodded to the boy, who was hovering at the edge of the
table. "Build up the fire, will you? Or the hypothermia will get to
her before I do."

The cut was ragged and ran from the crease of her ring finger
across her palm to the fleshy base of her thumb, which accounted
for the good amount of blood. Her thawing hands ached and
stung; he could see that, too. And before he thought about it, he
was massaging them some with his own, carefully, his skin feeling
husklike to him against the raw damp of hers. She was small-boned,
trembling. He dabbed at her palm with a corner of the towel, then
looked into her eyes, which gave him nothing. Without wiping his
own fingers clean, he began to irrigate the wound.

"I can fix this good enough to get you to the clinic. You going up
to the Soo?"

Neither of them answered him at first, though the girl dropped
her head so he could see its delicate oval crown, the pale scar of
her part.

"St. Ignace," the boy said from where he was squatting by the stove. "She's from there."

"They got a Indian clinic there, somewhere she can get stitches?"

"It'll get taken care of." The boy's voice was harder than it needed to be, and he wondered if they'd both been scared out there, truly afraid they were up against it, and that was what was holding them in so tight. Then again, maybe he'd made some kind of mistake. Maybe the girl wasn't Indian at all.

"Good," he said. "You take care of it. Because I can sew it up here and now if you're planning on getting stupid on me, or lazy."

The girl flinched so hard her knuckles knocked against the table-top. The boy, Frank, stood halfway and took on a look that read mad-as-hell, which made him feel solid to see because he knew how to deal with an angry man, whereas this other, this unprepared for ministering, had brought a floating feeling to his stomach and beneath his words that he did not care for.

"Don't do no more." The boy moved up against the table again. "She's all right. Shelley, you all right?"

She nodded and began to push away from the heavy oak table, her hand stained orange with disinfectant but unbandaged, gaping. She seemed caught in the swift stream of the boy's assurance. Her legs failed her, though, faster than even he'd foreseen, because they'd been half-assed, all of them, and hadn't stripped her of her wet boots and clothes. She sank toward the chair, faltered, fell against the boy. He caught her under the arms and lifted her as though he'd cradled her before, then carried her to the bunk without asking. That was fine, though, he thought. It was the right thing to do.

"We need to get her dry," he said to the boy, aware that his voice had gone solemn and whispery, though the girl was very much awake. "I've got some clothes. See if she'll undress." He went to the place he kept his chest and flipped open the smooth brass latches while they spoke in low voices behind him. Everything in the chest was neatly folded and held the warm, powdery scent of cedar. It was easy to find what he needed.

"She wants to dress herself," the boy said, and the girl, who was sitting upright now on his scarred bunk, swung her head in blank agreement. "You . . . we . . . ," the boy half coughed, "we make her nervous. Could we leave for a minute, let her take care of it?"

"Yes," he said, and that was all. He scooped up his cap and coat from the floor where they'd fallen and headed out the door. He'd forgotten to expect modesty from the young.

Frank Andrews closed the door behind them, and the clean, diffuse light the snow carried with it made it seem as though they'd stepped into a white, high-ceilinged room, one just large enough to handle their talk and commotion. He stepped over to the plump carcass of the beaver, knelt next to it. Its dead eyes and yellowed teeth were invisible, buried, yet he thought he could smell the oily, musky taint of panic.

"You planning to haul it out yourself?" The beaver was big, sixty pounds easy.

"She's strong," the boy said, tilting his head toward the cabin. "That's why I brung her along."

He laughed until the boy showed his well-spaced teeth, and then it was in him, fast and mean, to give his laugh an ugly twist. A girl like that shouldn't be out here, though he thought he understood why she'd come. The boy was rocking on his feet again, rippling with the unguided energy of a young man, an unbeaten one. Women would follow the stream of that energy as long as the boy had it, he thought. Follow it and try to drink it down.

Before he knew it he'd reached into his pocket for two cigarettes and a lighter. It amazed him, the way two people could make headway without words. He thought briefly of the girl drying her small, cold-clenched body with his bath towel, the live tinge that would come to her skin, the darkening smears of her blood. Then something about the way the boy handled his cigarette, his whole body sheltering the lighter's blue-whipped flame, brought a question to mind. "You play some basketball?" He tapped his own smoke on a thumbnail. "I think my nephew talked about that."

The boy narrowed his eyes as if he were measuring something. He raised one hand, cocked it at the wrist, then flipped it forward. He could see that it was all the answer he would get. It was over. The boy had left it behind. And even though his body remembered the moves, would forever remember them, he'd stopped tunneling into that game with his mind.

"We can stand out here and freeze, then, just standing here. Or we can load that beaver in my truck." He bent over and scythed the snow off the glossy pelt with the edge of his hand. "I'll take you out to your car."

The boy squinted at him through a scrim of smoke, then shrugged the way he did.

"Check on her first, maybe," he said. "Make sure she's using the blankets."

The boy grabbed at his frosted hat and stuck his head back inside the cabin. He could see that the boy's hair had been cut since he'd last seen him. It fell in a smooth, blunt line along the flat muscle of his jaw and the coppery nape of his neck.

"She's all right," the boy said, fitting his hat back onto his head. "Dressing."

They squatted as a pair and shared the beaver's weight as they lifted. He glanced up the track and made a guess that the Ford would get to the road all right; it would be a lot easier if they could travel in a heated cab. When the beaver was laid out in the truck bed, he found his fingers spidering through his pockets for more cigarettes. The boy seemed impressed that he had two trucks in the shed, plus the dozer and a good canoe. He wanted to know about the machines, if they drove well.

"Used to know your mother," he said to the boy instead, and right away the words hung from him like brittle ice from a branch. He felt foolish. The boy probably knew all he wanted to know about old Hermit Hansen. He had no business trying to make himself out to be another kind of man.

"Everybody knows my ma." The boy ran a hand along the searing green flank of the Ford, admiring the tires, the roomy bed. "Everybody from around here, anyway. Long time she's worked at the Chinook."

"I shot pool in there some, when I wasn't shipped out."

"Thought you hardly ever left this place." The boy blew some air into his hands, kept his eyes on the truck. "Guard it like a damn Doberman or something."

Hearing that strangled the bland words he'd aligned in his throat, and he stepped out of the shed into a dervish of snow that whirled off the roof. He tried to lock his mind onto the idea of the half-dressed girl, how she needed to be wreathed in warmth, gotten home.

"Hey, you want to tell me about my ma, go ahead." There was swagger in the boy's words now. "I've heard it before. One million times. So don't think you know a story that'll get to me. You don't know a story like that."

He turned on the boy, headed back to where he stood in the shelter of the shed. But he couldn't get his head to go all silky like it needed to before he went into a fight. He couldn't even bring Paula's smooth, silent commiserating face into focus, her sympathetic neck. He stopped, letting the wind split at his back.

"I guess now you're gonna tell me Ma's the reason you keep women's clothes way out here." The boy had his arms away from his sides, hands flexing. "Do it, then. Come at me with your weird-old-man shit. 'Cause no woman would ever come here for you. You can't tell me that."

It had been a long while since he'd been where the anger took him, riding roughshod through nerve and vein, howling within him louder than the words in his bitten throat could howl. Yet it came easily enough. He didn't bother to wait for the boy, who became like a broken-winged bird to him, clucking and fluttering in outrage. He went straight to the cabin, burst inside with his vision blanched by fury and the ungiving glare of snow. The girl was slumped on his bunk, drowsy maybe, wilted by comfort. He grabbed her where her shoulder met her collarbone, bent on flinging her to her feet, which he did. She gasped, and he felt her warm, shocked, caressing breath but didn't hear it. Didn't hear the boy tear into the cabin, either, though he knew when he was behind him, exactly there, and was able to meet him with a solid punch to the gut when it was time. He flung the girl's short-waisted coat after her and her false-furred boots and her wet, crumpled clothes. He flung them both out, into the world where they could keep their messes to themselves. The girl began to cry, but he was deaf to that also. He did see the boy's face, though, and he knew what it meant, the black lines of brows, the jagged, uncentered glint in the eyes. It meant the boy had been cornered for the first time. That he'd just about found a new edge to plunge over.

He barely heard the bleating curses and crude battering of his truck as they tore at the tailgate and took their beaver back. They would have stolen the truck if they could have, maybe even wrecked it. It's what he would have done. He watched them hump up the track with the beaver bowing the boy's infuriated young body, the girl stumbling along behind. He noticed that the girl had left her soaked garments strewn between the cabin and the shed, and he thought he could either burn them or fold them into his sea chest — that it wouldn't matter which he did. He saw, too, that she'd wrapped her hand with the gauze he'd laid out for her. There was the blankness of a bandage on her, just as there was the resin color of corduroys on her legs, the noon-blue print of a turtleneck on her slender torso and arms, the musky linger of her sweat. What he didn't know and couldn't give a good history to were those vagabond clothes, what she'd taken from him. He did not recall who they'd once belonged to or whether he'd known her name at all.

The nights became as long as they ever get, and as stark, and the wave-etched ice shelved itself around the bay and out into the lake until the shipping channels were closed. Snow came in sheets and squalls and perfect geometric drifts. On clear days he hauled wood in the restless company of crows, skidding pallets of poplar and deadfall oak in from the far-off places he'd stacked them. On days when the sky seemed no higher than the treeline and the smoke from his chimney fumed at his door, he stayed in, flipped cards, listened to the insistent radio. He spent some complicated hours with a T-square, drawing up plans for a sauna, but he did not keep at it.

One night he pried open a carton of cigarettes and thought about the boy. He hadn't been back for his traps. It was no way to run a line, but laziness of that sort was up to the boy and his uncle, if there really was an uncle. He considered how he'd once connected the boy with Henderson and what a mistake that had been. Henderson had a sense of humor and a bolt-tight sense of himself as a man. Henderson had never thrown anything in another man's face, which was where the boy's weakness was, in his impetuous, assuming pride. Good sailors withheld almost all there was to withhold aboard ship — it was how any crew avoided murder — and if a sailor was smart, he behaved much the same way when he had to be on land. Surviving. Two legs to stand on.

Henderson on the *McCurdy*. They'd been aboard together, hauling a capacity load of taconite out of Duluth, running to make St. Marys River before she froze. On his first watch they took white water across the bow, and some of the vessels ahead — especially the empty ones — heaved to in the lee of Keweenaw Point or short of the river, where thick fog was said to be mothering chunk ice and sleet. The *John C. McCurdy* steamed on. He had little trouble driving her into the black, foaming swells and keeping her trim. At next watch, though, things were different.

The old man was on the bridge by then, sleepless, thin-lipped. The wind screeched through the gangways, and the water they took across the bow began to rivet itself into a crystal armor of ice. Radio reports put them on the near side of a full-blown gale. The captain was an able man, overly cautious but never stupid. He ordered a change of course designed to run with wind and current alike. But *McCurdy* began to wallow under the extra weight of the ice. Two hours later the propeller gave way, unable to take the strain of being pitched into open air, then slammed into the mad roil of a twenty-foot crest. They all felt it, the wrench and give, and they hated the loss of momentum, the wheezing surge that had been the one force under their control. The captain radioed the Coast Guard and prepared for a merciless wait.

A twin-screw freighter from Canada offered to backtrack and give *McCurdy* a line to keep her off the shoals. But the captain told the freighter to tend to her own needs; he was nearly far enough east to be safe. And this was how Third Mate Hansen left things when he climbed from the bridge. Square-shouldered men not thinking ahead. Stoic.

He came into the officers' mess dripping and swearing. The air in the galley was stale with breath and sweat and the soggy smell of food no one wanted. He coughed into his hands, tasting the layered man-stink while he exhaled the arctic swipe of the storm. He noticed there was a passenger in the galley, a smallish withered man who was trying to read a magazine. It bothered him that the man was not in his cabin, puking into his steel bowl and staying clear of a crew that had trouble on its hands, but he said nothing.

"Sandwich," he called to Henderson, and he shed his rain gear behind the chair that was his. Sloppy, irregular, but he did it anyway. The ship fell off into a trough; each man braced himself for dive and recovery. Devil's pride, he told himself, all of them pretending that this cork-tossing was normal.

"I got some fish and some ham," Henderson said, his dark arms crossbarred in the doorway. "Your choice, sir."

That made them both laugh. "Make me four hams to run topside with some coffee. I can't stay here."

"Sure you can. No man is that everlasting important." The words came from the passenger, sudden and taunting. He glanced at Henderson for confirmation of the man's impertinence, but Henderson had turned to his work, bowed and uninvolved, so he angled his body across the long, tilting table toward the stranger.

"Maybe I don't care if I'm important. It's my job."

"No, it's not, Mate Hansen. You've pulled your watch. You were off at twelve bells."

"This is a bad time, sir."

"This," the man said delightedly, "is what a freshwater sailor would call a bad time."

The old fellow, he decided, was crazy with worry, or simply crazy. He yanked his slicker from the floor while the *McCurdy* balanced atop yet another wind-shorn crest. He moved into the galley as she paused, looking for a place to steady himself because he didn't like the way she felt, bovine, resigned. The ship plunged hard, then submarined. He found himself pressed next to Henderson in the tight space below the ovens. The Indian showed clenched teeth. The passenger, it sounded like, was flung against a wall. Seconds later the bow pulled free of the water, and they were afloat again. They'd need worse luck to lose her — he knew that — but the captain would want him to ready the boats just the same.

Henderson went to help the passenger while he tucked his pockets full of sandwiches and a thermos. He listened as the passenger insisted he was unhurt. "I am fine," he chided the cook. "You men have been through nothing if you can't chin up to this." Henderson said something inaudible, and the passenger began to cackle, then cough. "I've been washed ashore bare-arsed twice in my life. You ever sail Torpedo Alley off Cape Hatteras? Ever hear of the bloody hell called Dunkirk?" He paused long enough to hear the man's hollow accent become more British than it had been before. The captain had passed along a name at one point — Burley? Billingsley? — a joyrider, the captain said, with plenty of money. He fastened his slicker and made his way to the corner, where Henderson had propped the man upright.

"Ready to take to the boats, are you?" He leaned into the yellowish, translucent face that up close seemed shrunken by illness. He hadn't seen that before, or the blood dribbling from a split lip, and he felt pity mix with frustration in his gut, a blend he didn't like. "If that's what you're after, I'll make it my business to see you don't get it. Not on this ship."

"You don't give the orders." The man bared his pinkened teeth for a laugh.

He grabbed the man's throat, sank his fingers into slack, wattled flesh, and shoved until the galley wall banged, then banged again. "I give the orders needed, you bastard. Go back where you came from and do it while you can."

He stood and wiped the spit from his lips. The *McCurdy* chose that moment to slither and spasm beneath them. He could sense the massive torque along her keel.

"There it is, Mate Hansen," the voice at his feet wheezed. "You feel it. You'll be my man before all's well and done."

He struck the man outright. With the flat of his hand at first, then his rapid fist. The old fellow closed his eyes, and his head went loose on his neck, as though he'd been beaten before and knew how to take it. Three punches, maybe four. He stopped when the cartilage of the thin, arrogant nose gave way beneath his knuckles.

It was Henderson who surprised him. The cook looked like he planned to drive his own fist into the man's sunken gut. Yet he somehow fell away from the scarecrow collapse of the passenger, every glint of irritation and resolve drained from his eyes. His grim mouth moved in silence. He watched Henderson hard until the cook gasped as if he'd just discovered air. It was the ship, he thought. The damned strangling ship. Or the garrote of the storm. Henderson had caught something in the confluence of the two, something chill and speechless, and he had not.

It wasn't long before the cook came back into himself, ran his blade-nicked hands across his white apron, and offered to haul the passenger to his quarters, clean him up. Henderson's voice was low and easy, as always. Neither of them mentioned what had just yawed between them. If they spoke of it, they'd do so after the *McCurdy* had docked and unloaded and the time for stories had come. He left the galley in silence, turning his thoughts to his stubborn crew and what he would ask of them. The lifeboats would be frozen hard to their tackle, and the one on the bow might not be there at all. They'd have to go out — on lines or not — and see. And he would go out among them.

Some days later he found himself back in Frieda's kitchen, feeling browbeaten for reasons that were mucky in his own head. He hadn't been in touch with his sister for almost a month, a fact he registered when he emptied his box at the post office, searching for his pension check and finding letters from charities and colored fliers for the Christmas craft fair. He'd missed the holidays. He stopped at the hardware store and bought his nephews gifts. It would be okay, he thought, to give Frieda money as he usually did. Perfume, a sweater, a scarf — it wouldn't feel right to buy something like that for her. He planned for them to handle one another as they always had, without decoration.

It was the middle of the week, so Frieda put coffee on and allowed him his cigarette, but there was no food. The boys were still at school. The Christmas decorations, which his sister lavished on every surface of her small house, were gone, stored for another year. The brown paper bag that held the unwrapped gifts for his nephews mocked him from the kitchen countertop. A stupid idea. Weak. He smoked in silence, trusting he could hold fast longer than the nervy glimmers of his embarrassment could. The boys deserved something. He watched Frieda take things out of the refrigerator and the pantry. She stooped and bent, but even in a sweatshirt and purplish jeans, she didn't appear old to him. She was nimble, still concerned with the visitations of failure or success. He was the one who'd aged. He'd run from so many things, he'd pretty much run his way to the end of his life.

"You talk to them?"

"Marge and Otto? Oh, sure. They were here for —" She shook her head in disbelief. "We all got together for the holidays. Just once, but it was nice. Marge brought the ham, and the girls got along all right with C.J. and Chad. Otto complained about the government, as usual, and the bank, too, if you can believe that. He's on the G.D. board there. I thought Cecil would just bust."

They laughed, both of them, at the vision of Otto preaching about money. Their good brother, so sure of his restraint.

"Sorry I missed the party."

"No, you're not. And I'll tell you again what I told you last year. We've got so we don't miss you. Don't even bring up your name." Frieda was behind him, sweeping the floor. He could hear the hasty, scritching strokes of the broom.

"Makes it easier."

"Yes, it does."

He stood and drifted into the den, into the crabbed and narrow hallway that was so much like the hallways of his youth, drifted into the yellow-tiled bath looking for something to tinker with. When he asked Frieda where he might find replacement screws for the hinges of the clothes hamper, she handed him a shoebox of junk — buttons, paper clips, hardware — and told him to get on with it. He wanted to thank her for taking him up again, but he didn't. He thought about the jaundiced bathroom instead. How his sister never had anything unspoiled or new. He was sorting nails and scrap when his nephews charged into the house, faces stung red from the cold, their cheap, oversized parkas flapping.

They launched into competing stories about teachers and bus brawls before they saw him. C.J., the young one, clammed up at once. Chad dropped his backpack on the table and took up as much space as he could between his uncle and his mom.

"Did you tell him yet?" Chad pinned him with a squint, like he was studying long words on a sign.

"No." Frieda gathered the coats, knocked the slushy boots into a corner. "Hasn't come up."

"Well, I'm bringing it up. Everybody's talking about it."

"Just to be gross," C.J. said, edging out of the room. He was a large-eyed kid, and shy. "You like to think about him underwater all winter, down there with the pike and stuff."

"That's enough." Frieda waved an arm as though she was good-humored and tolerant, but he could see the creases around her mouth deepen and how she wouldn't look his way. "Out of here, and keep it down. Uncle John and me are talking."

"Then talk to him, will you?" Chad strode into the den. "It's like he lives in the desert or something."

He did a calm inventory in his head. The family was fine — he knew that. Something local, then. A thing spectacular to people who decided to share their tragedies.

"It's just one of those sad messes kids get caught up in because it bothers them. Maybe it'll bother you, too. It was the one you know, Paula's boy. He was running hay out to Mackinac, for the horses there, and the ice broke in a freak way. He's so far down, they can't even dive for him. Driving a Sno-Cat. The guys on Ski-Doos are all fine."

He looked at her, reacquainted himself with the wrinkles around her eyes.

"Plain bad luck is what they say. A squall got them off track, and they say one of the snowmobilers — some relative — was drunk, but they didn't do anything stupid. People make that run all the time."

"Been making it for years," he said.

"Yeah," she said, looking at him like she couldn't quite bring his hairline into focus. "Horses have to eat just like the rest of us. Some guy in St. Ignace has the contract, and he let this kid, what's his name, drive the Cat because he asked to. The paper said some nice things."

"Same as dying in a car wreck," he said.

"Maybe so. All the way to the bottom, though, that's different. Feels different to me."

She went on then — to a salting and pounding of meat, stopping once to ask if he wanted to stay for dinner. He didn't. He stood and rinsed his mug, emptied the green glass ashtray into the trash, found his hat and gloves on top of the refrigerator where he'd left them. Only when he went to put on the gloves did he realize his left fist was clenched. When he opened it he saw two wood screws pressed deep into his callused skin, so deep they ought to hurt.

"I'm sorry," his sister said. Her arms were folded tight over her chest, but her face was elongated, soft.

"About what?"

"You know what I mean." And she moved after him to shut the door, sealing her house again from the cold.

When he pulled in across from the Chinook, he realized that his mouth was wet and drooling for a drink while his throat was wrung dry. Divided up, he told himself. Same old story. He went inside, nodded to the men playing eight ball, then slid onto a stool at the bar. He ordered a Coke, and the bartender, a red-haired guy he didn't know, brought it to him right away. He left a good tip and moved to an empty round table against the wall. A stuffed salmon bucked on the wall above him. The air smelled of fry grease and sleep.

He finally thought to slip his coat off so he wouldn't look like he was on the run. Chewed on the ice in his Coke and watched the pool players circle the table like boxers, high-shouldered and flat-faced. He didn't have to wait long. She brought him a second Coke in a highball glass and sat down across from him.

"Hello, John." She'd always said it the same.

"Hello, Paula. Thought I'd come see the sights." He took in her face, which was thinner; he looked for gray in her hair or any bad sign of grief. What he could see right away were diamond-chip earrings and lipstick and the way she hid her hands.

"New jukebox. We got that for big dancers like you. And the kitchen's been redone. You want some food?"

"No," and he shook his head as her wide-set brown eyes smiled. He'd been puke-sick in front of her in the old days, there was that humiliation. He'd touched her some as well, as much as she'd allowed from an earnest drunk, since she had three or four kids already. That had happened maybe half a dozen times in ten years of drinking, shipping out, moving on. What he'd kept with him most was what hung before him now — her lovely, unassailing face.

"I heard about your boy."

She sat back in her chair and brought a hand up along her neck and ear. Her nails were still short-bitten. "I knew you were here because of that. You remembered, didn't you? That time with the puppy. It's good for me to think of times like that." She began to cry a little, even while she was trying not to, and the tears ran alongside her small, blunt nose. "I didn't see much of Frankie lately. He was living with his father's people. Wanted to do for himself."

He looked down, saw that his distant fingers were shredding a napkin.

"He loved when you sent me home with that crazy pup. Thought it was pure German shepherd and told everybody that, bragging. He was gonna train that dog, too, but it got killed on the road."

All those kids, tangled shapes of her kids, tangle of what she said about them, and him never bothering to sort them out by name or size or worry. No one in the Chinook had. And one of them was Frank, into his life then out of it like an ass-whipped bad dream. He sat there knowing he'd never given any kid a dog.

"He shouldn't have been on no Sno-Cat," he said. "That was plain stupid."

Paula tensed, looked at the wall next to them, then back.

"He was stupid about laying his traps, too. I could have told him if he listened one damn —" He choked up on his loud words as he realized the redhead bartender was watching him, and Paula was watching, too, but not in the right way.

"You come in here for whiskey, I won't sell you whiskey." She wept openly, with the light of temper rising in her eyes. "Don't talk down my boy, neither. It was an accident. Nobody meant no harm."

"I knew him." He felt terribly hot under his clothes, like he needed to tear them open. "We got along, and then we didn't, and I tried —"

"Say you're sorry, John. Then move on like we both got to. I'm marrying Pete Norlund." She sniffled and drew her arms tight to her sides. "Frankie hated I was with Pete. And now I don't got that battle to fight."

He took hold of his riptide mind, grappled and thought about Norlund, a barrel of a Swede older than himself, made rich off timber and real estate. There'd been a stout wife around, last he'd heard, but something had clearly been done about her.

"Maybe it'll go good, Paula. You deserve it if anybody does."

"Still know how to make sweet, do you? I didn't never forget you or the things you did." She stood and covered one of his hands with hers while she reached for his empty glasses. A brush light and warm, but he could feel it go deep just before it left him. Saw her ring, too, set with hard, permanent diamonds. Norlund had a big glassy house on the lakefront. He would work to imagine her in there.

"Sorry about your boy."

She swung her head as if she could fling it empty of tears and walked from him. A black, sleeveless blouse that was more modest than it needed to be. Good boots, tight jeans. Her long, thick hair fanning out from a silver conch clip that he immediately recognized, so like the ones he'd almost brought to her after his trips away, the ones he'd fingered and never bought in those smiling, jostling marketplaces far from home.

He took note of the ragged cuticles of snow left by the plows. Of the snapped-off tree branches. Of the convoyed clouds to the south. There was a way to carry on that every sailor learned after his first few watches — a way to remain alert but separate, never mesmerized or confused by the shape-shifting of fool water or the sky. Peering ahead, looking for decisions to make — that was the way a man remained clear.

He parked on the track, leaving room to swing the canoe out of the shed. He looked her over carefully first, eyeing the seams, checking where he'd patched her in the fall with a square of cloth from a shirt and some ambroid glue. She rested cleanly on her braces, a beamy wood-canvas shell. He'd bought her from an old steam tender who'd foulhooked the end of his luck, gave the man a sluggish Grumman and a hundred dollars in exchange. The steam tender said she came from Minnesota and was made the old-time trapper way, to last forever. Whatever the truth, she handled well in light water and was easy enough for one man to portage. He slid her off the braces, flipped her, then worked her up on end until he could yoke up between the varnished, seat-worn thwarts. The snow was crusty and deep. It would be a long, panting carry.

By the time he could see the wide silver scuff of the bay, he'd begun to sweat through his second shirt.

He took the canoe to the place he always took her, next to a great smooth log that had washed ashore in a spring storm not long after he'd moved into the shack for good. In summer he chained the canoe along the far side of the log, but he did not chain her now. He merely nestled her into her accustomed place, protected as much from wind and weather as she could be. He was months early. Porcupines or others might do her some mischief, though it was not a possibility that bore thinking about. He'd make up a special buoy before long, get together a good anchor and plenty of strong line. What he needed to consider now was when he would next be out on the water, stroking through the rocky blue shallows of the bay into the lake.

He made his way downshore to a natural cairn of porous, fossil-etched stones, swept them clean of snow, leaned against them. Mackinac Island was a tired mirage beneath the translucent clouds, a smudge of dirtied crystal. Winter had leveled it, as it leveled them all. The boy he'd known had done nothing but take on a few jobs, try on his shifting attitudes. It hurt Paula plenty that he'd died, more than anything had ever hurt him. He knew he wouldn't set foot in the Chinook again, not even to recast his words to her, the ones he'd meant to say better. If he took up liquor, he'd go to the next town to drink it, or drink it in the hidy-hole of his shack like he was expected to.

The sun drifted west until the snow on the lake was shadowed in lavender and blue, and the trees drew themselves into a phalanx of darkness at his back. He had always cared for this, the way the lake

sealed itself off, flat and silent and hidden. There was nothing
practical to be done about the boy. He could walk the ponds and try
to locate the beaver traps, though the uncle would surely come
after them before long — maybe he'd come with the girl — and he
had no business pretending he was a help to anyone. He was not.

His sweat cooled but did not dry, and there was a chill against his
skin. Then the vast hush of an unhindered night brought Henderson back into his mind. Strong, private Henderson, who should
have been a cook on the lollygagging, sweet-tempered *Pontiac* with
its simple runs to Buffalo, but who kept manning the slipshod
McCurdy in his mind. It had been Henderson who'd done the
visceral thing.

He'd run his gang out along the decks, captain's orders, as they
needed to know how bad things were with the boats and hatches
and rails. Most of them went on safety lines — the decks were slick,
the air burned with sleet — but he and Quillian, a true Newfound-
land bastard, went footsure and unfettered. They'd discovered the
worst, and he was on his way to report to the captain when he saw a
man peering at him through a sclerous portal. Henderson. Broad
and searching in his foul-weather gear, face pressed against the
murky glass. He feared the cook wanted to volunteer for his crew,
and he did not want that to happen.

He took his tidings to the old man on the bridge. The bosun
would need a look at the number-three hatch; he'd take him there.
There was some relief in the orders that followed, the risks, the
sleight of hand it would take to get through the remainder of the
storm. There was a kind of march to the whole thing that he
relished — a sailor's muster and charge — all done to the drum-
beat of weather and damage.

Quillian was waiting for him belowdecks, his face and cap beaded
with melting sleet. "The Indian's gone out there. I told him not to."
Quillian spoke with neither urgency nor judgment. Narrow talk,
the speech of an islander.

"I'll get him. He has some crazy idea about helping."

"Don't know about that," Quillian said. "Had his duffel with him,
like he meant to leave."

He pushed his way out then. The deck lights flickered in the
thick spray and wind, teasing his sense of balance. He clutched a
rail as the *McCurdy* bucked through a shallow trough, water spewing

green and black across his face. They'd been spared by the genius
of the chief engineer so far, but if she caught beam seas again,
caught them hard enough, the decks would be carried under. He
looked midships for Henderson, thought again of the blackjacked
look in the cook's eyes when the passenger had sworn them off,
and made his way down an accursedly icy ladder and aft. Henderson was on the fire crew. Maybe he was crazy enough to take his drill
station. If he was still onboard at all.

He found him leaning over a beaten section of railing, sweeping
his arms above the frenzied leap of water. Madness. Or an Indian
thing, maybe. Or just madness. He'd ask him to come back with
him, to the galley for coffee, but if he wouldn't come, so be it. The
lake knew her business. He did not move, however, when he saw
Henderson lift his duffel — stuffed and heavy — onto the rail. A
clumsy shove and the bag went overboard, and while he waited a
pitiless moment for Henderson to follow the duffel, it did not
happen. The cook turned and saw him through the dim shower of
spray and nodded, his rain hat tied tight beneath his squarish chin.
It was as though he'd known he was being watched. Henderson
then passed by and made his way up the ladder with slow purpose.
He followed the cook until he met up again with Quillian and the
hard-pacing bosun. There were no words exchanged. They all went
on with their jobs.

He didn't hear about the passenger until the next day. Awake for
thirty hours until the weather broke, out dead for four hours' sleep,
then back into the crowded mess for some breakfast. He didn't
hear about it from Henderson, who was preparing a sherry soufflé
for the captain, his apron starched flat, his black hair drawn into a
neat, foreign-looking knot at the base of his skull. He heard it from
the chief steward, who'd been to the passenger's cabin with clean
towels and linens. The fellow was gone; the cabin as tidy as a com-
mander's. They were looking for him in every bunk and locker,
knowing how panic could make a rat out of any man, but some
who'd met him or seen him walking the decks before the storm did
not expect to see him again. This was what the steward said, working the tale slowly around his soft Caribbean vowels, savoring it for
the drinks that a longer, more lush version would someday buy.

He knew. And could feel the knowledge loop about him like a
fresh manila line, connecting him hard to Henderson and that

damnable yakking man. To Quillian, too, no doubt, though the Newfie would never speak of what he'd seen, as he lived ancestrally in the gap between what he witnessed and what he needed to act upon.

Now, standing on a plain of sharded dark and light, at the edge of water and his land, he could not remember what it had been like to look Henderson in the eye after that moment. He could not recall what they'd said to each other, though he knew they must have spoken — each of them — and let the words wrap the shroud on tight. Had they ever gone that far? He knew well how the *McCurdy* had been towed back to Duluth by a Coast Guard vessel with a belligerent crew. He knew Henderson had left the ship, as all the crew did, off to sign onto other freighters while the *McCurdy* underwent repairs. Henderson in his massive pea jacket, his oft-healed hands, a neatly packed duffel like a rolled sail across his shoulder. They had said goodbye to one another in the usual brief way, as there were always things left unspoken when a man passed by another man. He remembered that he never questioned Henderson's reasons. The passenger may have died on that pitching galley floor, or, good Christ, he may have begged to taste the saltless water of their particular sea. There *had* been a reason, he was sure of it — one that meant everything to the assembled heart that worked inside Henderson.

He walked onto the ice. First to where it laced around the lifeless rocks. Then to where the water of the bay deepened and he could have fished if he cared to and speared his share of whitefish and pike. Beyond, the ice grew thinner and might have groaned and pealed beneath him, but it did not. He went on, to the point where his canoe would begin to feel the draw of the great lake, its deep currents and cold logic. He would plant a hand-painted buoy when the ice broke, pay his delayed respects. The boy was out there, open-eyed and washed and preserved, a victim of risk and channel water, but all he could see were the pitiful man-lights that necklaced Mackinac and adorned her property. He turned back only when the wind rose from the black distance and drove into him, squalling with snow and bitterness. Only when he could be driven ashore like a sail with no good hull or keel beneath him. It was a motion he understood, for it was how his watery heart now worked within him.

TIM GAUTREAUX

Little Frogs in a Ditch

FROM GENTLEMEN'S QUARTERLY

OLD MAN FONTENOT watched his grandson draw hard on a slim cigarette and then flick ashes on the fresh gray enamel of the front porch. The boy had been fired, this time from the laundry down the street.

"The guy who let me go didn't have half the brains I got," Lenny Fontenot said.

The old man nodded, then took a swallow from a can of warm beer. "The owner, he didn't like you double-creasing the slacks." He wouldn't look at the boy. Instead, he watched a luminous cloud drifting up from the Gulf.

"Let me tell you," Lenny said with a snarl, his head following a dusk-drawn pigeon floating past the screen, "there's some dumb people in this world."

"Give it a rest," the old man said, looking down the street to the drizzle-washed iron roof of the laundry. His grandson was living with him again, eating his food, using all the hot water in the mornings. "If you work on your attitude a little bit, you could keep a job."

Lenny stood up and put his nose to the screen. "I didn't need a laundry job anyway. I'm a salesman."

"You couldn't sell cow cakes to a rosebush."

Lenny threw down his cigarette and mashed it with the toe of a scuffed loafer. "Hey, I could sell a pigeon."

His grandfather picked up his cap and looked at him. "Who the hell would buy a pigeon?"

"I could find him."

"Lenny, if someone wanted a pigeon, all he'd have to do is catch him one."

"A dumb man will buy a pigeon from me." He clopped down the steps to the side yard. At the rear of the lot was a broad, unused carport, swaybacked over broken lawn mowers and wheelbarrows. He looked up into the eaves to the ragged nests dripping dung down the side of a beam. With a quick grab he had a slate-blue pigeon in his hands, the bird blinking its onyx eyes stupidly. He turned to his grandfather, who was walking up. "Look. You can pluck them like berries under here."

Old man Fontenot gave him a disgusted look. "Nobody'll eat a pigeon."

Lenny ducked his head. "Eat? I ain't said nothing about eat." He smiled down at the bird. "This is a homing pigeon."

"Come on. That thing's got fleas like a politician. Put it down." The old man pulled at his elbow.

Lenny's eyes came up red and filmy. "Your Ford's got a crack in the head and you can't afford to get it fixed. I'm gonna make some money for you."

His grandfather knew Lenny wanted the car for his own but said nothing. He looked at the bird in his grandson's hands, which was pedaling the air, blinking its drop of dark eye. "I told your parents I wouldn't let you get in any more trouble." He watched Lenny make a face. The grandfather remembered the boy's big room in his parents' air-conditioned brick rancher, the house they sold from under Lenny to buy a Winnebago and tour the country. One day the boy had come home from a long weekend and everything he owned was stacked under the carport, a Sold sign out front.

Two days later, the old man watched Lenny fold back the classified section to his ad, which read, "Homing pigeons $10 each. Training instructions included." His grandfather read it over his shoulder, then went into the kitchen to cook breakfast. Lenny came in and looked down at the stove.

"You gonna cook some eggs? Annie likes eggs."

"She coming over again?" He tried to sound miffed, but in truth he liked Annie. She was a big-boned, denim-clad blonde who worked in a machine shop. He felt sorry for the girl because Lenny made her pay for their dates.

Lenny rumbled down the steps, and the grandfather watched him through the kitchen window. From behind the carport he pulled a long-legged rabbit cage. He shook out the ancient pellets and set it next to the steps. With his cigarette-stained fingers, he snatched from the carport eaves a granite-colored pigeon and clapped him into the cage. Most of the other birds lit out in a rat-tat-tat of wings, but he managed to snag a pink-and-gray. The old man clucked his tongue and turned up the fire under the peppery boudin.

Annie came up the rear steps lugging a toolbox. At the stove, she took a helping, then sat at the kitchen table spooning grits and eggs into herself.

"Annie, baby." Lenny plopped down across from her with a plate of smoking sausage. After they finished eating, she asked him why he was going into the pigeon business. He told her he was doing it for her, so they could use the car. Then the doorbell jittered, and everyone got up to see who it was.

On the front porch, they found a white-haired gentleman staring at a torn swatch of newsprint. He was wearing nubby brown slacks and a green-checkered cowboy shirt.

"I'm Perry Lejeune from over by Broussard Street. About five blocks. I saw your ad."

Mr. Fontenot gave his grandson a scowl and pulled off his cap as if he would toss it.

Lenny straightened out of his slouch and smiled, showing his small teeth. "Mr. Lejeune, you know anything about homing pigeons?"

The other man shook his head. "Nah. My little nephew Alvin's living at my house and I want to get him something to occupy his time. His momma left him with me and I got to keep him busy, you know?" Mr. Lejeune raised his shoulders. "I'm too old to play ball with a kid."

"Don't worry, I'll fill you in," he said, motioning for everyone to follow him back to the carport. He put his hand on the rickety rabbit cage and made eye contact with Mr. Lejeune. "I've got just two left. This slate," he nodded toward the plain bird, "is good in the rain. And I got that pink fella if you want something flashy."

Mr. Lejeune put up a hand like a stop signal. "I can't afford nothing too racy."

"The slate's a good bird. Of course, at this price, you got to train him, you know."

"Yeah, I want to ask you about that." Mr. Lejeune made a pliers of his right forefinger and thumb and clamped them on his chin. Annie came around close, and the grandfather looked at the bottom of his back steps and shook his head.

Lenny put his hands in the cage and caught the pigeon. "You got to build a cage out of hardware cloth with a one-way door."

"Yeah, for when he comes back, you mean."

Lenny gave Mr. Lejeune a look. "That's right. Now to start training you got to hold him like a football, with your thumbs on top of him and your fingers underneath. You see?"

Mr. Lejeune put on his glasses and bent to look under the pigeon. "Uh-hun."

"Stand exactly where your property line is. Then you catch his little legs between your forefingers and your middle fingers. One leg in each set of fingers, you see?" Lenny got down on his knees, wincing at the rough pavement. "You put his little legs on the ground, like this. You see?"

"Yeah, I got you."

"Then you walk the bird along your property line, moving his legs and coming along behind him like this. You got to go around all four sides of your lot with him so he can memorize what your place looks like."

"Yeah, yeah, I got you. Give him the grand tour, kinda."

Annie frowned and hid her mouth under a bright hand. His grandfather sat on the steps and looked away.

Lenny waggled the bird along the ground as the animal pumped its head, blinked and tried to peck him. "Now it takes commitment to train a bird. It takes a special person. Not everybody's got the character it takes to handle a homing pigeon."

Mr. Lejeune nodded. "Hey, you talking to someone's been married forty-three years. How long you got to train 'em?"

Lenny stood and replaced the bird in the cage. "Every day for two weeks, you got to do this."

"Rain or shine?" Mr. Lejeune's snowy eyebrows went up.

"That's right. And then after two weeks, you take him in a box out to Bayou Park and set his little butt loose. He might even beat you home, you know?"

The man bobbed his head. "Little Alvin's gonna love this." He reached for his wallet. "Any tax?"

"A dollar."

Mr. Lejeune handed him a ten and dug for a one. "Ain't the tax rate eight percent in the city?"

"Two percent wildlife tax," Lenny told him, reaching under the cage for a shoebox blasted with ice-pick holes.

That day Lenny sold pigeons to Mankatos Djan, a recent African immigrant, and to two children who showed up on rusty BMX bikes. By the twelfth day, he had sold twenty-six pigeons and had enough to fix the leaf-covered sedan. Lenny counted his money and walked up to the front porch, where his grandfather was finishing a mug of coffee in the heat. He looked at the cash in Lenny's outstretched hand. "What's that?"

"It's enough money to fix the car."

His grandfather looked away toward the laundry. "I saw you take twenty dollars from some children for a lousy pair of flea baits. You got no morals."

"Hey. It's for your car, dammit."

"That poor colored guy who couldn't hardly speak a word of English. Black as a briquette and he believed every damned thing you told him. My grandson sticks him for eleven bucks that'd feed one of his relatives living in a grass shack back in Bogoslavia for a year." He looked up at Lenny, his veiny brown eyes wavering from the heat. "What's wrong with you?"

"What's wrong with me?" he yelled, stepping back. "Everybody's getting money but me. I ain't even got a job, and I start a business, just like everybody else does."

"You don't know shit about business. You're a crook."

"All right." He banged the money against his thigh. "So I'm a crook. What's the difference between me and the guy that sells a Mercedes?"

The grandfather grabbed the arms of his rocker as his voice rose. "A Mercedes won't fly off toward the clouds, crap in your eye and not come back after you paid good money for it."

Lenny jerked his head toward the street. "It's all how you look at it," he growled.

"There's only one way to look at it, dammit. The right way." His grandfather stood up. "You get out of my house. Your parents got rid of you and now I know why. Maybe a few nights sleeping in the car will straighten you out."

Lenny backed up another step, the money still in his outstretched hand. "They didn't get rid of me. They moved out west."

"Get out." The old man brought his thin brows down low and beads of sweat glimmered on his bald head. "Don't come back until you get a job."

"I can't live out on the street," Lenny said, his voice softening, his face trying a thin smile.

"Crooks wind up on the street and later they burn in hell," the old man said.

Lenny kicked the bottom of the screen, and his grandfather yelled. Five minutes later, he was standing next to the sagging Ford, listening to the feathery pop of wings as the old man pulled pigeons out of the rabbit cage and tossed them toward the rooftops.

That night the grandfather couldn't sleep and rolled up the shade at the tall window next to his bed, looking into the moonlit side yard at his car parked against the fence. He knelt on the floor and folded his arms on the windowsill, thinking how Lenny should be back at the cleaner's, smiling through the steam of his pressing machine. Down in the yard, the Ford bobbled, and he imagined that Lenny was slapping mosquitoes off his face, that the boy was turning over, putting his nose into the crack at the bottom of the seat back, smelling the dust balls and old pennies and cigarette filters. The grandfather thought of Annie, her Pet milk skin, her big curves. Lenny talked with longing of her paychecks, nearly $2,400 a month, clear. Lenny had never made above minimum wage and complained often about how undervalued he was. His grandfather wondered if some dim sense of the real world of work would ever settle on him. The old man climbed into bed but couldn't sleep because he began to see people Lenny had sold birds to, the dumb children, the African, and wondered how the boy could sell his soul for $11.

At six o'clock, he went down into the yard and opened the driver's door to the car. The boy lay back against the seat and put an arm over his eyes. "Aw, man."

His grandfather pushed on his shoulder. "You get a job yet?"

Lenny cocked up a red eye. "How'm I gonna get a job smelling bad with no shave and mosquito bites all over me?"

The old man considered this a moment, looking his grandson in his sticky eyes. He remembered the inert feel of him as a baby. "Okay. I'll give you a temporary reprieve on one condition."

"What's that?" Lenny hung his head way back over the seat.

"St. Lucy has confessions before seven o'clock daily Mass. I want you to think about going to confession and telling the priest what you done."

Lenny straightened up and eyed the house. The old man knew he was considering its old deep bathtub and its oversized water heater. "Where in the catechism does it say selling pigeons is a mortal sin?"

"You going, or you staying outside in your stink?"

"What am I supposed to tell the priest?" He turned his hands up in his lap.

His grandfather squatted down next to him. "Remember what Sister Florita told you one time in catechism class? If you close your eyes before you go to confession, your sins will make a noise."

Lenny closed his eyes. "A noise."

"They'll cry out like little frogs in a ditch at sundown."

"Sure," Lenny said with a laugh, his eyeballs shifting under the closed lids. "Well, I don't hear nothing." He opened his eyes and looked at the old man. "What's the point of me confessing if I don't hear nothing?"

His grandfather stood up with a groan. "Keep listening," he said.

After Lenny cleaned up, they ate breakfast at a café on River Street, and later, walking home, they spotted Annie coming up the street carrying her toolbox, her blond hair splashed like gold on the shoulders of her denim shirt.

Lenny gave her a bump with his hip. "Annie, you're out early, babe."

She lifted her chin. "I came to see you. Somebody told me you were sleeping in the car like a bum." She emphasized the last word.

"The old man didn't like my last business."

"It wasn't business," she snapped. Annie looked at the grandfather, then at Lenny's eyes, searching for something. "You just don't get it, do you?"

"Get what?" When he saw her expression, he lost his smile.

She sighed and looked at her watch. "Ya'll come on." She picked up her toolbox and started down the root-buckled sidewalk toward Broussard Street. After five blocks, they crossed a wide boulevard, went one more block and stopped behind a holly bush growing next to the curb. Across the street was a peeling weatherboard house.

"This is about the time I saw him yesterday," Annie said.

"Who?" the grandfather asked.

"The old guy Lenny sold the pigeon to."

Lenny ducked behind the bush. "Jeez, you want him to see me?"

Across the street, there was movement at the side of the house, and Mr. Lejeune came around his porch slow, shuffling on his knees like a locomotive. The grandfather stood on his toes and saw that the old man was red in the face, and the pigeon itself looked tired and drunk.

"Man," Lenny whispered, "he's got rags tied around his knee-caps."

"Yesterday I saw he wore the tips off his shoes. Look at that." Behind Mr. Lejeune walked a thin boy, perhaps nine years old, awkward and pale. "Didn't he say he had a nephew?" The boy was smiling and talking down to his uncle. "The kid looks excited about something."

"Two weeks," Lenny said.

"Huh?" The grandfather cupped a hand behind an ear.

"Today's two weeks. They'll probably go to Bayou Park this after-noon and turn it loose."

Mr. Lejeune looked up and across toward where they were stand-ing. He bent to the side a bit and then lurched to his feet, waving like a windshield wiper. "Hey, what ya'll doing on this side the boulevard?"

The three of them crossed the street and stood on the walk. "We was just out and about," Lenny told him. "How's the bird doin'?" The pigeon seemed to look up at him angrily, blinking, struggling. Someone had painted its claws with red fingernail polish.

"This here's Amelia," Mr. Lejeune said. "That's what Alvin named him. Or her. We never could figure how to tell, you know." He looked at his nephew. The grandfather saw that the boy was trembling in spite of his smile. His feet were pointed inward, and his left hand was shriveled and pink.

"How you doing, bud?" The grandfather asked, patting his head.

"All right," the boy said. "We going to the park at four o'clock and turn Amelia loose."

Lenny forced a smile. "You and your uncle been having a good time training old Amelia, huh?"

The boy looked over to where his uncle had gone to sit on the front steps. He was rubbing his knees. "Yeah. It's been great. The first day, we got caught out in a thunderstorm and I got a chest cold, but the medicine made me feel better."

"You had to go to the doctor?" Annie asked, touching his neck.

"Him too," the boy volunteered in a reedy voice. "Shots in the legs." He looked up at Lenny. "It'll be worth it when Amelia comes back from across town."

"Why's it so important?" Lenny asked.

The boy shrugged. "It's just great that this bird way up in the sky knows which house I live in."

The old man struggled to his feet, untying the pads from his knees. "Come in the back yard and look at the cage." He shook out his pants and tugged the boy toward the rear of the house, to a close-clipped yard with an orange tree in the middle. Against the rear of the house was a long-legged cage, shiny with new galvanized hardware cloth.

"That took a lot of work to build, I bet," the grandfather said out of the side of his mouth to Lenny, who shrugged and said that he'd told him how to do it. The corners of the cage were finished like furniture, mortised and tenoned. In the center was a ramp leading up to a swinging door. The pigeon squirted out of the old man's hand into the cage, crazy for the steel-mesh freedom.

"We'll let him rest up for the big flight," Mr. Lejeune said.

Lenny glanced over at Annie's serious face. She looked long at the pigeon, then over at where the boy slumped against the orange tree. "You know," Lenny began, "if you decide you ain't happy with the bird, you can have your money back."

Mr. Lejeune looked at him quickly. "No way. He's trained now. I bet he could find this house from the North Pole."

The grandfather told Mr. Lejeune how much he liked the cage, then touched Annie's shoulder, and they said their goodbyes. On the walk home, she was silent. When they got to the grandfather's, she stopped, rattled her little toolbox, glanced back down the street and asked, "Lenny, what's gonna happen if that bird doesn't come back to the kid?"

He shook his head. "If he heads for the river and spots them grain elevators, he'll never see Broussard Street again, that's for sure."

"Two weeks ago, you knew he was buying Amelia as a pet for a kid."

Lenny turned his palms out. "Am I responsible for everything those birds do until they die?"

The grandfather rolled his eyes at the girl. She wasn't stupid, but when she looked at Lenny there was too much hope in her eyes.

Annie clenched and unclenched her big pale hands. "If I was a bad sort, I'd hit you with a crescent wrench." She looked at him the way she studied a gadget whirling in her lathe, maybe wondering if he would come out all right.

Lenny lit up a cigarette and let the smoke come out as he talked. "I'm sorry. I'll try to think of something to tell the kid if the bird don't come back."

She considered this for a moment, then leaned over and kissed him quickly on the side of his mouth. As the grandfather watched her stride down the sidewalk, he listened to the Williams sockets rattling in her toolbox, and then he saw Lenny wipe off the hot wetness of her lips.

That night, a half hour after dark, Annie, Lenny and his grandfather were watching a John Wayne movie in the den when there was a knock at the back screen door. It was Mr. Lejeune, and he was worried about Amelia.

"I turnt her loose about four-thirty, and she ain't come back yet," the old man told Lenny. "You got any hints?"

Lenny looked at a shoe. "You want a refund?"

"Nah." He pushed back his white hair with his fingers. "That ain't the point. The boy's gonna get a lift from seeing the bird come back." Alvin's pale face tilted out from behind his uncle's waist.

Annie, who was wearing shorts, peeled herself off the plastic couch, and the grandfather put a spotted hand over his eyes. Lenny turned a serious face toward the boy. "Sometimes those birds get in fights with other birds. Sometimes they get hurt and don't make it back. What can I tell you? You want your money?" He put a hand in his pocket but left it there.

The old man sidestepped out onto the porch. "Me and Alvin will go and wait. If that bird'd just come back once, it'd be worth all the crawlin' around, you see?" He held the boy's twisted hand and went down ahead of him, one step at a time. Annie moved into the kitchen and broke a glass in the sink. The grandfather tried not to listen to what happened next.

Lenny went to see what caused the noise, and there was a rattle of accusations from Annie. Then Lenny began to shout. "Why are you bitching at me like this?"

"Because you gypped that old man and the crippled kid. I've never seen you do nothing like that."

"Well you better get used to it."

"Get used to what?" She used a big, contrary voice better than most women, the grandfather thought.

"Get used to doing things the way I like."

"What, like stealing from old people and kids? Acting like a freakin' slug? Now I know why your parents left your ass in the street."

Lenny's voice came through the kitchen door thready and high-pitched. "Hey, nobody left me. They're on vacation, you cow."

"People don't sell their houses, leave the time zone and never write or call because they're on vacation, you retard. They left because they found out what it took me a long time to just now realize."

"What's that?"

And here a sob came into her voice, and the grandfather put his head down.

"That there's a big piece of you missing that'll never turn up."

"You can't talk to me like that," Lenny snarled, "and I'll show you why." The popping noise of a slap came from the kitchen, and the grandfather thought, Oh no, and struggled to rise from the sofa, but before he could stand and steady himself, a sound like a piano tipping over shook the entire house, and Lenny cried out in deep pain.

After the grandfather prepared an ice pack, he went to bed that night but couldn't sleep. He thought of the handprint on Annie's face and the formal numbness of the walk back to her house as he escorted her home. Now he imagined Mr. Lejeune checking Amelia's cage into the night, his nephew asking him questions in a resigned voice. He even formed a picture of the pigeon hunkered down on a roof vent above the St. Mary Feed Company elevator, trying with its little bird brain to remember where Broussard Street was. About one o'clock, he smacked himself on the forehead with an open palm, put on his clothes and went down to the old carport with a flashlight. In the eaves, he saw a number of round heads pop into his light's beam, and when he checked the section from which Lenny had plucked Amelia, he thought he saw her. Turning off the light for a moment, he reached into the straw and pulled out a bird that barely struggled. Its claws were painted red, and the grandfather eased down into a wheelbarrow to think, the bird in both hands, where it pecked him resignedly. He debated whether he should just let the animal go and forget the Lejeunes, but then he imagined how the boy would have to face the empty cage. It would be like an abandoned house, and every day the boy would look at it and wonder why Amelia had forgotten where he lived.

At two-fifteen the grandfather walked down the side of Mr. Lejeune's house, staying close to the wall and out of the glow of the streetlight. When he turned the corner into the back yard, he was in total darkness and had to feel for the cage, and then for its little swinging gate. His heart jumped as he felt a feathery movement in the palms, and the bird leaped for the enclosure. At that instant, a floodlight came on and the back door rattled open, showing Mr. Lejeune standing in a pair of mustard-colored pajama bottoms and a sleeveless undershirt.

"Hey, what'cha doing?" He came down into the yard, moving carefully.

The grandfather couldn't think of a lie to save his soul, but stood there looking between the cage and the back door. "I just wanted to see about the bird," he said at last.

The other man walked up and looked into the cage. "What? How'd you get ahold of the dumb cluck? I thought she'd be in Texas by now." He reached back and scratched a hip.

The grandfather's mouth slowly fell open. "You knew."

"Yeah," Mr. Lejeune growled. "I may be dumb, but I ain't stupid. And no offense, Mr. Fontenot, but that grandson of yours got used car salesman writ all over him."

"Why'd you come by the house asking about the bird if you knew it'd never come back?"

"That was for Alvin, you know? I wanted him to think I was worried." Mr. Lejeune grabbed the grandfather by the elbow and led him into his kitchen, where the two men sat down at a little enamel-topped table. The old man opened the refrigerator and retrieved two frosty cans of Schlitz. "It's like this," Mr. Lejeune said, wincing against the spray from the pull tabs. "Little Alvin's never had a daddy, and his momma's a crackhead that run off with some biker to Alaska." He pushed a can to the grandfather, who picked it up and drew hard, for he was sweating. Mr. Lejeune spoke low and leaned close. "Little Alvin's still in fairy-tale land, you know. Thinks his momma is coming back when school starts up in the fall. But he's got to toughen up and face facts. That's why I bought that roof rat from your grandson." He sat back and began rubbing his knees. "He'll be disappointed about the little thing, that bird, and maybe it'll teach him to deal with the big thing. That boy's got to live a long time, you know what I mean, Mr. Fontenot?"

The grandfather put his cap on the table. "Ain't that kind of a tough lesson, though?"

"Hey. We'll watch the sky for a couple days and I'll let him see how I take it. We'll be disappointed together." Mr. Lejeune looked down at his purple feet. "He's crippled, but he's strong and he's smart."

The grandfather lifted his beer and drank until his eyes stung. He remembered Lenny, asleep in the front bedroom with a big knot on the back of his head and a black eye. He listened to Mr. Lejeune until he was drowsy. "I got to get back home," he said, standing up and moving toward the door. "Thanks for the beer."

"Hey. Don't worry about nothing. Just do me a favor and put that bird back in its nest." They went out, and Mr. Lejeune reached into the cage and retrieved Amelia, dropping her into a heavy grocery bag.

"You sure you doing the right thing, now?" the grandfather asked. "You got time to change your mind." He helped fold the top of the bag shut. "You could be kind." He imagined what the boy's face would look like if he saw that the bird had returned to the cage.

Mr. Lejeune slowly handed him the bag. For a moment, they held it together and listened. Inside, the bird walked the crackling bottom, back and forth on its painted toes, looking for home.

Contributors' Notes

HA JIN has published two poetry books, *Between Silences* and *Facing Shadows*. His first short story collection, *Ocean of Words*, received the 1997 PEN/Hemingway Award for first fiction, and his second collection, *Under the Red Flag*, received the Flannery O'Connor Award in 1996 and is forthcoming from the University of Georgia Press. He teaches at Emory University in Atlanta.

▪ Some years ago, a friend of mine told me that hepatitis had recently broken out in his hometown in mainland China and that thousands of the citizens had contracted the disease. He mentioned that some workers began eating at different restaurants the moment they were informed that they carried the bacteria. They described their malign act as "Change your position after every shot." I was shocked and didn't know what to make of that.

A few months later, I read in a legal journal that in a small country town in northern China, the head of the police station had tied a lawyer to a tree because the lawyer was willing to represent a man the police had arrested. By turns the policemen slapped the lawyer, boasting that law only came out of their mouths. Such an occurrence was commonplace in China.

After I had finished a group of country stories, I decided to write some urban stories set in a remote frontier city in Manchuria. I began with "Saboteur," in which I combined the two aforementioned incidents and shaped them into the dramatic line of the story. In addition, two ideas decided the story's dramatic structure: (1) Crimes pursue criminals. This idea has been elaborately presented in Kafka's *Trial*. In "Saboteur," Mr. Chu is innocent in the beginning, but once he is labeled as a saboteur, he begins to change. In the end he becomes a true saboteur. (2) The distinction between oppressors and victims is not clear-cut. When I was a college student in Harbin, I saw with my own eyes how some intellectuals, who had been persecuted for over a decade, rapidly turned into cruel officials after they had been rehabilitated and given power again. Evil is innate. The Communists used to be victims, but given the opportunity, they have become oppressors.

I chose an intellectual as the main character because most Chinese intellectuals like whining about the brutality they have suffered, as though whoever has suffered is bound to be a better human being. The truth is that suffering doesn't necessarily improve humanity. Many, many intellectuals have connived with the Chinese government, and some are still willing to serve the government — to oppress and rule others. In a way, this story is a critique of their moral degradation.

ROBERT STONE is the author of many works of fiction, including *A Flag for Sunrise, Outerbridge Reach* and *Dog Soldiers,* for which he won the National Book Award. His most recent work is a collection of short stories, *Bear and His Daughter.* He lives in Connecticut and teaches at Yale University.

▪ The year before last, I was able to go sailing in the Windward Islands and enjoyed it very much. Of course the tradition and the stories of contrabanding and piracy are part of the local color, and the writer's imagination turns toward them in those surroundings. A few texts apply. The Coast Guard safety manual points out, "Mariners should take special precautions in securing mooring lines or in shallow anchorages when engaged in recreational swimming."

Customs forms remind us, "The importation or transportation for the purposes of importation with the intention to sell or distribute controlled substances is strictly forbidden by Federal law and by international treaties to which the United States is signatory. Fines, imprisonment, or confiscation of vessel may be pursuant to violation of these regulations."

Then there's the epigraph to the *Admiralty Sailing Routes of the World,* a Breton fisherman's prayer: "O Lord, thy sea is so big and my boat is so small."

CAROLYN COOKE was born on Mount Desert Island in Maine and now lives in Point Arena, California, with her husband, the poet Randall Babtkis, and their two children. Her fiction has appeared in *The Gettysburg Review, New England Review, The Paris Review, Puckerbrush Review,* and in *Prize Stories 1997: The O. Henry Awards.*

▪ When I lived in New York in the 1980s, my favorite novels were *The Portrait of a Lady* and *Lolita,* and I thought of innocence as something like tooth enamel — a veneer of whiteness that you had to scrub. Arguments between innocence and experience interested me then, and do now; I still wonder about the difference between naked and nude. "Bob Darling," which I first hoped would be the last word in cross-age tutoring, is finally about a couple of Americans who are eroded by a journey abroad, who wear each other down to what's called, in dentistry, the pulp. A few weeks after the story appeared I spent an afternoon lurking in my old neighborhood in Greenwich Village and ran smack into Bob Darling with a bag of dry cleaning on his arm. He had become, in the years since I last saw him, entirely fictional. Otherwise, he seemed the same.

JONATHAN FRANZEN is the author of the novels *The Twenty-seventh City* and *Strong Motion* and is a frequent contributor to *The New Yorker* and *Harper's Magazine*. He lives in New York.

■ "Chez Lambert" is a short story caught in the act of becoming the second chapter of a novel, a tadpole-with-budding-legs type of thing. In 1992, after a visit to the retirementland in which my parents lived, I wrote a long fragment that I called "The Chair." A few years later I took a break from my stalled third novel and tried to finish the story, but instead of rounding off neatly the fragment began to grow toward the novel. All the good tropes for such a tropism seem to be organic. The story was like a heart transplanted into a body whose immune system was considering: accept or reject? It was like a backwater neuron extending fresh dendrites in the brain of someone acquiring a new skill, a new language. It was like an insect struggling in a web — strands and nodes of fiber resonating urgently, a self-interested spider scrambling over to mummify the prey, inject its tissue-liquefying venom. The chapter was still mistakable for a story when I read it aloud in Manhattan last year, and George Plimpton was kind enough to publish it as a self-contained piece. But by then the donor heart was wedded to the recipient's body.

MICHELLE CLIFF is the author of several books, including the novels *Abeng, No Telephone to Heaven, Free Enterprise,* the forthcoming *Into the Interior,* and the short fiction collection *Bodies of Water.* She is the Allan K. Smith Professor of English Language and Literature at Trinity College, Hartford.

■ "Transactions" is a story that originates in my colonial past, in the decadent world into which I was born. There is a peculiar strangeness to that world: the more I dredge it, the stranger it reveals itself, and I become more of a stranger in it.

I sought an early exit from that world. Witness to the casual cruelty visited by individuals one on the other. Wary of the privileges I was expected to accept without question.

The little girl in the story represents a historical fact as well as a fantastic notion. There *is* to this day a colony of Germans in the countryside of Jamaica. They came in the nineteenth century, understudies to the manumitted slaves. An acquaintance, an African-American journalist, commented, "What kind of place is that? I went into the bush and found Heidi, complete with a flock of goats." Indeed.

As with my other work, I wanted to show how the landscape resonates against the transactions negotiated across its body, and across the bodies of those who inhabit it. The indentations, the damages, the places where a river remembers itself, and floods.

The figure of Emmett Till, forty years gone, is central to the soul of this story. In my childhood "that other world that was the world" (the words of Italo Calvino by way of Nadine Gordimer) was overseas; at first, the mother country, England. But that mother of a country was fast being overtaken by the United States.

I wanted to show the glamour of this other world that was the world, which lavished on us sweets and Coca-Cola, comic books and automobiles, and most especially movies, veiled its own decadence, but we were not privy to its secrets.

RICHARD BAUSCH's stories have appeared in *The New Yorker, Esquire, The Atlantic, Harper's Magazine, Playboy, The Southern Review, Story,* and other magazines. His 1984 novel *The Last Good Time* was made into a motion picture. In 1996, The Modern Library/Random House published his *Selected Stories.* His most recent novel is *Good Evening Mr. & Mrs. America, and All the Ships at Sea.* He has received the Award in Literature from the American Academy of Arts and Letters, and he was recently elected to the Fellowship of Southern Writers.

▪ "Nobody in Hollywood" began as a kind of challenge between me and my former student and friend Steve Amick, whose work has begun to appear in various magazines around the country. He and I were talking on the phone about childhood, our own, and one of us — I believe it was Steve — said, "I was pummeled as a teenager." We laughed. Over the years we have amused each other with lines like this ("We were delayed by a horrible, horrible accident"), lines that seem to be stretching for one thing while "unwittingly" accomplishing something else. This time, I said, "We ought to both try writing a story that opens with 'I was pummeled as a teenager.'" The whole thing became a kind of bet between us — which one would finish first. Steve won, with a hilarious story called "Fat Tracy." (I am certain that this story will inevitably make its way into print — its only problem is that it is longer than most magazines are able to do these days — and when it does, there will be matter for some curious reader to consider: two stories with identical opening lines.) The writing of "Nobody in Hollywood" became mostly trying to solve the problem of staying within the tonal considerations set up by that first line — one cannot, finally, get very serious in a story beginning with that sentence — and then, well, I thought I'd have a little fun with some of the pieties of this ridiculous age.

That, too. But I didn't plan a thing. I just went on letting the character speak, and watching what happened, until he got through. And so of course all the opinions expressed in the story are his. I wouldn't want anyone to think that I had any complaints.

CYNTHIA OZICK is the author of short stories, essays, novels, and a play. She is the recipient of numerous prizes and awards, including four O. Henry first prizes and the Rea Award for the Short Story. Her most recent books are *Fame & Folly,* a collection of essays, and *The Puttermesser Papers,* a novel.

KAREN E. BENDER grew up in Los Angeles and graduated from UCLA and the University of Iowa. Her fiction has appeared in *Granta, The Iowa Review, The Kenyon Review,* and has been reprinted in *Pushcart Prize XVIII, Feminism 3: The Third Generation in Fiction,* and other anthologies. She lives with her husband, the writer Robert Anthony Siegel, in New York City and is currently finishing her first novel.

- In this story, I wanted to teach myself new things about love. The germ of the story began a few years ago. I was not married, or a mother, but I was interested in someday becoming both. I wanted to tell the story from Ella's point of view because, through her perceptions, I thought I could learn some valuable things.

I am also drawn to writing about characters who have various kinds of disabilities. Lena intrigues me because, through her, I can explore questions such as: What is normal? How does she create her version of the world?

The story evolved over a few years, but it began with two scenes — the family's first meeting with Bob and the scene with the spatula. I've always liked the idea of a free gift, especially in emotionally charged situations — it seems like such a tender, hopeful offering.

For a while, I just had some scenes of Lena and Bob's courtship. When I added the separate-bedroom issue, the story started moving; it had an arc. Over time, odd items surfaced in the story, borrowed from memory or life. The wedding dress Lena sees in the window was an actual dress I saw in a store window in Manhattan, on Fourteenth Street.

I've been to Las Vegas a few times, and I love its pointless gaudiness, and how human beings become even stranger in the glow of its lights. I've also had some memorable culinary experiences at the $2.99 buffet.

LEONARD MICHAELS's most recent works are *A Cat,* a meditation on cats; *To Feel These Things,* a collection of stories and essays; and *Sylvia,* a memoir. He lives in California and Italy.

- "A Girl with a Monkey" came to be written when an old friend told me about his divorce and another old friend told me about her year as a prostitute. I married them in my story.

LYDIA DAVIS is the author of two collections of stories (*Break It Down* and *Almost No Memory*) and a novel (*The End of the Story*), and is the translator of numerous works from French. Her stories have appeared in *Harper's Magazine, Conjunctions, Antaeus, Grand Street, DoubleTake, Exquisite Corpse,* and *City Lights Review,* as well as many anthologies, including several volumes of *The Pushcart Prize.* Since 1986 she has been on the faculty of Bard College's Milton Avery School of the Arts in upstate New York, where she lives with her two sons and her husband, the painter Alan Cote.

▪ When I think about my story, "St. Martin," it seems to me it was the landscape that wanted to be the subject of it, though when I look at it again I see a great deal of human activity, a story about people, too. I had come from my own city to a foreign city, and then from the foreign city into the foreign countryside. I was there in the countryside for that year — we were there — in a house called St. Martin, for the sake of the place, not for a job or a friend or an education. The house and the animals, my activities and our activities, were tied up with the place, and it was the land that I watched all the time and that moved me. Without signs of human habitation — the ruined farmhouses and the intact poor farms, the prosperous new country houses and the village houses, poor and prosperous — and the activities of the people themselves, the land would not have moved me in the same way, but the people were always in the same relationship to the land, to the actual dirt of the land, at that time and in that place.

Particularly because it was new to me and because I would be leaving it, there was a greater urgency about describing it to myself, which was my way of seeing it clearly, discovering the way in which I saw it, and so I wrote things down exactly as I could, as I saw them, and took away with me when I left small pieces of writing about elements or moments of it, separate sentences surrounded by sentences about other things. It was only years later, wanting to write a story of that whole year, wanting to have that year again in written form, that I put the separate sentences together, remembered more, rearranged, wrote, erased whole parts, and invented, until there was one continuous story. I saw this story, after it was finished, as a dark one that grew darker around the incident of the dog, because it was a dark year despite the beauty of the place. I also saw the story as a very even, very level story, without much of a climax anywhere along the way because that was also the shape of the year and the shape of the land.

JUNOT DÍAZ was born and raised in Santo Domingo, the Dominican Republic. Díaz now lives in Brooklyn, New York. His first story collection, *Drown,* was published by Riverhead and has also been published in Spanish, in the United States, by Vintage Español, entitled *Negocios*. His story "Ysrael" appeared in *The Best American Short Stories 1996*. Diaz is now working on his first novel.

▪ I'd been trying to write this one for the longest time. At first I had Yunior whipping stones at the windows of his father's new van on the sly — something I had once tried in my younger days, but my aim was shitty and my neighbor's eyesight was not — but this plot ploy didn't work out. And then, on an interminable bus ride from Ithaca, New York, I had an attack of motion sickness which, I realized later in front of my computer, I hadn't had since I was young. The rest fell together. I wish I could have written more about Perth Amboy, a city I felt a strong connection to, and the Puerto Rican woman, but these things don't always work out. It was enough that I could talk a little about those parties my parents used to take us to, the ones where we kids always fell asleep in the room with the coats while they partied their asses off until four in the morning. Our folks were people who were working fifty, sixty hours a week, doing the worst of the worst. Parties like these were necessary, I think, for survival.

DONALD HALL lives on an old family farm in New Hampshire. He has published several volumes of poetry (*The Old Life*, 1996) as well as textbooks, anthologies, plays, collections of essays (*Principal Products of Portugal*, 1995), and children's books (*The Milkman's Boy*, 1997). In 1997 the Audio Bookshelf brought out *Donald Hall Prose and Poetry* in two cassettes. He published his one collection of short stories, *The Ideal Bakery*, in 1987. Hall made his first appearance in *The Best American Short Stories* in 1963.

▪ "From Willow Temple" spent at least a decade inside my head, altering and expanding. I started to write it in a man's voice, then set it aside for two years while my mother still lived. Neither of Camilla's parents resembles my own, but my mother had a beloved cousin who hanged himself, and I could not work on the story until my mother died.

The story takes place in southern Michigan because I lived in Ann Arbor from 1957 to 1975, often explored the little towns and farmland around it, and wanted to imagine this countryside in an earlier time. Perhaps I told the story as a female because I wanted to keep something female alive. My mother had died, and my wife was dying as I wrote "From Willow Temple." I worked on the story at Jane Kenyon's bedside in a hospital or at home while I took care of her during the fifteen months of her illness. Leukemia makes a brief appearance here. Sometimes when Jane felt well enough I read aloud to her what I was writing. Although I made a few changes after her death — with help from her old friend Alice Mattison — the story was virtually done when I read it to her at Dartmouth-Hitchcock Hospital in March of 1995. She died at home on April 22.

Though he still has most of his teeth and a brittle, unforgiving remnant of his hair, T. CORAGHESSAN BOYLE is feeling as ancient and decomposed as the immemorial muck at the bottom of the sea. Still, it hasn't yet prevented him from inditing various novels (7) and story collections (4), including most recently *The Road to Wellville* ('93), *Without a Hero* ('94), and *The Tortilla Curtain* ('95). His new novel, *Riven Rook,* will appear early next year, followed in the fall by a volume of selected stories, including fifty or so gleaned from the earlier collections.

▪ I don't believe in turning the other cheek: fight hate with hate and violence with violence. Anger was the impetus behind "Killing Babies" — that, and a brilliant and harrowing essay by Verlyn Klinkenborg that appeared in *Harper's* in January of 1995 and detailed some of the excesses of the "pro-lifers" at a Milwaukee abortion clinic. What interests me in the way "Killing Babies" evolved is that it really doesn't address the issue of abortion, but rather the violence that surrounds it. In a more conventional telling, Rick might have become enlightened on the issue and taken sides in a rational and heartfelt way, but what makes this telling more convincing — and, I hope, chilling — is his moral nullity. I get the sense that if Rick's brother were on the other side of the street, a banner waver and shouter, the violence would have gone the other way. Rick knows one thing: which team he's on. And he knows, with his twisted logic, what to do when someone violates you. You fight back. You lash out. You kill.

As I write this, I'm reeling round the room in the punch-drunk daze of a man who's just finished a long and complex novel, only now beginning to grope toward the ideas that will hopefully bloom into the stories that will complete the "Killing Babies" collection. The companion pieces I wrote at the time of "Killing Babies" are somewhat atypical for me, in that they are for the most part realistic and grimly rather than joyously comic, and I wonder if the new stories will follow in this direction or go somewhere else altogether. But then, that's the beauty of writing stories — each one is an exploratory journey in search of a reason and a shape. And when you find that reason and that shape, there's no feeling like it.

CLYDE EDGERTON lives in Orange County, North Carolina, with his wife, Susan Ketchin, and their daughter, Catherine. He is the author of seven novels.

▪ When I was five or six years old, my mother took me to Central Prison in Raleigh, North Carolina, to see the electric chair. The purpose of the trip was educational: if I was bad, I would die. I soon forgot about our trip, oddly enough, until about three years ago, when I was fifty and she was ninety, when for some reason she mentioned it. I don't remember why she mentioned it — perhaps we were eating lunch and she said, "Son, if you don't stop driving so fast they gon fry your ass." In any case, the memory inspired the story, and after writing it I remembered a great blues song, "Send Me to the Electric Chair," and used that as the title.

The story seemed to imply a novel, which I went on to write — and it should soon be available in bookstores everywhere. It's called *Where Trouble Sleeps*.

JUNE SPENCE was born and grew up in Raleigh, North Carolina, and has recently returned there to live. Her short story collection, *Nice Men and Good Girls*, won the 1995 Willa Cather Award (judged by Leonard Michaels), and a collection including many of the stories from that volume is slated for publication by Riverhead Books in 1998. Her short fiction has appeared in *Seventeen*, *The Oxford American*, *Puerto del Sol*, *The Crescent Review*, and *The Southern Review*.

▪ This story grew out of a strange summer spent in my college town after graduation. Three women had inexplicably disappeared from a house not far from my own. The town was baffled by this, is how I recalled it, and a town likewise becomes a sort of entity in my story's narrative, though a split one, in that it puzzles over the women's absence while at the same time carries the secret somewhere within it.

I was working evenings as an editorial assistant for the local newspaper at the time, and I spent my days walking around, following the railroad tracks that ran through a series of old neighborhoods. I was walking home from the grocery store one day, and an old woman sitting in her car called out to me, "You're not afraid?" meaning, You're not afraid to walk here alone after all this with the women? I told her no, but what I felt was more complicated. I'd been, like everyone else, unnerved, but was defiantly venturing out because it seemed wrong to have to live otherwise — and besides, it was broad daylight. "If you get gone," the old woman reassured me, "I'll tell them I saw you."

Working at the paper, I was privy to all manner of possible facts and odd details and downright misinformation about the women. The way the local media presented every tidbit, aired every theory available, seemed sensationalistic at times, but it was just as much a way of keeping those lost women at the front of all our minds when there were so few actual clues to what happened. The media seemed to answer our collective need to ponder over it, to not forget. I have never told a story in this manner before or since, but years later it seemed the right way to tell this one. The mystery remains.

JEFFREY EUGENIDES is the author of *The Virgin Suicides*. His fiction has appeared in *The New Yorker*, *The Paris Review*, *The Yale Review*, *Conjunctions*, *The Gettysburg Review*, and *Granta*'s "Best of Young American Novelists." He is the recipient of fellowships from the Guggenheim Foundation and the

National Endowment for the Arts, a Whiting Writers' Award, an Ingram-Merrill Foundation grant, the Aga Khan Prize for fiction, and the Harold D. Vursell Award from the American Academy of Arts and Letters. He lives in Brooklyn, New York, with his wife, the artist Karen Yamauchi.

▪ I wrote the first paragraph of "Air Mail" clandestinely at work, in 1991 or thereabouts, while purportedly typing my boss's correspondence. My clever, Mata-Hari-ish method was to roll a sheet of paper into the type-writer, assign a date in the upper right-hand corner, type the address of either a hoary philanthropist or deified poet (I was employed by a non-profit arts organization) and, after the salutation, start writing fiction. ("Dear James Merrill," those letters began, "In the days after the funeral, our interest in the Lisbon girls only increased.") A fair amount of my first novel was composed in this fashion, and I commend it to any aspir-ing writers who might be reading this right now in the prison cells of their own corporate cubicles. (Note: the method works even better on a computer, as you can use the split-screen function to toggle from fiction to business correspondence at the slightest sound of the boss's foot-steps.)

Not surprisingly, I was soon fired. I cleaned out my desk, including the large folder containing my fictional tesserae — bits of stories, openings of novels never written — and took this folder home. Years passed. I finished my first novel. I wrote a few short stories and began a second book. But I always came back to that paragraph about the sick budget traveler lan-guishing on an island in the Gulf of Siam. I kept coming back to it for the following reason. In 1982, I myself had taken a year off from college to travel the world. I had brought with me a change of clothes and a portable library of theology books and arcane mystical treatises. I visited twenty-seven countries in Europe, Africa, and Asia. I sat in all kinds of churches. I got sick. I wrote letters home that alarmed my parents. The reason there was such a thing as the Peripatetics is that wandering is conducive to reverie and self-transformation.

Thirteen years after my own travels and four years after my furtive writing-at-work, I pulled the paragraph out of my desk and wrote "Air Mail." I began with that first paragraph and a goal: to write a story wherein death and enlightenment would be indistinguishable. It took me a long time to get from point A to point B.

PAM DURBAN grew up in South Carolina and now lives in Atlanta, where she teaches at Georgia State University. She is the author of a book of short stories, *All Set About with Fever Trees*, and a novel, *The Laughing Place*.

▪ In the summer of 1958 I attended a family reunion at my great-aunt's summer place near Highlands, North Carolina. The reunion lasted three days but I remember it in great detail, a series of particular moments and faces and happenings. A visit to an elderly relative and his invalid wife in their dark house on the mountainside. My father's case of food poisoning and his boisterous recovery after several doses of my aunt's home-brewed blackberry wine. My aunt herself, with her doctorate in metaphysics, her reputation as a clairvoyant, her dietary theories. An enormous rattlesnake in a roadside ditch. Then, almost thirty years later, on a trip to Highlands, I found the house again, abandoned as it is in the story, and like the woman in the story, I stood on the porch and looked in through the front window and was surprised by a rush of feelings so intense it was as if I had just been told startling and disturbing news. The freshness and intensity of those feelings became the nucleus of this story, and other things began to collect around that center. In a way, I think I wrote the story in order to track those feelings to a source, to understand what that moment was about. In thinking about that moment, I was struck by how events and circumstances are always trying to come together to make a coherent story, and it's that motion I was after in writing the story: the way things come together and break apart and come together again. This story was also the first short fiction I wrote after finishing my novel, and I wrote it for the pleasure of being able to run again after a long march.

MICHAEL BYERS grew up in Seattle, graduated from Oberlin College, and received his M.F.A. from the University of Michigan. He now lives in San Francisco, where he is a Stegner Fellow at Stanford University. His stories have appeared in various literary magazines and anthologies, including *The Missouri Review, The Indiana Review, Prairie Schooner,* and *Prize Stories 1995: The O. Henry Awards.*

▪ *Shipmates Down Under* was the title of a real book that sat on my shelf when I was a kid. It had a green cover, with pulleys or nets or something on it, and I deduced the rest — that the story had to do with some seagoing adventure, and that it happened in or around Australia, but for one reason or another I never took the book off the shelf. The title intrigued me, sort of, and I always meant to get around to it, but I never did, and then, after a while, *not reading* the book came to seem very important. Unread, the book contained any number of stories, and I liked that — I later recognized the feeling as the same one you get from unwritten stories, at least when you imagine them beforehand: the way they're always multitudinous and dense and brilliant, and then of course you write them and screw them up completely.

Years later, I learned about Fatal Familial Insomnia, which sounded to me like just about the worst way to die, though not without its own sort of Borgesian interest. I hadn't thought of the book in years by that time, and I didn't know where it was, but through some process I don't exactly understand, the two things attached themselves to each other and began a sort of confabulation of their own, and this story is the result. I'm indebted to Charles Baxter and Eileen Pollack for their help with the drafts.

TOBIAS WOLFF has published three collections of stories, *In the Garden of the North American Martyrs, Back in the World,* and most recently, *The Night in Question,* in which "Powder" appears. He has also written a novel, *The Barracks Thief,* and two memoirs, *This Boy's Life* and *In Pharaoh's Army: Memories of the Lost War.* He teaches at Stanford University.

▪ "Powder" is not a memoir, though certain elements of the story have their beginnings in memory, particularly the figure of the father. My own father has been dead some thirty years now, and as time goes on I miss him not less but more. I want him to know my wife and sons and daughter, see his pleasure in their ways. I want to see him pull up to my house in one of his cool, unpaid-for sports cars. I want him to sit down with me after dinner and drink Scotch and listen to Louis Armstrong sing "Black and Blue." This story is a way, my only way, of having him back for a while in all his outlaw charm and maddening, tragic irresponsibility.

ALYSON HAGY was raised on a farm in the Blue Ridge Mountains of Virginia. She has published two collections of fiction, *Madonna on Her Back* and *Hardware River,* and her work has recently appeared in *Shenandoah, Mississippi Review,* and *The Virginia Quarterly Review.* She lives and teaches in Laramie, Wyoming.

▪ My stories often begin with a place, a blue valley or the rusty stones of an abandoned homestead. I'll be outdoors somewhere — near an alpine lake, in a canoe in an estuary, on the edge of the high desert — and I'll suddenly sense the rush and roil of a story. My reaction is physical, heated, unbidden. It makes me an exasperating person to hike or fish with. Sometimes characters will immediately rise up to inhabit the landscape that stirs me; sometimes I have to wait on them, raise them slowly from bits of speech and memory.

There really is a Search Bay, and you can see the dark glide of freighters from its shores. There is a man who lives alone nearby. I've been told he was a merchant seaman. I've seen his tidy handwriting on a scroll of silver birch bark. The truth of his life is undoubtedly more intriguing than the life I've made for John Hansen, yet my story owes a great deal to his apparent resilience. Why do we live where we live? What sort of America do we build at the margins of the continent? These questions didn't occur to me until later . . . until I was indoors and the story had been drafted for the lake and its characters . . . but they pursued me to the end.

TIM GAUTREAUX was raised in Morgan City, Louisiana. He earned a doctorate in English at the University of South Carolina and now lives in

Hammond, Louisiana, with his wife and two sons. His fiction has appeared in *The Atlantic, Harper's Magazine, Story, New Stories from the South, The Best American Short Stories,* and other places. He is the recipient of a National Endowment for the Arts fellowship as well as the National Magazine Award for fiction. Recently he was the John and Renee Grisham Southern Writer in Residence at the University of Mississippi. For many years he has directed the creative writing program at Southeastern Louisiana University. St. Martin's Press has recently published his book of short stories, *Same Place, Same Things,* and will bring out a novel, *Machinery of Dreams,* early next year, as well as another collection of stories.

▪ I listen to local talk radio too much. One morning the topic of discussion was "the meanest trick you played on someone when you were a kid." One man called in and bragged that he had bagged a batch of common roof pigeons and advertised them in the paper as untrained homing pigeons, "instructions included." People had actually shown up to purchase the birds, and the caller laughed as he described the two-week training regimen he made up to tell his customers.

I don't remember the other callers because I couldn't stop thinking about the bird trick. Much later, I began to wonder what type of person would sell these birds to folks who would waste fourteen days of their lives following the bogus training instructions. What would it be like to put up with such a person in my family or to have him as a friend? To find out, I put together Lenny Fontenot and had him lose his job. A character needs something out of the ordinary to happen to set him in motion. Otherwise there'd be no story. Lenny makes his long-suffering girlfriend pay for their dates, he sponges off his grandfather, and he takes money from naive children and old codgers for worthless birds. His girlfriend beats him up, his grandfather throws him out of the house, and even his saddest victim, the deceptively simple Mr. Lejeune, turns a ten-dollar pigeon into a valuable lesson for both his crippled nephew and Lenny's grandfather as well.

Lenny's big talent is taking advantage of people he meets and making life a little harder for them. He's the type who never seems to see that he makes life hardest for himself.

100 Other Distinguished Stories of 1996

SELECTED BY KATRINA KENISON

Editorial Addresses of American and Canadian Magazines Publishing Short Stories

When available, the annual subscription rate, the average number of stories published per year, and the name of the editor follow the address.

African American Review
Stalker Hall 212
Indiana State University
Terre Haute, IN 47809
$24, 25, Joe Weixlmann

African Voices
270 West 96th Street
New York, NY 10025
$10, 12, Carolyn A. Butts

Agni Review
Creative Writing Department
Boston University
236 Bay State Road
Boston, MA 02115
$12, 13, Askold Melnyczuk

Alabama Literary Review
Smith 253
Troy State University
Troy, AL 36082
$5, 21, Theron E. Montgomery

Alaska Quarterly Review
Department of English
University of Alaska
3211 Providence Drive
Anchorage, AK 99508
$8, 28, Ronald Spatz

Alfred Hitchcock's Mystery Magazine
1540 Broadway
New York, NY 10036
$34.97, 130, Cathleen Jordan

Alligator Juniper
Prescott College
220 Grove Avenue
Prescott, AZ 86301
$7.50, rotating editorship

American Letters and Commentary
Suite 56
850 Park Avenue
New York, NY 10021
$5, 4, Jeanne Beaumont, Anna Rabinowitz

American Literary Review
University of North Texas
P.O. Box 13615
Denton, TX 76203
$15, 14, Barbara Rodman

American Short Fiction
Parlin 108
Department of English
University of Texas at Austin
Austin, TX 78712-1164
$24, 32, Joseph Krupa

American Voice
332 West Broadway
Louisville, KY 40202
*$15, 20, Sallie Bingham, Frederick
Smock*

Analog Science Fiction/Science Fact
1540 Broadway
New York, NY 10036
$34.95, 70, Stanley Schmidt

Another Chicago Magazine
Left Field Press
3709 North Kenmore
Chicago, IL 60613
$8, 16, Sharon Solwitz

Antietam Review
82 West Washington Street
Hagerstown, MD 21740
$5, 8, Suzanne Kass

Antioch Review
P.O. Box 148
Yellow Springs, OH 45387
$30, 11, Robert S. Fogarty

Apalachee Quarterly
P.O. Box 20106
Tallahassee, FL 32316
$15, 4, Barbara Hamby

Appalachian Heritage
Berea College
Berea, KY 40404
$18, 6, Sidney Saylor Farr

Arkansas Review
Department of English
P.O. Box 1890
Arkansas State University
State University, AR 72467
$20, 12, Norman Lavers

Ascent
P.O. Box 967
Urbana, IL 61801
$9, 8, W. Scott Olsen

Asimov's Science Fiction Magazine
Bantam Doubleday Dell
1540 Broadway
New York, NY 10036
$39.97, 27, Gardner Dozois

Atlantic Monthly
77 N. Washington Street
Boston, MA 02114
$15.94, 12, C. Michael Curtis

Bellingham Review
MS 9053
Western Washington University
Bellingham, WA 98225
$10, Robin Hemly

Baffler
P.O. Box 378293
Chicago, IL 60637
$16, Thomas Frank, Keith White

Bellowing Ark
P.O. Box 45637
Seattle, WA 98145
$15, 7, Robert R. Ward

Beloit Fiction Journal
Beloit College
P.O. Box 11
Beloit, WI 53511
$9, Fred Burwell

Big Sky Journal
P.O. Box 1069
Bozeman, MT 59771-1069
$22, 4, Allen Jones, Brian Baise

Black River Review
855 Mildred Avenue
Lorain, OH 44052
12, Jack Smith

Black Warrior Review
P.O. Box 2936
Tuscaloosa, AL 35487-2936
$11, 13, Jim Hilgartner

Blood & Aphorisms
P.O. Box 702
Toronto, Ontario
M5S ZY4 Canada
$18, 20, Michelle Alfano, Dennis Block

BOMB
New Art Publications
10th floor
594 Broadway
New York, NY 10012
$18, 6, Betsy Sussler

Border Crossings
Y300-393 Portage Avenue
Winnipeg, Manitoba
R3B 3H6 Canada
$23, 16, Meeka Walsh

Boston Book Review
30 Brattle Street
Cambridge, MA 02138
$24, Theoharis Constantine

Boston Review
Building E53
Room 407
Cambridge, MA 02139
$15, 6, editorial board

Boulevard
4579 Laclede Avenue #332
St. Louis, MO 63108
$12, 17, Richard Burgin

Briar Cliff Review
3303 Rebecca Street
P.O. Box 2100
Sioux City, IA 51104-2100
$4, 4, Phil Hey

The Bridge
14050 Vernon Street
Oak Park, Ml 48237
$8, 10, Helen Zucker

BUZZ
11835 West Olympic Blvd.
Suite 450
Los Angeles, CA 90064
$14.95, 12, Renee Vogel

Callaloo
Dept. of English
Wilson Hall
University of Virginia
Charlottesville, VA 22903
$32, 6, Charles H. Rowell

Calyx
P.O. Box B
Corvallis, OR 97339
$18, 11, Margarita Donnelly

Capilano Review
Capilano College
2055 Purcell Way
North Vancouver,
British Columbia
V7J 3H5 Canada
$25, 12, Robert Sherrin

Carolina Quarterly
Greenlaw Hall 066A
University of North Carolina
Chapel Hill, NC 27514
$10, 13, Shannon Wooden

Century
P.O. Box 150510
Brooklyn, NY 11215-0510
$33, 10, Robert J. Killheffer

Chariton Review
Division of Language & Literature
Northeast Missouri State University
Kirksville, MO 63501
$9, 6, Jim Barnes

Chattahoochee Review
DeKalb Community College
2101 Womack Road

Dunwoody, GA 30338-4497
$15, 21, Lamar York

Chelsea
P.O. Box 773
Cooper Station
New York, NY 10276
$13, 6, Richard Foerster

Chicago Review
5801 South Kenwood
University of Chicago
Chicago, IL 60637
$15, 20, Andrew Rathman

Cimarron Review
205 Morrill Hall
Oklahoma State University
Stillwater, OK 74078-0135
$12, 15, Gordon Weaver

Cities and Roads
P.O. Box 10886
Greensboro, NC 27404
$15.75, 20, Tom Kealey

Clockwork Review
Department of English
Illinois Wesleyan University
Bloomington, IL 61702-2900
$8, 6, James Plath

Colorado Review
Department of English
Colorado State University
Fort Collins, CO 80523
$15, 8, David Milofsky

Columbia
404 Dodge
Columbia University
New York, NY 10027
$13, 14, Ken Foster,
 Justin Peacock

Commentary
165 East 56th Street
New York, NY 10022
$39, 5, Neal Kozodoy

Concho River Review
English Department
Angelo State University
San Angelo, TX 76909
$12, 7, Terence A. Dalrymple

Confrontation
English Department
C. W. Post College of Long Island
 University
Greenvale, NY 11548
$8, 25, Martin Tucker

Conjunctions
Bard College
Annandale-on-Hudson, NY 12504
$18, 6, Bradford Morrow

Crab Creek Review
4462 Whitman Avenue N.
Seattle, WA 98103
$8, Linda Clifton

Crazyhorse
Department of English
University of Arkansas
Little Rock, AK 72204
$10, Judy Troy

Cream City Review
University of Wisconsin, Milwaukee
P.O. Box 413
Milwaukee, WI 53201
$12, 30, Andrew Rivera

Crescent Review
P.O. Box 15069
Chevy Chase, MD 20825-5069
$21, 23, J. Timothy Holland

Critic
205 West Monroe Street, 6th floor
Chicago, IL 60606-5097
$20, 4, Julie Bridge

Crucible
Barton College
College Station
Wilson, NC 27893
12, Terence Grimes

Cut Bank
Department of English
University of Montana
Missoula, MT 59812
$12, 20, Marcus Hersh, Amanda E. Ward

Denver Quarterly
University of Denver
Denver, CO 80208
$25, 5, Bin Ramke

Descant
P.O. Box 314, Station P
Toronto, Ontario
M5S 2S8 Canada
$20, 20, Karen Mulhallen

Descant
Department of English
Texas Christian University
Box 32872
Fort Worth, TX 76129
$12, 16, Neil Easterbrook

DoubleTake
Center for Documentary Studies
1317 West Pettigrew Street
Durham, NC 27705
$32, 10, Robert Coles, Alex Harris

Eagle's Flight
P.O. Box 832
Granite, OK 73547
$5, 10, Rekha Kulkarni

Elle
1633 Broadway
New York, NY 10019
$24, 2, John Howell

Epoch
251 Goldwin Smith Hall
Cornell University
Ithaca, NY 14853-3201
$11, 23, Michael Koch

Esquire
250 West 55th Street
New York, NY 10019
$17.94, 12, Rust Hills

Eureka Literary Magazine
Eureka College
P.O. Box 280
Eureka, IL 61530
$10, Loren Logsdon

event
c/o Douglas College
P.O. Box 2503
New Westminster, British Columbia
V3L 5B2 Canada
$15, 18, Christine Dewar, Maurice Hodgson

Farmer's Market
Elgin Community College
1700 Spartan Drive
Elgin, IL 60123
$10, 18, Rachael Tecza

Fiction
Fiction, Inc.
Department of English
The City College of New York
New York, NY
$7, 15, Mark Mirsky

Fiction International
Department of English and
     Comparative Literature
San Diego State University
San Diego, CA 92182
$14, Harold Jaffe, Larry McCaffery

Fiddlehead
UNB Box 4400
University of New Brunswick
Fredericton, New Brunswick
E3B 5A3 Canada
$16, 20, Don McKay, Bill Gaston

Fish Stories
5412 N. Clark, South Suite
Chicago, IL 60640
$10.95, Amy G. Davis

Five Points
Department of English
Georgia State University
University Plaza

Atlanta, GA 30303-3083
$15, Pam Durban

Florida Review
Department of English
University of Central Florida
P.O. Box 25000
Orlando, FL 32816
$7, 14, Russell Kesler

Flying Horse
P.O. Box 445
Marblehead, MA 01945
$7, Dennis Must

Folio
Department of Literature
The American University
Washington, D.C. 20016
$10, 12, Cynthia Lollar

Four Quarters
LaSalle University
20th and Olney Avenues
Philadelphia, PA 19141
$8, 10, John J. Keenan

Fourteen Hills
Department of Creative Writing
San Francisco State University
1600 Holloway Avenue
San Francisco, CA 94132
$12, Elsa Dixon

Frank
Association Frank
32, rue Edouard Vaillant
93100 Montreuil, France
$38, 6, David Applefield

Fugue
Department of English
University of Idaho
Brink Hall, Room 200
Moscow, ID 83844-1102
$10, Eric P. Isaacson

Geist
1062 Homer Street #100
Vancouver, Canada

V6B 2W9
$20, 5, Stephen Osborne

Georgetown Review
400 East College Street, Box 227
Georgetown, KY 40324
$10, 5, John Fulmer

Georgia Review
University of Georgia
Athens, GA 30602
$18, 10, Stanley W. Lindberg

Gettysburg Review
Gettysburg College
Gettysburg, PA 17325
$18, 22, Peter Stitt

Glimmer Train Stories
812 SW Washington Street
Suite 1205
Portland, OR 97205
$29, 40, Susan Burmeister, Linda Davies

Good Housekeeping
959 Eighth Avenue
New York, NY 10019
$17.97, 7, Arleen L. Quarfoot

GQ
350 Madison Avenue
New York, NY 10017
$19.97, 12, Ilena Silverman

Grain
Box 1154
Regina, Saskatchewan
S4P 3B4 Canada
$23.95, 21, Connie Gault

Grand Street
131 Varick Street
New York, NY 10013
$40, 20, Jean Stein

Granta
2-3 Hanover Yard
Noel Road Islington
London, England N1 8BE
$32, 12, Ian Jack

Great River Review
211 West 7th Street
Winona, MN 55987
$12, 8, Pamela Davies

Green Mountain Review
Box A 58
Johnson State College
Johnson, VT 05656
$12, 23, Tony Whedon

Greensboro Review
Department of English
University of North Carolina
Greensboro, NC 27412
$8, 16, Jim Clark

Gulf Coast
Department of English
University of Houston
4800 Calhoun Road
Houston, TX 77204-3012
$22, 10, Marsha Recknagel, Merrill Greene

Gulf Stream
English Department
Florida International University
North Miami Campus
North Miami, FL 33181
$4, 6, Lynne Barrett, John Dufresne

Habersham Review
Piedmont College
Demorest, GA 30535-0010
$12, Frank Gannon

Harper's Magazine
666 Broadway
New York, NY 10012
$18, 9, Lewis H. Lapham

Harvard Review
Poetry Room
Harvard College Library
Cambridge, MA 02138
$12, 6, Stratis Haviaris

Hawaii Review
University of Hawaii
Department of English
1733 Donagho Road

Honolulu, HI 96822
$25, 40, Lisa Chang

Hayden's Ferry Review
Matthews Center
Arizona State University
Tempe, AZ 85287-1502
$10, 10, Melissa Olson,
Verania White

High Plains Literary Review
180 Adams Street, Suite 250
Denver, CO 80206
$20, 7, Robert O. Greer, Jr.

HR
1733 Donagho Road
University of Hawaii, Manoa
Honolulu, HI 96822
$25, Robert Sean Macbeth,
S. Gonzalez

Hudson Review
684 Park Avenue
New York, NY 10021
$24, 8, Paula Deitz, Frederick Morgan

Hyphen
3458 W. Devon Ave., No. 6
Lincolnwood, IL 60659
$12, 8, Matthew Adrian, Margaret Lewis

Ibis Review
P.O. Box 133
Falls Village, CT 06031
$8.95, group editorship

Image
323 S. Broad Street
P.O. Box 674
Kennett Square, PA 19348
$30, 12, Gregory Wolfe

Indiana Review
316 North Jordan Avenue
Bloomington, IN 47405
$12, 13, Shirley Stephenson

Ink
P.O. Box 52558
St. George Postal Outlet
264 Bloor Street
Toronto, Ontario
M5S 1V0 Canada
$8, 10, John Degan

Interim
Department of English
University of Nevada
4505 Maryland Parkway
Las Vegas, NV 89154
$8, A. Wilber Stevens

International Quarterly
P.O. Box 10521
Tallahassee, FL 32302
$22, 20, Van K. Brock

Iowa Review
Department of English
University of Iowa
308 EPB
Iowa City, IA 52242
$18, 20, David Hamilton

Iowa Woman
P.O. Box 680
Iowa City, IA 52244
$18, 15, Marianne Abel

Iris
Box 323 HSC
University of Virginia
Charlottesville, VA 22908
$17, 4, Kristen Staby Rembold

Italian Americana
University of Rhode Island
College of Continuing Education
199 Promenade Street
Providence, RI 02908
$15, 6, Carol Bonomo Albright

Jewish Currents
22 East 17th Street, Suite 601
New York, NY 10003-3272
$20, 8, editorial board

Journal
Department of English
Ohio State University
164 West 17th Avenue
Columbus, OH 43210
$8, 5, Kathy Fagan, Michelle Herman

Journal of African Travel Writing
P.O. Box 346
Chapel Hill, NC 27514
$10, Amber Vogel

Kalliope
Florida Community College
3939 Roosevelt Blvd.
Jacksonville, FL 32205
$10.50, 12, Mary Sue Koeppel

Kansas Quarterly
Department of English
Denison Hall
Kansas State University
Manhattan, KS 66506
$20, 8, Norman Lavers

Karamu
English Department
Eastern Illinois University
Charleston, IL 61920
$6.50, 8, Peggy L. Brayfield

Kenyon Review
Kenyon College
Gambier, OH 43022
$22, 18, Marilyn Hacker

Kiosk
English Department
306 Clemens Hall
SUNY
Buffalo, NY 14260
$6, 9, Lia Vella

Laurel Review
Department of English
Northwest Missouri State University
Maryville, MO 64468
$8, 20, Craig Goad, David Slater,
  William Trowbridge

Lilith
250 West 57th Street
New York, NY 10107
$16, 4, Susan Weidman

Literal Latté
Suite 240
61 East 8th Street
New York, NY 10003
$25, 12, Jenine Gordon

Literary Review
Fairleigh Dickinson University
285 Madison Avenue
Madison, NJ 07940
$18, 10, Walter Cummins

Louisiana Literature
Box 792
Southeastern Louisiana University
Hammond, LA 70402
$10, 8, David Hanson

Lynx Eye
1880 Hill Drive
Los Angeles, CA 90041
$20, 12, Pam McCully, Kathryn Morrison

McCall's
110 Fifth Avenue
New York, NY 10011
$15.94, 6, Laura Manske

Madison Review
University of Wisconsin
Department of English
H. C. White Hall
600 North Park Street
Madison, WI 53706
$15, 8, Joley Wood

Malahat Review
University of Victoria
P.O. Box 1700
Victoria, British Columbia
V8W 2Y2 Canada
$15, 20, Derk Wynand

Manoa
English Department
University of Hawaii
Honolulu, HI 96822
$18, 12, Ian MacMillan

Many Mountains Moving
2525 Arapahoe Road
Suite E4-309
Boulder, CO 80302
$18, Naomi Horii,
  Marilyn Krysl

Massachusetts Review
Memorial Hall
University of Massachusetts
Amherst, MA 01003
$15, 6, Mary Heath, Paul Jenkins

Matrix
1455 de Paisonneuve Blvd. West
Suite LB-514-8
Montreal, Quebec
H3G IM8 Canada
$15, 8, Terence Byrnes

Michigan Quarterly Review
3032 Rackham Building
University of Michigan
Ann Arbor, MI 48109
$18, 10, Laurence Goldstein

Mid-American Review
Department of English
Bowling Green State University
Bowling Green, OH 43403
$12, 11, Rebecca Meacham

Midstream
110 East 59th Street
New York, NY 10022
$21, Joel Carmichael

Midwesterner
Big Shoulders Publishing
343 S. Dearborn Street
Suite 610
Chicago, IL 60604
$20, 12, David Schabes

Minnesota Review
Department of English
State University of New York
Stony Brook, NY 11794-5350
$12, 10, Jeffrey Williams

Mirabella
200 Madison Avenue
New York, NY 10016
$17.98, 2, Kathy Medwick

Mississippi Review
University of Southern Mississippi
Southern Station, P.O. Box 5144
Hattiesburg, MS 39406-5144
$15, 25, Frederick Barthelme

Mississippi Valley Review
Department of English
Western Illinois University
Macomb, IL 61455
$12, 16, John Mann,
Tama Baldwin

Missouri Review
1507 Hillcrest Hall
University of Missouri
Columbia, MO 65211
$19, 23, Speer Morgan

Modern Words
350 Bay Street #100
San Francisco, CA 94133
$20, 10, Garland Richard Kyle

Monocacy Valley Review
Mount Saint Mary's College
Emmitsburg, MD 21727
$10, William Heath

Ms.
230 Park Avenue
New York, NY 10169
$45, 7, Marcia Ann Gillespie

Nassau Review
English Department
Nassau Community College
One Education Drive
Garden City, NY 11530-6793
Paul A. Doyle

Nebraska Review
Writers' Workshop, ASH 212
University of Nebraska
Omaha, NE 68182-0324
$10, 10, Art Homer, Richard Duggin

New Delta Review
Creative Writing Program
English Department
Louisiana State University
Baton Rouge, LA 70803
$7, 9, Mindy Meek

New England Review
Middlebury College
Middlebury, VT 05753
$18, 16, Stephen Donadio

New Letters
University of Missouri
4216 Rockhill Road
Kansas City, MO 64110
$17, 21, James McKinley

New Orleans Review
P.O. Box 195
Loyola University
New Orleans, LA 70118
$18, 4, Ralph Adamo

New Quarterly
English Language Proficiency
   Programme
University of Waterloo
Waterloo, Ontario
N2L 3G1 Canada
$14, 26, Peter Hinchcliffe,
Kim Jernigan, Mary Merikle,
Linda Kenyon

New Renaissance
9 Heath Road
Arlington, MA 02174
$11.50, 5, Louise T. Reynolds

New Yorker
25 West 43rd Street
New York, NY 10036
$32, 45, Tina Brown

Nimrod
Arts and Humanities Council
of Tulsa
2210 South Main Street
Tulsa, OK 74114
$15, 10, Francine Ringold

North American Review
University of Northern Iowa
1222 West 27th Street
Cedar Falls, IA 50614
$18, 13, Robley Wilson, Jr.

North Dakota Quarterly
University of North Dakota
P.O. Box 8237
Grand Forks, ND 58202
$25, 13, William Borden

Northeast Corridor
Department of English
Beaver College
450 S. Easton Road
Glenside, PA 19038-3295
$10, 6, Susan Balee

Northwest Review
369 PLC
University of Oregon
Eugene, OR 97403
$20, 10, John Witte

Notre Dame Review
Department of English
University of Notre Dame
Notre Dame, IN 46556
$15, 8, Valerie Sayers

Oasis
P.O. Box 626
Largo, FL 34649-0626
$22, 14, Neal Storrs

Ohio Review
Ellis Hall
Ohio University
Athens, OH 45701-2979
$16, 10, Wayne Dodd

On the Make
127 Academy Hill Road

Boston, MA 02135
$16, Nicholas Patterson

Ontario Review
9 Honey Brook Drive
Princeton, NJ 08540
$12, 8, Raymond J. Smith

Open City
38 White Street
New York, NY 10013
$24, Thomas Beller, Daniel Pinchbeck

Orion
136 East 64th Street
New York, NY 10021
$20, Emily Helstand

Other Voices
University of Illinois at Chicago
Department of English
(M/C 162) Box 4348
Chicago, IL 60680
$20, 30, Sharon Fiffer,
Lois Hauselman

Oxford American
115¼ South Lamar
Oxford, MS 38655
$16, 12, Marc Smirnoff

Oxygen
Suite 1010
535 Geary Street
San Francisco, CA 94102
$14, 10, Richard Hack

Pangolin Papers
P.O. Box 241
Nordland, WA 98358
$15, 6, Pat Britt

Paris Review
541 East 72nd Street
New York, NY 10021
$34, 14, George Plimpton

Paris Transcontinental
Institut du Monde Anglophone,
Sorbonne Nouvelle
5, rue d'École de Médecine

75006 Paris, France
$20, *Claire Larriere*

Parting Gifts
3006 Stonecutter Terrace
Greensboro, NC 27405
Robert Bixby

Partisan Review
236 Bay State Road
Boston, MA 02215
$22, 4, *William Phillips*

Passages North
Kalamazoo College
1200 Academy Street
Kalamazoo, Ml 49007
$10, 8, *Michael Barrett*

Pearl River Review
P.O. Box 8146
Mobile, AL 36689-0416
$15, *Kimberly Kelly*

Playboy
Playboy Building
919 North Michigan Avenue
Chicago, IL 60611
$24, 23, *Alice K. Turner*

Pleiades
Department of English
Central Missouri State University
P.O. Box 800
Warrensburg, MO 64093
$10, *R. M. Kinder*

Ploughshares
Emerson College
100 Beacon Street
Boston, MA 02116
$19, 20, *Don Lee*

Porcupine
P.O. Box 259
Cedarburg, WI 53012
$13.95, *group editorship*

Potpourri
P.O. Box 8278

Prairie Village, KS 66208
$12, 20, *Polly W. Swafford*

Pottersfield Portfolio
The Gatsby Press
5280 Green Street, P.O. Box 27094
Halifax, Nova Scotia
B3H 4M8 Canada
$18, 12, *Ian Colford*

Prairie Fire
423-100 Arthur Street
Winnipeg, Manitoba
R3B 1H3 Canada
$24, 8, *Andris Taskans*

Prairie Schooner
201 Andrews Hall
University of Nebraska
Lincoln, NE 68588-0334
$20, 20, *Hilda Raz*

Press
125 West 72nd Street
Suite 3-M
New York, NY 10023
$24, *Daniel Roberts*

Prism International
Department of Creative Writing
University of British Columbia
Vancouver, British Columbia
V6T 1W5 Canada
$16, 20, *Rick Maddocks*

Provincetown Arts
650 Commercial Street
Provincetown MA 02657
$10, 4, *Christopher Busa*

Puerto del Sol
P.O. Box 3E
Department of English
New Mexico State University
Las Cruces, NM 88003
$10, 12, *Kevin McIlvoy*

Quarry Magazine
P.O. Box 1061
Kingston, Ontario
K7L 4Y5 Canada
$22, 20, Mary Cameron

Quarterly West
317 Olpin Union
University of Utah
Salt Lake City, UT 84112
$12, 6, Lawrence Coates,
Margot Schilpp

RE:AL
School of Liberal Arts
Stephen F. Austin State University
P.O. Box 13007
SFA Station
Nacogdoches, TX 75962
$15, 10, Dale Hearell

The Recorder
991 Fifth Avenue
New York, NY 10028
4, Christopher Cahill

Red Cedar Review
17 Morrill Hall
Department of English
Michigan State University
East Lansing, MI 48823
$10, 12, Tom Bissell

Redbook
959 Eighth Avenue
New York, NY 10017
$11.97, 10, Dawn Raffel

River Styx
Big River Association
14 South Euclid
St. Louis, MO 63108
$20, 30, Richard Newman

Rosebud
P.O. Box 459
Cambridge, WI 53523
$10, 20, Roderick Clark

Salamander
48 Ackers Avenue
Brookline, MA 02146
$12, 10, Jennifer Barber

Salmagundi
Skidmore College
Saratoga Springs, NY 12866
$18, 4, Robert Boyers

San Jose Studies
c/o English Department
San Jose State University
One Washington Square
San Jose, CA 95192
$12, 5, John Engell, D. Mesher

Santa Barbara Review
104 La Vereda Lane
Santa Barbara, CA 93108
$16, 8, Patricia Stockton Leddy

Santa Monica Review
Center for the Humanities
Santa Monica College
1900 Pico Boulevard
Santa Monica, CA 90405
$12, 16, Lee Montgomery

Saturday Night
Suite 400
184 Front Street E
Toronto, Ontario
M5V 2Z4 Canada
$26.45, 4, Robert Weaver

Seattle Review
Padelford Hall, GN-30
University of Washington
Seattle, WA 98195
$9, 12, Charles Johnson

Sewanee Review
University of the South
Sewanee, TN 37375-4009
$18, 10, George Core

Shenandoah
Washington and Lee University
P.O. Box 722
Lexington, VA 24450
$11, 17, R. T. Smith

Shooting Star Review
7123 Race Street
Pittsburgh, PA 15208
$10, 12, group editorship

Snake Nation Review
110 #2 West Force Street
Valdosta, GA 31601
$20, 14, Roberta George

Sonora Review
Department of English
University of Arizona
Tucson, AZ 85721
$10, 12, Hannah Hass

So to Speak
4400 University Drive
George Mason University
Fairfax, VA 22030-444
$7, 10, Wendi Kaufman

South Carolina Review
Department of English
Clemson University
Clemson, SC 29634-1503
$10, 8, Frank Day,
  Carol Johnston

South Dakota Review
University of South Dakota
P.O. Box 111 University Exchange
Vermillion, SD 57069
$15, 15, Brian Bedard

Southern Exposure
P.O. Box 531
Durham, NC 27702
$24, 12, Jo Carson

Southern Humanities Review
9088 Haley Center
Auburn University
Auburn, AL 36849
$15, 5, Dan R. Latimer, Virginia M.
  Kouidis

Southern Review
43 Allen Hall
Louisiana State University

Baton Rouge, LA 70803
$20, 17, James Olney, Dave Smith

Southwest Review
Southern Methodist University
P.O. Box 4374
Dallas, TX 75275
$20, 15, Willard Spiegelman

Story
1507 Dana Avenue
Cincinnati, OH 45207
$22, 52, Lois Rosenthal

Sun
107 North Roberson Street
Chapel Hill, NC 27516
$30, 30, Sy Safransky

Sycamore Review
Department of English
Heavilon Hall
Purdue University
West Lafayette, IN 47907
$10, 5, Jon Briner

Talking River Review
Division of Literature
Lewis-Clark State College
500 8th Avenue
Lewiston, ID 83501
$10, 10, group editorship

Teacup
P.O. Box 8665
Hellgate Station
Missoula, MT 59807
$9, group editorship

Thema
Box 74109
Metairie, LA 70053-4109
$16, Virginia Howard

Thin Air
P.O. Box 23549
Flagstaff, AZ 86002
$9, Jeff Huebner,
  Rob Morrill

13th Moon
Department of English
SUNY at Albany
Albany, NY 12222
$18, Judith Emlyn Johnson

Threepenny Review
P.O. Box 9131
Berkeley, CA 94709
$16, 10, Wendy Lesser

Tikkun
5100 Leona Street
Oakland, CA 94619
$36, 10, Michael Lerner

Trafika
Columbia Post Office
Box 250413
New York, NY 10025-1536
$35, 27, Dorsey Evans

Treasure House
Suite 3A
1106 Oak Hill Avenue
Hagerstown, MD 21742
$15, 11, J. G. Wolfensberger

TriQuarterly
2020 Ridge Avenue
Northwestern University
Evanston, IL 60208
$20, 15, Reginald Gibbons

Unmuzzled Ox
105 Hudson Street
New York, NY 10013
$8.95, Michael Andre

Urbanus
P.O. Box 192561
San Francisco, CA 94119
$8, 4, Peter Drizhal

Vignette
4150-G Riverside Drive
Toluca Lake, CA 91505
$29, 4, Dawn Baille,
  Deborah Clark

Virginia Quarterly Review
One West Range
Charlottesville, VA 22903
$15, 14, Staige D. Blackford

Voices West
West Los Angeles College
4800 Freshman Drive
Culver City, CA 90230
Rafael Weinstein

Wascana Review
English Department
University of Regina
Regina, Saskatchewan
S4S 0A2 Canada
$10, 8, J. Shami

Weber Studies
Weber State College
Ogden, UT 84408
$10, 2, Neila Seshachari

Wellspring
770 Tonkawa Road
Long Lake, MN 55356
$8, 10, Meg Miller

West Branch
Department of English
Bucknell University
Lewisburg, PA 17837
$7, 10, Robert Love Taylor,
  Karl Patten

Western Humanities Review
University of Utah
Salt Lake City, UT 84112
$20, 10, Barry Weller

Whetstone
Barrington Area Arts Council
P.O. Box 1266
Barrington, IL 60011
$6.25, 11, Sandra Berris

William and Mary Review
College of William and Mary
P.O. Box 8795
Williamsburg, VA 23187
$5, 4, Forrest Pritchard

Wind
RFD Route 1
P.O. Box 809K
Pikeville, KY 41501
$7, 20, Quentin R. Howard

Windsor Review
Department of English
University of Windsor
Windsor, Ontario
N9B 3P4 Canada
$19.95, 12, Alistair MacLeod

Witness
Oakland Community College
Orchard Ridge Campus
27055 Orchard Lake Road
Farmington Hills, MI 48334
$12, 24, Peter Stine

Worcester Review
6 Chatham Street
Worcester, MA 01690
$10, 8, Rodger Martin

Writers Forum
University of Colorado
P.O. Box 7150
Colorado Springs, CO 80933-7150
$8.95, 15, Alexander Blackburn

Xavier Review
Xavier University
Box 110C

New Orleans, LA 70125
$10, Thomas Bonner, Jr.

Yale Review
1902A Yale Station
New Haven, CT 06520
$20, 12, J. D. McClatchy

Yalobusha Review
P.O. Box 186
University, MS 38677-0186
$6, Al Dixon

Yankee
Yankee Publishing, Inc.
Dublin, NH 03444
$22, 4, Judson D. Hale, Sr.

Yemassee
Department of English
University of South Carolina
Columbia, SC 29208
$15, Stephen Owen

Zoetrope
AZX Publications
126 Fifth Avenue, Suite 300
New York, NY 10011
free, Adrienne Brodeur

ZYZZYVA
41 Sutter Street, Suite 1400
San Francisco, CA 94104
$28, 12, Howard Junker